Organizational Change: Themes and Issues

Organizational Change

THEMES & ISSUES

Jim Grieves

OXFORD
UNIVERSITY PRESS

OXFORD
UNIVERSITY PRESS

Great Clarendon Street, Oxford OX2 6DP

Oxford University Press is a department of the University of Oxford.
It furthers the University's objective of excellence in research, scholarship,
and education by publishing worldwide in

Oxford New York

Auckland Cape Town Dar es Salaam Hong Kong Karachi
Kuala Lumpur Madrid Melbourne Mexico City Nairobi
New Delhi Shanghai Taipei Toronto

With offices in

Argentina Austria Brazil Chile Czech Republic France Greece
Guatemala Hungary Italy Japan Poland Portugal Singapore
South Korea Switzerland Thailand Turkey Ukraine Vietnam

Oxford is a registered trade mark of Oxford University Press
in the UK and in certain other countries

Published in the United States
by Oxford University Press Inc., New York

British Library Cataloguing in Publication Data
Data available

Library of Congress Cataloging in Publication Data
Data available

Typeset by MPS Limited, A Macmillan Company
Printed in Italy
on acid-free paper by
L.E.G.O. S.p.A

ISBN 978–0–19–921488–4

1 3 5 7 9 10 8 6 4 2

Preface

The subject of organizational change has become a central theme for management, as it has for social science discourses over the years. Each discipline has made a significant contribution to various interweaving debates, but the management discourse has often been seen by critics to lack academic rigour by favouring a focus on managerialism. This is due, in the main, to the assumption that management is neutral, adopted by the structural-functional perspective. The result has been a process in which organizational change is treated mechanistically. One can see this today on the shelves of popular book shops, in which books by consultants and populist authors provide prescriptive strategies for change. The dominant tendency has been to describe the management of change as a mechanistic grand narrative in which the author's expertise is presented as the accumulation of wisdom and never as the result of contestable debates. This type of mechanistic thinking is often represented by the phrase 'management of change', which may be as apocryphal as the famous saying ascribed to Archimedes, 'Give me a lever long enough and a fulcrum on which to place it, and I shall move the world'. Furthermore, it is quite common to read newspaper articles about communities, consumers, clients, and employees who have had change thrust upon them by chief executives acting as leviathans in a world in which their own egos or motivations simply echo the desires of their poorly informed appointments panels. The result is often a mess of exploitation or chaos. For this reason I have chosen the title *Organizational Change: Themes and issues*—I wanted to open up the debate by encouraging a more nuanced appreciation of the subject.

I wish to argue that organizational change requires a sophisticated appreciation of *themes and issues*. For this reason the book is divided into two parts. Part One focuses on five core themes related to *understanding change*. Each theme is presented as a chapter. Chapter 1 exposes the problems with the managerialist approach by exploring four pathways to change, defined by four contrasting perspectives that contribute to our understanding of change—the structural-functional perspective, the multiple constituencies perspective, Organizational Development, and Creativity and Volition: a Critical Theory of Change. What we discover is that each perspective contains its own assumptions, preferences, and limitations, and each is informed by different theoretical approaches. Sometimes these theories overlap, but more often than not they compete for our attention by providing cautionary tales or illuminating insights. The result is that no one pathway to change is enough to explain the complexity of organizational change.

The second theme is described in Chapter 2, which argues that most interventions with individuals, groups, and organizations carry ethical implications. To understand this, one need only reflect on the captains of industry who, in recent years, failed to understand their obligations to their stakeholders and ignored the consequences of their actions on others—consumers, clients, employees, and even entire societies.

Chapter 2 explores this theme by considering the place of ethics in organizational change. It reflects on how the four pathways introduced in Chapter 1 address ethical awareness. The result is that only two perspectives—the multiple constituencies perspective and the Organizational Development (OD) perspective—overtly express an ethical commitment. The main theme of the chapter is to explain why it is dangerous to make change interventions as if we were dealing with merely technical problems. Chapter 2 takes our understanding of organizational change further by arguing that governance is central to effective change strategies.

The third theme—planned change—is addressed in Chapter 3. Essentially, we need to confront two difficulties. The first is that most managerialist accounts of planned change present the subject uncritically as a matter of rational planning. The second difficulty is that the critics of planned change (the processual or emergent change writers) present credible arguments indicating that planned change does not work, but they fail to provide a coherent alternative to fill the void they leave. To some extent this is caused by a lack of conceptual clarity about what constitutes planned change. Many fail to appreciate that there is more than one type of planned change and each carries very different implications. The first type is characterized by empirical–rational approaches to change: strategies designed in linear stages that have a clear beginning and end. The second type is characterized by normative-re-educative models of change. These are not the same as the previous type, because they are designed by those involved. Whereas the former can be described as 'top-down' approaches, the latter focus on a collective organizational problem that is resolved through a process of organizational learning. Unlike the managerialist empirical–rational approaches the normative re-educative type are diagnostic rather than prescriptive. Critics of planned change tend to conflate these two approaches, which leads to the assertion that all planned change contains the same problems. The *impasse* they impose on planning change is the theme we must confront in order to proceed.

Chapter 4 addresses the fourth theme—strategic change—which is concerned with external forces for change. We discover that four dominant approaches to strategic management have influenced the concept of the strategic manager. These are the planning approach, the outcomes approach, the pluralistic approach, and finally the emergent approach. These approaches raise different dilemmas. For example, to what extent can we identify a suitable strategy simply by examining the structure of the industry and markets within which the organization competes? Alternatively, might we wish to consider the impact of a corporate strategy upon a range of external and internal stakeholders, who may be involved in very different markets that the organization serves? Furthermore, might we need to consider how relevant contingencies affect the strategic plan, and the need to balance planning for change and innovation with the need for flexibility? The main thrust of this chapter is to enable managers to understand how to deal with changes forced upon them.

Chapter 5 brings Part One of the book to a conclusion by providing a theme of internal development in contrast to dealing with external forces, as discussed in Chapter 3. The theme of building and developing competitive advantage is essential to organizations in both the public and private sectors. For example, we need to understand how organizations innovate and how to create forces for competitive advantage. We examine high-performance practices, and address whether it is possible to construct a learning organization, or if we should focus on organizational learning instead. Each of these issues leads to a better understanding about what we can do to build proactive change in organizations.

Part Two deals with six issues related to change interventions. These are the role of culture in managing change, the way that power and control influence change, the role of leaders in managing the change process, the purpose of organizational diagnosis, the relevance of change models, and resistance to change. These issues are critical to organizational change, because they each represent a means by which change takes place. Each has the potential to influence change interventions, for success or failure. In Chapter 6 we are forced to confront a conceptual issue about the role of organizational culture. The predominant functional-fit model appears to provide an effective means to manage change. This approach (which is located in the structural-functional perspective) places culture in a prominent position as the corporate glue that binds the other functions together. This is favoured by the 'strong corporate culture' and OD writers. This view—that culture change offers a simple solution by arguing that cultural integration is necessary, that consensus is required and is actually achievable—is regarded as a myth by the *critical perspective,* which, in contrast, argues that culture is an analytical device not a management tool. Once more, we are presented with an insightful argument by critical theorists who again present us with a managerial problem. They do not seek cultural change because they are not interested in organizational performance. The questions we must confront therefore are: is our analytical framework objective? And how does culture change benefit the organization?

The issue of power is addressed in Chapter 7, which focuses on the nature of compliance. Thus, whether people are compelled by force to comply, or compliance is by voluntary agreement, is a central question for us. All interventions are political and this process involves change managers making assumptions about the way change should be managed. Many of these assumptions are derived from consultants who have often adopted a particular structural theory of change. But they are also derived from a corporate ideology. Power informs how people perceive change. An investigation of psychodynamics suggests that power used badly may amplify conflict. We might even discover examples of neurotic organizations in which people who hold positions of power create structures that disable effective performance. We discover this when, for example, attitudes become rigid and distorted. The role of leaders in managing change is an issue that is directly related to organizational culture and to the use or abuse of power. Thus, in Chapter 8 we are forced to confront the qualities of leadership. Once we have dispensed with the idea of the great heroic leader, we can learn to appreciate different types of approach raised by management scholars. These include behavioural research into leadership, strategic leadership, leadership attributes, transformational leadership, and results-based leadership. We can see the overlap with the issue of power when we discover how some chief executive officers influence the cultural psychodynamics of their organizations. We need to consider how dominant personalities influence organizational outcomes.

The issue at the heart of all well-constructed interventions is, of course, that of organizational diagnosis (Chapter 9). Can we identify the nature of organizational problems? Can we distinguish between cause and effect? Furthermore, by adopting the wrong analytical frame, might we inadequately diagnose the real problem? One of the difficulties is that, whilst the signs that indicate the existence of a problem may be obvious, many require analytical skill and judgement. Chapter 10 provides examples of other change models that might be used in introducing change, but the central issue here is that they should not be used as a substitute for careful analysis. Nor can they be used as a replacement for experience, knowledge, and skills. Nowhere is this more apparent than with the topic of resistance to change. The issue of resistance (Chapter 11) has often been treated in the managing change literature as unproblematic. This literature can tend to view resistance as a matter of faulty perception, arising from inappropriate organizational design, or resulting from anxiety. There are, however, more intellectually challenging ideas to pursue. For example, can we find examples of tipping points, and under what circumstances do these occur? Are some occupations and some situations more prone to stress and resistance than others? Can managers or change leaders cause resistance as a result of their behaviour? Finally, I sincerely hope that you read the final chapter, which reflects on the themes and issues of future organizational change, by which time you will have become more enlightened.

Jim Grieves

Walk through preface

There are many key features included in the chapters of *Organizational Change* that are designed to help you both to learn, and organize information.

Learning objectives

Following the introduction, each chapter opens with a bulleted outline of the main concepts and ideas. These serve as helpful signposts to what you can expect to learn from each chapter.

By the end of this chapter you will:

- Understand the place of ethics in organizational change.
- Recognize the limitation of technical solutions to complex problems.
- Appreciate the role of stakeholders and social contracts.
- Be aware of the consequences of organizational decisions for stakeholders.
- Appreciate why we need a clear personal understanding for our own ethical position.
- Recognize critical issues in managing change in a multinational global environment.
- Understand governance and commitment to social responsibility.
- Become sensitive to rationalizations and understand the process of defensive reasoning.

Stop and think boxes

These are short questions and examples that give you the opportunity to 'pause for thought' and relate the topic to your own experience.

❶ Stop and think 2.1

From your knowledge of one organization, list the stakeholders. Then examine their needs. Identify how similar or different these needs are. Indicate whether differences cause tensions and, if they do, suggest what might be done to resolve these. Say what type of power each stakeholder possesses. For example, is it formal or informal? Finally, state what the organization's ethical responsibilities should be to each stakeholder, as well as the pressure they may exert on the organization.

OD reflects a more recent but non-philosophical approach to the link between organizational change and ethics. It is proactive, being the only perspective that has articulated humanistic commitment to developing organizations through their people. The OD code of ethics recognizes a professional commitment to values, as discussed in 1.1 above and demonstrated in the following case example.

Case examples

The book is packed with examples and case studies that link topics to real-life situations.

❯❯ Case Example 4.1

Haier's successful strategic drivers

Competing in globalized markets, such as in consumer electrical 'white goods', is an increasingly difficult environment in which to secure a sustainable advantage. Consider, however, the experience of the Chinese domestic goods manufacturer Haier. A young organization founded in 1984, part of its success has come from a strategic focus on both product and market needs through observed product use, which has shaped its emergent corporate strategy. For example, in the 1990s engineers at Haier observed users of their washing machines washing clothes and vegetables together in their machines. A few minor product changes ensured that the machines were capable of performing this unexpected task on a regular basis and Haier rapidly became the number one brand in rural China.

They have also applied this ability to listen to the market by translating it into

Chapter summary

Each chapter ends with a précis that summarizes the most important arguments developed within that chapter.

3.6 Summary

In this chapter we have undertaken a critical reflection of planned change. We noted three theoretical positions with different knowledge claims: the empirical–rational, normative re-educative, and processual or emergent approaches. Each represents a different approach to change. For example, empirical–rational methods were defined as managerialist, prescriptive, and, in the case of strategic change, tend to be driven by unitarist assumptions. Both at a strategic and an operational level, empirical–rational approaches are task-driven and pursued for pragmatic reasons. Consequently, these are constructed in discrete linear stages from beginning to end. We noted that a process can be regarded as the means by which something (a physical object or an idea) is transferred so that value can be added. At a strategic level, as we noted with Case Example 3.1 'Putting the Customer First',

End-of-chapter study questions

Check your understanding by working through these questions after you have read each chapter. Suggested answers are available on the Online Resource Centre.

■ Study Questions

1. What is planned change?
2. What is Action Research and how does it characterize Organizational Development?
3. What arguments would you put to suggest that Action Research may be a more sophisticated change approach than a linear managerialist approach?
4. State the contribution of the open-systems model to analysing change processes.
5. If Organizational Development encouraged an ethical humanist perspective in the twentieth century, how might we extend this to a new position for the twenty-first century?
6. Define empirical–rational approaches and contrast these with normative re-educative approaches.
7. Can all planned change be described as linear destination-oriented change?
8. What is a critical path analysis?

End-of-chapter case study

A longer case study at the end of each chapter provides an opportunity to apply what you have learnt and analyse a real-life example.

✪ Case study

Planning, why bother?

On 12 February 2009, after weather reports the previous day had stated that the weather would be 'cold but sunny', unexpected blizzard conditions hit parts of the UK. Six inches of snow fell within two hours. Although road managers in county councils stated that they had planned for changing conditions by gritting all major roads, many roads became jammed as a consequence of several unforeseen events. As one county roads manager stated, 'no matter how well one plans for these events unexpected things happen'. The driver of a snow plough stuck in a traffic jam stated that, 'when they first noticed a build-up of traffic the police should have closed the road and allowed the snow ploughs and gritters to do their jobs'.

Why did jams occur on such an unexpected scale? The answer is that small incidents occur which can be resolved with coordination, patience, and cooperation.

End-of-chapter exercises

Exercises have been included at the end of every chapter to check you have grasped the key concepts.

■ Exercises

Exercise 1
Identify an example of a contemporary change initiative from the business section of a newspaper you have read in the last month. If you have not found any then go to the library in search of one. Identify what changes were made to this organization and place them in one of the three categories: people, systems, and structures. Then explain the interrelationships between them to a friend or colleague.

Exercise 2
Four types of threat were identified by Case Example 3.4. These were non-traditional threats; and irregular, catastrophic, and disruptive challenges. These characterize uncertainty and unpredictability, which make it difficult to instigate planned strategic change. Apply these to an organization known to you, such as a bank, hospital, insurance broker, furniture manufacturer, or an oil company. Explain how such threats might arise and illus-

Key terms with definitions

Key terms that appear throughout the chapters are highlighted and defined in the end-of-book glossary.

and clear strategic intent, its implementation and clarity of outcomes were not (Allison, 2006; Allison and Waters, 2007).

Should strategic leaders need or seek out consensual support, then? This had been a key question in the development and implementation of the HP–Compaq merger (Waters, 2006) and is a much more critical question and activity to pursue than the articulation of the vision of an organization might be, especially when vision and mission statements are often so generic. One solution is proposed by Coyle (2004) through the methodology of a congruence analysis. This requires the strategist to consider corporate intent by establishing the advantages and disadvantages for key stakeholders. In other words, it considers directly the impact of strategic change of intent upon outcomes. The proposed outcomes are evaluated by means of a *gestalt* interpretation, where 'gestalt' means the strategic manager must consider the overall patterns in the analysis of the major beneficiaries (or losers) in the strategic proposal. We might consider, for example, what a congruence analysis of the Finnish organization

Further reading

An annotated list of recommended reading on each subject will help guide you through further reading on a subject area.

■ Further reading

Blosch, M. and Preece, D. (2000), 'Framing Work Through a Socio-technical Ensemble: The Case of Butler Co.', *Technology Analysis & Strategic Management*, 12(1). A useful example of processual analysis.

Buchanan, D. and Dawson, P. (2007), 'Discourse and Audience: Organizational Change as Multi-Story Process', *Journal of Management Studies*, 44(5). The authors provide a method for unearthing the political and historical dimensions of change by investigating unofficial accounts.

Casey, C. (2002), *Critical Analysis of Organizations, Theory, Practice, Revitalization*, London: Sage. Casey provides one of the strongest criticisms of modernist organizational analysis.

Hughes, M. (2007), 'The Tools and Techniques of Change Management', *Journal of Change Management*, 7(1), 37–49. A simple example of the arguments for and against tools

How to use the Online Resource Centre

www.oxfordtextbooks.co.uk/orc/grieves/

To support this text, there is a wide range of web-based content for both students and registered adopters. Students can go to the Online Resource Centre to find web links, updates to case studies and references to seminal papers. Tutors will be able to access a suite of teaching and discussion notes, alongside a bank of diagrams, figures and tables from within the text.

All of these resources can be incorporated into your institution's existing virtual learning environment.

For registered adopters

Diagrams, figures and tables from the text

All figures and tables from the text have been provided for you to download for lecture presentations, or to include in handouts.

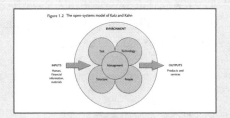

Guidance notes for case studies

Guidance on how best to use the case studies in class or assignments are provided to help you prepare for each term's teaching.

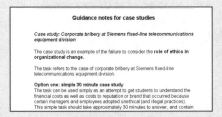

Teaching and discussion points

Additional ideas for seminar and tutorial work have been provided to save you time and provide you with a ready-to-use bank of material.

> **Lecturer Discussion Points**
>
> **Starting point: the role of ethics in organizational change**
> The main learning point from this chapter is that all interventions carry ethical implications. But there is one central question: why should we be concerned to create and nurture ethical organizations?
>
> **The Place of Ethics in Organizational Change (Section 2.2)**
> There are two answers to the question stated above. Students should therefore be invited to consider:
>
> 1. The unintended consequences that may occur if a strategy is not thought through.
> 2. Your own ethical position about a change initiative.
>
> **The limitation of technical solutions to complex problems (Section 2.2.1)**

For students

Web links

A series of annotated web links to key research and organizations provide a useful guide for further study.

> Web links
>
> **Ethical Issues and Green Business**
>
> The Organizational Development Credo can be found at the website:
> <http://www.....................>
>
> The International Organization Development code of ethics
> (December, 1991; 22nd Revision) refers to the values for an Organization Development consultant. This can
> <http://www....................>
>
> *Deeper Luxury* Report written by Jem Bendell and Anthony Kleanthous, and published by WWF-UK in Novem
> <http://www.....................>
>
> **Green Business**
> It is worth exploring the official business link to the US Government for what it recommends and commits itself
> <http://www....................>

Glossary

These flashcards have been designed to help you understand and memorize the key terms used in the book. You can even download them to your iPod® or other small-screen device for revision on the move!

Answers to end-of-chapter questions

Check your understanding by comparing your answer with the one the author has prepared.

> **Answers to end of chapter questions**
>
> *Check your understanding by comparing your answer with the one the author has prepared.*
>
> 1. *Explain with a diagram how the structural-functional perspective helps us to understand how inputs are transformed into outputs.*
>
>   Your diagram should be similar to figure 1.2 - the open-systems model of Katz and Kahn. The inputs to an organization you choose will be related to the type of organization you identify. In general terms the inputs that apply to most organizations include people, materials, technology, and information. However, if you provide a more specific example, such as a university, then you will be likely to clarify the inputs by providing more specific examples which include students, staff, customers, chemistry and physics materials, teaching materials and resources, books and electronic

References to seminal papers

This resource provides references to seminal academic papers to further develop your understanding of a particular concept or theory.

> References to seminal papers
>
> **Approaches to change**
>
> Beugelsdijk, S., Slangen, A., van Herpen, M. (2002), 'Shapes of organizational change: The case of Heineke *Management*, 15(3), 311–326. A good example of change strategies and leadership.
>
> Buchanan, D. and Dawson, P. (2007), 'Discourse and Audience: Organizational Change as Multi-Story Proc (5). A good example of research into processual issues.
>
> Collins, H. and Wray-Bliss, E. (2005), 'Discriminating ethics', *Human Relations* 58, 799. Illustrates critical the
>
> Kersten, A. (2007), 'Fantastic performance and neurotic fantasy: A case-based exploration of psychodynam Makes an interesting argument that organizations stage their own grand dramas and come to believe in the
>
> Sun, Y. and Wen, K. (2007), 'Environmental Challengers for Foreign R&D in China', *Asia Pacific Business R* relationship between companies looking to locate to China and cultural expectations of the host country.

Contents

Detailed contents

Part One: Understanding change   1

Acknowledgements

I would like to express my gratitude to the following reviewers, who were meticulous in their critical review of earlier drafts of the manuscript. Their ideas and critiques were both challenging and stimulating: Dr Sue Williams, University of Gloucestershire; Louise Fitzgerald, Visiting Professor, University of Manchester; Dr Alex Weich, Westminster Business School at the University of Westminster; Dr Louise Grisoni, University of the West of England; Dr Stefan Sveningsson, Lund University; Emma Roberts, Leeds Trinity University College; John Summers, Ashcroft International Business School, Anglia Ruskin University; Ian Pyper, University of Ulster; Dr Staffan Furusten, Stockholm School of Economics and Score; Dr Peter Critten, Institute for Work Based Learning, Middlesex University; Simon Gurevitz, University of Westminster; Dr Alasdair Galloway, University of the West of Scotland; Miriam Green, London Metropolitan University; Jim Cheetham, previously of Robert Gordon University; Dr Ann Davis, Aston University; Dr Martin Brigham, Lancaster University; and Willem Vrakking, Erasmus University.

In addition, I would like to thank two people whose contribution was enormously helpful. First, Dr. Ian Pownall who wrote Chapter 4 on Strategic Change, and for whose expertise I am indebted. Second, I would like to thank OUP's Publishing Manager, Francesca Griffin, who steered me in the right direction on more than one occasion.

Publisher's note

List of tables

List of figures

List of case examples

List of case studies

List of abbreviations

BPR	Business Process Re-engineering
CCM	Cultural Climate Measure
CPA	Critical Path Analysis
CSF	critical success factors
CSR	corporate social responsibility
FAR	Field Anomaly Relaxation method
FFA	Force Field Analysis
Gurt	Genetic Use Restriction Technology
HPWS	high-performance work systems
HRD	human resource development
HRM	human resource management
IOE	industrial organizational economics approach to strategy
MNE(s)	multinational enterprise(s)
OD	Organization Development approach
OESP	Organization–Environment–Strategy–Performance view
OL	organizational learning
PCAOB	Public Company Accounting Oversight Board (USA)
PDCA	plan, do, check, and act (Deming cycle)
PESTLE	political, economic, social and technological, legal, and environmental factors for analysis
RBV	resource-based view (RBV) approach to strategic thinking
SCP	Structure–Conduct–Performance view
SCT	Social contract theory
SMART	specific, measurable, attainable, realistic, and timely
SSP	Structure–Strategy–Performance view
SWOT	Strengths, Weaknesses, Opportunities, Threats
TA	Transactional Analysis
TQM	Total Quality Management
VRIN	Valuable/Rare/Imperfectly Imitable/Non-substitutable framework

PART ONE
Understanding change

CHAPTER 1

Perspectives on change

1.1 Introduction

This chapter lays the framework for this book by arguing that organizational change is developed within models and frameworks that inform our understanding of the subject. In this chapter we will learn that knowledge and practice of organizational change are influenced by assumptions derived from the models or perspectives we use. For example, if we regard change as a matter of systemic structural arrangements we can make in an organization, then we can see how the analogy of organism or biological system helps to inform our judgements. Because perspectives offer ways of seeing, they will inevitably organize our perception in line with the dominant analogy used. However, analogies are only partial knowledge claims. Four perspectives on change are cited in this chapter: why four perspectives in particular? The answer to that question is straightforward but you need to understand at this point that a perspective is an overarching approach that contains a variety of theories that have become associated with it. You will see why these are the dominant perspectives once you have read the remainder of this section.

First, the structural-functional perspective is the oldest approach to organizational design and therefore change. Like each perspective, it contains a variety of theories that attempted to resolve some of its difficulties as it developed. These theories include the hard systems, systems dynamics, cybernetics, soft systems, critical-systems heuristics, and postmodern systems thinking (Jackson, 2003). The structural-functional perspective encourages us to think about structural arrangements and functional interrelationships within organizations. The development of the open-systems model in the 1950s assisted our understanding further by focusing on how inputs to an organization are transformed into outputs. This is useful for thinking about how we might change tasks and relationships in a production process. The value of the structural-functional perspective lies in its ability to change the arrangement of tasks and procedures in relation to the customer or client specification. The advantage of the perspective lies in its ability to look at an organization as a control mechanism: that is, to understand the important structural components and to articulate the functional interrelationships between the parts. Inevitably, structural redesign will therefore influence the functions that each part produces for the whole. But the perspective has disadvantages also. Because it is a model for controlling operations, it is therefore mechanistic. It tends to ignore how motivations, behaviours, attitudes, and values contribute to effective performance.

The multiple constituencies perspective emerged from dissatisfaction with the structural-functional perspective. Although it was initially associated with the work of Cyert and March (1963), it increasingly came to adopt a range of theories associated with the action and motives of individual actors rather than with the action of systems per se. The multiple constituencies perspective refers to the way that complex organizations have to negotiate objectives with different groups of stakeholders who have overlapping and often conflicting needs. When we consider hospitals, health trusts, postal services, public bodies, local government, and transnational companies, then we come to recognize that the organization's needs are inextricably linked to various stakeholder groups. This affects how resources are managed and distributed, as well as how change might be facilitated to maximize efficiency and effectiveness. An investigation of how multiple constituencies bring their own interests and motivations into the organizational arena will help us to provide an informed approach to managing change by recognizing the various resource needs of different groups. We can recognize the advantage of this perspective in drawing attention to the various stakeholder needs but we can also recognize that it is limited to a partial analysis. It is less concerned with developing people. It also has a limited view of power. Consequently this reduces organizational change to consensual negotiation between pluralities of groups.

Those academics and practitioners that adopt the Organizational Development perspective would share much with the two previous perspectives because it embraces both a systems approach and a focus on stakeholders and governance. However, it is distinguished by its methodology of action research as much as it is by its ethical approach to developing organizations through people. For the first time we begin to see people as resources to be developed rather than as simply costs on a balance sheet. This perspective emerged from the human relations approach, which focused on personal and group development. However, unlike the two previous perspectives, it argues that maximum efficiency and effectiveness cannot be achieved by dealing with tasks, procedures, and customers' or clients' needs without looking at the quality of management, leadership, communication, culture, motivation, and values. Because the Organizational Development (OD) perspective on change emerged out of human resource theory, it became a synthesis of structural functionalism and behavioural research. The two main contributions of this approach are the focus on social characteristics and its methodology dedicated to a humanistic approach to change and development. OD is also associated with the idea of planned change and the need to clearly diagnose clients' needs before making an intervention. These provide major advantages in thinking about change but they are also partial and limited to conceptualizing change as a matter of consensus, as does each perspective mentioned so far.

The final perspective—Creativity and Volition: a Critical Theory of Change—reflects the challenges and assumptions of Critical Theory. It cannot be regarded as a unified perspective, as the others can, because it does not seek to offer solutions to change problems. But it does go further than any of the other perspectives in demonstrating that people, rather than systems, are the main element of analysis in any change theory. Each of the other perspectives tends to reify human action. By contrast, this perspective seeks to redress the balance by arguing that people are active agents of change. It also brings another important element under scrutiny. That is, each of the other perspectives focuses on rational change. This has implications for designing and planning change as a linear sequence of events. However, if change programmes ignore emergent processes that result more from conflict, flux, and uncertainty than from consensus and stability, then intervention strategies will have a limited and often unintended effect. Because this perspective is derived from Critical Theory we should not assume that it is immune to criticism. The main criticism is that it does not offer solutions. It does not provide useful intervention strategies. It does, however, make us stop and think before we act.

You should now be clear that each perspective contains a range of theories that share assumptions, methods, and approaches. These can be stated simply as:

1. A focus on *systems and structures* (the structural-functional perspective).

2. A focus on *governance* (the multiple constituencies perspective).

3. A focus on *behavioural improvement* through personal and Organizational Development (the OD perspective).

4. A focus on *constant critique* (Creativity and Volition: a Critical Theory of Change).

A simple reminder of the focus is: *systems, governance, behaviour,* and *critique.* The argument throughout the book is that to manage change you need to understand these interweaving debates.

In this chapter we will:

- Explain the benefits and limitations of change contained within the structural-functional perspective.

- Examine how a multiple constituencies perspective provides arguments for involving stakeholders in complex change initiatives.

- Explore the value of human resource and organization development interventions as well as their limitations in planned change initiatives.

- Appreciate why organizational change may be characterized better by conflict, flux, and uncertainty.

- Consider the source of creativity.

- Appreciate the role of Critical Theory in understanding organizational change.

1.2 Perspectives on change

1.2.1 Modernity, progress, and change

It is important to contextualize the four perspectives of this chapter by illustrating that each emerged from, or in reaction to, the process of modernism. The term 'modernism' was originally used to describe the new machine age of the early twentieth century, which reflected progress through the application of scientific principles, order, and control. Scientific principles emerged from the pursuit of rationality embedded in the philosophy of the Enlightenment. The twentieth century was influenced by progressive movements in art and architecture, but the new age was eventually associated with negative qualities that, paradoxically, were linked to its greatest triumph—the machine age. The new machine age was characterized by large-scale movements, revolutions, and world wars which all proclaimed progress through the application of machine technology or through the metaphor of the machine as the embodiment of efficiency and effectiveness. This was no more apparent than in business and management, where modernity reflected the task of controlling large-scale organizations. Techniques or processes such as bureaucracy, Taylorism, and Fordism came to reflect the new managerialism of the machine age in which the principles of measurement and calculation came to dominate thinking. This emphasis on rational calculation had advantages in the form of mass production of cheap goods but, to achieve this, the human cogs in the machine were alienated by a technology that largely ignored social practices.

You should therefore be aware that the structural-functional perspective emerged at the time when modernism suggested progress through the application of rational principles. It should be no surprise, then, that it tended to focus on task and throughput by using the metaphor of organism as machine. The perspective referred to as multiple constituencies emerged in the 1960s. It was the first to challenge the naive rationalism of the structural-functional perspective by arguing that an organization is not equivalent to a biological entity and that therefore the organic model was not appropriate to organizations. An organization was better conceived as a 'legal fiction' (Shafritz and Ott, 1991). This had the advantage of persuading us that progress is simply a result of social processes and that all organizations are no more than devices to achieve certain objectives. The perspective helped to establish the idea of change through governance. Organizational Development has been the main tradition of organizational change and has much to recommend it, such as a declared humanistic commitment to change. It has also developed useful techniques and methods, but its use of the biological model limits its critique. The perspective we call 'Creativity and Volition: a Critical Theory of Change' is united only by its objection to modernism. It therefore provides a useful counterbalance to the other perspectives by offering criticism of the conventional wisdom. But it also suggests that human volition and creativity are a long way from the modernist assumptions of progress.

1.2.2 Pathways to change

Each perspective contains theories that lead to a change intervention. The phrase 'change intervention' refers to change actions taken at a strategic level to help an organization become more effective. A perspective can therefore be regarded as a model for understanding how a subject can be understood.

Advocates of a perspective develop theories to inform their views and they construct methodologies to test the accuracy of their various theories within a perspective. However, each perspective is open to criticism precisely because it contains assumptions about organizational reality. Each is therefore valuable as a framework

Figure 1.1 Pathways to change

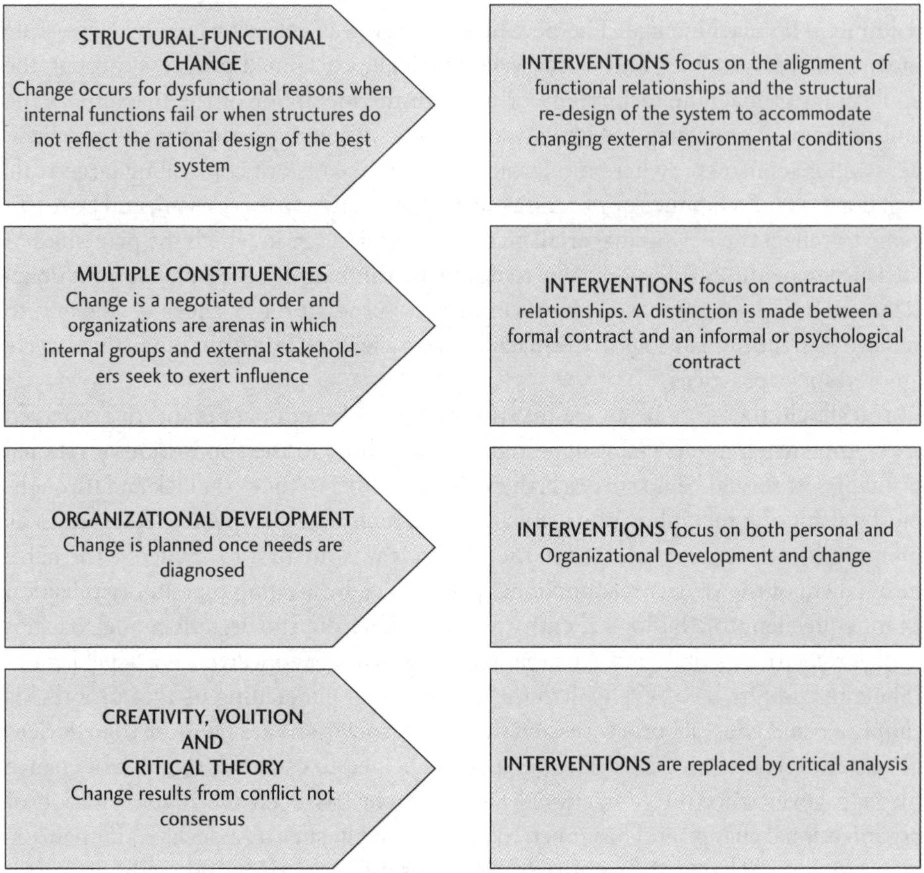

STRUCTURAL-FUNCTIONAL CHANGE Change occurs for dysfunctional reasons when internal functions fail or when structures do not reflect the rational design of the best system	**INTERVENTIONS** focus on the alignment of functional relationships and the structural re-design of the system to accommodate changing external environmental conditions
MULTIPLE CONSTITUENCIES Change is a negotiated order and organizations are arenas in which internal groups and external stakeholders seek to exert influence	**INTERVENTIONS** focus on contractual relationships. A distinction is made between a formal contract and an informal or psychological contract
ORGANIZATIONAL DEVELOPMENT Change is planned once needs are diagnosed	**INTERVENTIONS** focus on both personal and Organizational Development and change
CREATIVITY, VOLITION AND CRITICAL THEORY Change results from conflict not consensus	**INTERVENTIONS** are replaced by critical analysis

for change, but in the interest of validity we need to be cautious about the claims to certainty that each makes. We would be wise, therefore, to view these perspectives as pathways to understand organizational change. We can take the analogy further and suggest that each perspective represents a pathway through a minefield of conceptual difficulties. Each perspective is illustrated in Figure 1.1.

1.3 Structural-functional change: changing structures and functions

Structural-functional change is the oldest perspective on organizational change. This perspective is also known as structural-functional analysis. It is effectively a social-systems view of organizations as opposed to the mechanistic or closed-systems perspective of physics. Henry Fayol was one of the first writers to make the link between structure and function. In his 1916 book *General and Industrial Management*, he describes the relationship between organizations and biology in terms of an analogy. Thus he points out that, just as organisms evolve and become more sophisticated in their structural properties, so do organizations. We can see why the organic analogy is important to organizations when we consider Fayol's description of specialization and differentiation. For example,

> [s]pecialization belongs to the natural order; it is observable in the animal world, where the more highly developed the creature the more highly differentiated its organs; it is observable in human societies where the more important the body corporate the closer its relationship between structure and function. As a society grows, so new organs develop destined to replace the single one performing all functions in the primitive state.
>
> (Fayol, 1916: 19)

Thus, as organizations grow and develop, they become much more complex and require new types of structure. In order to deal with this complexity, work has to be simplified through the division of labour. Some years later, structural-functional analysis viewed the study of organizations as the analysis of both structural and functional interrelationships between elements in an organizational system. Structural-functional analysis of an organization begins with the assumption that organizations are cooperative systems. Whilst they are constituted by individuals, this is less relevant than the fact that they are systems designed to coordinate the actions of individuals. They are better viewed, therefore, as adaptive organisms. This means that any organizational system 'is deemed to have basic needs... related to self-maintenance... and... self-defence' (Selznick, 1948: 26). Selznick suggests that organizations, as systems, maintain themselves by means of five essential imperatives, described as follows:

1. The *security* of the organization as a whole in relation to social forces in its environment. This imperative requires continuous attention to the possibilities of encroachment and to the forestalling of threatened aggressions or deleterious (though perhaps unintended) consequences of the actions of others.

2. The *stability* of the lines of authority and communication. One of the persistent reference points of administrative decision is the weighing of consequences for the continued capacity of leadership to control and to have access to the personnel or ranks.

3. The stability of informal relations within the organization. Ties of sentiment and *self-interest* are evolved as unacknowledged but effective mechanisms for adjustment of individuals and subgroups to the conditions of life within the organization. These ties represent a cementing of relationships which sustains the formal

authority in day-to-day operations and widens opportunities for effective communication. 'Consequently, attempts to "upset" the informal structure… will normally be met with considerable resistance.'

4. The *continuity* of policy and of the sources of its determination. For each level within the organization, and for the organization as a whole, it is necessary that there be a sense that action taken in the light of a given policy will not be placed in continuous jeopardy. Arbitrary or unpredictable changes in policy undermine the significance of (and therefore the attention to) day-to-day action by injecting a note of caprice. At the same time, the organization will seek stable roots (or firm statutory authority, or popular mandate) so that a sense of the permanency and legitimacy of its acts will be achieved.

5. A *homogeneity of outlook* with respect to the meaning and role of the organization. To minimize disaffection requires a unity derived from a common understanding of what the character of the organization is meant to be. When this homogeneity breaks down, as in situations of internal conflict over basic issues, the continued existence of the organization is endangered. On the other hand, one of the signs of a 'healthy' organization is the ability to orient new members effectively and readily slough off those who cannot be adapted to the established outlook.

(Selznick, 1948)

These imperatives are the mechanisms of a stable 'organic' system that is applied by analogy to an organization. One particularly relevant assumption of this analogy, and indeed of structural functionalism in general, is that of compulsion. There is little room for individuals to exercise imagination because organizations are viewed as constraining mechanisms that compel people to act in a particular way. When viewed through a structural-functional frame, organizational analysis proceeds by following three basic assumptions, as indicated below.

1. Organizations are cooperative systems with adaptive social structures, made up of interacting individuals, subgroups, and formal and informal relationships.

2. Organizations contain variable aspects, such as goals, which are linked to needs and self-defence mechanisms.

3. Organizations are determined by constraints and characterized by transformations when adjustments to needs are required. Such adjustments are required to deal with dysfunctions caused by instability in the operating environment.

The biological sciences were seen as rescuing social science from the laws of traditional Newtonian physics, which saw everything as a closed system (Katz and Kahn, 1966: 16). Consequently, the emergence of the open-systems model, which was influenced by von Bertalanffy's 'general system theory', enables us to view organizations as continuous flows of inputs, transformations, and outputs beyond their own boundaries. In 1966 Katz and Kahn articulated the concept of an organization as an open system. This was reinforced by Thompson's systems contingency perspective in 1967. What emerged was an idea of an organizational system as an artificial rational construction designed to improve work performance. Unlike the closed systems of physical sciences, social (and biological) systems depend on, and interact with, their external environments. For Katz and Kahn, the main difficulty in proactively managing strategic change results from the fact that organizations have in-built protective devices to maintain stability. Changing these patterns is very difficult. Unintended change often occurs when organizations drift from their original aims. As Katz and Kahn indicate:

> [t]he major misconception is the failure to recognize fully that the organization is continually dependent upon inputs from the environment and that the inflow of materials and human energy is not a constant. The fact that organizations have built-in protective devices to maintain stability and that they are notoriously difficult to change in the direction of some reformer's desires should not obscure the realities of the dynamic interrelationships of any social structure with its social and natural environment. The very efforts of the organization to maintain a constant external environment produce changes in organizational structure. The reaction to changed inputs to mute their possible revolutionary implications also results in changes.

(Katz and Kahn, 1966: 278)

The open-systems model expresses the relationship between the elements as indicated by Figure 1.2.

Figure 1.2 The open-systems model of Katz and Kahn

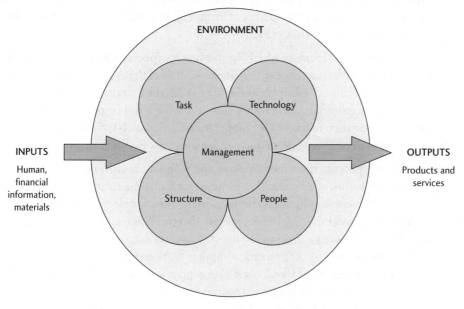

The organization has inputs that are then transformed through a variety of management functions. These are designed to achieve the best possible organizational design by coordinating the *task*, through the use of *technology* by *people* who are *structured* or organized in a way that is both efficient and effective.

> ❶ **Stop and think 1.1**
>
> Identify an organization and illustrate its inputs, outputs, and transformational processes. Provide details on how the internal processes are managed and controlled.

Following Katz and Kahn, the open-systems model contains eight characteristics:

1. *Importing energy* from the external environment. Thus, just as the biological cell receives oxygen from the bloodstream or the body takes in oxygen from the air and food from the external world, the organization draws energy from other institutions.

2. *Throughput* is a phrase used in many organizations, meaning that, as open systems, organizations transform the energy available to them. Just as the body converts starch and sugar into heat and action, an organization takes raw inputs such as materials and people and transforms them by producing products or services. Katz and Kahn suggest that, just as the personality converts chemical and electrical forms of stimulation into sensory qualities, and information into thought patterns, so the organization creates a new product, or processes materials, or trains people, or provides a service.

3. *Output* is essentially the service or product. Just as the biological organism exports from the lungs physiological products like carbon dioxide that help to maintain plants in the immediate environment, the organization provides customers with an output they value.

4. *Systems are cycles of events* in which the product is exported into the environment, where it furnishes sources of energy for repetition of the cycle of activities. Thus energy is the exchange of inputs and outputs with the external environment. For example, raw materials and human labour are turned into products and services, which are then marketed for monetary return, which is then used to obtain more raw materials and labour and perpetuates the cycle of activities.

5. *Entropy* is a process described by Katz and Kahn as 'a universal law of nature in which all forms of organization move toward disorganization or death'. For example, 'all complex physical systems move toward simple random distribution of their elements and biological organisms also run down and perish'. Therefore the survival of the organization requires the 'arrest of the entropic process'. This is overcome because the organization imports more energy from its environment than it expends. In other words, 'social organizations will seek to improve their survival position and to acquire in their reserves a comfortable margin of operation'. Organizations do go out of business but they can replenish themselves. As

Katz and Kahn point out, 'social systems, however, are not anchored in the same physical constancies as biological organisms and so are capable of almost indefinite arresting of the entropic process. Nevertheless the number of organizations which go out of existence every year is large.'

6. *Information input*, *negative feedback*, and the *coding process* mean that all inputs are also 'informative in character and furnish signals to the structure about the environment and about its own functioning in relation to the environment'. Furthermore, the 'simplest type of information input found in all systems is negative feedback', which 'enables the system to correct its deviations from course'. Katz and Kahn see this as analogous to the digestive system, in which selective signals are absorbed or assimilated. Terms like *adaptation* and *assimilation* reflect the biological analogy because an organization responds only to those signals to which it is adapted, and reacts to the information signals to which it is attuned. Katz and Kahn argue that, rather like the selection process in nature, the term coding reflects the selective mechanisms of a system by which incoming materials are either rejected or accepted and translated for the structure.

7. Organizations, like biological systems, are not motionless, so there can never be a true equilibrium. Instead, we must understand that organizations, like organisms, develop a *steady state* or 'continuous inflow of energy from the external environment and a continuous export of the products of the system'. The biological analogy is illustrated by the 'catabolic and anabolic processes of tissue breakdown and restoration within the body' that 'preserve a steady state so that the organism from time to time is not the identical organism it was but a highly similar organism'. Related to this are what they call the 'homeostatic processes' for the regulation of body temperature. Thus, as external conditions of humidity and temperature vary, the temperature of the body remains the same because it is regulated by the endocrine glands. The steady state and *dynamic homeostasis* of organizations are regulated by the organization's subsystems.

8. Organizations 'move in the direction of *differentiation* and elaboration'. That is, in biological systems genetic change occurs: organisms move from primitive to complex arrangements in order to survive. Similarly, as organizations mature they become increasingly diffuse. Thus they 'move toward the multiplication and elaboration of roles with greater specialization of function'.

1.3.1 An organization is a complex whole

As Michael Jackson states, 'a system is a complex whole the functioning of which depends upon its parts and the interactions of those parts' (2003: 3). Broadly speaking, we can think of three types of system:

• Natural biological systems.

• Social systems, such as families and religious and political institutions, which are socially constructed entities designed to accommodate relationships between people.

- Artificial or mechanical systems, such as built environments and information systems, which are designed to make improvements to living or work arrangements.

One of the advantages of systems theory, as Jackson informs us, is that it is not reductive. That is, it does not seek to reduce complexity by breaking it down into its component parts. Systems theory seeks to understand phenomena as wholes and consequently the term 'holism' is sometimes used to illustrate that a system needs to be seen in its entirety.

The idea of holism is articulated by Thompson (1967):

> Approached as a natural system, the complex organization is a set of interdependent parts which together make up a whole because each contribute something and receive something from a whole, which in turn is interdependent with some larger environment. Survival of the system is taken to be the goal, and the parts and their relationships presumably are determined through evolutionary processes. Dysfunctions are conceivable, but it is assumed that an offending part will adjust to produce a net positive contribution or be disengaged, or else the system will degenerate.
>
> Central to the natural-systems approach is the concept of homeostasis, or self stabilization, which spontaneously, or naturally, governs the necessary relationships among parts and activities and thereby keeps the system viable in the face of disturbances stemming from the environment.

(Thompson, 1967: 283)

Systems theory seeks to explain complex interrelationships among organizational elements and external variables by using quantitative techniques. Because they see them as continually changing dynamic equilibria, systems theorists therefore view organizations as designed to cope with and manage change. An example of this is Weiner's model of an organization as an adaptive system. Weiner uses the term 'cybernetics' (from the Greek for 'steersman') to describe a study of structures and functions of control, and information processing systems in both animals and machines. Thus, such systems are able to regulate themselves. In biological systems this is a natural process, whereas an organization's systems must be designed.

The overly mechanistic approach to viewing artificial systems needs to be balanced against two concerns related to the environment in which the organization exists:

1. Organizations are also social systems: any technical system requires people to operate it. Consequently their needs must be designed into the technical system.

2. Organizations have contingencies. In other words, the technology used by the organization, the nature of the industry it operates in, the competences of the

staff who work for it, their motivations and leadership are also important contingencies that affect an organization's performance.

Each concern reflects the view that any change interaction must incorporate these constraints into the design of the new (changed) systems model. For example, if an organization is seen as a social system and not simply a technical system, then we must come to recognize the way in which people have to live, work, and engage in some way with the technical system. For systems designers such as architects and computer programmers it is therefore important to involve the people affected by the system.

---

❶ Stop and think 1.2

Think of a technical system that you might redesign if asked to do so by an organization. For example, this might be an IT system, a production system, use of a physical space, or an administrative system. If you do not involve in its design the people who will eventually use the system, what negative outcomes might emerge?

The link between organizational systems design and contingency theory illustrates how systems theory developed from a simple biological analogy. Galbraith's (1973) book made a clear link between the functional components, organizational structures, and contingent circumstances of an organization. For example, Galbraith's approach invites us to look for:

- The type and quality of information required in conditions of certainty or uncertainty.
- The degree of interdependence between the various functional components.
- Mechanisms that enable organizational adaptation.

Table 1.1 illustrates how information within the system affects an organization's ability to take action towards change. The degree to which change can be planned depends upon the amount of reliable information in the system. When the quality of information is high, changes can be planned but are unlikely to be major; when conditions are unpredictable, information is unreliable and the degree of success in any change initiative is low. We can therefore state that the greater the level of uncertainty, the more the organization must make provisional judgements and be ready to change things quickly.

Contingency theorists who work within this perspective view organizational change as the degree of control an organization has over circumstances. Thus we can formulate a simple question for this purpose: 'how wide is the gap between the amounts of information required by this organization at this time?' If we take the 2008 world banking crisis as an example, we can illustrate this point. During the month of

Table 1.1 Control over circumstances: situations where significant change is inevitable

The likelihood of major strategic change is low when:	The likelihood of major strategic change is high when:
The situation is highly predictable.	The situation is not predictable.
Traditional roles and procedures guide action.	New procedures are required.
The quality of information is high.	The quality of information is low.

October 2008, protracted negotiations between President Bush and the US Senate representatives, unhappy with his initial plans, eventually resulted in a rescue package for US banks. This was followed by the British Prime Minister, Gordon Brown, partly nationalizing some UK banks. Members of the G7 countries lowered interest rates around the world at the same time, also attempting to find a coordinated approach to the world economic crisis. The reality was that, at the time, no one could realistically estimate its extent: the information gap was simply too large. No one really knew who owed money to whom; nor did anyone know what impact the banking crisis was likely to have on other sectors of the world economy. Thus, attempting to steer change was impossible because there was insufficient information to make reliable decisions. Although this is an extreme example, many organizations face similar problems to varying degrees. In situations of severe unpredictability caused by lack of information, managing planned change becomes highly problematic. The solution, according to Galbraith, is to find new solutions:

> The ability of an organization to successfully coordinate its activities by goal setting, hierarchy, and rules depends on the combination of the frequency of exceptions and the capacity of the hierarchy to handle them. As task uncertainty increases, the number of exceptions increases until the hierarchy is overloaded. Then the organization must employ new design strategies. Either it can act in two ways to reduce the amount of information that is processed, or it can act to increase its capacity to handle more information. An organization may choose to develop in both of these ways.

(Galbraith, 1973: 312)

1.3.2 Structural theory

The structures of organizations are considered to be amenable to change. Organizations are viewed as rational and should be designed to achieve their objectives. The Classical School of Management argued that all organizations should be designed scientifically. The main contributors to the school were Henry Fayol,

Charles Babbage, Daniel McCullum, Frederick Winslow Taylor, and Max Weber. For these writers, organizational efficiency was achieved through the rational design of organizations. The Classical School assumed that there was a best structure for any organization, related to the environment in which the organization operated.

The design of an organization was related to *specialization* and to the *division of labour*. Specialization is the extent to which highly skilled operations and individuals are required. Because the design of organizations was seen as a purely rational activity, problems or dysfunctions were seen to result from structural imperfections or flaws that could be solved by changing the organization's structure. Furthermore, although the Classical School considered that a bureaucratic structure was the best means to achieve efficiency and effectiveness, by the 1950s this view was increasingly challenged. The first challenge emerged with the work of Burns and Stalker (1961), who were interested in the rapidly changing electronics industry in Britain, and in Scotland in particular. Their research revealed that organizations in stable operating environments are heavily dependent on control mechanisms and therefore require mechanistic structures. Conversely, the newer industries based on, or developing, micro-electronic technology required organic structures in order to meet situations that are changing. The message, therefore, was that the rate of organizational change is critical to organizations. Where they have to meet rapidly changing circumstances and conditions, and where technology is critical to their survival, then organic structures need to be designed. This would also be true today of the fashion industry, where styles change quickly and competition for change requires organizations to get goods into the high street quickly.

In the following year Blau and Scott (1962) argued that organizations have both a formal structure and an informal aspect to them. The formal structure determines the standard rules and regulations: for example, a highly structured organization operating bureaucratic procedures is managed through complex rules, policies, frameworks, and desk instructions. However, they argued that it is impossible to understand how organizations are structured by simply looking at rules and regulations without understanding the informal aspect of the organization. Their argument was heavily influenced by Barnard's (1938) book, *The Functions of the Executive*, and suggested that the informal organization reflects unconscious processes. In other words, habits, attitudes, and assumptions of people are critical to performance. This was clearly an early recognition that change requires more than structural redesign because it suggested that senior managers have to align the structure with what we call today the organization's culture.

The earlier work of Max Weber in the 1920s reflected his concerns with specialization. By the 1960s academics used the word 'differentiation' to reflect this but also to indicate how specialization is affected by increasingly complex environments. In relation to organizational change, we can note that the process of differentiation—increased complexity of organization—suggests that diverse forces are responsible for pulling organizations apart. This process of differentiation therefore means that organizational change is required in order to integrate the organization with its new environment. To put this more succinctly, differentiation requires integration. This particular concern was articulated by Lawrence and Lorsch (1969) in their book, *Developing Organizations: diagnosis and action*. It also reflects the emphasis on design since change planning is required to deal with uncertainty caused by rapidly changing circumstances. This was reinforced by Davis and Lawrence's (1977) argument that a matrix organization was required when external change was forced upon organizations. Accordingly, they argue that change in design is therefore determined by three conditions:

1. *Outside pressure for dual focus.* What they mean by this is that some companies need to focus attention both on complex technical issues and on the unique requirements of the customer; this dual focus requires a matrix structure.

2. *Pressures for high information-processing capacity.* The second reason to adopt a matrix structure is a requirement for high information-processing capacity among an organization's members. The failure to construct a matrix organization in such circumstances will lead to information overload.

3. *Pressure for shared resources.* When organizations are under pressure to achieve economies of scale, they need to find ways of utilizing scarce human resources to meet quality standards.

Both systems theory and structural theory share the view that organizations are rational and serve utilitarian purposes. That is, organizations are viewed as a means to achieve efficiency and effectiveness. They do this by identifying clear goals. The structural-functional systems perspective is therefore described as rational because it assumes a relatively simple cause and effect relationship among variables related to functional integration and structural change. As a perspective, it is clear about what it seeks to achieve. Organizational change is relatively straightforward: we either change functional relationships in order to achieve harmony or we change the design of the organization in order to meet the complexity of its environment.

1.4 Multiple constituencies: change by negotiation

In advancing a critique of the structural-functional perspective Michael Keeley (1983) argues that it is common to model organizations after biological systems. In most texts organizations are depicted as 'social actors' who possess the distinguishing features of living beings such as goals and needs. By contrast, individuals are portrayed as functional 'members' filling roles and serving as 'human resources' to further the organization's ends. The organic model is useful mainly for addressing survival needs, but one difficulty is that it tends to confuse the goals of an organization with the goals of powerful individuals. The structural-functional perspective presents a reified and over-rational picture of social systems.

By contrast, the multiple constituencies perspective does not assume that organizations exist independently from the people who work for them or interact with them. Multiple constituency theory was first outlined by Cyert and March in their book *A Behavioural Theory of the Firm* (1963), which describes organizations as coalitions of self-interested participants. Organizational goals, they argue, change as a result of bargaining processes because an organization is a dynamic coalition of individuals and groups, all of which have different demands. The perspective focuses on how goals are achieved and whose interests are satisfied and affected by the actions taken in the name of the organization. If we think, therefore, of an organization containing a number of groups and external stakeholders, all of which have differing interests, then we can consider how organizational change affects each different group, or alternatively how each may make demands on an organization to change its strategy. The multiple constituencies perspective focuses on the way in which resources are managed and distributed among organizational members and stakeholders in the interests of governance.

❶ Stop and think 1.3

Imagine that you start a new job as a travel executive and are required to visit overseas destinations six times a year. You chose this job because you were excited by the prospect of overseas travel. As an incentive, employees are permitted to stay in the destination for two days after they have completed their tasks. Consequently executives are motivated to choose an interesting destination. Your organization operates from two different sites in the UK. During your first year of employment you hear rumours that the person who allocates staff to destinations 'cherry picks' the best for herself and then for friends or colleagues who work with her at the main site. You begin to realize that the rumours have a ring of truth about them. What do you do? Try to ingratiate yourself with the decision maker by becoming friends? Offer to take on more work if she offers you one or two better destinations? Should you take the issue to her line manager at the risk of becoming unpopular? Or do you accept the situation for what it is and that life is not fair? How do you bargain for change?

The multiple constituencies perspective criticizes the structural-functional approach for making it difficult to achieve conceptual clarity about what constitutes organizational effectiveness. For example, Connolly, Conlon, and Deutsch argue that effectiveness statements are evaluative and descriptive. Generally they are not attempts to answer the question 'how is an entity X performing?' but usually 'how well is entity X performing?' and often 'how much better should entity X perform?'

The central differentiation among current effectiveness statements is how they specify the evaluation criteria used to define how well the entity is performing or could perform (Connolly, Conlon, and Deutsch, 1980: 211). As a result, the multiple constituency view treats organizations as systems with differential assessments of effectiveness by different constituencies. Although the interests of internal groups (for example, executives, managers, production workers, and so forth) and external stakeholders (for example, clients, shareholders, government regulators, suppliers, and so forth) may overlap, they each have specific interests and priorities or goals they seek to pursue. Each constituency brings its own interests and motivations into the organizational arena. We can therefore consider organizations as webs of fluid interactions between different groups of people whose interests keep changing. The multiple constituencies approach is therefore a means to identify the actions and motivations of people. More importantly, it reflects organizational change as a continuously negotiable order because interests and coalitions change over time.

Although the multiple constituencies perspective originated with Cyert and March, it is rooted in the social contract tradition of political and moral argument. The idea of contract theory emerged in the seventeenth century with the political theorists Thomas Hobbes, John Locke, and Jean-Jacques Rousseau. In the twentieth century such theories have become the basis for political theorists (as we will see in Chapter 7) and writers concerned with corporate ethics (see Chapter 2).

1.4.1 Stakeholder interests

Since stakeholders reflect dynamic interests, change agents need to learn how to interact with them. There are various ways of doing this. For example, Mitroff (1983) suggests seven approaches. These are:

1. *The imperative approach,* which identifies stakeholders who feel strongly about an organization's proposed policies or actions. This approach requires making a list of as many stakeholders as possible and interacting with them to resolve concerns.

2. *The positional approach,* which identifies stakeholders who occupy formal positions in a policy-making structure. For example, health trusts, schools, colleges, universities, and charities are required to have boards of governors who must oversee the operations of such organizations. Many boards of governors can be identified from organization charts or legal documents.

3. *The reputational approach* entails asking various knowledgeable or important people to nominate those they believe to have a stake in the organization.

4. *The social participation approach* identifies individuals or groups of stakeholders who may have an interest in a policy-related issue for the organization. For example, members of committees, and people who might normally be excluded because they are not so visible, or who do not normally have the opportunity to articulate their views, will be represented.

5. *The opinion-leadership approach* identifies individuals who have access to leverage of some sort. Examples include informed professionals, commentators, and editors of important newspapers or journals.

6. *The demographic approach* identifies stakeholders by characteristics such as age, sex, race, occupation, religion, place of birth, and level of education.

7. *The focal organization approach* seeks to identify individuals and organizations that have important relationships with the focal organization. That is, suppliers, employees, customers or clients, allies, competitors, regulators.

The multiple constituencies perspective suggests that, prior to any change initiative, change agents should analyse the following issues:

- The purposes and motivations of a stakeholder.
- The resources of a stakeholder. These will include material, symbolic, and physical resources, as well as informational resources and skills.
- Special knowledge and opinions of the stakeholder.
- Stakeholders' commitments to the organization and expertise.
- Relationships between stakeholders, focusing particularly on the amount of power (or authority), responsibility, and accountability they have.
- The extent of the network of interdependent relationships among stakeholders.
- The extent to which a change in strategy can be identified in the interests of any one particular stakeholder.

Such an analysis of stakeholder interests suggests that whilst stakeholders are generally supportive and have an interest in the organization, they can also become a negative influence on it. They might indeed reflect a threat and become a barrier to organizational change. Mitroff therefore suggests a number of options for influencing or changing the views and actions of particular stakeholders. We can:

- Simply exercise power and authority by commanding the stakeholder to comply.
- Appeal to reason and therefore attempt to persuade the stakeholder.
- Engage in tactical bargaining with a stakeholder.
- Negotiate in order to reach a compromise.
- Engage in problem solving by sharing information, debating, and arriving at mutually agreed perceptions.

The multiple constituencies perspective reflects a view of social systems in which people take actions and engage in activities to maximize their own interests. They also collude with others and engage in purposeful activity. Negotiation of organizational change revolves around three central issues:

1. Changing organizational objectives requires that leaders be able to re-evaluate the organization's current mission, purposes, objectives, and goals, and mobilize action through inspiration. Such leaders need to embrace inspirational leadership.

2. The ability to develop and mobilize intellectual capital by using the combined resources held by all stakeholders creatively. This should include the identification and cultivation of scarce resources, skills, and capital.

3. The ability to sustain cooperation and to eliminate conflict among stakeholders so that ethical, moral, and cooperative understanding is achieved.

The perspective argues that it is constituencies of people, rather than organizations, that have goals and objectives. Consequently, it moves us away from the problem of reification, because stakeholder interests must be negotiated. Yet it still assumes that people act rationally through an appeal to the common good. The perspective draws us towards interventions that focus on a concern with organizational and personal values, social justice, and the distribution of rights and obligations. It provides a useful way forward for organizations in the public domain that are subjected to public scrutiny through governance.

1.5 Organizational Development: the humanistic approach to change

Organizational Development (OD) is derived from human resource theory or organizational behaviour. It dates back to the Hawthorne experiments, which began in the Western Electrical Company in 1927. Elton Mayo and his team began these experiments by using the same assumptions as the structural-functional perspective: that is, they initially sought to investigate improvements to organizational efficiency by redesigning an organization's environment along scientific principles. The experiments focused on rational pragmatic concerns such as technology and work performance, the rate of flow of materials, and throughput of a factory system. One can therefore recognize the early development of open-systems theory and structural design within these experiments. Their lack of success meant that the problem of efficiency and effectiveness was refocused towards socio-psychological factors, such as group norms. One interesting source dating back to 1926 was Mary Parker Follett's description of 'The Giving of Orders' (1926). Follett argued that psychology could make an important contribution to understanding motivational relationships in the workplace. One example she discusses is the importance of understanding the law of the situation. Once this is discovered, better attitudes follow. She suggested that giving orders in a positive manner facilitated more harmonious attitudes within the workplace.

But related concerns that began with the Second World War later paved the way for a more sophisticated social science concerned with behaviour in organizations. In particular, a concern to identify effective leadership and to enhance workgroup relationships was paramount because of the American army's focus on morale. As a result, many academics emerged from this tradition with a clear focus on the relationship between leadership, motivation, and group dynamics. The investigation of individual and organizational needs was part of this use of applied social science. An early example was Maslow's research, which resulted in his paper 'A Theory of Human Motivation' (1943). The awareness that human needs impact on organizations was a theme developed further in McGregor's *The Human Side of Enterprise* (1957). By the late 1960s and 1970s OD emerged from this behavioural research as a distinct discipline. Whilst it focused on harmonizing individual and organizational needs, it also readily adopted the open-systems framework of the structural-functional perspective. French and Bell (1978) were largely responsible for articulating this approach when they characterized the perspective as a mixture of open-systems theory with humanistic values.

Today, we can discern six essential characteristics of OD. These are:

1. A methodology informed largely by Action Research—a term coined by Kurt Lewin in the 1940s.

2. Interventions should only result from careful organizational diagnosis (Tichy, Hornstein, and Nisberg, 1976).

3. A recognition that effective change requires process consultation (Schein, 1995) rather than negotiation through an individual in order to achieve corporate social responsibility in change initiatives. It should be noted that this is in line with OD's humanistic approach to change.

4. An awareness of barriers to personal growth and organizational change, championed largely by Elisabeth Kübler-Ross (1973).

5. An emphasis on personal and organizational learning in contrast to training, proposed by Reg Revans (1982).

6. A recognition that groups and culture will influence change initiatives, articulated by Lewin (1951) and Schein and Bennis (1965).

OD emerged as a distinctive discipline for managing change. It did so initially by adopting experiential approaches such as T-groups (training groups) and Lewin's Force Field Analysis as a technique for managing organizational transitions. Action Research encouraged employees to develop a collaborative approach to diagnosing problems and engaging in action learning. Argyris's book on *Intervention Theory and Method* (1970) is a comprehensive review of process-consultation techniques articulated by Schein (1995) and intervention techniques that became associated with the idea of planned, organization-wide change. Such change strategies were 'managed from the top' in order to 'increase organizational effectiveness and health' through interventions in the organization's processes using behavioural science knowledge (Beckhard, 1969). Lewin's (1951) three stages of change—unfreeze, change, refreeze—reflects the essence of the traditional OD approach through which a clear goal or destination is identified and cascaded to the organization's members. This has been described as a linear model of change (Marshak, 1993) that tends to omit the 'untidy parts of the process that do not fit neatly into Lewin's framework' (Inns 1996: 23). Most critics of Lewin's planned change model make this argument. However, we must be cautious about this since, as we will see in Chapter 3, Lewin did not apply this approach to organization-level change.

Often, OD proceeds with problem identification through the application of Action Research at the individual, the group, or the organizational level. Following careful diagnosis, intervention strategies are designed to deal with an organizational problem by applying various techniques. At the individual level, behaviour modification theory is often used to encourage personal growth. At the group level, intervention strategies are informed by analysis of group dynamics, whilst at the organizational level, strategic interventions are designed to manage strategic change through the application of technology, structural change, or change to human resources. We can understand how these interventions work by exploring them in greater depth.

1.5.1 Intervention strategies at the individual level

Strategies at the individual level were influenced by behaviour modification theory. The purpose of this technique is to increase the frequency of desired behaviours and reduce the frequency of undesired behaviours. Behaviour modification therefore seeks to modify the behaviours of individuals by training people to recognize a positive stimulus in order to provoke a desired response. It can also be used to change an individual's reaction to fears and phobias. Intervention strategies used instead of behaviour modification theory include personal and management development techniques such as Lewin's Force Field Analysis and learning interventions designed to improve personal learning.

---

❶ Stop and think 1.4

We rarely remember modifying our own behaviour but we do this all the time. Think about the last time you learned a new skill. How difficult was this at first? During the learning process how did you modify your own behaviour or attitudes? How did evaluation lead to improvement?

1.5.2 Intervention strategies at the group level

At the group level, intervention strategies originated from studies of group dynamics including armed forces personnel, industrial workers, and professional groups. Group dynamics was first defined by Kurt Lewin in the 1940s. Observations of groups led Lewin to note that groups develop personalities as a result of their unique composition. Change was therefore more likely when the group as a whole made a collective decision to have its members change their behaviours. This was far more effective in producing the desired changes than more formal techniques such as lectures and instruction. Lewin's work became the foundation for training in group skills, sensitivity training, teambuilding, and OD.

Groups therefore can be a major influence on change, or can inhibit change. However, the capability of a group to respond flexibly to change will depend on the degree to which its members:

- Explore problem-solving alternatives.
- Are motivated to achieve the objectives of the group.
- Make an effort to learn how to change.
- Discover what specifically needs to be changed to meet current demands.
- Are prepared to experiment.

1.5.3 Intervention strategies at the organizational level

At the organizational level, a greater depth was provided by a focus on planned change interventions. Planned change strategies, according to Chin and Benne (1976), emerged from the Enlightenment tradition with the application of rational thought to interventions in the modern world. In other words, changing things requires an application to reason. Associated with this was the pursuit of social progress. Chin and Benne describe a central element common to all planned change programmes as 'the conscious utilisation and application of knowledge as an instrument or tool for modifying patterns and institutions of practice' (1976: 22). Planned change interventions are therefore extremely varied but they fall under three broad headings:

1. *Empirical–rational interventions,* such as political interventions giving rise to new government policies.
2. *Normative re-educative interventions,* which involve organizational and group change and are usually made by OD consultants, change agents, and trainers.
3. *Power-coercive interventions,* which range from industrial relations strategies, protests, and the use of political institutions, to legislation.

Empirical–rational strategies reflect the Enlightenment desire for progress by replacing ignorance or superstition with more objective, or scientific, and rigorous methods for extending knowledge. This therefore implies:

- Basic research and dissemination of knowledge through general education.
- Personnel selection in order to engage the most appropriately experienced and qualified people for the post.
- Developing systems analysts who can identify the interconnections between people and processes in the pursuit of efficiency and effectiveness.

Examples of empirical–rational planned change strategies include the application of 'rational' planning to the design of the built environment (architecture) or of public services such as the National Health Service, education, social services; military interventions; and so forth. However, as we discover in Chapter 3, empirical–rational planned change strategies are also associated with mechanistic and managerialist versions of change. Such strategies assume that people are rational and will follow persuasion once the logic of the situation is revealed through discourse. Change occurs because a critical mass of people is motivated by improvement to change. It is also assumed that power, in some form, will involve a degree of compliance.

Normative re-educative strategies seek to enlighten through exploration. As Chin and Benne point out, Lewin's view of change 'required interrelations between research, training, and action' (Chin and Benne, 1976: 31). Re-education is a normative process because it requires agreement as well as changes to cognitive and perceptual elements. These ideas led Lewin to develop Action Research as a means to jointly explore problems and to find collaborative solutions. These strategies are designed to achieve organizational improvement by enhancing the problem-solving capabilities of the organizational system and also to develop the people who engage in planned change.

Normative re-educative strategies therefore contain four prerequisites:

1. The collection, analysis, and feedback of data about the nature of the 'organizational problem'.
2. Training of key personnel in methods of problem solving.
3. Developing research and development roles as a strategic necessity.
4. Training internal change agents to function within the organization.

Power-coercive strategies are designed to analyse the sources of power. They 'seek to mass political and economic power behind the change goals which the strategists of change have decided are desirable' (Chin and Benne, 1976: 39). Thus, analysis of legitimate or illegitimate power is exercised.

> **» Case example 1.1**
>
> The petrol war—a power-coercive strategy
>
> In 2000, Britain was in the middle of an oil crisis. By 13 September 90 percent of petrol stations were out of fuel; buses, trains and schools were affected, the National Health Service had to cancel operations, and food supplies were threatened.
>
> The crisis was caused by road hauliers who blockaded roads, thus preventing supplies of fuel from getting through to petrol stations. Many of the tanker drivers were either sympathetic to the road hauliers' complaints that the price of fuel was too high, or »

> were too frightened to drive out of refineries and oil depots. Britain's economy relies heavily on road transport, which was reported to have been less than 48 hours from total shutdown. A national crisis developed that affected the economy, emergency services, and public confidence in government.

Tony Blair, the Prime Minister, attempted to solve the problem by appealing to oil company executives to instruct tanker drivers to restore supplies of fuel to the nation's petrol stations. At the same time, the government ensured that police would provide protection to drivers of oil tankers. Police served an order on 20 pickets to leave private property and stop blocking refineries in Colwick, Nottinghamshire. The Police Superintendents' Association said officers would have no choice but to make sure that tankers were able to leave depots and deliver their fuel if oil companies decided to send them out.

Since the late 1980s there have been various criticisms of the planned change with which OD is associated. Planned organizational change initiatives such as Total Quality Management and Business Process Re-engineering have tended to use some OD concepts selectively, which results in mechanistic approaches. But such approaches do not usually employ the methodology of OD and often ignore the organizational learning implicit in the normative re-educative approach to planned change, as discussed in Chapter 3. This has led to the accusation that planned change has been too concerned with the mechanics of change at the expense of the historical, processual, and contextual issues that inform the underlying dynamics of the organization. For example, in their study of TQM programmes, Dawson and Palmer (1995) noted that unforeseen critical events during the change process could impede, hasten, or redirect the route to change. The most notable critiques of planned change are those of Pettigrew (1985), Dawson (1994), and Pettigrew and Whipp (1993). The alternative to planned change models that has gradually developed has been dubbed 'the emergent change model' (Burnes, 1996) or 'processual change' (Dawson, 1994). The criticisms suggest that change should not be treated as a series of linear events but as a complex, temporal, iterative, and non-linear patchwork of unfolding processes.

! Stop and think 1.5

Make a list of intervention strategies that you have been affected by. This list should include personal interventions at school or at work that were used to change your behaviour in some way. Then identify interventions that were applied to a group you were a member of and say what the dynamics were that required change. Finally, say what was successful or unsuccessful and why.

1.6 Creativity and Volition: a Critical Theory of Change

Each of the perspectives we have previously considered has tended to focus on the structures, functions, and practices of different groups in organizations. To varying degrees each perspective has accepted a rational and utilitarian view of organizations. The various strands identified in this section take an entirely different view of organizations. This section addresses what is missing from the previous accounts of organizational analysis and change. This perspective is informed by Critical Theory, which seeks to focus on the ways in which people interact as well as on their motives for doing so, and it suggests that creativity and critical analysis should become the focus for change interventions because this is missing from previous accounts. Central to this focus is the view that conflict, rather than consensus, is the driving force for change at an individual level, a group level, and an organizational level. The most important implications of this assumption are as follows:

1. Organizations, like the social world in general, are better characterized by conflict, flux, and change than by the stability and consensus typical of the structural-functional perspective. Indeed, creativity emerges from the challenge and conflict of ideas.

2. People in organizations do not simply follow orders, nor do they occupy roles as prescriptively as the structural-functional perspective assumes. People are therefore active agents within organizations. The social practice of creativity is therefore the driving force of organizational change.

3. Observations of organizational life should reject the spectator view of knowledge.

1.6.1 Conflict, flux, and change

The modern idea that organizations are better characterized by conflict, flux, and change can be traced back to the philosophy of Hegel. Hegel himself was influenced by the views of the Greek philosopher Heraclitus, who saw everything that exists in the world as part of some continuously changing process. Hegel argued that change is never arbitrary and is always intelligible, and that every complex situation contains the seeds of conflict. These conflicting elements destabilize the system. Consequently, no system, situation, or idea could simply exist indefinitely. Conflicts have to work themselves out until they achieve a resolution. But this resolution is never an end point because the whole process begins again. Hegel describes this as the dialectical process, which is made up of three stages: the description or *thesis*; the *antithesis*, which is the reaction or magnitude of countervailing forces or conflicting elements; and the *synthesis*, a new situation or idea that arises from a resolution of the previous conflicts.

An example of the way in which conflict leads to change can be gleaned from the following case example.

> ## » Case example 1.2
>
> ### Conflict and resolution in an organizational setting
>
> John and Mary attended regular monthly management meetings chaired by the chief executive Edward Strangeways. During the course of a meeting John and Mary were asked to report informally to Edward on the actions and views of close colleagues. Both John and Mary recognized that they were responsible to their line manager, Edward. However, they also felt that what had been asked of them placed them in a difficult situation. When they considered the ethics of this situation, Mary stated that 'basically what Edward wants us to do is spy on our colleagues'. John said that he felt uncomfortable with this request but recognized they had a responsibility to their line manager. As they observed their work colleagues, particularly during their own staff meetings, they noted that their staff had some potentially genuine grievances and personal views that either had not previously been addressed by the organization, or that the staff felt would not be taken seriously.
>
> Two days before the next monthly management meeting, John and Mary decided that they could not misrepresent the views of their colleagues, and to present a number of issues to Edward. Edward wanted the names of the staff who had expressed opinions and concerns but John and Mary refused on the grounds that this was unfair and potentially unethical to the individuals concerned. Edward decided to take action against John and Mary, both of whom had experienced a significant amount of stress during the previous month. He let John know that he would not be putting him forward for further promotion and he told Mary that her temporary position would not be made permanent. Both John and Mary took their case to an industrial tribunal, which decided in their favour, and this resulted in a severe reprimand to Edward on the ground of his leadership style. Eventually both John and Mary were promoted and Edward left the company. The Human Resources Department were concerned that no one had consulted them and, as a result, decided to promote training throughout the company on the subject of stress, bullying, and harassment.

The case example illustrates how Hegel's dialectic works. Stage one began with the demands of Edward (the thesis). Stage two was characterized by the stress and conflict experienced by John and Mary and their decision to challenge Edward (the antithesis). Stage three is the resolution (synthesis).

1.6.2 People are active agents

In contrast to other animals, humans are uniquely capable of creativity. This is because of the human being's ability to employ complex linguistic rules in everyday interaction.

As Noam Chomsky (1972) indicated, humans can create an infinite variety of novel constructions using a relatively small set of linguistic rules. Indeed, humans have the ability to construct a stream of new activity out of the old. Just as some individuals produce more creative outcomes than others, so do organizations.

The role of language is central to creativity. It is through the use of language that we are able to construct descriptions of events and things, process information, and symbolically manipulate the world in which we live by imposing order and meaning on it. In their 1966 book, *The Social Construction of Reality*, Berger and Luckmann point out that the social worlds we construct are possible only because of the meanings we impose. But just as we construct reality, we can also distort it when beliefs do not stand up to scrutiny. Such ideological distortions may also result from power differences caused by those who control situations to their advantage. Conflict might not always be inevitable in organizations, largely because people find ways of avoiding it or defusing it. Pfeffer (1981), for example, suggests that we need to understand the role of power in decision making. As he points out in the following paragraph, understanding the dynamics of decision-making situations is central to critical analysis:

> To understand organizational choices using a political model, it is necessary to understand who participates in decision making, what determines each player's stand on the issues, what determines each actor's relative power, and how the decision process arrives at a decision; in other words, how the various preferences become combined… A change in any one of these aspects—relative power, the rules of decision making, all preferences—can lead to a change in the predicted organizational decision.
>
> (Pfeffer, 1981: 31)

But language can also reflect the way some individuals manipulate discourse to their advantage. It is therefore possible to understand how power is not only a physical thing; it is also a property of the way in which language is used.

1.6.3 The critique of the spectator view of knowledge

One way of understanding what is meant by the spectator view of knowledge is to imagine oneself in an arena or a theatre in which a sports event or a play takes place. As a spectator you are aware of the rules of the context and, as you watch the performance unfold, you make judgements about the quality of the event and about the quality of the performances. This type of knowledge is contained within a set of rules that already exists. Such rules indicate what the players and actors can do, just as they indicate what the spectator can do. But just imagine if you wanted to challenge this convention of star *versus* spectator in the setting of the theatre. One thing you could do is to leave your seat, go up onto the stage, and take part in the play. By doing so you alter the boundaries of performance and the taken-for-granted interactional rules are challenged.

The perspective is critical of modernism. Although the concept carries a variety of meanings, one central theme is the construction of a grand narrative. For example, one of the conventions in the accumulation of scientific knowledge is the construction of a deductive theoretical model that is then put to the test. This principle emerged with Enlightenment thinkers and it was introduced into the discourse of science. The principle that we usually refer to as positivism was also adopted by management thinkers. Implicit in this process is the attempt to construct a grand narrative: essentially a causal story that takes the reader or the viewer from act one through to the final act. Similarly, management stories often carry an implicit grand narrative that simplifies complexity by creating a causal story for their readers. The management stories are usually related to efficiency and effectiveness. Academics who challenge this type of grand narrative are usually grouped together under the heading of 'post-modernists', despite the fact that many do not see themselves as such. These include Foucault, Derrida, and Lyotard. Foucault's analysis of power, for example, seeks to uncover the discontinuity in history and to discredit the belief in a holistic, universalistic theory of human social development (Casey, 2002: 125). In contrast to the idea of the grand narrative, Foucault argued for 'the suspension and interrogation of unities' because 'history is random and discontinuous' (ibid.). If we apply this idea to organizations, then we can argue that organizational change is not a linear process.

As spectators of organizations we therefore tend to collapse events into a sequence and ignore a variety of processes that will, in fact, be discontinuous. For example, if we consider organizational change as a neat linear sequence, which begins with a strategic plan produced by senior executives that is then cascaded down through the organization, what we are likely to notice is that, whilst senior executives appear to have the power and authority to manage this sequence, in reality it requires people to accept it. In other words, we can observe the appearance of formal power and authority as well as other forms that take shape throughout the organizational system. Thus we might discover resistance to change, cynicism about the change project, and fatigue from previous change initiatives, which impact on motivation and so on.

Derrida is also critical of modernism, although his critiques are focused on linguistic theory. According to Derrida (1978), all texts carry at least a double meaning. That is, we can deconstruct a text into at least two possible alternative viewpoints, but we should note that texts often contain multiple viewpoints. In other words, Derrida's technique of deconstruction allows us to see a plurality of meanings rather than a single objectively meaningful plot. If we therefore adopt Derrida's argument and method of deconstruction and apply it to an organization, we will discover a multiplicity of narratives. For example, if we were to analyse change in a particular organizational setting we might well come across significant differences between management discourse and a variety of other discourses. But Derrida's work employs more than *recognition* of multiple constituencies, because all reflect different power relationships. There is, furthermore, no single claim to truth and, as observers, we must question why such claims are made and whose interest they serve.

A third example is the work of Lyotard, who seeks to address *The Postmodern Condition* in his book (1984) of that name. Lyotard takes issue with various philosophers of science such as Kuhn, Lakatos, and Popper, and linguistic philosophers like Wittgenstein. He argues that because of modern information technology society can no longer be viewed as an organic system. Nor can it be conceived of as a simple two-party antagonistic field of conflict between opposing classes, as Marx saw it (Casey, 2002: 122). A consequence of modern information technology is that we can no longer subscribe to the myth of a single Enlightenment grand narrative. If we apply this argument to organizations, then we have to reject the biological, organic analogy of structural functionalism as a means of interpretation and analysis, and replace it with the investigation of multiple language games. In other words, who's doing what to whom and why. In the process we have to dispense with any questions pertaining to organizational efficiency and effectiveness.

We should note that postmodern Critical Theory is a generic term that embraces many disparate theorists who are nevertheless united in their objection to the modernist grand narrative. These include academics influenced by the Critical Theory of the Frankfurt School of social science, which was influenced by both the ideas of Marx about the origins of social structures and the psychotherapy of Freud; analysts of power, particularly Foucault (1977; 1980), Derrida (1978) and Lyotard (1984); the phenomenology of Berger and Luckmann and the ordinary-language philosophy of Wittgenstein (1953).

A useful example of postmodern Critical Theory is illustrated by the case example below:

> ## ≫ Case example 1.3
>
> ### Enron's 'spectacle theatrics'
>
> To analyze Enron's 'spectacle theatrics', we combine critical and postmodern theory, as recommended by Alvesson and Deetz... The genesis of our innovation comes from the work of Best and Kellner... which points to Debord's theory of spectacle as an archetype of critical postmodern theory. By using the concept of spectacle, we engage in 'critical dramaturgy', which (rather than social constructionism (or interpretivism) and what many think of as postmodern) considers the assessment of material conditions embedded in the political economy. We propose a critical dramaturgy theory based on Debord's... Critical Theory that extends Marx's theory of accumulation of production into an accumulation of spectacles in consumer society that produce and reap profit from illusions: pseudo-reforms, false desires, and selective sightings of progressive evolution... We expand the work of corporate theatre theorists... by combining Boal... with Debord to give Aristotle's *Poetics* a more critical and postmodern turn, thus a critical dramaturgy.
>
> In sum, in order to examine critically what we consider to be the suffering and oppression resulting from the antics of Enron as an exemplar of the above tactics, ≫

> we prefer Debord to Baudrillard (who rejects the real in favor of simulation and implosion) and to Lyotard (who rejects all grand narratives). Critical dramaturgy in organization studies 'shows' how corporate theatre 'presents' oppressive and often violent social control as a celebration of progress. Using critical dramaturgy concepts and methods we decode layers of theatrical spectacle that heroize global virtual corporations and free markets, while distancing transnational corporations, such as Enron, from responsibility over their far-flung global energy-supply chains, where particularly exploitive conditions flourish.
>
> Our critical dramaturgy explores how theatrical spectacles are produced, distributed, and consumed in ways to attract and retain investors, and theorizes 'spectacle theatrics' as *the* work of contemporary organizations.
>
> *from 'Enron Spectacles:* A Critical Dramaturgical Analysis' by David M. Boje, Grace Ann Rosile, Rita A. Durant and John T. Luhman, *Organization Studies* 25(5): 751–774.

This rather dense and complicated series of references makes a simple point. That is, that like many organizations, Enron created a series of fictions promoted through company reports and corporate stories. These often take the form of presentable facts or ideologies designed to cultivate a version of reality the authors want us to believe. For example, following the collapse of Enron the authors present a criticism of the standard empiricist research:

> Enron may come to be the most analyzed business case in the history of capitalism and, more than likely, in a fix-it Harvard case analysis style…

But their Critical Theory goes on to argue that 'Enron's "spectacle theatrics" of financial reports and other representations of economic reality… seduced spectators into a willing suspension of disbelief'. In other words, Enron used these devices not as factual reports that speak for themselves but as ideological devices that seek to justify the deregulation of industry markets, while securing monopolistic economic rents and even corporate welfare from the state (Boje *et al*, 2004: 751).

Critical Theory should be considered as change theory without an intervention strategy. As the name suggests, it is designed to criticize rather than to provide solutions. Its purpose is therefore to challenge the various language games that are presented by corporate business. In method, its purpose is not to expose the 'truth' because there is no such thing, but to challenge the discourses presented in the name of objectivity.

1.7 Summary

This chapter has articulated four perspectives that inform organizational change. We have discovered that each perspective makes claims to knowledge implying how change should be understood. The structural-functional perspective on change helped our understanding of the way that inputs are transformed into outputs. Change is thus related to the rational arrangement of tasks in an organization. We can therefore understand the throughput of any organizational system by considering what changes might be made to the structural arrangements and to their functional relationships. Whilst an analogy with organic processes is useful, we can see how this perspective excludes human processes, except in the most general way. For example, there is no examination of how cultural or political issues impinge upon the task.

The multiple constituencies perspective recognizes the manager's prerogative to manage but is aware that complex organizations require a more sophisticated approach, since external and internal stakeholders are critical to any change initiative. We can get a sense that cultural and political issues are apparent through the need to manage change by involving stakeholders in critical decisions. This perspective generally leads to a pluralist conception of power. Whilst change is still top-down, the perspective does, nevertheless, seek to involve people through an appeal to reason. Because stakeholders are central to strategic realignment, their interests and motivations are brought into the organizational arena. Stakeholder needs replace the organization's needs. Change is therefore a matter of good governance, ideally through consensual negotiation between pluralities of groups that each have resources they bring into the arena. The multiple constituencies perspective reflects the development of consent theories as illustrated in Chapter 7. These reflect the importance of effective governance, in which it is the job of leaders to avoid conflict by demonstrating participative management.

The third perspective, Organizational Development (OD), extends the utilitarian theme of efficiency and effectiveness. OD is essentially a synthesis of the systems thinking that characterizes the structural-functional perspective with the behavioural research of human resource theory. OD is characterized by its dedication to humanistic principles and a set of methods informed by Action Research, organizational diagnosis, process consultation, a desire to promote personal growth and organizational learning, and a focus on the roles of groups within an organization's culture. Central to OD is the idea of planned change. These characteristics mark out OD as the major tradition for managing organizational change. The disadvantages are what it shares with the multiple constituencies perspective by focusing on change as consensus and its desire to resolve conflict through participative management.

The final perspective—Creativity and Volition: a Critical Theory of Change—is not a unified perspective but reflects the contributions of Critical Theory. Whilst Critical Theory cannot be described as a unified approach to change, what its exponents do agree on is that change does not emerge from consensus. It goes further than any of the previous perspectives in arguing and demonstrating that people, rather than systems, should be the main element of analysis in any change theory. Whilst each of the previous perspectives reifies human action, Critical Theorists argue that people create change. Whilst the other perspectives focus on rational change, Critical Theorists argue that change cannot be planned effectively because of emergent processes that continuously reflect conflict, flux, and uncertainty. We are wise to remember that each perspective is partial and that, despite its valuable critique of other change theories, Critical Theory, or what we have come to call the perspective of Creativity and Volition: a Critical Theory of Change is not immune to criticism. One problem for a manager is its refusal to offer solutions to the problems it criticizes. Of course, we can regard this as a virtue but we should reflect on its contribution when we engage in change strategies.

■ Study questions

1. Explain with a diagram how the structural-functional perspective helps us to understand how inputs are transformed into outputs.

2. What is useful about the biological or organic analogy?

3. The structural-functional perspective characterizes change as a redesign of a system to facilitate functional integration. What does this mean?

4. Why should the multiple constituencies perspective be concerned with governance? What are the implications?

5. What are the advantages of analysing stakeholder interests in complex organizations?

6. What are the six characteristics of the Organizational Development (OD) perspective?

7. What might be the value of focusing on change at the individual, group, and organizational levels?

8. Name the three types of organization-level intervention strategy practised by OD consultants.

9. If the perspective—Creativity and Volition: a Critical Theory of Change—cannot be regarded as a unified perspective, then what are its virtues?

10. Why is the perspective—Creativity and Volition: a Critical Theory of Change—critical of modernism?

■ Exercises

Exercise 1
Think of an organization you are familiar with, then consider how you would analyse it from a structural-functional perspective by using the open-systems model of Katz and Kahn.

Exercise 2
Identify a complex organization in the public or voluntary sector such as a hospital, a university, local government, a police force, a fire service, social services, or a hospice, Using the multiple constituencies perspective, list as many coalitions as you can think of. You may wish to consider these as interest groups. Divide your list into internal and external constituencies. Then analyse their relative power by placing them in order of high to low power or influence. When you have done that, state the implications for governance.

Exercise 3
Adopting an OD perspective, identify an organizational problem. Make a list of potential causes of this problem. Then write another list of potential solutions. Then say how you would resolve it using Action Research.

Exercise 4
Consider a change problem you have experienced personally. This should be some feature of your own behaviour that you wanted to change. Identify the barriers to this change and say whether you overcame them, and what you would do differently if you were to do it again.

Exercise 5
Consider how power affects your interactions within your student experience. In undertaking this task, think of three arenas such as a lecture, an examination, or a social encounter with other students. In each case consider how the situation carries constraints on your own action or lack of it. Explain how this power appears invisible but can be regarded as an emergent process and not usually observable. Now apply this to a change situation at the organizational level and say how emergent processes might affect the progress of change.

■ Further reading

Casey, C. (2002), *Critical Analysis of Organizations—theory, practice, revitalization*, London: Sage. Provides useful critiques of organizational analysis from the perspective of Critical Theory.

Chin, R. and Benne, K.D. (1976), 'General Strategies for Effecting Change in Human Systems', in Bennis, W.G., Benne, K.D., and Chin, R. (eds), *The Planning of Change* (Fourth edition), Fort Worth, TX: Holt, Rinehart and Winston, 22–47. A classic, and should be read for its contribution to planned change.

French, W.L. and Bell, C.H. (1995), *Organization Development: Behavioral Science Interventions for Organization Improvement* (Fifth edition), Englewood Cliffs, NJ: Prentice-Hall. A classic text for an introduction to Organizational Development.

Mitroff, I.I. (1983), *Stakeholders of the organizational mind*, San Francisco, CA: Jossey-Bass. This illustrates the multiple constituencies perspective.

Shafritz, J.M. and Ott, J.S. (1991), *Classics of Organization Theory* (Third edition), Pacific Grove, CA: Brookes/Cole. Although their focus is organizational analysis rather than change, the authors provide a good account that addresses many of the themes in this chapter.

■ References

Argyris, C. (1970), *Intervention Theory and Method*, Reading, MA: Addison-Wesley.

Barnard, C.I. (1938), *The Functions of the Executive*, Cambridge, MA: Harvard University Press.

Beckhard, R. (1969), *Organization Development: Strategies and Models*, Reading, MA: Addison-Wesley.

Berger, P. and Luckmann, T. (1966), *The Social Construction of Reality*, New York: Anchor Books.

Blau, P.M. and Scott, W.R. (1962), *Formal Organizations: A Comparative Approach*, San Francisco, CA: Chandler Publishing.

Boje, D.M., Rosile, G.A., Durant, R.A., and Luhman, J.T. (2004), 'Enron Spectacles: A Critical Dramaturgical Analysis', *Organization Studies*, 25(5), 751–774.

Burnes, B. (1996), 'No such thing as a "one best way" to manage organizational change', *Management Decision*, 34(10), 11–18.

Burnes, B. (2007), *Managing Change*, London: Pitman.

Burns, T. and Stalker, G.M. (1961) *The Management of Innovation*, London: Tavistock Publications.

Casey, C. (2002), *Critical Analysis of Organizations— theory, practice, revitalization*, London: Sage.

Chin, R. and Benne, K.D. (1976), 'General Strategies for Effecting Change in Human Systems', in Bennis, W.G., Benne, K.D., and Chin, R. *The Planning of Change* (Fourth edition), Fort Worth, TX: Holt, Rinehart and Winston, 22–47.

Chomsky, N. (1972), *Language and mind*, New York: Harcourt, Brace, Jovanovich.

Connolly, T., Conlon, E.J., and Deutsch, S.J. (1980), 'Organizational effectiveness: a multiple constituency approach', *Academy of Management Review*, 5, 211–217.

Cyert, R.M. and March, J.G. (1963), *A Behavioural Theory of the Firm*, Englewood Cliffs, NJ: Prentice-Hall.

Davis, S. and Lawrence, P.R. (1977), *Matrix*, Reading, MA: Addison-Wesley.

Dawson, P. (1994), *Organizational Change: A Processual Approach*, London: Paul Chapman.

Dawson, P. and Palmer, G. (1995), *Quality Management*, Melbourne: Longman.

Derrida, J. (1978), *Writing and Difference*, London: Routledge.

Fayol, H. (1916), *General and Industrial Management*, trans. Constance Storrs, London: Pitman, 1949.

Follett, M.P. (1926), 'The Giving of Orders', in Metcalf, H.C. (ed), *Scientific Foundations of Business Administration*, Baltimore, MD: Williams and Williams.

Foucault, M. (1977), *Discipline and Punishment*, London: Tavistock.

Foucault, M. (1980), *Power/Knowledge*, Brighton: Harvester.

French, W.L. and Bell, C.H. (1978), *Organization Development: Behavioral Science Interventions for Organization Improvement*, Englewood Cliffs, NJ: Prentice-Hall.

—— (1995), *Organization Development: Behavioral Science Interventions for Organization Improvement* (Fifth edition), Englewood Cliffs, NJ: Prentice-Hall.

Galbraith, J. (1973), *Designing Complex Organizations*, Reading, MA: Addison-Wesley.

Inns, D. (1996), 'Organization Development as a Journey', in Oswick, C. and Grant, D. (eds) *Organization Development, Metaphorical Explorations*, London: Pitman, 20–32.

Jackson. M.C. (2003), *Systems Thinking: Creative Holism for Managers*, Chichester: John Wiley & Sons.

Katz, D. and Kahn, R.L. (1966), *The Social Psychology of Organizations*, Chichester: John Wiley & Sons.

Keeley, M. (1983), 'Values in Organizational Theory and Management Education', *Academy of Management Review*, 8(3), 376–386.

Kübler-Ross, E. (1973), *On Death and Dying*, London: Routledge.

Lawrence, E.R. and Lorsch, J.W. (1969), *Developing Organizations: diagnosis and action*, Reading, MA: Harvard University Press.

Lewin, K. (1951), *Field Theory in Social Science*, New York: Harper and Row.

Luthans, F. and Kreitner, R. (1985), *Organizational Behavior Modification and beyond: An Operant and Social Learning Approach*, Glenview, IL: Scott Foresman & Co.

Lyotard, J.F. (1984), *The Postmodern Condition: a report on knowledge*, Minneapolis, MN: University of Minnesota Press.

McGregor, D.M. (1957), *The Human Side of Enterprise*, New York: McGraw-Hill.

Marshak, R.J. (1993), 'Managing the metaphors of change', *Organisational Dynamics*, 22(1) 44–56.

Maslow, A.H. (1943), 'A Theory of Human Motivation', *Psychological Review* 50, 370–396.

Mitroff, I.I. (1983), *Stakeholders of the organizational mind*, San Francisco, CA: Jossey-Bass.

Pettigrew, A. (1985), *The Awakening Giant, Continuity and Change in ICI*, Oxford: Blackwell.

Pettigrew, A. and Whipp, R. (1993), 'Understanding the environment', in Mabey, C. and Mayon-White, B. (eds), *Managing Change* (Second edition), London: The Open University/Paul Chapman.

Pfeffer, J. (1981), *Power in Organizations*, Boston, MA: Pitman.

Revans, R. (1982), *The Origins and Growth of Action Learning*, Bromley: Chartwell Bratt.

Schein, E.H. (1995), 'Process consultation, action research and clinical inquiry: are they the same?' *Journal of Managerial Psychology*, 10(6), 14–19.

—— (1997), 'The concept of "client" from a process consultation perspective, a guide for change agents', *Journal of Organizational Change Management*, 10(3), 202–235.

Schein, E.H. and Bennis, W.G. (1965), *Personal and Organizational Change Through Group Methods: The Laboratory Approach*, New York: Wiley.

Selznick, P. (1948), 'Foundations of the Theory of Organization', *American Sociological Review* 13: 25–35.

Shafritz, J.M. and Ott, J.S. (1991), *Classics of Organization Theory* (Third edition), Pacific Grove, CA: Brookes/Cole.

Thompson, J.D. (1967), *Organizations in Action*, New York: McGraw-Hill.

Tichy, N.M. (1983), *Managing Strategic Change: Technical, Political and Cultural Dynamics*, New York: John Wiley & Sons.

Tichy, N.M., Hornstein, H., and Nisberg, J. (1976), 'Participative organization diagnosis and intervention strategies: developing emergent pragmatic theories of change', *Academy of Management Review*, April, 109–221.

von Bertalanffy, L. (1956), 'General system theory', in *General Systems: Yearbook of the Society for the Advancement of General System Research*, 1, 1–10.

Wiener, N. (1948), *Cybernetics*, Cambridge, MA: MIT Press.

Wittgenstein, L. (1953), *Philosophical Investigations*, Oxford: Blackwell.

 Take your learning further: Online Resource Centre
http://www.oxfordtextbooks.co.uk/orc/grieves/

Visit the Online Resource Centre that accompanies this book to enrich your understanding of this chapter. Explore case study updates and answers to questions, test yourself using an interactive flashcard glossary, and keep up to date with the latest developments in the area.

CHAPTER 2

The ethics of organizational change

2.1 Introduction

This chapter is concerned with the role of ethics in organizational change.

The most important issue to understand is that all interventions with individuals and organizations are political; and, as they are political, they are ethical. The failure to consider ethical responsibility can turn what was intended as an innocent change strategy into a tyrannical leviathan. This chapter begins by considering the place of ethics in organizational change. It reflects on how the four perspectives introduced in the previous chapter deal with change. Note that only two overtly express ethical commitment: the multiple constituencies perspective and the Organizational Development (OD) perspective. In particular, we will come to understand why technical solutions to complex problems are limited and, on occasions, dangerous. Indeed, the black swan theory suggests exactly this, because assumptions built into perspectives or paradigms lead to errors of judgement.

The multiple constituencies perspective is central to the argument for ethical consideration. It derives from analysis of the role of social contracts that can be located in political theory dating back to seventeenth- and eighteenth-century attempts to define the legitimate exercise of authority, but is also related to contemporary contractual relationships. With these we need to look in two directions. First, we need to consider stakeholders and issues of governance, which are clearly articulated by the multiple constituencies perspective. Second, contemporary social contract theory raises concerns with social justice and corporate morality.

Organization Development can claim a more recent and clearly articulated humanistic commitment to developing organizations through their people. The OD code of ethics recognizes a professional commitment to values. It requires that practitioners act to demonstrate responsibilities to self; to clients and significant others; to the profession; to take responsibility for professional development and competence; and, finally, to be accountable for social responsibility. Consideration of the perspective Creativity and Volition: a Critical Theory of Change suggests that it does not seek to promote a theoretical position on organizational ethics. Instead, it raises difficult questions for those who seek to manage change because it questions how the social reality of the organization is constructed. Social structuring in relation to gender relationships and the role of conflict as a dynamic for change raises ethical questions, such as how governance is constructed.

The consequences of organizational decisions for stakeholders suggest the need to question and probe the relevance of ethical responsibility in the management of change. You need to consider your own position before you engage in managing change. We should proceed with the knowledge that developing sensitivity to ethical issues will avoid the charge of being mechanistic, task-driven, and alienating. But why should you be concerned about ethics? One answer is to suggest two major concerns for organizations that are likely to act as drivers for ethical change in the future. The first is sustainable development and whether we should take an oath to act responsibly.

The second is that managing change in a multinational global environment carries serious implications that we need to consider in relation to the challenge of responsible leadership. The interconnectedness of the world economy raises questions about effective governance requiring that organizations should act responsibly.

Adopting an ethical position on organizational change requires that we understand the rationalizations that occur when people seek to justify indefensible actions. These are cognitive strategies that enable managers and employees to justify their illegal or unethical behaviour. Becoming aware of these and their subsequent defence routines is essential for any knowledgeable practitioner of change. Knowledge of these issues enables you to build an ethical climate.

By the end of this chapter you will:

- Understand the place of ethics in organizational change.
- Recognize the limitation of technical solutions to complex problems.
- Appreciate the role of stakeholders and social contracts.
- Be aware of the consequences of organizational decisions for stakeholders.
- Appreciate why we need a clear understanding of our own ethical position.
- Recognize critical issues in managing change in a multinational global environment.
- Understand governance and commitment to social responsibility.
- Become sensitive to rationalizations and understand the process of defensive reasoning.
- Recognize the importance of building an ethical climate.

2.2 The place of ethics in organizational change

It will be useful to start by considering issues related to strategic change and leadership of ethical policy. We can begin with a simple question: why should we be concerned to create and nurture ethical organizations? To answer this question we need to consider two things. First, we need to be aware of the consequences of organizational decisions for stakeholders (this is the position of the multiple constituencies perspective), otherwise effective governance cannot occur. Second, we need to have a clear personal understanding of our own ethical position. Do we, for example, adopt the values-driven, humanistic charter advocated by OD practitioners in the pursuit of personal or organizational improvement? Alternatively, should we adopt the position of Critical Theory and be permanently sceptical of rationalism and capitalism?

2.2.1 The limitation of technical solutions to complex problems

If the perspective of structural functionalism is used to investigate problems in order to manage organizational change, then attention will be limited to task-related issues to the exclusion of ethical issues. One therefore needs to be absolutely certain that ethical issues do not impinge upon the task. The difficulty for managers is that absolute certainty is hard to rule out in any decision-making model. This is illustrated in the following case example.

》 Case example 2.1

The limits of technical solutions—the case of the Ford Pinto

In the 1970s the Ford motor company produced the Ford Pinto. Over time it was reported that, in certain situations involving collisions a significant number of the cars tended to burst into flames. Many of these were described as low-impact collisions. Consequently, a number of serious injuries and deaths forced Ford to investigate this problem.

The company regarded this as a purely technical matter to be solved. In other words, ethical awareness did not fit the paradigm of the decision-making process that was supposed to drive the change required. It is possible that this was simply down to costs, since to acknowledge liability and responsibility for a dangerous vehicle had serious financial implications for Ford, as doing so would render the company liable to compensate all the victims of its negligence.

Sources: Anand, Ashfoith, and Joshi (2005); Butterfield, Klebe Trevino, and Weaver (2000).

This case example suggests that perception was limited by a perspective that relied on technical solutions to the exclusion of anything else. With hindsight, it is not difficult to see how the exclusion of ethics from the decision-making process limits consideration purely to costs of production changes. Indeed, we can see how it is difficult to engage in effective planned change with a limited frame of reference, because of the possibility that unforeseen processes will impinge upon the situation. This suggests that, whilst we may not be able to plan for every contingency, we should be cautious with our metaphors (in this case, the organic) when diagnosing problems. The example also supports the emergent or processual change argument.

As we have discovered, the four perspectives discussed in the previous chapter adopt different positions on organizational change. They also carry different consequences or implications for an ethical or values-driven position (see Table 2.1 on p. 50).

We can avoid ethics altogether by limiting our approach to technical solutions: that is, by pretending we are dealing with nothing more than technical systems in which change is related to the most appropriate operational structure and the integration of task elements in the chain of processes. Contemporary examples include Business Process Re-engineering and project management, which seek to examine core processes to make them more efficient and effective. They are essentially performance systems and are the modern equivalents of scientific management. Consequently, any task-related change is derived from managers who, in theory, are equipped to make either strategic or operational decisions. The problem that emerges is one of omniscience. In other words, very bad or dangerous decisions emerge from strategy designed by well-meaning people and for the very best possible motives. This is the difficulty when we simply apply rational solutions (defined as efficiency and effectiveness) to technical problems, as the case example below makes clear.

>> **Case example 2.2**

Compliant workers or happy slaves?

Recent experiments conducted on rhesus monkeys demonstrate how animal (and therefore human) behaviour can be altered permanently. For example, it is possible to turn aggressive animals into compliant ones. Scientists have discovered how to block the effects of a gene in the brain (known as D2) by cutting off the link between motivation and reward. By manipulating the gene, the researchers found they could get the monkeys to work harder and faster over long periods of time without any sign of discontent. The experiments were performed at America's National Institute of Mental Health and reported in the journal *Nature Neuroscience* in October 2004.

Humans have a D2 gene identical to that in to rhesus monkeys. The experiments have huge implications for work and society. For example, people could be 'enabled' to work enthusiastically for long periods of time without a reward other than the obvious comfort breaks. As in the experiments with monkeys, people could perform boring and repetitive tasks by working harder and faster with fewer mistakes. There would be no sense of alienation. The team leader stated that 'most people are motivated to work hard and well only by the expectation of reward, whether it's a pay cheque or a word of praise', but these experiments show that 'we could remove that link and create a situation where repetitive, hard work would continue without any reward'.

The research was originally set up to find new treatments for mental illness: for example, a state of depression causes people to think that no reward is worthwhile; and with obsessive compulsive disorder individuals never feel satisfied by what they have done. The research suggests ways such conditions can be treated.

In this case example the very fact that a neuroscientific research-team leader can imply there are benefits for workers and organizations from such changes suggests that his thinking is dominated by the pursuit of scientific rationality. This was the concern expressed in Aldous Huxley's futuristic novel, *Brave New World,* which imagined a society of castes ranging from Alpha at the top to Epsilon at the bottom. The Epsilons were plodders able to perform boring tasks because their brains were numbed by drugs. We can extend this analogy to the problem of alienation. Social theorists such as Marx argued that capitalist rationality caused workers to be alienated from themselves, from others, and from the products of their labour. Critical theorists such as the psychologist Eric Fromm (1941) saw alienation as an expression of dissatisfaction or lack of fulfilment, which emerged as a direct result of industrial technology. By contrast, positivistic sociologists such as Blauner (1966) used the concept of alienation differently (and rationally) to measure the extent to which workers suffered from four dimensions of deprivation in their work: powerlessness; meaninglessness; isolation; and self-estrangement. However, unlike Marx's political economy, these empirical studies were generally interested in the relationship between technology and work satisfaction or deprivation. In other words, if we are simply interested in creating *compliant workers or happy slaves,* then we assume omniscience in the pursuit of our goal and we simply apply rationality by asking the question: how can we make the system more efficient and effective? By asking only this question, or, as critical theorists would put it, by privileging this text above all others, we are excluding other ways of seeing, such as a values-driven approach.

2.2.2 The black swan problem

Nassim Nicholas Taleb's (2007) theory of the black swan refers to events that are hard to predict, are rare, and have a large impact on situations. He argues that when we examine history we discover that most consequential events are unexpected, never predicted, nor planned. Yet, paradoxically, we convince ourselves that these events are explainable because we apply retrospective logic.

Taleb refers to John Stuart Mill's use of the term black swans to discuss the scientific process of falsification. The metaphor illustrates how some Western cultural assumptions led to errors of judgement. For example, the observation that all swans are white may become a 'true' universal statement because contradictions are not searched for, though it is not objectively true because we can never know with certainty that contradictions will not emerge. The discovery of black swans in Australia in the eighteenth century is an example of such a contradiction to the conventional wisdom.

In management situations where we only ask questions about task design and integration of internal components, we can create a scientific model by applying statistical and applied probabilistic knowledge. As Taleb argues:

> statistics is what tells you if something is true, false, or merely anecdotal; it is the 'logic of science'; it is the instrument of risk-taking; it is the applied tools of epistemology; you can't be a modern intellectual and not think probabilistically— but… let's not be suckers. The problem is much more complicated than it seems to the casual, mechanistic user who picked it up in graduate school. Statistics can fool you. In fact it is fooling your government right now. It can even bankrupt the system (let's face it: use of probabilistic methods for the estimation of risks did just blow up the banking system).

(Taleb, 2007: 57)

The real problem arises when people use statistical models designed to measure causal variables for nonlinear situations with complicated variables that do not possess direct and observable causality. As Taleb states, when we do this, 'we are riding in a bus driven by a blindfolded driver' (2007: 57). The desire to force complex data into neat causal categories, and to model problems to provide solutions, is the drawback we encounter with the structural-functional perspective.

2.2.3 Stakeholders and social contracts

The multiple constituencies perspective focuses on governance. Governance is promoted by both stakeholder theory and social contract theory (SCT). Stakeholder theory is meant to guide organizations by applying ethics to governance. In his book *Strategic Management: A Stakeholder Approach*, Freeman (1984) recommends procedures for governance. Stakeholder theory is also a critique of the structural-functional approach in which the open-systems model focuses on inputs and outputs to the exclusion of wider issues. Thus, by simply converting inputs of investors, employees, and suppliers into outputs consumed by customers, the needs of the organization are defined purely in terms of the input–output process. In contrast, the stakeholder approach identifies interested groups such as communities, trades unions, professional associations, and others. Stakeholder theory originated with strategic management and reflects the resource-based view of the firm, but came to reflect ethical issues through an examination of governance. Other writers, such as Donaldson and Preston (1995: 71), refer to ethics when they state that the 'identification of moral or philosophical guidelines for the operation and management of the corporation' is the central aspect of stakeholder theory. Three implications are relevant to organizational change. These are:

1. That an examination of stakeholder needs indicates that each has different implications for an organization.

2. That, as Friedman and Miles (2002) indicated, contentious relationships between different groups of stakeholders raise questions about the best way to resolve differences.

3. That different stakeholders display differences in power. This was indicated by Mitchell, Agle, and Wood (1997), who suggest that three issues are important in relation to stakeholder power: the type of power (its attributes); the type of legitimacy, such as how their power is sanctioned—formally or informally; and the urgency with which their needs should be addressed.

SCT originated in the seventeenth and eighteenth centuries with the political theories of Thomas Hobbes, John Locke, and Jean-Jacques Rousseau, each of whom was interested in the legitimate exercise of political authority. SCT has been influential in providing a moral and political base for debates about democracy. Contemporary theories influenced by John Rawls have focused on principles of social justice and corporate morality. SCT is claimed to have superior empirical and norma-tive bearings (Keeley 1988: 12–20) and to be better in its capacity to guide business actions than more 'general' ethical theories such as Kantianism, Pragmatism, or Utilitarianism (Wempe, 2008). SCT argues that legitimacy is derived from formal agreements that are accepted by all parties. It therefore goes further than stakehold-er theory by arguing that a contractual relationship goes beyond the organization. For example, an organization has contractual responsibilities to society. These involve environmental concerns, community interests, safety of customers, and equality of opportunity within the organization for diverse members of society (Anshen, 1980). SCT also suggests a rights-based approach to organizational eth-ics (Keeley, 1988), to replace the dominant goal-based view of stakeholder theory (Wempe, 2008: 1340).

One way of thinking about social justice is in relation to human resource policy. Consideration of equality of opportunity, anti-discrimination practices, gender and diversity issues, and occupational health are examples of governance. Both the stake-holder approach and the social contract approach are therefore useful for thinking about effective management of human resources and protecting the organization from unwanted litigation.

❶ Stop and think 2.1

From your knowledge of one organization, list the stakeholders. Then examine their needs. Identify how similar or different these needs are. Indicate whether differences cause tensions and, if they do, suggest what might be done to resolve these. Say what type of power each stakeholder possesses. For example, is it formal or informal? Finally, state what the organization's ethical responsibilities should be to each stake-holder, as well as the pressure they may exert on the organization.

OD reflects a more recent but non-philosophical approach to the link between organizational change and ethics. It is proactive, being the only perspective that has articulated humanistic commitment to developing organizations through their people. The OD code of ethics recognizes a professional commitment to values, as discussed in 1.1 above and demonstrated in the following case example.

❯❯ Case example 2.3

The International Organization Development Code of Ethics (December, 1991, 22nd Revision)

Our purpose in developing an International OD Code of Ethics is threefold: to increase professional and ethical consciousness among OD professionals and their sense of ethical responsibility; to guide OD professionals in making more informed ethical choices; and to help the OD profession itself function at the fullness of its potential. ❯❯

>> We recognize that for us to exist as a profession, a substantial consensus is necessary among the members of our profession about what we profess, particularly our values and ethics. This statement represents a step toward such a consensus.

Values of OD professionals

As an OD professional, I acknowledge the fundamental importance of the following values both for myself and my profession:

1. quality of life—people being satisfied with their whole life experience;

2. health, human potential, empowerment, growth and excellence—people being healthy, aware of the fullness of their potential, recognizing their power to bring that potential into being, growing into it, living it, and, generally, doing the best they can with it, individually and collectively;

3. freedom and responsibility—people being free and responsible in choosing how they will live their lives;

4. justice—people living lives whose results are fair and right for everyone;

5. dignity, integrity, worth and fundamental rights of individuals, organizations, communities, societies, and other human systems;

6. all-win attitudes and cooperation—people caring about one another and about working together to achieve results that work for everyone, individually and collectively;

7. authenticity and openness in relationships;

8. effectiveness, efficiency and alignment—people achieving the maximum of desired results, at minimum cost, in ways that coordinate their individual energies and purposes with those of the system-as-a-whole, the subsystems of which they are parts, and the larger system of which their system is a part;

9. holistic, systemic view and stakeholder orientation—understanding human behavior from the perspective of whole system(s) that influence and are influenced by that behavior; recognizing the interests that different people have in the system's results and valuing those interests fairly and justly;

10. wide participation in system affairs, confrontation of issues leading to effective problem solving, and democratic decision making.

Ethical guidelines for OD professionals

As an OD professional, I commit myself to supporting and acting in accordance with the following ethical guidelines: »

❯❯I. Responsibility to Self

A. Act with integrity; be authentic and true to myself.

B. Strive continually for self-knowledge and personal growth.

C. Recognize my personal needs and desires and, when they conflict with other responsibilities, seek all-win resolutions of those conflicts.

D. Assert my own economic and financial interests in ways that are fair and equitable to me as well as to my clients and their stakeholders.

II. Responsibility for Professional Development and Competence

A. Accept responsibility for the consequences of my acts and make reasonable efforts to ensure that my services are properly used; terminate my services if they are not properly used and do what I can to see that any abuses are corrected.

B. Strive to achieve and maintain a professional level of competence for both myself and my profession by developing the full range of my own competence and by establishing collegial and cooperative relations with other OD professionals.

C. Recognize my own personal needs and desires and deal with them responsibly in the performance of my professional roles.

D. Practice within the limits of my competence, culture, and experience in providing services and using techniques.

E. Practice in cultures different from my own only with consultation from people native to or knowledgeable about those specific cultures.

III. Responsibility to Clients and Significant Others

A. Serve the long-term well-being, interests and development of the client system and all its stakeholders, even when the work being done has a short-term focus.

B. Conduct any professional activity, program or relationship in ways that are honest, responsible, and appropriately open.

C. Establish mutual agreement on a contract covering services and remuneration.

D. Deal with conflicts constructively and avoid conflicts of interest as much as possible.

E. Define and protect the confidentiality of my client–professional relationships.

F. Make public statements of all kinds accurately, including promotion and advertising, and give service as advertised.

IV. Responsibility to the Profession

A. Contribute to continuing professional development for myself, other practitioners, and the profession.   ❯❯

⟫B. Promote the sharing of OD knowledge and skill.

C. Work with other OD professionals in ways that exemplify what our profession says we stand for.

D. Work actively for ethical practice by individuals and organizations engaged in OD activities and, in a case of questionable practice, use appropriate channels for dealing with it.

E. Act in ways that bring credit to the OD profession and with due regard for colleagues in other professions.

V. Social Responsibility

A. Act with sensitivity to the fact that my recommendations and actions may alter the lives and well-being of people within my client systems and the larger systems of which they are subsystems.

B. Act with awareness of the cultural filters which affect my view of the world, respect cultures different from my own, and be sensitive to cross-cultural and multicultural differences and their implications.

C. Promote justice and serve the well-being of all life on Earth.

D. Recognize that accepting this Statement as a guide for my behavior involves holding myself to a standard that may be more exacting than the laws of any countries in which I practice, the guidelines of any professional associations to which I belong, or the expectations of any of my clients.

Notes

The process which has produced this statement (currently in its 22nd version) was in being in 1981. It has been supported by most OD-oriented professional organizations, associations, and networks in the United States. It was also supported unanimously by the participants at the 1984 OD World Congress in Southampton, England. To date, more than 200 people from more than 15 countries have participated in the process. (Note: The endorsements are of the process and not the statement.) The process has included drafting a version, sending it out with a request for comments and suggestions, redrafting based on the responses, sending it out again and so on. Our aim has been to use the process to establish a substantial consensus including acknowledgment of the differences among us.

By providing a common reference for OD professionals throughout the world, we seek to enhance our sense of identity as a global professional community. Because this statement was initially developed within the United States, adapting it to other cultures has been necessary. ⟫

> ❯❯ *Editor's Note*: A more complete discussion of Organization Development values and ethics can be found in:
>
> Gellermann, William, Frankel, Mark S. and Landenson, Robert F., *Values and Ethics in Organization and Human Systems Development*, Jossey-Bass, 1990.
> Frankel, Mark S., *Values and Ethics in Organization and Human Systems Development: An Annotated Bibliography*, AAAS Publication, October, 1987
> White, Louis P. and Wooten, Kevin C., *Professional Ethics and Practice in Organization Development*, New York, Praeger Publishers, 1986.
> For further information on the credo visit: <http://www.odnetwork.org/aboutod/credo.php>.
>
> *Source*: Reproduced with kind permission from the Organizational Development Network.

Both the multiple constituencies perspective and the OD perspective suggest that, at a global level, governance requires cooperation and a values-driven commitment by multinational enterprises (MNEs) because they have considerable power that must be exercised responsibly. If it is not, then we encounter potentially negative consequences for stakeholders from organizational decisions. Each perspective carries consequences. These are identified in Table 2.1.

Table 2.1 The consequences for multinational enterprises of perspectives on change

Perspective	Consequences
Structural-functional—No ethical consideration.	Technical, related to the most appropriate operational structure, and the integration of task elements in the chain of processes.
Multiple constituencies—ethical focus on governance through negotiation of stakeholder concerns, and examination of contractual relations.	Manage change by negotiating and agreeing objectives with different groups of stakeholders who have overlapping and often conflicting needs.
Organizational Development—the only proactive stance.	Manage planned change through a values-driven commitment to personal and organizational growth.
Creativity and Volition: a Critical Theory of Change—serves as a critique by examining discursive practice.	Act as sceptical observer, focusing on emergent processes, conflict, flux, and change. Capitalism requires mediation through governance because social, material, and mental well-being are just as important as economic value.

Critical Theory is derived from social constructivism and postmodernism, which are sceptical about universal claims to truth and therefore of the implicit neutrality of truth claims made by rational science applied to social situations. This raises difficult questions for those who seek to manage change. The perspective seeks what Collins and Wray-Bliss (2005) call an **anti-foundationalist** approach because 'it has a deep suspicion of appeals to authority'. It rejects 'universal laws or codes as a way of resolving, or avoiding, ethical differences'. Consideration of Critical Theory suggests that it does not seek to promote a theoretical position on organizational ethics. Instead, it raises difficult question for those who seek to manage change because it questions how the social reality of the organization is constructed. Social structuring of gender relationships and the role of conflict as a dynamic for change raise ethical questions such as how governance is constructed.

> **❶ Stop and think 2.2**
>
> Imagine that you are a consultant to an MNE. Which perspective would you adopt and why?

2.3 The consequences of organizational decisions for stakeholders

There is a clear case to make for acting responsibly. This runs through all activities in an organization. Decisions made in the boardroom may have serious implications for investors, customers, and employees. Consider the example of Northern Rock in 2008: when the bank was caught up in the US sub-prime market, and unable to raise capital because other banks feared it was in too deep, this lack of confidence caused a sharp deterioration in share price. The problem escalated when people with savings accounts formed lengthy queues outside high-street branches. Because such large numbers of small savers formed queues, they forced the British government to act. But why should we consider this an ethical issue? The answer lies in the company's failure to behave ethically towards its stakeholders. For example, it failed to consider whether governance was lacking, and to provide responsible leadership. There were two essential problems of poor ethical practice that could have been avoided. First, Adam Applegarth, the chief executive, adopted a policy of moving Northern Rock from making steady investments out of savings, as it had done when it was a building society, to speculating in the volatile short-term money markets, which resulted in catastrophe.

The result was that Northern Rock had to beg the Bank of England for help with its 'liquidity' problem. Second, Applegarth sold £2.6m of shares in Northern Rock at high prices while urging investors and employees to purchase more.

Financial management is no different from any other area of management, in that most practices of a sensitive nature should be audited. Some examples will illuminate the implications for strategic change and leadership:

- An environment portfolio should indicate how environmental emissions will be controlled. If a company commits itself to an ethical marketing policy, then it cannot be seen to engage in contradictory practices, as Coca-Cola did with its Dasani brand of bottled water (see the case example below).

- Research and development must be carried out responsibly so that products are safe, and made increasingly from sustainable sources.

- Project planning must take account of environmental issues. For example, if the development of a new road would wipe out a variety of natterjack toad, then developers would be challenged for a solution by green campaigners or other pressure groups.

- Manufacturing processes must be safe. Good-quality working life and personnel-related issues are all features of a progressive organization. In *The Green Business Guide*, Elkington, Knight, and Hales (1991) illustrate how all of these features are driven by changing world views. In 1981 we began to notice a change from 'dominance over nature' to 'harmony with nature', or away from viewing the natural environment simply as a resource to be exploited to a resource that must be replenished. But we now need to ask how far this agenda has moved on, and what changes we are likely to encounter in future.

> **》 Case example 2.4**

When a bottle of water led to a strategic management disaster

In January 2004 Coca-Cola marketed a brand of bottled water called Dasani. This turned out to be a disaster for the company. The problems emerged when Coca-Cola recalled all bottles of Dasani in the UK after bromate was found to exceed legal levels, meaning that the product was potentially carcinogenic. Public outrage was articulated in the press, first by *The Independent* newspaper in March 2004, followed quickly by BBC News. The problem was compounded by labelling that advertised Dasani as 'pure' water. This was contradicted when it was discovered that the water was actually from the River Thames and treated by reverse osmosis. Consequently, the Dasani brand name became disreputable. As examples of strategic management disasters go, this ranks as one of the worst.

2.3.1 Why we need a clear understanding of our own ethical position

The decisions we make have consequences for the organization. But they also have personal consequences. Therefore we need to have a clear personal understanding of our actions. We can, of course, simply adopt a position of expediency in this regard, purely maximizing success rather than committing ourselves to ethical or humanistic principles. But even if we adopt a position of personal expediency without a commitment to values, we are likely to encounter organizations with a moral compass. Such organizations are said to be in the ascendancy. Hatcher, for example, argues that there is growing evidence from surveys and reports that 'companies without a moral compass will be left adrift in a sea of organizations charting an ethical course' (Hatcher, 2002: 3). These reports reveal that:

- Employees are turning their backs on employers with no sense of moral responsibility. Ethical issues are becoming crucial in the recruitment process. Companies with tarnished reputations face problems in recruiting top talent.

- A total of 85 of the London Stock Exchange (FTSE) 100 companies (UK's Dow) have a code of ethics. And even though many observers see such statements as mere rhetoric, companies that focus on ethics actually do better. A 1999 survey showed that companies with codes of ethics outperformed those with none. Even the stock market is getting into the act. Companies listed on two indices, the Dow Jones Group Sustainability Index and the FTSE4Good index, appear to outperform the average by over 35 percent.

- Companies with good reputations enhance their brand image. The proportion of corporate value obtained from intangible assets like reputation rose over 50 percent from 1981 to 1998.

- Customer loyalty is enhanced. A recent study found that almost 100 percent of the population wants companies to focus on more than profit and over 50 percent of the respondents said they form an impression of a company based on its social responsiveness, or lack thereof.

- Assets in socially screened investment portfolios rose by almost 40 percent between 1999 and 2001. A total of 33 percent of stock analysts consider that environmental issues affect the value of investments.

- Ethical companies enhance their productivity and improve the quality of their products and services. They also expend fewer resources on regulatory supervision.

- Companies with environmental management systems substantially reduce their operating costs. Operational efficiencies are enhanced through reductions in material waste and energy consumption.

- Even MBAs, young Turks taught well to count beans, are getting into the socially responsible act. A survey of graduate programmes in the United States, Asia, Europe, and the Americas by the Aspen Institute reveals a growing dedication to the inclusion of social and environmental issues in MBA programmes.

(Hatcher, 2002: 4).

There are clearly drivers for change in the world today but we cannot be sure whether they will be effective. For example, globalization and sustainable development are issues that have become a matter of international focus. The main concern is international regulation in order to avoid exploitation and to encourage genuine economic development rather than dependency. The world economy is changing, and so are the processes of globalization. However, will this lead to the development of an ethical social framework for organizations? This will depend on whether economics is the only driver for change. There are others, such as:

- High-speed technological changes.
- Demographic changes.
- Investment in skills training.
- Greater levels of education.
- Concern over the environment.
- Sustainable development.

There are some negative possibilities also, such as:

- Unstable economic change.
- The impact of climate change.
- A contentious international political climate.
- Political change and dominance in the world economy.

The argument that organizations with a moral compass are increasing due to these pressures suggests that international leadership will require a focus on corporate ethics and social responsibility. But whether this moral compass is in the ascendancy at an international level depends upon an intervening variable—the power of MNEs to engage with sustainable development and ethical social responsibility. We therefore need to explore this possibility.

2.3.2 Drivers of ethical change

There are two major concerns for business that are likely to act as drivers for ethical change in the future. These are:

1. Sustainable development.
2. Whether we should take an oath to act responsibly.

Sustainable development is mediated by the power of corporations to exploit opportunities in a competitive world. For example, we might regard all advances in science and technology as unproblematic and neutral because we see scientists as such. However, when we consider who the scientists work for and what their objectives are, we discover that neutrality dissolves into ethical and political judgement. This is apparent in the case example below.

> ## ❯❯ Case example 2.5

Genetic engineering and the power of global corporations

An example of the power of global corporations can be illustrated by the science of genetic engineering. Advocates claim it can solve world poverty. The name given to the technology by advocates of genetic modification is Genetic Use Restriction Technology, or Gurt. Its main advantage is resistance to drought or pests; however, the technology makes crops produce sterile seeds.

Critics produce two main arguments against the technology. The first is that the technology is potentially dangerous. As a result they have nicknamed it the 'Terminator' technology. Furthermore, they argue that the technology still produces pollen and its genes are likely to pose a particular hazard by threatening to make non-GM crops sterile. The second is an economic argument: crops produced by this method, they aver, may be sowing the seeds of starvation for poor farmers in the developing world.

In order to address the first argument, in the year 2000 under the UN Convention on Biological Diversity the world's governments imposed a *de facto* moratorium on developing and testing the technology. Pro-GM countries such as Australia, New Zealand, Canada, and the United States attempted to lift the moratorium in favour of a case-by-case risk assessment. The UK government, for example, has given approval on a case-by-case basis.

The second, economic, argument has three strands. First, because the technology can be applied to any crop, such as maize or rice, which are the staple diets of people in developing countries, there is a danger that it might destroy traditional farming methods. Second, in view of the power of global corporations to seek large rewards, it might damage livelihoods. Third, it might be a danger to food security in developing countries since such economies could move towards the production of luxury food products for the rich rather than actually helping people out of dependence on subsistence agriculture.

The point for anyone involved in organizational change is whether it is possible to identify an ethical position in relation to the two essential arguments for the application of this new technology. From the case example above we can identify two arguments:

1. Bio-tech companies claim the Gurt technology is a green solution to genetically modified crops.

2. Conversely, critics claim two distinct problems: one based on science and the other related to the economics of development. As the technology still produces pollen, both concerns are exacerbated by the question whether genes could migrate to non-GM crops.

The difficulty is to know how we should formulate our own position in relation to this debate. How would you resolve this ethical dilemma?

> **❶ Stop and think 2.3**
>
> If you were a consultant with a GM company and you were asked to recommend an ethical position for the company in relation to each of these debates, what would you recommend? Provide a reasoned argument to address the issue of the power of global corporations to exploit their own interests or to assist in the progress of economic development.

The second major driver for potential change is the rise of wider ethical concerns. Many professions have adopted a code of practice to regulate their activities. The oldest is medicine, which developed its professional code from the Hippocratic oath. This is taken upon graduation in most medical schools and has had a major influence on medical practice for the last 2,500 years. As Emiliani (2000: 263) argued, 'without doubt, there have been many corrupt physicians who have failed to honor the Hippocratic oath. But the majority of physicians appear to have honored it in recognition of their profound responsibility.' Nevertheless, we often discover contradictions between professional ethics and organizational ethics. Consequently, whistleblowing occurs. This practice appears to be increasingly accepted and even becoming institutionalized, as the following extract makes clear:

> Whistleblowing—the unauthorized disclosure of illegal or unethical conduct within an organization—has an ancient lineage, although the first known use of the term rather than the concept was in 1963. Far from being subversion, it is a vital, almost indispensable control device. This is seen in case study examples of the *Challenger* disaster, the North Sea oil rigs and international banking. Despite this, whistleblowers experience discrimination and retaliation. One way forward is to set up codes of practice that will distinguish valid from invalid forms of whistleblowing, and ensure that the contribution of whistleblowers to the organization is maximized and public interest is not sacrificed.
>
> (Vinten, 1995: 26)

We may reach a point at which managers, as well as consultants, take an oath to act responsibly. Other areas that can provide examples of ethical responsibility include industrial disasters. It has also been suggested that many destructive outcomes occur because of contradictions between legitimate value-systems (Schneider, 2000). Marketing is also considered to be one of the most unscrupulous areas giving rise to contradictions in decision making. For example, Townsend (2000) argues that, as the Western markets for tobacco decline, companies use unscrupulous marketing methods to sell cigarettes in other parts of the world. Thus, whilst tobacco companies claim not to encourage new smokers, evidence suggests that marketing campaigns directly target overseas markets without legal frameworks similar to those in the developed world.

2.4 Managing change in a multinational global environment

One of the difficulties for organizations with global corporate power is the challenge of responsible leadership. There are significant consequences for international corporate governance as we can see in the following case example.

» Case example 2.6

The Penalties for Abusing the Global Consumer

A report on *Pet Food Politics* by Marion Nestle (2008), a professor of sociology, nutrition and public health at New York University, illustrates the impact of globalization in terms of the consequences for senior decision makers as well as for the company's profits.

For two months from March 2007, a significant number of leading US dog and cat food manufacturers recalled products from retailers. The products included several brands familiar to consumers in the UK, including those at the costly end of the market such as Eukanuba, IAMS, and Royal Canin. This was the largest recall of consumer products in US history. In the aftermath, as many as 5,000 pet cats and dogs were found to have died from kidney failure owing to a toxic chemical cocktail in their food. US pet owners' faith in many pet-food manufacturers was shaken, as contamination had been traced back through the supply chain, revealing connections in the sources both for pet food and for products fed to agricultural animals, including animals raised for meat, milk, and eggs to be consumed by humans. In China, where the toxic compounds were inserted into the pet-food supply chain, Zeng Xiaoyu, the former head of China's State Food and Drug Administration, was executed. In the USA, pet-food sales fell by 30 percent and animal advocates aimed to 'take pet liability damages into the stratospheric heights of compensation for human liability'.

Source: Times Higher Education Supplement, 22 January 2009, review of Nestle, M. (2008), Pet Food Politics: The Chihuahua in the Coal Mine, Berkeley, CA: University of California Press.

Failing to act responsibly is not an option, but MNEs, the drivers of globalization, need to ensure that all employees are aware of their responsibilities and of the consequences of corruption.

2.4.1 Governance and commitment to social responsibility

Managing change in a multinational global environment raises questions about commitment to corporate social responsibility. A consultant with a responsibility for managing change in an MNE is likely to face contradictions. Some examples can be illustrated with the selling of luxury goods. According to the Worldwide Fund for Nature (WWF) report *Deeper Luxury,* 'certain markets are driving sustainable goods'. Consequently, '[l]uxury-brand executives should care about their company's social and environmental performance for two reasons: first, because the challenge of global sustainability is clear and urgent; second, because it makes good business sense for them to improve this performance.' However, the report exposes many major luxury brands, such as designer jewellers and fashion houses, as 'barely passable in the ethical and environmental stakes'. The report examines the environmental damage caused by the production of the world's top brands. It seeks to put pressure on the world of celebrity by forcing stars to lead by example, because celebrity stars have a moral responsibility to ensure that the brands they endorse are not damaging the planet. As a result, none of the top ten labels in the study scored more than a C+ on the report's A to F scale and two of the labels failed the test, with F grades. You may wish to undertake exercise 5 at the end of the chapter (*Rank the top ten luxury holding companies against their own claims*) to discover the ranking of the world's luxury products and to assess their claims to support sustainability.

The examples cited in the *Deeper Luxury* report might suggest that it is difficult to practise corporate social responsibility (CSR) and that doing so may be confined to developed economies because it is a 'luxury' that developing economies cannot afford. Indeed, this argument has been put in relation to the development of new clean, green technologies. This argument limits organizational change in relation to ethics and sustainability to advanced capitalist economies largely because they have more sophisticated or enlightened consumers. Consequently, this suggests that such consumers are becoming more conscious of the environment and the need for sustainability, as well as concerned about quality products. For example, we can identify public concern about chickens bred in battery conditions and sold cheaply in supermarkets. In the West, organic foods are popular, Fairtrade is now established, and recycling of waste has increased as a result of the drive for sustainable products. In 12 months between 2003 and 2004 the market for ethical buying increased by 30 percent to £43m, according to the *Ethical Consumption Report* (2005) published by the Co-operative Bank, which states that 'ethical shopping for everything from energy-efficient fridges to organic food is rising steadily year on year'.

---

❶ Stop and think 2.4

Consider the difficulties of managing change at a macro level by looking at the website for the Organisation for Economic Co-operation and Development (OECD). You can find this at: <http://www.oecd.org/>

Critical Theorists are likely to argue that capitalism is inherently selfish and has to be continuously challenged because it is essentially exploitative. That is, it requires governance to prevent its worst excesses; it increases the wealth of the wealthy, and provides little trickle-down effect (James, 2008). This argument contends that the idea of free-market capitalism is a myth and essentially dangerous to our social and mental health if it is not subjected to critical scrutiny and mediation with the aim of forcing governments and transnational corporations to develop awareness that social, material, and mental well-being are just as important as economic value. A further concern is related to the enormous power and influence of multinational corporations. Because globalization requires the internationalization of financial markets, the power of the nation state to regulate environmental standards is significantly reduced. The consequence is that power is concentrated in the hands of relatively few individuals, leading to the influence of a new power elite, the actions of which must be scrutinized critically.

A second difficulty with commitment to social responsibility is related to industry-sector barriers to change. These usually occur when industry lead-bodies seek to resist change by influencing the media or government policy. One of the main factors driving this today is pressures to improve environmental performance and to find sustainable solutions. Recent examples include companies in the airline business, chemical manufacturers, mining, oil extraction industries, wood, pulp and paper industries, and so on. Such industries face tough challenges in overhauling operations to promote environmental sustainability. The main reasons why companies in such industries resist change are related to the perceived burdens of increased costs for new green technologies, and regulatory barriers that are seen as possible restrictions to performance. It is possible that some of these industries have such a major impact on natural resources that they may be incompatible with the principles of sustainable development. Examples of industry-sector barriers to change include:

- Capital costs of improvement which reduce the internal rate of financial return.
- Response to public concerns that threaten key products. Recent examples include the airline industry's concern with fuel duties or the car industry's concern with the media portrayal of 4×4s as 'Chelsea tractors'. The location of types of industry such as fireworks and oil storage depots near to residential communities has also given rise to regulation or elimination of such plants.
- Legal regulations perceived as restricting the ability of an industry to regulate itself—feared loss of regulatory control. This has occurred in relation to newspapers and the advertising industry.
- Difficulties with technical knowledge such as the inability to eliminate risks.

Despite such barriers to social responsibility, many organizations appear to have clear views about an ethical position. A useful example is provided in the following case example.

›› Case example 2.7

Arguments for corporate social responsibility

The Times[1] sought the views of leaders holding significant positions in contemporary organizations to explain why we should be concerned to develop corporate social responsibility (CSR). Because the public increasingly expects ethical standards in ››

❯business—especially with regard to the environment and fair trade—does the business case require that organizations should shape their ethical policies?

Erica Hauver—the lead partner of the sustainability and climate-change practice at PricewaterhouseCoopers—argues that 'attention on environmental protection and the scarcity of resources has improved the business case for CSR. Organizations that are more environmentally efficient can be financially efficient too and should be able to cut costs. Consumers want affordable sustainable products; that's a challenge, but equally it presents a business opportunity. Companies must understand what the issues are in their sector. These could be about raw materials or labour and human rights issues in the supply chain.'

Ty Jones—head of corporate responsibility, Bank of Scotland Corporate—argues that 'CSR policies are now closely related to corporate reputations so they're a part of business risk. In shaping CSR policies, organizations must have a clear vision of what they want to do and be realistic about their goals. Ambitions can mushroom and be difficult for smaller enterprises, especially, to manage. Getting an independent assessment of your policies is useful and you need to maintain the dialogue with key stakeholders to keep abreast of public expectations.'

Brendan May—managing director of Planet 2050, the corporate and sustainability practice of Weber Shandwick—argues that 'CSR affects a wide range of business relationships. A vital factor now is the ability of companies to attract and retain talent. People want to know about the ethical credentials of potential employers—they don't want to work for companies who end up with bad press on page one of newspapers. And investors want to move away from businesses that are high-risk to those that are more sustainable and don't fall foul of regulation.'

Jessica Sansom—head of sustainability, Innocent Drinks Company—argues that 'minimizing the negative impact your company has on the environment and the communities it deals with helps you save money and improve your business relationships—from suppliers to employees. We sell drinks on the basis of taste and health. If consumers like our ethics too, that's good. People also need to be aware of the accusations that can be made against them. We've been accused of "greenwash" recently over transport. We blend drinks in Holland and bottle in the UK. We think it's actually more efficient and environmentally sound transporting in bulk, but we've had this challenged. You have to be able to explain your policies.'

Richard D. North—writer and broadcaster, Media Fellow, Institute of Economic Affairs—argues that 'CSR policies can bring companies peace and quiet with consumers and regulators, so in that sense there's a business case for it. But consumers can be suspicious now that CSR programmes are used to justify the charging of premiums for goods and that it's just a business "bolt-on". Businesses should not pretend to be something they are not and consumers are now asking who is actually paying for some of these policies. I believe that there's a growing appetite for people to speak honestly to their own self-interests.'

[1] *The Times,* 7 September 2008.

2.5 Rationalizations: justifying the indefensible

The world economic crisis began in 2008 with the sub-prime market. This appears to have resulted, in large part, from the failure to regulate institutional investors, including the world's largest banks. Lax regulation may have enabled corruption scandals that may be defined sociologically as white-collar crime. However, the scale of recent illegal or unethical practice in companies as varied as Siemens and Stanford International Bank suggests that such actions become legitimized through learned behaviour. That is, employees are encouraged to learn to avoid moral and ethical standards. Fraudulent acts often become institutionalized by deliberate collusion between employees and, in some cases, are sanctioned by senior managers. Whilst the motives may vary from case to case, what does appear to be a common feature is the way participation in illegal or unethical behaviour is rationalized.

Rationalizations are cognitive strategies that enable managers and employees to justify their illegal or unethical behaviour. When these become institutionalized in an organization they tend to sanction deviant group dynamics. What we know about rationalizations is that they are encouraged through a process of socialization. Employees, therefore, learn tactics that 'allow perpetrators of unethical activities to believe that they are moral and ethical individuals, thereby allowing them to continue engaging in these practices without feeling pangs of conscience' (Anand, Ashfoith, and Joshi, 2005: 10). Often, people in such situations do not see themselves as corrupt. Established research suggests that the reason for this is that individuals respond to institutionalized precedents, work routines and pressures, and organizational dilemmas that do not allow sufficient time for critical reflection (Chambliss, 1996; Jackall, 1988). In Table 2.2 we note various rationalizations that people use to legitimize their actions.

The process of group dynamics described by Anand, Ashfoith, and Joshi (2005) includes:

1. *Incrementalism*—a form of socialization in which new members are gradually introduced to deviant practices. Usually the initial act is 'only slightly deviant' but it 'creates some cognitive dissonance' which is relieved when the newcomer learns to rationalize the process through the help of colleagues. Eventually, the individual learns to accept a practice as normal. Instrumentalism is therefore a sliding scale of immoral or illegal behaviour.

2. *Co-opting*—a process that rewards a change of attitude towards unethical behaviour. Anand, Ashfoith, and Joshi illustrate examples such as 'financial brokers who push offerings with high commissions', and 'contract researchers who spin their findings to support their sponsor's preferences', or 'public officials in regulatory agencies who take pro-industry stands in the hope of getting jobs'. An example of this process is how Merrill Lynch executives were co-opted in Enron's efforts to 'cook the books'.

Table 2.2 Rationalizing corruption

Strategy	Description	Examples
Denial of responsibility	The actors engaged in corrupt behaviours perceive that they have no other choice than to participate in such activities.	'What can I do? My arm is being twisted.' 'It is none of my business what the corporation does overseas.'
Denial of injury	The actors are convinced that no one is harmed by their actions; hence the actions are not really corrupt.	'No one was really harmed.' 'It could have been worse.'
Denial of victim	The actors counter any blame for their actions by arguing that the violated party deserved whatever happened.	'They deserved it.' 'They chose to participate.'
Social weighting	The actors assume two practices that moderate the salience of corrupt behaviours: 1. Condemn the condemner. 2. Selective social comparison.	'You have no right to criticize us.' 'Others are worse than we are.'
Appeal to higher loyalties	The actors argue that their violation of norms is due to their attempt to realize a higher-order value.	'We answered to a more important cause.' 'I would not report it because of my loyalty to my boss.'
Metaphor of the ledger	The actors rationalize that they are entitled to indulge in deviant behaviours because of credits they have accrued (time and effort) in their jobs.	'We've earned the right.' 'It's all right for me to use the internet for personal reasons at work. After all, I do work overtime.'

3. *Compromise*—occurs when individuals are corrupted by dilemmas or role conflict. In other words, the attempt to be honest is compromised by the need to do deals. For instance, by forming networks and supporting causes that require deals leads to actions that might compromise personal values. Politicians are obvious examples.

2.5.1 Defensive reasoning

To change the perceptions of employees we require a moral awareness built into the decision-making process (Butterfield, Klebe Trevino, and Weaver, 2000). A model for moral awareness in an organization involves four stages, as suggested by Rest (1986):

1. Recognize the moral nature of a situation (*moral awareness*).
2. Decide what is morally right in the situation (*making a moral judgement*).

3. Decide to give priority to moral values over other values (*establishing moral intent*).

4. Follow through on moral intention with moral behaviour (*engaging in moral action*).

If we build a moral sensitivity into our decision-making criteria, then we begin with the premise that we know we are looking for moral issues. The goal now becomes to identify potential ethical problems, but to do this we need a frame that informs our judgements. A frame can be described as a method of viewing the problem in different ways in order to arrive at multiple interpretations. This is exactly what the four change perspectives enable us to do. However, we need to remember that each perspective contains a variety of theories that share the same assumptions. Framing therefore influences our interpretations. The problem with viewing organizations as organisms, or machines, is that such frames limit perception to technical matters. Decisions may appear neutral but they rarely are. As Butterfield, Klebe Trevino, and Weaver (2000) state, the initial internal reports about the Pinto referred to the word 'condition' and avoided the word 'problem' because, to Ford's legal department, it implied culpability. Neutralizing or sanitizing language is, of course, political. Ford decision makers referred to Pintos as 'lighting up', rather than 'catching fire' or 'bursting into flames'. Bandura (1999) suggests that psychologically this is 'euphemistic labelling', which is designed to neutralize any moral responsibility.

A moral sensitivity requires an ethical climate, but this is not always easy to achieve. Siemens is a case in point. In Siemens' own case study—*Creating a high performance culture*—the company states that the case study looks at 'how the Siemens organization is built on a high performance culture' which is 'shared by everyone from the most senior executive to the newest trainee'. A full account can be found at <http://www.thetimes100.co.uk>. What is therefore astonishing is the widespread corporate corruption scandal that emerged in 2008. The company has acknowledged a €1.3bn scandal involving bribery, the creation of a network of secret payments through Swiss bank accounts, and widespread cultural practices that are completely at odds with the transparency and openness required by a high-performance culture. Referring to the practices, the presiding judge, Peter Noll, said, 'one can assume that Mr Siekaczcek [a senior manager] was part of a system of organized irresponsibility that was implicitly condoned'. The presiding judge was critical of Siemens' organization and control mechanisms, and said that the responsibilities of the former head of compliance, Albrecht Schäfer, were 'too narrowly drawn'. Summing up (29 July 2008), he stated that '[i]t's as if you were to equip the fire department with a toothbrush cup to extinguish fires'.[1]

Although there are a number of aspects to this case, the most noteworthy is that the scandal illustrated deviant practices in many of its companies throughout the world. If we compare the two accounts (see the case study at the end of this chapter), then we

---

1 David Gow, *The Guardian*, 27 May 2008; Maria Marquat, *The Huffington Post*, 26 May 2008; Carter Dougherty, *New York Times*, 26 May 2008.

can find examples of defensive reasoning. This case illustrates a cover-up intended to hide the facts, but defensive reasoning can be seen as an example of the process of rationalization. As in the Siemens example, many organizations experience a gap between their 'espoused theory' (what the organization formally states) and the 'theory in practice' (what really happens). Defensive reasoning can therefore be seen as the psychological process behind the sociological practice of making rationalizations.

The process works by individuals deflecting the potential problem of operating within an actual value system at odds with the formally espoused system. Defensive reasoning is a means to protect the guilty by avoiding embarrassment, threat, or the feeling of vulnerability or incompetence. It 'encourages individuals to keep private the premises, inferences, and conclusions that shape their behavior and to avoid testing them in a truly independent, objective fashion' (Argyris, 1997: 206).

In discussing an example of defensive reasoning, Argyris cites managers who continually attribute the problem elsewhere rather than recognize their own contribution to it:

> Because the attributions that go into defensive reasoning are never really tested, it is a closed loop, remarkably impervious to conflicting points of view. The inevitable response to the observation that somebody is reasoning defensively is yet more defensive reasoning. With the case team, for example, whenever anyone pointed out the professionals' defensive behavior to them, their initial reaction was to look for the cause in somebody else—clients who were so sensitive that they would have been alienated if the consultants had criticized them or a manager so weak that he couldn't have taken it had the consultants raised their concerns with him. In other words, the case team members once again denied their own responsibility by externalizing the problem and putting it on someone else... Needless to say, such a master program inevitably short-circuits learning. And for a number of reasons unique to their psychology, well-educated professionals are especially susceptible to this.
>
> (Argyris, 1997: 207)

If these are inevitable human behaviours, then how can organizations break out of this vicious circle? Argyris' first point is motivational. That is, 'despite the strength of defensive reasoning, people genuinely strive to produce what they intend' because they 'value acting competently' and because their 'self-esteem is intimately tied up with behaving consistently and performing effectively' (ibid.). His second point is about method. That is, individuals 'can be taught how to recognize the reasoning they use when they design and implement their actions' and they can begin by identifying the 'inconsistencies between their espoused and actual theories of action' (ibid.). Inevitably, as with all human learning, there is no quick fix or recipe for personal change. There is, however, a growing awareness among practitioners that organizational learning and change are intertwined and need to begin with reflective awareness. As Argyris argues, the first step is for managers at the top to critically examine and change their own theories-in-use.

The Siemens example illustrates a tension between espoused values and values-in-practice. Whilst we can guess at motives, the real concern here is that the practices are grounded in employees' experiences and interpretations that, following Argyris, require bringing to the surface. Building an ethical climate is therefore a means to do this.

2.5.2 Building an ethical climate

Whilst ethical issues in organizations can be addressed from a variety of perspectives, and raise complex theoretical issues, it would be more instructive to consider how you would address them. This applies to your own position as well as to the contradictions that emerge from organizations' procedures and guidelines. Where guidelines and ethical codes of practice exist, you will be obliged to be guided by them. Employees are likely to be informed by an organization's values, as well as by its rules and guidelines. But many are also governed by professional codes of practice. However, as a general principle, it is recommended that organizations review their own activities in relation to interventions, which always have the consequence for action.

There are, nevertheless, some dilemmas when we make interventions. The first is the extent to which the pursuit of humanistic values is contradicted or compromised by the desire to achieve organizational effectiveness. As Cummings and Worley argue, 'more practitioners are experiencing situations in which there is conflict between employees' needs for greater meaning and the organization's need for more effective and efficient use of its resources' (Cummings and Worley, 1997: 57). As a result, it is important to identify any areas of potential concern at the point of agreeing a contract with the client system. It should be clear, therefore, that any contract must make it transparent that organizational efficiency and effectiveness will depend upon an open and democratic concern for improvement through the organization's employees. And this, of course, has not always been the case where more task-focused interventions predominate (for example, TQM, BPR), with instrumental and formulaic approaches to their interventions.

A second dilemma is related to value conflicts we often face in relation to the different perspectives of stakeholder groups. This inevitably means that different stakeholders may need to be consulted and their views explored in order to arrive at a workable intervention strategy. But it is also important to identify potential value conflicts. As a result, you may wish to consider ethical guidelines such as clarifying:

- The needs of the client system, in its widest possible sense, which, of course, might include all stakeholders and/or different employee groups.

- The extent to which compromises are possible in relation to organizational efficiency and effectiveness *vis-à-vis* humanistic values.

- The purpose or remit of the intervention, in order to achieve its defined objectives.

A code of ethics is a general guide to actions in relation to appropriate conduct. This usually seeks to elaborate key issues and responses through scenario planning, as well as drawing attention to regulatory issues such as laws and regulations. Issues relate to both conformance and proactive behaviour. The code of conduct should be made public so that everyone has access to it. Whilst it is not possible to cover all contingencies, it is important to address potential ethical dilemmas. A code of ethics can have a positive impact assuming that it: (1) is distributed to every employee; (2) is firmly supported by top management; (3) refers to specific practices and ethical dilemmas likely to be encountered by stakeholders; (4) is evenly enforced with rewards for compliance and strict penalties for noncompliance; (5) reinforces ethical behaviour and punishes unethical behaviour; and (6) contains procedural guidance in order to guide behaviour.

2.6 Summary

You should now be clear that ethics plays a very important role in organizational change. It should be apparent that interventions carry political and ethical consequences. This tends to be the problem with the structural-functional perspective, which is devoted to technical solutions and largely ignores ethical issues. We can see this in the case example, *The limits of technical solutions—the case of the Ford Pinto,* and we can also note how the black swan theory is evident in that case. Perception was limited by relying on technical solutions to the exclusion of anything else. Avoidance of ethical issues can turn what at first appears to be an innocent change strategy into a tyrannical leviathan. Indeed, this is the message of the case example *Compliant workers or happy slaves?* You should now understand why the application of technical solutions to complex problems (structural-functional perspective) may have limitations that, on occasion, are dangerous.

The multiple constituencies perspective is central to the argument for ethical consideration. Stakeholder theory suggests that it is important to link change initiatives to an examination of stakeholder needs and their implications for an organization, as well as to contentious relationships between different groups of stakeholders, and to the power differences between stakeholders. The role that social contracts play has become important to the governance of organizations. Both the stakeholder approach and the social contract approach are useful for thinking about effective management of human resources and protecting the organization from unwanted litigation. Organization Development reflects a more recent but non-philosophical approach to the link between organizational change and ethics. It is proactive, being the only approach that has articulated humanistic commitment to developing organizations through people. The case example *The International Organization Development Code of Ethics* provides a good example of the principles involved. Consideration of Critical Theory suggests that this does not seek to promote a theoretical position on organizational ethics. Instead, it raises difficult questions for those who seek to manage change by questioning how the social reality of the organization is constructed. Social structuring of gender relationships and the role of conflict as a dynamic for change raise ethical questions such as how governance is constructed.

Your own position on engagement should also be questioned and you need to be clear where you stand before you engage in managing change. Sensitivity to ethical issues should enable you to avoid the pitfall of being mechanistic and task-driven. And, as a result, you should avoid alienating people in the process. But if you have any doubt about why you should be concerned about ethics, then hopefully you found an answer in the future drivers for ethics-based interventions: sustainable development and whether all employees, and managers in particular, should take an oath to act responsibly. Alternatively, you might consider how managing change in a multinational global environment carries serious implications for responsible leadership. The case example *Genetic engineering and the power of global corporations* is a clear indication that many issues are not straightforward because they involve values. But the status of multinational corporations also means that power intervenes and forces moral dilemmas.

Every individual responsible for managing change should be aware of, and in adopting an ethical position understand, the rationalizations that occur when people seek to justify indefensible actions. The defence routines people engage in are clearly demonstrated in the end-of-chapter case study, which requires consideration of problems within Siemens. Finally, any knowledgeable practitioner of change should be aware that it is important to build an ethical climate.

⊛ Case study

Corporate bribery at Siemens fixed-line telecommunications equipment division

On 26 May 2008 a former Siemens senior manager admitted building an elaborate system of slush funds and shell firms at the request of his superiors. This enabled Siemens to win huge overseas contracts through institutional bribes. The senior manager Reinhard Siekaczek told a Munich court that he had informed his divisional board about the illegal system. He also stated that he assumed the whole group executive board had been aware of this from at least 2004. The elaborate scheme involved managers signing off 'commissions' on yellow Post-it® notes. These could easily be removed if raids or investigations occurred. His testimony alleged that his efforts to stop the widespread bribery had fallen foul of his superiors, who didn't want to hear. Siekaczek is the first of at least 300 staff who are accused of complicity. The scandal involves six divisions in which at least €1.3bn (£1bn) was siphoned into slush funds that extended across the world. The former chairman Heinrich von Pierer and his successor Klaus Kleinfeld have lost their jobs. Siekaczek, the former sales manager, said he had not received promotion or bonuses but had simply acted for the benefit of ❯❯

❯Siemens. He added that 'this was the only means we could use once overseas bribery was outlawed'. The slush funds employed phoney consultants, shell firms, contracts, and false bills. Siemens' own investigations and others have widened beyond the telecoms unit to include transport and power divisions.

US authorities may also impose fines, and Siemens has set aside €1bn to cover these. In addition, the Siemens group is being investigated in many countries for allegedly paying huge sums to governments and officials in order to win lucrative contracts. The group's Austrian chief executive, Peter Loescher, has pledged to make Siemens 'squeaky clean' and has introduced new compliance officers to enforce strict observance of corporate governance rules.

Task

Consider this case of corporate bribery. Then read Siemens' own case example, 'Creating a high performance culture', which sets out the culture the company aspires to. This can be found at <http://www.thetimes100.co.uk>.

Explain why there is a gap between the company's formal statement and the actual internal work practices that have led to the German court investigating the company. To do this answer the following questions:

1. Identify the manifest problems.

2. Say why there appears to be a gap between the espoused values of the company and the practices that led to the current problem. State whether there is evidence of defensive reasoning.

3. Make a case for acting responsibly. What would you suggest the company should address?

▪ Study questions

1. Explain how the case example—*The limits of technical solutions—the case of the Ford Pinto*—illustrates the argument for processual or emergent change.

2. Explain the black swan theory and say how it affects our perception of problems.

3. Explain how the multiple constituencies perspective addresses ethics through governance.

4. Why can we regard Organization Development as a non-philosophical but proactive approach to the ethics of change? State the implications.

5. There is a clear case to make for acting responsibly. What is it? List as many reasons as you can think of and justify your argument.

6. Examine the case example—*When a bottle of water led to a strategic management disaster*—and explain how an ethical consideration of the product would have avoided that disaster.

7. Draw up your own arguments for a sustainably developed product; then do the same for a service.

8. Should managers take an oath to act responsibly? If you agree, outline what areas of the business you would include. If you disagree, then make a case saying what areas ethics should be applied to, and how the process should be managed.

9. Make a case for or against the argument of Critical Theory that capitalism is inherently selfish and has to be continuously challenged because it is exploitative.

10. Explain how defensive reasoning works and identify its potential ethical dangers.

■ Exercises

Exercise 1: The ethics of intervention
Read the case example *Compliant workers or happy slaves?* at the beginning of this chapter; then answer the following questions:

1. Does genetic manipulation have any advantages for organizations?

2. Could it ever be justified on ethical grounds?

3. If applied to humans, is this an ethical approach to the treatment of mental patients?

4. What are the implications if power rested with a non-elected government, and if companies of the future wanted compliant employees?

Exercise 2: Economic drivers for developing sustainable business
Read the *Guardian Unlimited* talk-board session (Wednesday 13 December 2000—<http://www.guardian.co.uk>—please consult the ORC for the weblink).

When you have done this, identify the processes that are claimed to be driving economic change, and provide an argument that illustrates the process of development and raises questions about other possibilities and contradictions.

Exercise 3: The role of governance in an MNE
Look at the speech of Donald Johnston, Secretary-general of the Organisation for Economic Co-operation and Development (OECD), on the website below. Then come to a reasoned decision about what you consider to be arguments for *governance* in an MNE. For example, you might consider how this can be represented in each company, awnd what needs to be controlled and coordinated. You should also consider the dysfunctional consequences of poor leadership. What are the issues and how might you deal with them? <http://www.oecd.org/> (Please see the ORC for a more detailed weblink.)

Exercise 4: Managing change with the local farming community
Read the scenario below first. Then say how you would manage change at a national level with the local farming community. There are three obvious positions you can take. Identify which one you believe is ethically acceptable and argue your case. Provide a reasoned argument for one of the following:

- You accept the challenge on the grounds that the decision is a political one.
- You refuse to accept the challenge on the grounds that the position is unethical.
- You will accept the challenge providing that a clear position is defined that you personally find acceptable.

Scenario
A government that had previously signed up to the 2000 World governments' moratorium on developing and testing of GM technology plans to reverse its decision. Government ministers have refused to meet a coalition of ten environment groups to discuss their current policy. They have also failed to publicize their position. Furthermore, the previous minister, who had resigned from the government, stated that 'for the first time in the history of the world, farmers would be stopped from using their own seeds. This would undermine food production and cause starvation.'

Exercise 5: Rank the top ten luxury holding companies against their own claims.
Go to the WWF report *Deeper Luxury* (<http://www.wwf.org.uk/deeperluxury/index.html>) and rank the companies, with the highest performing at the top and the lowest performing at the bottom.

Exercise 6: How difficult and practical is it for companies to practise corporate social responsibility given the international competition in certain industries?
Working in pairs or as a small group, identify a particular industry, discuss the statement above, and produce a written list of:

- arguments for change;
- arguments against it;
- approaches for pursuing an ethical policy demonstrating social responsibility.

■ Further reading

Ethical issues related to the perspective of multiple constituencies are influenced by governance, which is informed by the stakeholder approach and by the social contracts approach. Therefore, useful sources are:

Phillips, R. and Freeman, E. (2003), *Stakeholder Theory and Organizational Ethics*, San Francisco, CA: Berrett-Koehler Publishers.

Wempe, B. (2008), 'Contractarian Business Ethics: Credentials and Design Criteria', *Organization Studies* 29: 1337–1355.

For an account of the values for an Organization Development consultant see:

Gellermann, W., Frankel, M.S., and Landenson, R.F. (1990), *Values and Ethics in Organization and Human Systems Development*, San Francisco, CA: Jossey-Bass.

The values for an Organization Development consultant can also be found at: <http://www.odinstitute.org/ethics.htm>.

White, L.P. and Wooten, K.C. (1986) *Professional Ethics and Practice in Organization Development*, New York: Praeger Publishers.

Governance and commitment to social responsibility

The top ten luxury holding companies are discussed and analysed in the Worldwide Fund for Nature report *Deeper Luxury*. This can be found at the website: <http://www.wwf.org.uk/deeperluxury/index.html>.

All aspiring managers should look at the role of governance in an MNE. This can be found at: <http://www.oecd.org/>.

Green Business

It is worth exploring the official business link to the US Government for what it recommends and commits itself to. See this at: <http://www.business.gov/expand/green-business/>.

If you are interested in starting your own green business, then the BT site below helps you to address the issue involved: <http://insight.bt.com/guides/Understanding-green-business-practices/>.

For Critical Theory see:

Collins, H. and Wray-Bliss, E. (2005), 'Discriminating ethics', *Human Relations* 58, 799.

■ References

Anand, V., Ashfoith B.E., and Joshi, M. (2005), 'Business as usual: The acceptance and perpetuation of corruption in organizations', *Academy of Management Executive*, 19(4), 9–23.

Anshen, M. (1980) *Corporate strategies for social performance*, London: Macmillan.

Argyris, C. (1997), 'Teaching Smart People How To Learn' in Carnal, C.A. (ed.), *Strategic Change*, Oxford: Butterworth-Heinemann.

Bandura, A. (1999), 'Moral disengagement in the perpetration of inhumanities', *Personality and Social Psychology Review,* 3(3), 193–209.

Blauner R. (1966), *Alienation and Freedom*, Chicago, IL: University of Chicago Press.

Butterfield K.D., Klebe Trevino L., and Weaver G.R. (2000), 'Moral awareness in business organizations: Influences of issue-related and social context factors', *Human Relations*; 53, 981.

Chambliss, D.F. (1996), *Beyond caring: Hospitals, nurses, and the social organization of ethics*, Chicago, IL: University of Chicago Press.

Collins, H. and Wray-Bliss, E. (2005), 'Discriminating ethics', *Human Relations* 58, 799.

Co-operative Bank (2005), *Ethical Consumption Report*.

Cummings, T.G. and Worley, C.G. (1997), *Organization and Change*, Minneapolis/St. Paul, MN: West.

Donaldson, T., and Preston, L.E. (1995), 'The Stakeholder Theory of the Corporation: Concepts, Evidence, and Implications', *Academy of Management Review* 20(1), 65–91.

Elkington, J., Knight, P., and Hales, J. (1991), *The Green Business Guide*, London: Victor Gollancz.

Emiliani, M.L. (2000), 'The Oath of Management', *Management Decision* 38(4), 261–262.

Freeman, R.E. (1984), *Strategic Management: A stakeholder approach*, Boston, MA: Pitman.

Friedman, A.L. and Miles, S. (2002), 'Developing Stakeholder Theory', *Journal of Management Studies* 39(1), 1–21.

Fromm, E. (1941), *Escape from freedom*. New York: Farrar and Rinehart.

Hatcher, T. (2002), *Ethics and HRD: A New Approach to Leading Responsible Organizations*, New York: Perseus Publishing.

Jackall, R. (1988), *Moral mazes: The world of corporate managers*, New York: Oxford University Press.

James, O. (2008), 'Selfish Capitalism is Bad for our Mental Health', *The Guardian*, 3 January.

Keeley, M. (1988). *A social contract theory of organizations*. Notre Dame, IN: University of Notre Dame Press.

Mitchell, R.K., Agle, B.R., and Wood, D.J. (1997), 'Toward a Theory of Stakeholder Identification and

Salience: Defining the Principle of Who and What Really Counts', *Academy of Management Review* 22 (4), 853–886.

Nestle, M. (2008), *Pet Food Politics: The Chihuahua in the Coal Mine*, Berkeley, CA: University of California Press.

Phillips, R. and Freeman, E. (2003), *Stakeholder Theory and Organizational Ethics*, San Francisco, CA: Berrett-Koehler Publishers.

Rest, J.R. (1986), *Moral Development: Advances in Research and Theory*, New York: Praeger.

Schneider, R.O. (2000), 'Knowledge and Ethical Responsibility in Industrial Disasters', *Disaster Prevention and Management*, 9(2), 98–105.

Taleb, N.N. (2007), *The Black Swan: The Impact of the Highly Improbable*, New York: Random House.

Townsend, A. (2000), 'Misplaced marketing—Dangers for misplaced tobacco marketing in Eastern Europe', *Journal of Consumer Marketing* 17(2), 103–106.

Vinten, G. (1994), *Whistleblowing—Subversion or Corporate Citizenship?* London: Paul Chapman.

—— (1995), 'The whistleblowers' charter', *Executive Development*, 8(2), 25–28.

Wempe, B. (2008), 'Contractarian Business Ethics: Credentials and Design Criteria', *Organization Studies*, 29, 1337–1355.

■ Useful Websites

Deeper Luxury website: <http://www.wwf.org.uk/deeperluxury/index.html>.

 Take your learning further: Online Resource Centre
http://www.oxfordtextbooks.co.uk/orc/grieves/

Visit the Online Resource Centre that accompanies this book to enrich your understanding of this chapter. Explore case study updates and answers to questions, test yourself using an interactive flashcard glossary, and keep up to date with the latest developments in the area.

CHAPTER 3

Planned change and its critics

3.1 Introduction

In Chapter 1 we noted that different perspectives make claims to knowledge, implying how change should be understood. This chapter illustrates the nature of planned change, but this is related to the nature of knowledge. The chapter discusses three theoretical positions making different knowledge claims: the *empirical–rational*, *normative re-educative*, and *processual or emergent* approaches. The first is a product of the structural-functional perspective, which focuses on rational solutions to problems. The second is the product of the Organizational Development (OD) perspective, which seeks collaborative learning solutions. The third is derived from the perspective Creativity and Volition: a Critical Theory of Change, which forces us to think about change issues much more carefully. The chapter should be read as a critical reflection on planned change.

The difficulty with many accounts of planned change is their lack of conceptual clarity. Accordingly, let us begin by clarifying the three main approaches to organizational change. The first is a form of planned change that is sometimes referred to as mechanistic, managerialistic, or linear change. We will use the term 'empirical–rational' to illustrate the change strategies employed. The second approach is intended to develop an organization's capacity to learn: it is referred to as 'normative re-educative' change. The third has more to do with the small but significant change processes that emerge once planned change is implemented: processual or emergent change. This third approach to change is critical of planned change, although it is not always clear which type of planned change it is criticizing. What often emerges is that various approaches to planned change are often bundled together as if they are driven by the same agendas or are characterized by the same deficiencies. This is unfortunate, because we need to be alert to the fact that different approaches are embedded with contrasting, as well as overlapping, assumptions. For example, it is common to regard all planned change as linear or sequential. Yet this is true only of the most mechanistic versions, in which change is characterized by managerialism. This term carries cynical associations, such as the employment of prescriptive strategies in which management adopt unitarist assumptions and plan actions in a top-down manner. At a strategic level these are rigid formulaic strategies, aiming to achieve objectives identified by senior managers and cascaded down to others. The means by which a destination-oriented strategic plan is constructed is one aspect of it; another is its execution. Thus, rigid adherence to a plan that is empirically unsound demonstrates naivety of the highest order. Often these plans are nothing more than 'off-the-shelf' packages designed by consultants and applied indiscriminately to a variety of organizations. At an operational level, the pursuit of technical expediency is designed into the change strategy. This is usually undertaken by process redesign and a critical path analysis typical of project management. The stages reflect the controlled throughput of products or services until they are received by a customer or client.

If empirical–rational approaches are prescriptive, normative re-educative approaches are diagnostic. These are commonly applied by OD practitioners, who are interested in identifying a clear need before a change intervention is introduced. Empirical–rational and normative re-educative approaches reflect opposite extremes of the structural-functionalist continuum: at one extreme, mechanistic approaches that originated in Taylor's prescriptive scientific management; at the other, more reflective, learning-oriented approaches typical of the open-systems model. The adoption of this model by the OD discipline implies subjective and humanistic concerns governing interventions. The OD approach was also less rigid than previous versions of systems theory, as is illustrated in the punctuated equilibrium model. This is different from linear change models because it is designed as a learning system: Kurt Lewin's Action Research model is one example. Normative re-educative methods therefore involve collaborative approaches by teams who collectively seek to learn by discovering and experimenting to reap new strategic or operational advantages.

Despite the differences in approach to planned change, a problem remains. Planned change models are aligned to a management agenda and are therefore driven by a concern to reduce complexity through planning. This reductionist tendency is amplified by the structural-functional epistemology's tendency to view change as resulting from control and consensus. In contrast, processual or emergent change theory is characterized by an epistemology that suggests that change results from conflict. Processual theorists, as we shall see, focus on historical, political, and contextual processes that unfold as change progresses. Despite the value of their contribution, processual theorists cannot provide a model for managing change, because their epistemological position, particularly their reluctance to be aligned to the needs of management, and their methodology negate planning change.

Each stage of a change programme carries potential risks, but the main problem faced by planned change programmes is that many things cannot be anticipated and planned for in advance. These include threats posed by non-traditional foes, and irregular, catastrophic, or disruptive challenges. One attempt to limit this problem is to practise scenario planning. This is a method for dealing with change in times of crisis or for an unpredictable future. Scenarios provide alternative images of how the future might unfold and what the consequences of our responses might be.

In this chapter we will:

- Elucidate the nature of planned change by contrasting empirical–rational approaches with normative re-educative approaches to planned change.
- Clarify managerialist approaches to change.
- Demonstrate functional integration by examining the redesign and management of critical processes.
- Describe the problems of planned change.
- Evaluate the approach of processual or emergent change theorists.

3.2 Empirical–rational approaches to change

3.2.1 Prescriptive managerialist approaches to change

Empirical–rational approaches to change are characterized by planned, linear stages that have a clear beginning and end. These are often described as top-down change strategies because the strategic manager or team leader acts as designer, planner, and implementer of planned change. Such approaches are therefore mechanistic. Change is viewed as a rational arrangement of tasks in an organization. The most obvious empirical–rational approaches are often described as managerialist. An example of these is the five-year strategic plan common in some public sector organizations and universities. The term 'managerialist' carries cynical associations suggesting a lack of empowerment and an inflexible approach to implementing change. Consequently, they limit collaboration to formal roles in a bureaucratic process. Carnall (2007) suggests that linear change is characterized by two things: managerialist approaches to change and the lack of stakeholder involvement. In his discussion of managerialist approaches he cites Stacey (1996) to argue that such approaches are typical of situations in which managers lead change ahead of environmental changes, and/or where perceptions of change are informed by a systems model that tends towards a static equilibrium. He qualifies the first point by suggesting that such 'models of change tend to view the process as operating within the existing organizational system, that is with senior executives starting and then dominating the process' (Carnall, 2007: 69). This does appear to be the case in some respects. However, we should be careful not to regard all such attempts to lead from the top as political domination. That may well be the end result, and how people experience change initiatives, but it may also happen because of naivety due to incompetence or lack of experience. The point that Carnall is making is that such change is imposed in some way. There are three main reasons why this may happen:

1. Overt political domination.
2. Use of a prescriptive (rather than diagnostic) formula by managers, following previous patterns of behaviour or systems as Carnall suggests, or bought-in management consultancy advice involving expert systems or off-the-shelf change packages.
3. Expediency when time is short, and staff have a high trust in the leadership's skills.

The first point needs no explanation, other than that this fits with a lack of stakeholder involvement and is driven by unitarist assumptions (see Chapter 7 for a comprehensive description). The second point appears to be common to many organizations, since linear change models appear to fit one of these patterns and off-the-shelf programmes have been sold by consultants offering expert packages. The third point suggests that expediency drives the need for prescriptive change, but that the leader may be more skilled because s/he is trusted.

Linear, managerialist programmes are composed of sequential stages that take the change from beginning to end. Thus the change journey ends at the final stage in the plan. Linear managerialist models are usually easy to use and can be modified to fit the bespoke requirements of clients. But these always feature a mixture of strategic and operational planning managed in sequential stages. The main disadvantage to using a linear managerialist model is that it drives change as if this were a project composed of simple tasks or phases. Because the stages are sequential they are considered to be continuously progressive, but this is rarely the case. At an operational level this approach to change has its place when speed is required and technical skills are applied routinely. This is rarely successful at a strategic level, because the greater the complexity the greater are the opportunities for conflict, instability, and disequilibrium.

❗ Stop and think 3.1

When Stuart Rose became chief executive of Marks & Spencer, the company appeared to be in terminal decline and was close to being taken over. Pressure from shareholders and financial institutions created a situation that appeared to require a new chief executive with proven imaginative flair. The planned change strategy he introduced was a top-down series of initiatives that proved very successful in the short term.

When used for more complex change initiatives, linear managerialist approaches tend to be viewed as a series of events rather than a series of complex processes. Such approaches often lack commitment from the people who have to implement the plan. An example of a linear managerialist model is the use by The Training Agency in the 1980s of a five-stage process to implement change (see the following case example). A model essentially similar to project management—a 'Five-Stage Project Control' model—was used in this case to manage strategic organization-wide change. An example of how the stages of change may be managed by using a Gantt chart is illustrated in Figure 3.1, which follows the case example.

≫ Case example 3.1

'Putting the customer first'

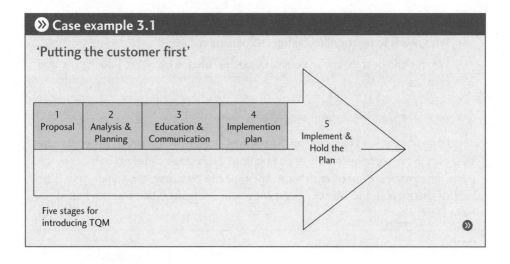

| 1 Proposal | 2 Analysis & Planning | 3 Education & Communication | 4 Implemention plan | 5 Implement & Hold the Plan |

Five stages for introducing TQM

❯❯ Stage 1: Proposal

The proposal asks two questions:

1. Who owns the project and who will be accountable for its success?
2. What is it intended to address?

Addressing these requires a statement of *objectives*, *membership* and *resources*. Thus, objectives refer to the development of a specified outcome, at a specified cost, and within a specified time. Objectives must form a realistic compromise between these three interdependent attributes. They are the means of measuring progress on the specific quality improvement you intend. These are developed in the next stage and are critical if progress and success are to be measured. 'Membership' and 'resources' refer to the need to consider the resources required to complete the project, including the team members. Other aspects to consider are timing and links to other initiatives.

Stage 2: Analysis and Planning

This stage involves identifying the activities of each stage. Therefore it requires details of:

- What is going to be done.
- When it is going to be done.
- What is needed to carry out the work.
- What is going to be produced.
- How variances at any stage will affect later stages.

Stage 3: Education and Communication

This stage is a simple matter of informing and educating people about what is required. The following questions are essential:

- Whose support/agreement is required to ensure success?
- Who needs to be consulted, informed, and/or involved?
- What is the best means to communicate the what, why, when, how, where, and by whom questions?

Stage 4: Detailed Implementation Plans

This stage is regarded as fine-tuning the planned change by outlining how people play their part in the implementation. At completion of this stage, detailed implementation plans for all staff are specified. That is, they specify how people will undertake their part of the project and obtain agreement about implementation from the management team. ❯❯

> **Stage 5: Implementation**

The final stage requires measuring and assessing results. Deviations from conformance may occur and the project may develop problems along the way. This stage is essentially about monitoring progress to ensure that quality improvements are recognized and maintained.

Figure 3.1 Gantt chart detailing timing and tasks completed in phases

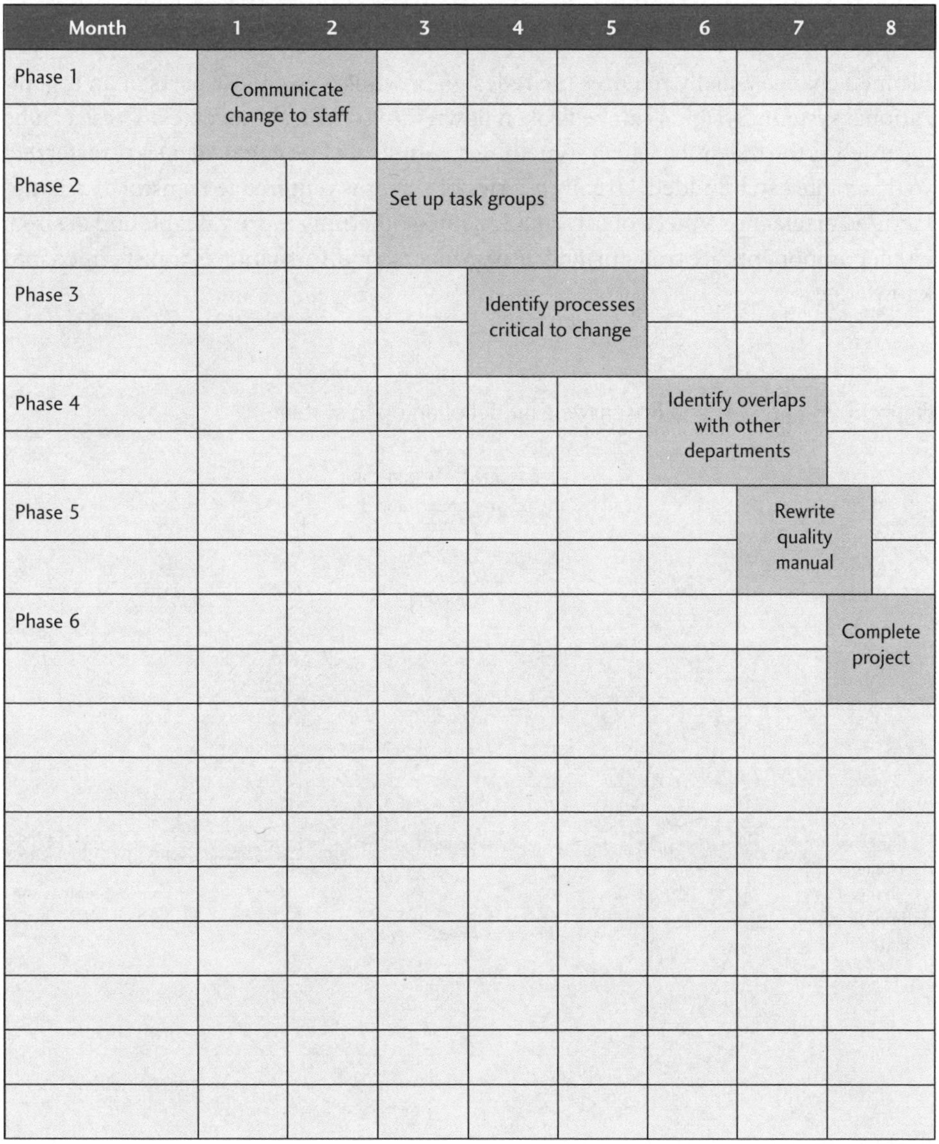

Month	1	2	3	4	5	6	7	8
Phase 1	Communicate change to staff							
Phase 2			Set up task groups					
Phase 3				Identify processes critical to change				
Phase 4						Identify overlaps with other departments		
Phase 5							Rewrite quality manual	
Phase 6								Complete project

Prescriptive approaches are central to many forms of strategic change, as well as many types of operational change. We can think of mechanisms in terms of either a physical mechanical object such as a clock, or a biological mechanism such as an organism. The emergence of structural functionalism during the early twentieth century led to this mechanical *versus* organic dualism, yet both were seen as analogies by which organizations should be managed or changed. If we choose to design an organization to operate like a clock, then we must to examine its component parts to make their operation more efficient. In considering below the redesign and management of critical processes and Critical Path Analysis, we examine this dualism.

3.2.2 Redesigning and managing critical processes

Planned change usually requires the redesign of whole systems or parts of an organizational system. Systems can be broken down into technical processes. These can be regarded as the means by which something (a physical object or an idea) is transferred, so that value can be added. Usually a series of stages is required to transform a manufactured artefact or a piece of information into something more valuable and desired: either components are transformed into products, or information is transformed into knowledge.

Figure 3.2 The Kast and Rosenzweig model of an open system

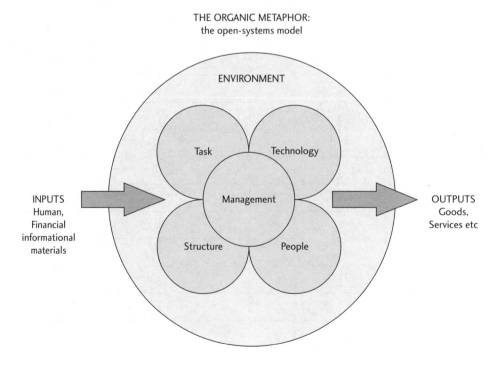

As the Kast and Rosenzweig model (Figure 3.2) illustrates, processes are transformed by the application of knowledge, skills, and effort. A series of transformations has to be managed in order to produce an output desired by the customer or client. We can see therefore how the whole process adds value.

❗ Stop and think 3.2

Apply the descriptions stated above to a product or service. Identify the transformations and consider how these are managed.

The purpose of redesigning critical processes is to ensure that each process in the sequence adds value. The questions for the redesign of processes are as follows:

1. Is the process clearly outlined and understood by all engaged in it?
2. How are efficiency and effectiveness measured?
3. What systems are used?
4. What benefits does the customer or client receive?

Change requires the identification of critical processes. These are the core processes that drive the sequence and are usually referred to as critical success factors (CSF). Performance measures determine expectations of the change process. This is illustrated in Figure 3.3 below.

3.2.3 Critical Path Analysis

Critical Path Analysis (CPA) is a tool for scheduling and managing projects. It was originally developed to control defence projects but has been applied routinely to any project with complex tasks in order to control the flow of work through a number of stages. Its purpose is to plan resources. Its advantage is that it enables the clear identification of a critical path; that is, problem junctures that could delay a project.

Figure 3.3 Redesigning processes

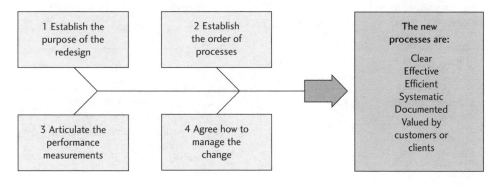

Although projects can also be managed using a Gantt chart, the CPA has the advantage of displaying the tasks to be achieved together with the processes critical to each stage. It also enables those involved in managing a change project to establish how much time each stage or event requires. All activities must be undertaken in a logical sequence and a distinction should be made between dependent tasks (that is, those with a causal relationship to others in the sequence) and non-dependent tasks that can be carried out alongside the causal chain. This is facilitated by writing a list of activities and related processes on a chart. As an example, we can imagine a student project

Table 3.1 Critical Path Analysis chart illustrating tasks and processes

Task	Start	Complete	Parallel processes that must be achieved
1) Define the project and agree the rules for performance.	Week 1	5 days	1) Establish an effective team. 2) Clarify objectives. 3) Undertake preliminary field work and desk research. 4) Write an ethical statement.
2) Meet sponsor and confirm or renegotiate the project definition.	Week 2	3 days	1) Determine and agree the outcomes and expectations. 2) Agree resources and funding. 3) Document discussion and send copy to sponsor.
3) Establish a framework for analysing the results.	Week 2	Day 4	Agree which model(s) should be used.
4) Agree roles and responsibilities of each member.	Week 2	Days 4 and 5	Establish responsibility for each task. These will include research, writing up, and reporting back to the sponsor.
5) Undertake empirical research and further desk research if required.	Week 3	Week 7	Agree methodology, scope, and boundary or limits of the research.
6) Write up results.	Week 8	End of week 8	
7) Report back to sponsor.	Week 9		1) Report findings and clarify contradictions if required. 2) Provide recommendations and outline possibilities for future research if required.

and attempt to identify all processes that lead to each stage (event). This is detailed in Table 3.1. Each step is sequential because it is causally related. However, there are some parallel processes that must be addressed and the team must be satisfied with these, or else they will become potential risks. For example, to ensure that task 1 is performed effectively, the team must attend to four parallel processes. These are to operate as an effective team; to clarify objectives; to undertake preliminary field work and desk research; and to write an ethical statement. Parallel processes are therefore what the team agree to in relation to the performance of the task.

The next step is to outline the critical flow of the activities. Figure 3.4 illustrates the Critical Path Analysis of the same student team project. The numbered circles in the figure represent the tasks or events and the arrows show that all previous processes that lead to the task should have been completed. The parallel processes can be defined as risks that might impact on the project.

A CPA, as a mechanical tool for organizing the sequence of activities, might be one reason why mechanisms are viewed as amenable to simple linear change. For this reason, it would appear that the concepts of tools and techniques are subject to some disapproval by some academics.

Figure 3.4 Plotting the course of a student team project using Critical Path Analysis

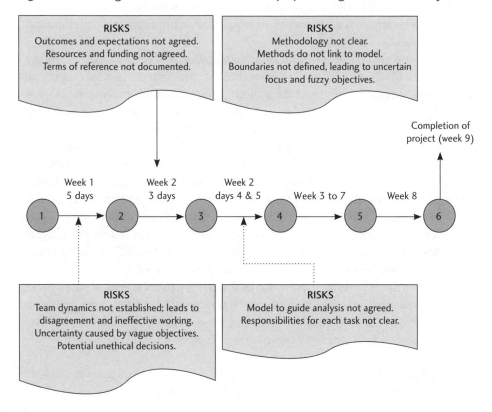

3.2.4 Tools and techniques

Popular tools and techniques include brainstorming, flowcharts, cause-and-effect diagrams, checklists, histograms, Pareto analysis, Force Field Analysis, graphs, statistical process control, quality circles, task forces, and departmental purpose analysis. However, academic texts appear reluctant to discuss change tools and techniques, apart from change models derived from TQM, project management, and, to a lesser extent, from business strategy. This reluctance is no doubt related to a dislike of less sophisticated prescriptive approaches. However, the terms tools, models, and techniques are sometimes used interchangeably. For example, academics tend to refer to 'models'—e.g. Lewin's three-stage model (Force Field Analysis)—whilst practitioners often refer to this as a 'tool' or a 'technique'. Furthermore, some academics refer to the processual change model, but as we will see later there is no model we can identify to manage change from this approach. Tools, techniques, and models can also be confused with methods.

A useful way forward is to distinguish a tool from a technique, as indicated by Dale and McQuater (1998), who suggest that a tool should be viewed as a stand-alone application. In contrast, a technique should be viewed as a more comprehensively integrated approach to problem solving that might rely on a number of supporting tools (Hughes, 2007). An example of this difference can be gleaned from Bjørnson, Wang, and Arisholm (2008), who sought a method to improve the quality of post mortem analyses. They sought to combine three techniques: brainstorming, group performance, and causal maps.

They begin with a particular form of brainstorming in which each participant was provided with five Post-it® notes. They were then asked to write down what they regarded as significant experiences from the project. At the end of this process, participants placed their notes on a whiteboard and explained what they meant by each note. Once the notes had been placed on the whiteboard, the group discussed them in terms of conceptual similarity. Each group of notes was then named and potential connections between groups of notes were marked with arrows. The process was repeated twice, for positive experiences followed by negative experiences. Brainstorming was then analysed using a fishbone diagram (alternatively known as a cause-and-effect or Ishikawa diagram) to establish root causes. A facilitator then asked the group to select a positive or negative experience and attribute causes, which were recorded on a whiteboard. Finally, the group discussed the potential cause of the experience. Several tools were therefore combined to produce a new technique. What emerged enabled the researchers to improve upon a previous technique by discovering that the level of participation could be increased if a cognitive mapping tool was introduced. As they suggested, group dynamics were better facilitated by introducing a less controlled technique, which they refer to as causal mapping, derived from strategic decision making:

> In order to better accommodate the nominal brainstorm technique, we needed a more free-form diagrammatic technique for presenting the results. For this,

we examined the technique of causal mapping… one of the most popular methods for investigating individuals' cognitive representations in strategic decision making.

(Bjørnson, Wang, and Arisholm, 2008: 153)

3.3 Normative re-educative models of change

3.3.1 Diagnostic approaches—planning, Action Research, and Force Field Analysis

Normative re-educative models of change require a higher degree of reflexivity than rational–empirical models because attention is focused on an organizational problem and resolved through collective action, which requires learning to progress change. For example, if we look at two of the first Organizational Development (OD) models of planned change (see Figure 3.5) we notice that, whilst the planning model appears closer to a linear programme of change, similar to the prescriptive linear destination models, the Action Research model focuses on both developing the skills and knowledge of participants, and solving a problem. It is, in effect, a heuristic device for organizational learning. The fundamental purpose of the Action Research model is to impart the knowledge, skills, and experience of the behavioural science expert. In other words, it is intended as a method for collective learning.

Many authors refer to Lewin's Force Field Analysis, or three-step model (see Figure 3.6), as an example of linear change. Yet this claim is contentious because his work was concerned with changing behaviours in individuals and groups. It was never intended as an organizational model, as is frequently implied. Unfortunately, many management writers or consultants have turned Lewin's method into a simplistic mechanistic device for managing organizational change.

For Lewin, all change is complex and none should be treated mechanistically. Indeed, we know this from his method of Action Research. He argued that 'any planned social change will have to consider a multitude of factors and characteristics for any particular case' and that all change situations have their own 'unique combination of educational and organizational measures'. These may 'depend upon quite different treatments or ideology, expectation, and organization' (Lewin, 1999: 279). We should note his concern with learning. Lewin saw the idea of a force field as a tension (or series of related tensions) that affects the personal (psychological) or social (group) context. It is his analytical method for enabling change. Lewin was interested in the emotional and cognitive forces that block change and devised FFA as a voluntary means to influence habits and routines which block personal change. For example, cultural norms often influence an individual's attitudes to and behaviours towards hygiene, food, social relationships, and taboos. Working methodically through these by challenging old assumptions enabled individuals and groups to make transitions by overcoming psychological and social barriers. Others who later followed these research interests include Kübler-Ross (1973), who researched psychologically extreme transitions such as bereavement, and Menninger (1975), who was concerned with discontinuity and transition.

FFA can be described as a method for focusing on forces that either drive us towards a goal (Lewin describes these as helping forces) or that restrict, block, or hinder achievement of the goal (restricting forces). For example, in 'Group Decision and Social Change' (Lewin, 1948; 1999), he makes the following explicit statement:

Figure 3.5 Comparison of two OD models: the planning model and the Action Research model

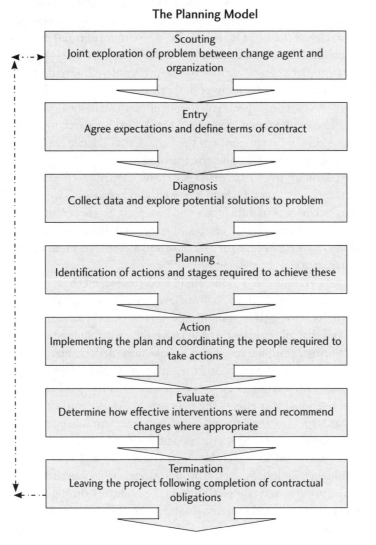

The Planning Model

Scouting
Joint exploration of problem between change agent and organization

An OD model that focuses on a particular task

Entry
Agree expectations and define terms of contract

Diagnosis
Collect data and explore potential solutions to problem

Planning
Identification of actions and stages required to achieve these

Action
Implementing the plan and coordinating the people required to take actions

Evaluate
Determine how effective interventions were and recommend changes where appropriate

Termination
Leaving the project following completion of contractual obligations

Figure 3.5 (Continued)

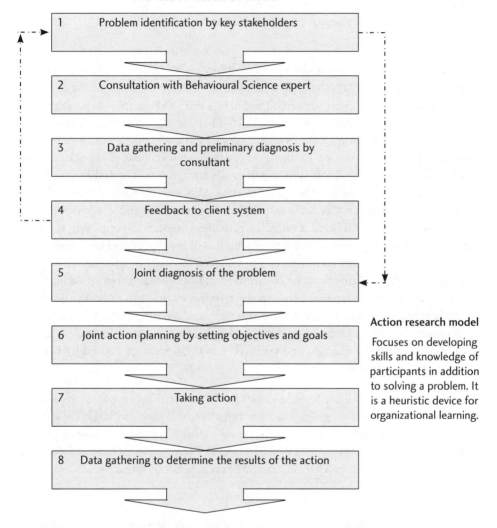

The Action Research Model

Action research model

Focuses on developing skills and knowledge of participants in addition to solving a problem. It is a heuristic device for organizational learning.

The objective of social change might concern the nutritional standard of consumption, the economic standard of living, the type of group relation, the output of a factory, the productivity of an educational team. It is important that a social standard to be changed does not have the nature of a 'thing' but of a 'process'.

(Lewin, 1999: 279)

The starting point for understanding social change, according to Lewin, is to understand equilibrium. He was at pains to describe this, not as a situation of 'no change', but as a slow and often imperceptible movement. Thus, his more exacting terminology is 'quasi-stationary equilibrium':

we do not refer to a stationary but to a quasi-stationary equilibrium, that is, to a state comparable to that of a river which flows with a given velocity in a given direction during a certain time interval. A social change is comparable to a change in the velocity or direction of that river.

(Ibid.).

In his discussion of food and education within social groups he refers to a quasi-stationary equilibrium as a balance of conflicting forces. For example, he describes an experiment on group decision into food habits and food channels as a comparison of different ethnic and economic groups in a Midwestern town. In this study he states that 'the buying situation' of the housewife 'can be characterized as a conflict situation' in which the motivation to buy food is a positive force that changes in relation to (a) how valued the food is (that is, whether it is attractive and desirable) and (b) the price of the food in relation to the family income. Although the food may be desirable, it may also be expensive. Consequently there is both a driving and an opposing force. In most situations of this kind it might be possible to reduce the opposing force. As he states, 'for any type of social management, it is of great practical importance that levels of quasi-stationary equilibria can be changed in either of two ways: by adding forces in the desired direction or by diminishing opposing forces' (Lewin, 1999: 281). There is usually tension between the two forces that can only be minimized by finding ways to increase the driving force and reduce the resisting force. This is best undertaken by unfreezing, moving, and refreezing at a new level. The biggest difficulty in achieving change, he observed, was the resistance caused by habitual behaviours. For example:

a change toward a higher level of group performance is frequently short lived: after a 'shot in the arm', group life soon returns to the previous level. This indicates that it does not suffice to define the objective of a planned change in group performance as the reaching of a different level. Permanency of the new level, or permanency for a desired period, should be included in the objective.

(Ibid.)

A successful change involves unfreezing existing behaviours by challenging assumptions and prejudice. But clearly this was not the so-called rationalist tendency that some critics charge him with. The application of Lewin's FFA to organizations came later, as a procedure adopted by others searching for a simple tool to manage change.

3.3.2 The punctuated equilibrium model

A second reason why we should not treat Lewin's three-step planned change model as linear is because his view of equilibrium was not static. For Lewin, change was only possible because of a 'quasi-stationary equilibrium'. That is, change looked

Figure 3.6 Lewin's model of Force Field Analysis

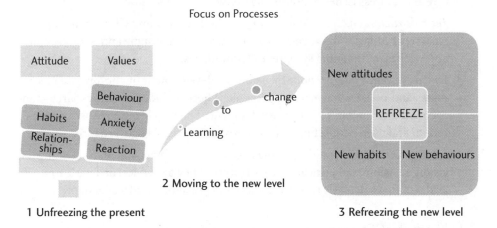

stationary only because small changes and their consequences usually go unnoticed. The paradox is that Lewin recognized that it was the small processes related to habits and attitudes that cause problems with behavioural change.

The OD perspective adopted FFA as well as his focus on Action Research. It also modified the structural-functional organic model by qualifying the types of intervention that we are likely to encounter, and then it humanized that model. OD is therefore not restricted to a static view of equilibrium. Indeed, many OD researchers adopted what Tushman and Romanelli (1985) called the punctuated equilibrium model, which they developed in arguing that organizations progress through convergent periods (relatively stable periods) punctuated by periods of uncertainty that challenge and reorientate the strategic direction for the next convergent period. However, convergent periods are not stable but are relatively long periods of incremental change and adaptation. The reorientations, by comparison, are relatively short periods of radical and discontinuous change. Furthermore, Romanelli and Tushman more recently (1994) considered that organizational change occurs within five domains of activity: (1) organizational culture; (2) strategy; (3) structure; (4) power distributions; and (5) control systems.

3.3.3 Interventions and organizational issues

Although interventions are usually interrelated, Cummings and Worley (1993) describe them under four headings:

1. *Human process interventions* address interaction processes, such as communication, decision making, leadership, motivation, and group dynamics within organizations. Human process issues are dealt with by undertaking a variety of interventions that involve psychological training and mentoring. Human

process interventions also seek to make improvements to the organization's culture and address issues of power and politics.

2. *Technostructural interventions* require methods for dealing with technology and structural issues. These relate to organization redesign, and sociotechnical approaches to designing systems and procedures.

3. *Human resource interventions* focus on the development of appropriate mechanisms and policies for managing people. These include human resource management and human resource development. The organization must be able to recruit and train people but it must also practise effective governance.

4. *Strategic interventions* address issues in the external environment by creating the vision, mission, and critical success factors. They are concerned with strategic leadership, particularly transformational and results-based leadership.

Although the OD perspective views organizations as open systems, it is much more sophisticated in its approach than the original structural-functional perspective because it adopts a diagnostic approach to change instead of focusing simply on throughput. Nevertheless, as Cummings and Worley point out, the focus on functional integration is central to OD:

> because organizations are systems, the issues are interrelated and need to be integrated with each other. The double-headed arrows connecting the different issues... represent the fits or linkages... Organizations need to match answers to one set of issues with answers to other sets of questions in order to achieve high levels of effectiveness. For example, decisions about gaining competitive advantage need to fit with choices about organization structure, setting goals for and rewarding people, communication, and problem solving.

(Cummings and Worley, 1993: 164)

❶ Stop and think 3.3

Think of an intervention you have experienced and consider which of the four categories listed above it falls into. State what this involved, what could be planned for in advance, and what could not.

Whilst Cummings and Worley provide a typology for interventions, it is clear that the changing nature of work raises a range of issues that illustrate the interactive complexity of this typology. In the twenty-first century a number of factors have emerged that are necessary for encouraging the development of internal forces for change. First, because many organizations have restructured from hierarchical command-and-control systems, employees organize their actions through process teams instead of through departments. This requires different skills and competences. Many non-functional skills such as group problem solving, cooperation, negotiation, and leadership are required for effective team interaction. Thus, if people are to be innovative they require the means to develop creative solutions to organizational problems. A second aspect of managing the transition to innovation is the reorganization of jobs around projects rather than through departments. Such projects require groups who develop organizational learning. The third aspect is the performance standards set by the process teams. The use of methodologies to facilitate performance improvements in delivery time, cost reduction, and quality enhancement can only work effectively in highly motivated work environments. The fourth issue is the need to identify the new skills required for tomorrow. Project teams must take responsibility for developing self-regulating skills.

3.4 Processual and emergent change

Various writers have challenged the linear destination-oriented models of planned change from a phenomenological and critical perspective. These newer approaches have argued that change emerges from unplanned processes that could not be anticipated. This argument was originally put by Pettigrew (1985) in his study of ICI. More recently (2000) he has argued for a more sociological investigation focusing on different levels of analysis in which temporal and contextual factors play their part. Consequently, a variety of researchers have developed his arguments further and have demonstrated a gap between the claims of planned change interventionists and the reality experienced by those undertaking the change. Burnes (2007), for example, argues that the planned change approach:

- is simplistic because it follows formulaic recipe-driven approaches;
- does not focus on relationships between individuals, groups, and organizations;
- largely ignores decision-making processes, individual perceptions, political struggles, and coalition building.

Although Burnes talks about an emergent approach that stresses the 'developing and unpredictable nature of change' (Burnes, 2007: 293), to date no clearly articulated alternative approach to planned change has emerged. There are essentially two reasons for this: the first epistemological and the second methodological.

3.4.1 Epistemology

In addressing the first point we need to be clear that all change has to be planned. However, once we recognize this it becomes obvious that the knowledge we apply is central to planning and implementing change. For example, we have noted that empirical–rational approaches seek a linear progress towards their destination, whilst normative re-educative approaches, typical of OD, are cyclical. Prescriptive approaches are mechanistic whilst OD approaches are humanistic. Despite that, both share the central assumptions of the structural-functional perspective, that change involves structures and mechanisms. Structures and mechanisms either can be treated mechanistically or can include cultural components such as the 7S framework of Peters and Waterman discussed in Chapter 6. Because both approaches focus on efficiency and effectiveness, they ignore any activity that is not related to these. Consequently they:

- ignore historical processes;
- ignore processes that emerge from context;
- either ignore political processes or view them as problematic and dysfunctional.

In contrast to empirical–rational and normative re-educative change approaches, critical approaches are not interested in efficiency and effectiveness. But far more important is critical epistemology, which contends that structures and mechanisms, like the concept of organization itself, are artificial constructs and exist only in the minds of those who seek pragmatic convenience. By seeking such, they reify reality (simplify it by abstraction). Because the structural-functional perspective from which both the empirical–rational and normative re-educative change approaches are derived seeks solutions related to efficiency and effectiveness, it emphasizes a desire to predict and control things. The problem is that things do not always turn out as planned, as the folowing case example makes clear.

❯❯ Case example 3.2

Not everything turns out as planned

After years of putting other people through the agonies of reorganization, redundancy, expansion, harmonization, re-grading and process re-engineering, I was about to come face to face with major personal change, and I was laughably insouciant about the whole thing. This is because I had been brought up, in common, I suspect, with many managers, to believe in the predominant model of organizational change as a linear, purposive process. I had planned my changes meticulously, I had clear objectives and I would project manage the whole transition to meet those objectives. Why would it be anything other than painless? This goal-setting, programmatic approach to change, rooted in the machine metaphor of organizations (Morgan, 2004), is a tempting one for hard-pressed managers charged with bringing order and control to businesses. It is no surprise that it remains a powerful influence still. Like many, I clung to this picture rather like we all accept air travel safety instructions, in spite of an inner voice telling us that reality is likely to be a whole lot messier. The truth is that organizational changes, in my experience, rarely, if ever, pan out entirely as planned, and yet we find it hard to relinquish the hope that they might.   ❯❯

> ◈ It helps to reduce our anxiety. The appeal of five-step change models (or eight-step or ten-step) lies partly in the usefulness of the structure they provide, but mainly in the comfortable illusion that this structure is all you need to change things successfully. It is reassuring to have that little light and whistle on your life-jacket, just so long as you do not think too much about what use they will be.
>
> *Source:* Gravells (2006).

Processual researchers refer to 'processual' (Dawson, 1994), 'emergent' (Burnes, 2007), or 'integrationist' (Kimble and McLoughlin, 1995) models of change, which they contrast with planned change models. These models 'view major change as a non-linear, interactive process in which outcomes are shaped by the way people interpret and act on their contemporary and historical contexts' (Boddy, 2000: 284). Processual accounts therefore articulate volition, action, and choice through the three interpretive lenses of history, context, and politics. For example, in his study of implementing inter-organizational IT systems, Boddy (2000) contrasts his approach with planned change by stating that his strategic choice model places greater emphasis on volition. That is, 'on the influence that human beings have on the technology' and the way people shape its application:

> Managers have minds of their own, as do the people who work with and for them. They decide which technologies to develop, promote and install to further their interests. Others decide the details of how they will use or react to it—again in the light of their interests. In this view, technology is a dependent variable, reflecting the interplay of forces within and around the organization. The effects are uncertain, as they are heavily influenced by human choices.

(Boddy, 2000: 31)

Despite the reference to processual or emergent models of change, these are not clearly defined and, consequently, are not intended to manage change. For example, we will not find the equivalent to Lewin's Force Field Analysis. In his study of technology in call centres, Boddy argues that the continual process of action, reaction, and synthesis produces results 'quite different from those which the people promoting the change originally expected' (ibid.). The implications are that:

- Technology is not viewed as a constraint limiting human action. Indeed the opposite is the case because technology is shaped and designed by people at the design stage.

- Technology can become a constraint on stages after the design stage but this becomes a political process in which technology can be deliberately used to facilitate or constrain human action. It is also the case that the further away one gets from the design stage, the less control one has.

- Human action is also shaped by the organizational context. This gives rise to different interpretations and uses of the technology involved.

- Human interaction with technology shapes the context of the organization through culture or through the use of power.

Political processes are central to the processual account of organizational change. In their account of the NHS-inspired Patient Advice and Liaison Services (PALS) model, Buchanan *et al* (2005) use a processual perspective to demonstrate how a fluid, networked, and diversified context isolates PALS structures from management decision making, constraining the management power base, and inhibiting the promotion of substantive change agendas. Evidence from their discussion forums and interviews with PALS officers in London acute, primary care, mental health, and specialist trusts suggested that organizational instability, boundary disputes, variable management support, resource limitations, financial insecurity, and multi-site working characterized the context in which PALS operated. The study revealed that a major change initiative was marginalized whilst the existing system continued to work correctly.

Because some actors and groups have greater access to, and control over, information, they can manipulate situations to their advantage. Technology can be used to control people. An example of the discrete exercise of power by managers seeking to control sales staff is provided by Blosch and Preece (2000). Managerial control over technology can lead to surveillance and control, as the following case example illustrates.

» Case example 3.3

The technological imperative

Once a week each sales representative receives a printout of his/her performance for the previous week from his/her area manager. The analysis compares each representative against the others in the region on key factors such as days worked, surveys made (sales calls), 'out of stocks' encountered, 'out of stocks' rectified, new introductions (new brands taken on by the retailer). This is also captured in simple statistics. Often the area manager will include comments on the weekly performance. A representative observed: 'It makes me laugh, *1984* isn't a work of fiction—it's our management handbook. Big Brother watches us all the time, we have only one objective, determined by the party, and any contradictory thoughts we may have we must submerge with doublethink. But the sweetest paradox of this is our desperate compliance, we engage in this insanity because our very lifestyle depends on it, we cannot believe this is the best way to work, and yet we must preserve this way of working because we do so well out of it. We are trapped by our own greed!'

Source: Blosch and Preece (2000), 97.

The point made by Blosch and Preece is that, because area managers had access to the detail through their control of IT systems, they were able to control interpersonal communication to their advantage. This often led to surveillance and control. As the authors imply, the 'panoptic eye of senior management' can lead to a manipulative form of performance measurement.

> ❶ **Stop and think 3.4**
>
> Write your own example of why things often do not turn out as planned. State what was planned, what went wrong, and how you dealt with the unanticipated.

3.4.2 Methodology

The second point concerns methodology. Both the empirical–rational and the normative re-educative approaches start by seeking to implement change whereas approaches recommending emergent change first undertake longitudinal or retrospective analysis. In other words, their purpose is entirely different. Because the processual analysis of change seeks to examine specific historical, political processes that affect change initiatives, these must be studied through ethnographic analysis. This means that, because linear planned-change initiatives conceptualize change in terms of relatively simple variables to be transformed—they reduce complexity to structures and functions—such initiatives ignore underlying processes.

Processual or emergent change accounts detail the historical, contextual, and political influences on change, but such accounts are not meant to provide guides to change, but to illustrate the processes that enhance or limit change initiatives. Most studies of this kind are therefore longitudinal and ethnographic accounts of dynamics. An ethnographic example of the political dimension is illustrated by examining the gap between rhetoric and reality. This is illustrated by Badham and Garrety (2003) in their five-year study of a coke-making plant in Australia:

> Cokemaking OZ is part of a traditional hierarchical and paternalistic steel plant in Australia. Under pressures from an increasingly competitive international steel industry, and a need to improve 'return on capital', the company has sought over the last seven years to remove some of the rigidities, secrecy, game-playing and macho-management style that has dominated the culture of the past. If the pronouncements of the Organizational Development (OD) publicity were believed, the plant has undergone a significant cultural transformation. Even a brief set of visits to different sections of the plant are, however, enough to give a somewhat different impression—one of a traditional culture successfully resisting and undermining many of these OD initiatives—an impression that was itself communicated to members of the research team by some of the old personnel in their more pessimistic moments.

(Badham and Garrety, 2003: 23)

Badham and Garrety considered that planned change might be clearly articulated by rhetoric, but in reality the stages of change are never clear, are usually confusing, and are much more like the 'buffoonery of the social spectacle' or carnival:

> The process, as it appeared to us, was more akin to the 'buffoonery of the social spectacle' described by Berger [1991: 187]. Control, in this view, and as illustrated in this paper, is a multifaceted phenomenon... an ongoing theme in organizational relations, but one that is enacted, played with, rhetorically presented, imagined and faked—an amusing and fun, yet also hurtful and wounding, carnival not easily reducible to an underlying 'real' control dynamic.
>
> (Ibid.).

Because the methodology of processual accounts is largely ethnographic, processes are examined in detail to reveal the dynamics of change. But this form of reporting or storytelling carries a potential problem for the researcher. That is, how can researchers be sure that their accounts are reliable? One solution is to undertake what Buchanan and Dawson (2007) call poly-vocal pluralistic accounts. One uncovers political and historical dimensions by investigating accounts that are normally silent in official versions of change: 'the researcher should reveal all silenced and otherwise excluded voices, and not just report the "loud, articulate, respectable, or directive" ones'. Processual researchers should therefore learn how to articulate the resultant narratives and illustrate competing narratives and struggles between various groups with different interests. What often emerges is a study of unintended consequences. Buchanan and Dawson call their method dialogic discourse. This seeks to:

> unpack taken-for-granted realities, to uncover their complexities, lack of shared meaning, and hidden resistances. There are no conflicts of assessment or interpretation as different accounts are equally valid. Attributions are defined from different standpoints. Audiences must be aware of the motives and purposes of those who speak to them. Conflicting accounts in this discourse represent narrative fragments, elements in a kaleidoscopic tapestry. Closure cannot be achieved as the notion of a single reality is illusory, and such truth claims are suspect.
>
> (Buchanan and Dawson, 2007: 273)

Consequently, Buchanan and Dawson suggest that we can combine four elements to produce a processual narrative approach. This approach seeks to:

1. Identify how a particular event sequence can be explained by identifying *conflicts of attribution* that often occur between different stakeholders. Such groups or individuals have different concerns about events that must be identified.
2. Identify *conflicts of assessment*, or 'what went well, what went wrong', and 'what other organizations can learn from that experience'. In particular, such investigation reveals the contestable quality of change outcomes.

3. Identify *conflicts of interpretation* in order to identify both differences and collusion. 'These often work together. For example in his longitudinal study of
   plant-level change at an automotive manufacturer, Dawson (2003) illustrates
   how narratives reflect the political interests of key actors. The plant manager's
   account involved the creation of a stakeholder coalition comprising managerial
   and supervisory staff, union officials, and outside experts. Although union officials
   viewed his account as "inaccurate", claiming that his role as change champion
   was overstated, they did not undermine his story.'

4. Identify how different rationalizations are constructed for different audiences
   by investigating *conflicts of audience*. This requires identifying the underlying
   motives for such rationalizations.

Advocates of processual or emergent change argue that organizational change is so
complex that it must be studied through processes. It may therefore be argued that if
the epistemology of the structural-functional perspective limits its ability to manage
change, then the processual or emergent approach offers little help with the planning
of change. One solution suggested by Carnall (2007) is that managers become more
sophisticated in their ability to understand the complexity of change processes and
develop core skills in managing change.

3.5 Problems faced by planned change programmes

Empirical–rational, prescriptive change strategies are characterized by linear planned
change (see Figure 3.7). In Chapter 2 we noted the limits of technical solutions in
Case Example 2.1, the case of the Ford Pinto. This case highlighted how Ford deliberately avoided dealing with the real problem and therefore engaged in 'euphemistic
labelling'—Bandura (1999). One of the dangers of prescriptive change strategies is
that avoidance of social and political problems leads to rationalizations being made to
neutralize moral responsibility.

---

❶ Stop and think 3.5

Make a list of as many potential risks to a change strategy that you can think of for
each stage.

Each stage of change carries risks; some can be anticipated but others cannot. At
stage one (problem definition) those that can be anticipated may include:

- Different groups who hold different, but equally legitimate, perspectives. This
  is, of course, the argument presented by the multiple constituencies perspective,
  which argues that complex organizations include a variety of stakeholders

Figure 3.7 Stages in a linear planned change strategy

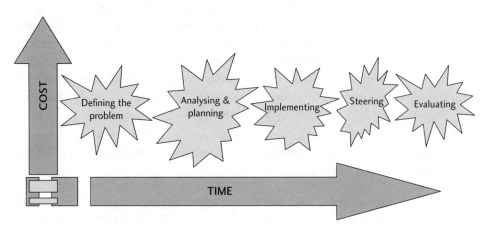

with overlapping but occasionally contradictory views. Thus, ignoring such views may lead to dissatisfaction with the change initiative, impairing commitment.

- An initiative that is not based on a clear identifiable need. This reflects the importance of the OD perspective, which argues that change should only proceed once a felt need is clearly defined. This is likely to lead to a lack of clarity in the subsequent stages.

Difficulties at stage two (analysing and planning) may reflect:

- Problems with the accuracy of data or insufficient data to make a qualified analysis.
- Lack of expertise among those responsible for managing the change process.

At stage three (implementation) difficulties may include:

- Resistance to change.
- Lack of management support.
- Lack of resources.

Difficulties at stage four (steering) may be characterized by:

- The loss of the change manager or team.
- Change adopted for the wrong reasons.
- Loss of momentum.

Finally, difficulties at stage five may include:

- The failure to involve relevant knowledgeable people in the evaluation.
- People with different political agendas.

Managing planned change is problematic, but consider how much more difficult it is to plan change in unpredictable circumstances. An example of planning for the unpredictable is indicated by the problems of planning US defence strategy, the predictability of which was thrown into disarray as a result of the attacks on the Twin Towers on 9/11. Subsequently, the American Forces Information Service stated that the 'Quadrennial Defense Review, to be delivered to Congress Feb. 6, will be dominated by two words: uncertainty and unpredictability' (United States Department of Defense, 5 January 2007). This problem is examined in the case example below.

≫ Case example 3.4

The problem of planning change in US defence strategy after 9/11

QDR Dominated by Uncertain, Unpredictable World

By Jim Garamone, American Forces Press Service

WASHINGTON, Jan. 25, 2006—The Quadrennial Defense Review, to be delivered to Congress Feb. 6, will be dominated by two words: uncertainty and unpredictability, senior defense officials said today.

'We cannot predict with any certainty whatsoever how our forces may be used in the future,' one official said. 'We can say with a very high probability that in the next 10 years, US forces will be employed somewhere in the world where they are not today.'

Speaking on background, the officials said the attacks of Sept. 11, 2001, forced a change in US security and military strategies. While transforming the Defense Department was already a priority, the attacks imposed a 'powerful sense of urgency' on all in the department.

The United States is now in the fifth year of a different war, and 'we need to shift our balance and (the) capabilities we have,' one official said. Congress mandates that DoD conduct the QDR every four years to ensure the armed forces have the right mix of people, skill sets and capabilities to meet current and future challenges to national security.   ≫

❯❯ The officials said the 2005 review discusses four major challenges. The first is threats posed by traditional foes. 'This basically involved major combat ops and state *versus* state conflicts, and we looked at everything else as a lesser included case to be able to meet that,' one official said.

In the future, irregular challenges will be more common. The official cited Iraq and Afghanistan as examples of irregular threats facing the United States, but included operations in areas such as the Horn of Africa, the Philippines and Haiti in this challenge. The enemy in this case would be within the state, but not sponsored by the state.

A third challenge is what he called a 'catastrophic set of challenges.' These are unacceptable blows to the United States and attacks such as Sept. 11 or Pearl Harbor. 'Getting hit by a nuclear (improvised explosive) device in one of our cities would be an example of that,' the official said.

The fourth is a 'disruptive' challenge. 'That is a challenge or threat that would come against us and neutralize the American military as a key instrument of national power,' he said.

The review looked at developing military capabilities to address all four challenges.

A second part of the review was a recognition that changing the makeup of forces in the field would mean revamping headquarters. He said the current headquarters setups are not sufficiently agile to command the fighting forces America has already deployed.

This review capitalized on the lessons the US military has learned around the world. Lessons from experiences in the Horn of Africa, Georgia and Africa's Pan Sahel region figured prominently because of the new way America had to deal with allies. Developing capabilities in allies is as important as developing capabilities in the US military, the officials said.

Humanitarian operations are another big area for the American military. The officials said that the 'biggest victories to date in the war on terrorism' have been in the US response to the tsunami in the Indian Ocean and to the earthquake in Pakistan. As a result of those operations the 'shift away from radical Islam has been very, very significant,' the official said.

Building capabilities and agility is more important than confronting specific threats from specific countries.

The review focuses on four areas:

- Providing defense in depth to the homeland;

- Hastening the demise of terror networks;

- Stopping hostile powers or rogue elements from acquiring weapons of mass destruction; and

- Influencing countries at strategic crossroads.   ❯❯

> ❱ The review looks to influence three countries that officials believe to be at these strategic crossroads: Russia, China and India.
>
> The review has 12 areas that cover everything from headquarters functions, to partnership capabilities, to recommending 'leading edge technologies' that could help warfighters in the fiscal 2007 budget request. The officials stressed that major shifts in acquisition funding must be part of the Future Years Defense Plan.
>
> Finally, the force-planning construct is basically a refined version of the 2001 review. The US military will be able to do two near simultaneous major conflicts, one of which involves regime change, one official said.
>
> 'Going forward, we want one of them to be a prolonged irregular campaign,' he said. 'The analysis we did in the QDR clearly proved that the most stressing thing on the force is not the high-intensity major combat operations, but the prolonged irregular campaign that requires a rotational base to support it.'
>
> United States Department of Defense, 5 January 2007
> (<http://www.defenselink.mil/news/newsarticle.aspx?id=14525>) Accessed: 14/06/2009.

As the case example illustrates, by analogy organizations face threats from unpredictable circumstances for which they cannot plan in advance. These include:

- Threats posed by non-traditional foes.
- Irregular challenges.
- Catastrophic challenges.
- Disruptive challenges.

The case example illustrates an interesting dilemma. On the one hand, too much structure carries serious implications for the flexibility required by logistics and procurement (both of which may be simplified as costs to the organization). Conversely, too little structure carries dangers of failing to act rapidly to meet changing environmental conditions.

3.5.1 Scenario planning

A method for dealing with change for an unpredictable future is to construct possible scenarios that might emerge at some point in the future. Scenarios are alternative images of how the future might unfold. An example of this is provided by the Intergovernmental Panel on Climate Change (IPCC) which, in September 1996, decided to develop a new set of emissions scenarios to predict climate change. The IPCC was established by the World Meteorological Organization (WMO) and the United Nations Environment Programme (UNEP) to 'assess the scientific, technical and socio-economic information relevant for the understanding of the risk of human-induced climate change' (Foreword of the IPCC Special Report on Emissions Scenarios). The scenarios constructed were intended to 'cover a wide range of the main driving forces of future emissions, from demographic to technological and economic developments. The scenarios encompass different future developments that might influence greenhouse gas (GHG) sources and sinks, such as alternative structures of energy systems and land-use changes' (IPCC Special Report on Emissions Scenarios). The use of scenarios suggests that we use models to predict some aspect of the future that we either wish to change or, if that is not possible, at least to manage effectively. At an individual level we use mental models that are relevant to us. With groups, teams, and organizations these mental models become shared and great care is necessary to ensure that we each define and comprehend them in the same way. The example of the IPCC case illustrates how complicated this can be. The team who constructed the scenarios consisted of more than 50 members from 18 countries who represented 'a broad range of scientific disciplines, regional backgrounds, and non-governmental organizations'. This involved six major steps, illustrated below.

1. Analysis of existing scenarios in the literature.
2. Analysis of major scenario characteristics, driving forces, and their relationships.
3. Formulation of four narrative scenario 'storylines' to describe alternative futures.
4. Quantification of each storyline using a variety of modelling approaches.
5. An 'open' review process of the resultant emission scenarios and their assumptions.
6. Three revisions of the scenarios and the report subsequent to the open review process, i.e. the formal IPCC Expert Review and the final combined IPCC Expert and Government Review.

The emissions scenarios were formulated to identify possible driving forces of future emissions. These included sociodemographic, technological, and economic developments. The problem defined was the likely impact of greenhouse gas sources and the variations that might result from alternative uses of new energy systems.

In the same way that scientists can model the future, we can produce models to warn us of the dangers ahead and to manage change more effectively in the future. However, we must be mindful of the negative consequences. First, the models that emerge from the scenarios to manage change may be too rigid and remain unchanged as new evidence emerges to contradict the scenario. Second, all evidence, including scientific and statistical data, has to be interpreted and a story told in order to make this comprehensible to others. In other words, facts do not speak for themselves. They have to be interpreted, expressed, emphasized, and warnings have to be given. The question is therefore: 'how representative is the story that links the data?' The problem is, the stories we tell to represent change contain rhetoric, hyperbole, and figures of speech. This is one of the major difficulties in communicating change. Using scenarios to predict aspects of the future is more of an art than a science, but consideration of future scenarios is really a matter of reducing risk by involving what Buchanan and Dawson (2007) call poly-vocal pluralistic accounts.

3.6 Summary

In this chapter we have undertaken a critical reflection of planned change. We noted three theoretical positions with different knowledge claims: the empirical–rational, normative re-educative, and processual or emergent approaches. Each represents a different approach to change. For example, empirical–rational methods were defined as managerialist, prescriptive, and, in the case of strategic change, tend to be driven by unitarist assumptions. Both at a strategic and an operational level, empirical–rational approaches are task-driven and pursued for pragmatic reasons. Consequently, these are constructed in discrete linear stages from beginning to end. We noted that a process can be regarded as the means by which something (a physical object or an idea) is transferred so that value can be added. At a strategic level, as we noted with Case Example 3.1, 'Putting the customer first', such approaches are instrumental and universally applied to a variety of organizations. These prescriptive approaches are sometimes referred to as 'off-the-shelf' or 'packaged approaches' and do not reflect diagnostic evaluation as expected by OD practitioners. At an operational level the pursuit of technical expediency is designed into the change strategy. This is usually undertaken by means of process redesign and a critical path analysis typical of project management. The stages reflect the throughput of products or services in a controlled manner until they are received by a customer or client.

In contrast to prescriptive change approaches, normative re-educative approaches to planned change embody greater reflexivity because collective learning, diagnosis, and problem resolution are central to such initiatives. It is also common to find feedback loops reiterating a concern with organizational learning. The perspective of OD is typical of this approach and is usually characterized by the methodology of Action Research to enable the development of participants' skills and knowledge. We noted in particular that, whilst many authors viewed Lewin's Force Field Analysis, or three-step model, as an example of linear organizational change, this is contentious because Lewin did not work at the organizational level, nor did he recommend the method for organizational change. We therefore have to conclude that his work with individuals and groups was applied to organizations by others. This has had the unfortunate effect of turning his methodology into a simplistic mechanistic device used by some consultants as a tool disembodied from its behavioural methodology. Normative re-educative strategies seek to *discover, experiment,* and *develop* new opportunities to enable strategic advantages through human resources. However, because such strategies for change are also concerned with efficiency and effectiveness, there is a danger that they reflect the agenda of management to the detriment of other stakeholders. One potential solution to this lies in process consultation and the investigation of the plural client system that have come to characterize OD methodology. However, despite their significant differences, each approach supports a management agenda that becomes the focus for criticism from more dispassionate observers who focus on processual change.

The main objection to planned change by processual theorists is its reductionist tendency to link objectives to formulaic strategies and to employ a methodology driven by managerial expediency. Thus, processual change theory highlights its own epistemological distinction, which contends that structural and functional integration perpetrate the myth of a reified reality. Processual theorists point out that planned change ignores specific historical, political, and contextual processes that affect change initiatives. Furthermore, these can only be studied by means of ethnographic analysis. We therefore end with a paradox. That is, although planned change is methodical but problematic, processual change does not provide an alternative change strategy because its method of ethnography relies on observation of contemporary experience. This impasse requires that we become skilled analysts able to plan but also able to observe and criticize our own assumptions and interventions.

We noted that problems of planned change emerge at each stage in a linear sequence. Each stage of a change programme carries potential risks, but the main problem faced by planned change programmes is that there are many things that cannot be anticipated and planned for in advance. These include threats posed by non-traditional foes, irregular challenges, catastrophic challenges, and disruptive challenges. Scenario planning is one method for dealing with contingencies, but it is not adequate to deal with crises that arise from the unanticipated processes of an unpredictable future. Knowledge and skills are more important and, as we have learned from the processual theorists, we need to focus on history, organizational context, and the exercise of power and control. To understand this you should read Chapters 6, 7, and 8.

⭐ Case study

Planning, why bother?

On 12 February 2009, after weather reports the previous day had stated that the weather would be 'cold but sunny', unexpected blizzard conditions hit parts of the UK. Six inches of snow fell within two hours. Although road managers in county councils stated that they had planned for changing conditions by gritting all major roads, many roads became jammed as a consequence of several unforeseen events. As one county roads manager stated, 'no matter how well one plans for these events, unexpected things happen'. The driver of a snow plough stuck in a traffic jam stated that, ❯❯

>> 'when they first noticed a build-up of traffic the police should have closed the road and allowed the snow ploughs and gritters to do their jobs'.

Why did jams occur on such an unexpected scale? The answer is that small incidents occur that can be resolved with coordination, patience, and cooperation. However, people have different motives for not using these methods. In one typical situation the causes of the jam can be explained: a car slid into a roadside sign at approximately 15 miles per hour and the sign fell over and crashed through the windscreen of an oncoming car, hitting one of its passengers. The driver called the ambulance service, which could not get through the jammed vehicles on the road until, some time later, the police moved vehicles one by one. Meanwhile, at the crash site some motorists gave first aid to the injured passenger, but others waiting in queues on each side of the road became impatient. Some tried to drive around the crashed vehicles but became stuck in deeper snow. Others who had been waiting patiently became angry at impatient drivers. Sporadic verbal abuse broke out in various places and a great deal of anger was vented. Normal rules of courtesy broke down. The roads manager was interviewed on the radio during the jam and defended himself against the charge that 'things could have been planned better'. One caller who was stuck in the traffic phoned in and stated that 'if this was the result of the county's best planning efforts, then why bother?' Another caller said that 'all that had been achieved was planned chaos and confusion' and that 'those responsible for planning roads in adverse weather conditions should be sacked because it was a waste of taxpayers' money'. A third caller criticized the radio station for 'turning a disaster into a programme of light entertainment which no one stuck in the chaos would appreciate'. A fourth caller, a local clergyman, said that he was also caught up in the jam and, whilst he was not enjoying the experience, appealed for calm, stating that 'whilst people may not want to hear it, this should be seen as a learning opportunity'.

Questions

1. Should planning for roads in adverse weather conditions be abandoned on the ground that it rarely achieves its intended result?

2. Is there a simple technical solution that can be planned-in to ensure that this does not happen again?

3. What social characteristics may have amplified the problems? Furthermore, could these ever be avoided?

4. Think of features in an organization. List as many as you can think of that would disrupt coordination, patience, and cooperation, and obstruct simple resolution of a problem.

5. If we can learn from this scenario, what lessons would you identify?

■ Study questions

1. What is planned change?

2. What is Action Research and how does it characterize Organizational Development?

3. What arguments would you put to suggest that Action Research may be a more sophisticated change approach than a linear managerialist approach?

4. State the contribution of the open-systems model to analysing change processes.

5. If Organizational Development encouraged an ethical humanist perspective in the twentieth century, how might we extend this to a new position for the twenty-first century?

6. Define empirical–rational approaches and contrast these with normative re-educative approaches.

7. Can all planned change be described as linear destination-oriented change?

8. What is a critical path analysis?

9. What is the punctuated equilibrium model of change?

10. How is processual or emergent change different from planned change?

■ Exercises

Exercise 1
Identify an example of a contemporary change initiative from the business section of a newspaper you have read in the last month. If you have not found any, then go to the library in search of one. Identify what changes were made to this organization and place them in one of the three categories: people, systems, and structures. Then explain the interrelationships between them to a friend or colleague.

Exercise 2
Four types of threat were identified by Case Example 3.4. These were non-traditional threats; and irregular, catastrophic, and disruptive challenges. These characterize uncertainty and unpredictability, which make it difficult to instigate planned strategic change. Apply these to an organization known to you, such as a bank, hospital, insurance broker, furniture manufacturer, or an oil company. Explain how such threats might arise and illustrate some imaginative examples.

Exercise 3
Write an organizational story in at least 300 words, stating why planning is necessary. The storyline should outline a critical incident and identify unintended consequences that could not be foreseen by those planning it. Finally, you should illustrate the social dynamics of the change processes and say whether they can be resolved.

Exercise 4

Identify a student project you have worked on or intend to work on in a team. Undertake a critical path analysis of this. When you have completed a diagram to illustrate how you will achieve the key tasks, identify as many things as possible that could prevent or minimize the successful achievement of the project. When you have examined these, identify how many are technical and how many are social processes. Finally, state what conclusions you draw from this.

Exercise 5

Look at the processual narrative approach suggested by Buchanan and Dawson (2007), which seeks to identify how a particular event sequence can be explained by identifying various conflicts. These are conflicts of attribution, assessment, interpretation, and audience. This requires identifying the underlying motives for such rationalizations. Apply this method to any change situation you are aware of and report your results. Alternatively, apply it to this chapter's case study.

■ Further reading

Blosch, M. and Preece, D. (2000), 'Framing Work Through a Socio-technical Ensemble: The Case of Butler Co.', *Technology Analysis & Strategic Management*, 12(1), 92–102. A useful example of processual analysis.

Buchanan, D. and Dawson, P. (2007), 'Discourse and Audience: Organizational Change as Multi-Story Process', *Journal of Management Studies*, 44(5), 670–686. The authors provide a method for unearthing the political and historical dimensions of change by investigating unofficial accounts.

Casey, C. (2002), *Critical Analysis of Organizations, Theory, Practice, Revitalization*, London: Sage. Casey provides one of the strongest criticisms of modernist organizational analysis.

Hughes, M. (2007), 'The Tools and Techniques of Change Management', *Journal of Change Management*, 7(1), 37–49. A simple example of the arguments for and against tools and techniques.

Lewin, K.A. (1999), 'Group decision and social change', in *The complete social scientist: A Kurt Lewin reader* by Lewin, K.A. and Gold, M. (eds) Washington, DC, 265–284.: American Psychological Association. A classic text that should always be read by students of change, if only to see what he really advocated rather than the way he is often represented by various authors: as the founder of planned change.

Pettigrew, A.M. (2000), 'Linking change processes and outcomes: a commentary on Ghosal, Bartlett and Weick', in Beer, M. and Nohria, N. (eds), *Breaking the Code of Change*, Boston, MA: Harvard Business School Press, 243–265. A useful survey of the processual field.

■ References

Alvesson, M. and Deetz, S. (1996), 'Critical Theory and Postmodernism, Approaches to Organizational Studies', in Clegg, S., Hardy, C., and Nord, W. (eds), *Handbook of Organization Studies*, London: Sage.

Badham, R. and Garrety, K. (2003), 'Living in the Blender of Change: The Carnival of Control in a Culture of Control', *Tamara, Journal of Critical Postmodern Science*, 2(4), 22–38.

Bandura, A. (1999), 'Moral disengagement in the perpetration of inhumanities', *Personality and Social Psychology Review*, 3(3), 193–209.

Berger, P. (1991), *Invitation to Sociology: A Humanistic Perspective*, Harmondsworth, Middx: Penguin.

Berger, P. and Luckmann, T. (1966), *The Social Construction of Reality*, New York: Anchor Books.

Bjørnson, F.O, Wang, A.I., and Arisholm, E. (2008), 'Improving the effectiveness of root cause analysis in post mortem analysis: A controlled experiment', *Information and Software Technology*, 51(1), 150–161.

Blosch, M. and Preece, D, (2000), 'Framing Work Through a Socio-technical Ensemble: The Case of Butler Co.', *Technology Analysis & Strategic Management*, 12(1), 91–102.

Boje, M.D. (1995), 'Stories of the Story-telling Organization: A Postmodern Analysis of Disney as "Tamara-land" ', *Academy of Management Journal*, 38(4), 997–1035.

Boje, M.D., Gephard, R.P., and Thatchenkery, T.J. (eds) (1996), *Postmodern Management and Organization Theory*, London: Sage.

Boddy, D. (2000), 'Implementing interorganizational IT systems: lessons from a call centre project', *Journal of Information Technology*, 15, 29–37.

Boselie P., Paauwe, J., and Richardson, R. (2003), 'Human resource management, institutionalization and organizational performance: a comparison of hospitals, hotels and local government', *International Journal of Human Resource Management*, 14, 1407–1429.

Buchanan, D., Abbott, S., Bentley, W.J., Lanceley, W.A., Meyer, W.J. (2005), 'Let's be PALS: User-Driven Organizational Change in Healthcare', *British Journal of Management*, 16, 315–328.

Buchanan, D. and Dawson, P. (2007), 'Discourse and Audience: Organizational Change as Multi-Story Process'. *Journal of Management Studies* 44(5), 670–686.

Burnes, B. (2007), *Managing Change*, London: Pitman.

Carnall, C. (2007), *Managing Change in Organizations*, Fifth edition, London: Prentice Hall/ FT.

Casey, C. (2002), *Critical Analysis of Organizations, Theory, Practice, Revitalization*, London: Sage.

Chin, R. and Benne, K.D. (1976), 'General Strategies for Effecting Change in Human Systems', in Warren, G.B., Benne, K.D., and Chin, R., *The Planning of Change*, Fourth edition, Fort Worth, TX: Holt, Rinehart and Winston, 22–47.

Clark, S. (2001), *Information Systems Strategic Management—An Integrated Approach*, London: Routledge.

Colomy, P. (1998), 'Neo-functionalism and neo-institutionalism: human agency and interest in institutional change', *Sociological Forum*, 13(2), 265–300.

Colomy, P. and Rhoades, G. (1994), 'Toward a micro corrective of structural differentiation theory', *Sociological Perspectives*, 37, 547–83.

Cummings, T.G. and Worley, C.G. (1993), *Organizational Development and Change*, Fifth edition, Minneapolis/St. Paul, MN: West Publishing Company.

Daft R.L. (1998), *Essentials of Organization Theory and Design*, Florence, KY: South-Western College Publishing.

Dale, B.G. and McQuater, R.E. (1998), *Managing Business Improvement and Quality: Implementing Key Tools and Techniques*, Oxford: Blackwell Publishers.

Dawson, P. (1994), *Organizational Change: A Processual Approach*, London: Paul Chapman.

—— (2003), *Reshaping Change: A Processual Perspective*, London: Routledge.

Dean, J. and Bowen, D. (1994), 'Management theory and total quality: improving research and practice through theory development', *Academy of Management Review*, 19(3), 392–418.

Delaney, J.T., Lewin, D., and Ichniowski, C. (1989), *Human resource policies and practices in American firms*, Washington, DC: US Government Printing Office.

Gravells, J. (2006), 'The Myth of Change Management: A Reflection on Personal Change and Its Lessons for Leadership Development', *Human Resource Development International*, 9(2), 283–289.

Hamel, G. and Prahalad, C.K. (2002), 'Competing for the Future' in Henry, J. and Mayle, D., *Managing Innovation and Change*, London: Sage, 23–35.

Hughes, M. (2007), 'The Tools and Techniques of Change Management', *Journal of Change Management*, 7(1), 37–49.

IPCC Special Report on Emissions Scenarios: available at <http://www.grida.no/climate/ipcc/emission/501. htm>.

Kimble, C. and McLoughlin, K. (1995), 'Computer-based information systems and managers' work', *New Technology, Work and Employment*, 10(1), 56–67.

Kübler-Ross, E. (1973), *On Death and Dying*, London: Routledge.

Lewin, K.A. (1999), 'Group decision and social change', in *The complete social scientist: A Kurt Lewin reader* by Lewin, K.A. and Gold, M. (eds), Washington, DC: American Psychological Association, 265–284 .

Menninger, W.X. (1975), 'The meaning of morale: a Peace Corps model', in Moyniham, D.P. (ed), *Business and Society in Change*, New York: American Telephone and Telegraph Co.

Morgan, G. (2004), *Images of Organisation*, London: Sage.

Pettigrew, A.M. (1985), *The Awakening Giant: Continuity and Change in ICI*, Oxford: Blackwell.

—— (2000), 'Linking change processes and outcomes: a commentary on Ghosal, Bartlett and Weick', in Beer, M. and Nohria, N. (eds), *Breaking the Code of Change*, Boston, MA: Harvard Business School Press, 243–265.

Prahalad, C.K. and Hamel, G. (1990), 'The core competence of the corporation', *Harvard Business Review*, May–June, 71–91.

Romanelli, E. and Tushman, M.L. (1994), 'Organizational transformation as punctuated equilibrium: an empirical test', *Academy of Management Journal*, 37(5), 1141–1166.

Stacey, R. (1996) 'Management and the science of complexity: if organisational life is non-linear, can business strategies prevail?', *Research and Technology Management*, 39(3), 2–5.

Tushman, T.V.L. and Romanelli, E. (1985), 'Organizational evolution: a metamorphosis model of convergence and reorientation', *Research in Organizational Behavior*, 7, 171–222.

Wilkinson, A. and Witcher, B. (1991), 'Quality concerns for managers', *International Journal of Quality & Reliability Management*, 9(2), 64–67.

Wittgenstein, L. (1953), *Philosophical Investigations*, Oxford: Blackwell.

Take your learning further: Online Resource Centre
http://www.oxfordtextbooks.co.uk/orc/grieves/

Visit the Online Resource Centre that accompanies this book to enrich your understanding of this chapter. Explore case study updates and answers to questions, test yourself using an interactive flashcard glossary, and keep up to date with the latest developments in the area.

CHAPTER 4

Strategic change

4.1 Introduction

This chapter focuses on external forces for change. We begin with a broad overview of the development and evolution of the strategic management discipline, giving consideration to the four dominant approaches to strategic management that have shaped the strategic manager. These broadly encompass the mechanisms and systems required for strategic management (the *planning approach*), the scope of aims and objectives to be achieved (the *outcomes approach*), the consideration of those deciding and being affected by strategies (the *pluralistic approach*), and the development of unforeseen and unexpected outcomes (the *emergent or processual approach*). The pluralistic approach is related to the multiple constituencies perspective discussed in Chapter 1, which, you will recall, seeks to address organizational change by tackling the concerns of different stakeholders. As we see later, the emergent approach is more generally concerned with determining both strategic intent and strategic outcome in strategic management, and continues to guide more recent debate and practice in strategy generally.

The discussion of these approaches raises concerns for the strategic manager that are also considered in this chapter. For example, to what extent can we identify a suitable strategy simply by examining the structure of the industry and markets within which the organization competes? Or consider the impact of a corporate strategy upon a range of external and internal stakeholders who might be involved in very different markets that the organization serves. Furthermore, we may need to consider whether and how relevant contingencies affect the strategic plan, and the need to balance planning for change and innovation with the need for flexibility.

The chapter then attempts to contextualize the approaches to strategic change in volatile global environments. Managers need to know how to deal with changes forced upon them and, equally, what actions they can take before problems emerge, or in order to exploit new opportunities. Managing strategic change is not possible without the ability to understand and analyse factors in both the industry and the organizational environments. We identify a range of simple environmental analysis tools such as Porter's Five Forces of competition; PEST(LE) analysis, which helps to analyse the forces that drive change; FAR analysis, which builds on the PEST(LE) outcomes and helps the strategic manager to understand the development and evolution of the external competitive environment; and congruence analysis, which supports an exploration of the potential outcomes of a given corporate strategy for a range of identified strategic stakeholders. A wise manager will attempt to deploy these insights to support, sustain, and potentially to lead strategic changes and (re)alignment of their competitive activities in a changing external context.

In this chapter we will explore external forces for strategic change by:

- Considering the role of rational planning.
- Distinguishing between strategic intent for change and strategic outcomes of change.

- Discussing the development of strategic change analysis.
- Understanding the importance of the industry environment and the organizational environment.
- Examining the importance of conducting an effective PEST (PESTLE or BPEST) analysis.
- Learning how to use Porter's five forces of competition.
- Understanding how external forces of an organization can be forecasted and identified.
- Learning the importance of strategic realignment for organizations.

This chapter addresses strategic change. In order to understand the relevance of this subject you will also need to read Chapter 8 and consider the role of the leader in managing change. Furthermore, whist this chapter focuses on external forces that drive change, it is important to understand arguments that focus on developing internal forces for change. You will therefore need to consider Chapter 5. In this chapter, then, we will explore the arguments for and against rational planning.

4.2 Rational planning and organizational change

Whatever type of change we encounter, whether historical accounts of change, economic changes within the world economy, personal, or organizational change, it is traditional to distinguish between long periods of stable activity (equilibrium), and activity punctuated by short periods of intense change in which there is a flurry of motion and a transformation in ideas, processes, and procedures, invention and creativity. To a certain extent, this traditional perception is an artificial view of reality, yet it provides a strong pedagogical vehicle for exploring key concepts of strategic change (see, e.g., Staton-Reinstein, 2008). For example, during the twentieth century, change occurring in organizations has been well documented. The major implications of this are twofold: first is the realization that strict controls of the Fordist process of manufacturing are no longer able to give contemporary organizations the productivity gains so easily achieved in the past, when the economy was not characterized by the intense global competition we see today. We may, in this sense, argue that the low-hanging competitive fruit of this strategic orientation has all been 'picked', i.e. that scale alone (via lower unit costs) is no longer sufficient to support competitive advantage. In the twentieth century, advantages through economies of scale were easier to achieve in this way. Second is the awareness that the modern global marketplace is increasingly dominated by flexible organizations that present new competitive challenges. Individuals able to adopt a flexible and contingent approach to management and problem solving, therefore, are better equipped to achieve, survive, and sustain a competitive position for their organizations.

Consequently, in recent years a distinction has been made between planned change dominated by rational planning, and processual change. Processual change argues that the reality of change is influenced more by processes that are too small or difficult to identify, because they occur on a daily basis, than large, stable, and anticipated factors. Planned programmes of change, associated with rational planning models, create an illusion of change that appears as episodes rather than processes. Organizations can appear to undergo periods of change in this approach, whereas processual change approaches stress a more continual view of these actions. It would be wise to consider both approaches as having merit and value for an organization and its strategic managers.

Before we begin a more detailed discussion, a focused consideration of the simple question 'what is strategy?' will help frame our understanding of external forces of change. Whittington (1993), for example, generated a holistic framework (Figure 4.1) to identify and then characterize the differing approaches to strategy that organizations can pursue.

In Whittington's framework, the two major axes stress the competing scope of external factors shaping strategic decision making. The horizontal axis describes the extent to which, through its strategic managers, an organization can seek to pursue a particular objective or goal (the *organizational intent*—which can be sought on a planned and designed basis or on one more responsive to unplanned, disruptive changes

Figure 4.1 Whittington's (1993) generic approaches to strategy

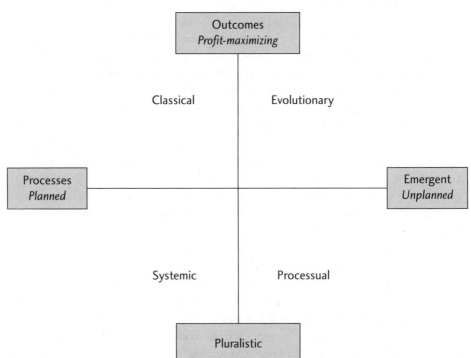

shaping the organization). The planned/designed basis for achieving a strategic goal was shaped largely by early views of effective military and organizational strategy, whilst the unplanned form of strategic change might be identified with competing in globalized, turbulent, and complex markets. We explore this dimension in Case Example 4.1. The vertical axis in Figure 4.1 stresses the focus on outcomes—i.e. who is the beneficiary of the goal. Classically, this might be the shareholder—as the organization seeks to maximize profit—but it is increasingly common to see a more pluralistic view of outcomes, which embraces triple bottom-line goals, for example, such as social, environmental, and profit objectives. The differences between planned and emergent (or processual) change in organizations, and a consideration of the outcome of strategy (whether profit-maximizing or seeking to achieve more pluralistic stakeholder outcomes), are therefore plainly identified in Figure 4.1 and hence strategic managers have these two broad considerations structuring their actions. The 'strategic manager' blends resultant analytical methods with creativity and vision for an organization (Bourgeois, 1984). This is illustrated in the following case example.

≫ Case example 4.1

Haier's successful strategic drivers

Competing in globalized markets, such as in consumer electrical 'white goods', is an increasingly difficult environment in which to secure a sustainable advantage. Consider, however, the experience of the Chinese domestic goods manufacturer Haier. A young organization founded in 1984, part of its success has come from a strategic focus on both product and market needs through observed product use, which has shaped its emergent corporate strategy. For example, in the 1990s engineers at Haier observed users of their washing machines washing clothes and vegetables together in their machines. A few minor product changes ensured that the machines were capable of performing this unexpected task on a regular basis and Haier rapidly became the number one brand in rural China.

They have also applied this ability to listen to the market by translating it into desirable product innovations in the USA in particular. The US student segment articulated a need for compact refrigerators, a market long ignored by other, larger competitive rivals, but which Haier have pursued to success (Inunisono, 2008). They have also implemented subsequent product innovations for this segment, such as refrigerators with fold-out desktops for students to work on in their confined student accommodation (BQF, 2009). As we will see later, a focus on product, and in particular market needs, is a key contributing strategy that can drive how the organization seeks to develop and change competitively in its markets and environment, and shape the purpose of this process, but is very difficult to design and plan formally. When such a focus is combined with a complementary internal human resource strategy that explicitly recognizes achievement (unusual in an Asian organization (Inunisono, 2008)), it can provide a powerful combination of intent drivers for strategic change in the organization.

4.2.1 The evolution of strategic approaches to change

We can expand on these two axes of consideration (and the four resulting approaches to strategy) by considering the key developments in the field of 'strategic management and strategy'. Three simple questions can then be asked to expand this discussion:

1. What is strategy (in other words, what are the key steps that support the effective (and advantageous) order of work undertaken in the organization)?

2. How is strategy developed (in other words, what is the formulation of preferred actions for an organization to pursue, through a consideration of internal and external environmental factors at corporate, business, and operational levels in the organization)?

3. How is strategy used to improve the competitive position of an organization?

Interest in these three questions has driven the development of strategy. The analytical lens applied to this development, however, has shifted focus between these questions. There are common key research concerns focused upon understanding what appropriate strategic intent, outcomes, and methodology might be for different external environments. These have then been argued to be shaped by what were considered the dominant strategic concepts at those times in history and context, the directional orientation of strategic activities, and what is emphasized and coupled with those approaches. Importantly, this last point has been a major factor shaping analysis of strategy by managers as it directs us to consider and question whether an 'outside-in' (more commonly known as a Structure–Conduct–Performance (SCP) view—which we discuss later) or an 'inside-out' organizational focus is more important to the organization's strategic formulation, choice, and implementation (Farjoun, 2002). In other words, it tasks the manager with the problem of whether to prioritize industry-competitive factors, or look inside organizational operations and assets for potential competitive advantages. Indeed, Hoskisson, Hitt, and Yiu (1999) use the metaphor of the 'pendulum of strategic management' to describe the swings and shifts in strategic management interest between these three questions and this dual inside/outside competitive focus. Jenkins and Ambrosini (2007) observed that interest, at present, tends to lie with adopting a realist view of the organization and its context, through integrating practitioner viewpoints with those of academics.

It is useful to stress the distinction between strategic outcomes and strategic intent. Strategic outcomes, as outlined above, can be described as the results of an implemented organizational strategy. By contrast, strategic intent is evidenced by a manager who seeks to ensure organizational success at all levels (Mantere and Sillince, 2007 citing Hamel and Prahalad, 1989). The intent therefore provides the guiding framework shaping a given choice in organizational strategy and the associated expectation of the outcome.

For example, in turbulent environments it is often more useful to seek outcomes without a planned strategy. In considering external factors that influence strategic change, Mintzberg (1998) has described this scope as a 'strategy safari' in which the development of the strategic management discipline has led to a variety of approaches. In Figure 4.1 Whittington (1993) explored how change reflects a tension between planning/design and emergent/unplanned engagement with strategic intents. Emergent strategic intent (and resultant change) is famously illustrated by Pascale's (1988) discussion of the way that Honda entered the US motorcycle market in the late 1950s. Honda's success, as revealed by interviews with key informants at that time, was neither planned nor designed. The strategic intent guiding corporate actions was for market exploration and opportunistic engagement, and there was no attempt to achieve a 'best' market-entry strategy, as it is often portrayed. Honda's strategy was, in fact, a series of emergent solutions to problems encountered. Pascale (1988) describes it as 'strategic accommodation' or 'adaptive persistence'. In other words, a traditional strategic design and planning perspective promoted the view that the Honda US entry was a planned approach, which (given the limited organizational pressures for globalization and more stable market environments at that time) became the dominant focus for contemporary strategic analysts and managers. The reality was that Honda had a strategic intent that was emergent with outcomes broadly of interest to shareholders at that time. Honda achieved success through an unplanned, emergent need to place itself in the US marketplace.

Ice (2007) provides a summary of this relationship between strategic intent and outcomes. Taking inspiration from early work of Tregoe and Zimmerman (1980) in Table 4.1, managers in the organization must choose between strategic areas as the drivers for shaping the form and purpose of how the organization then seeks to develop in its markets and environment, through using its resources and capabilities to achieve those preferred outcomes. The cited nine reasons therefore reflect both external structural features of markets (such as their scale, size, and organizational influence) and the internal management of organizational assets (Mantere and Sillince, 2007).

4.3 Stakeholders and congruence analysis

Figure 4.1 stresses the two axes of strategic intent and outcomes. We have considered the scope of intent and now we turn to that of outcomes. It was previously mentioned that, for the manager, strategic outcomes must identify the beneficiaries of the strategic intent, and latterly have expanded beyond shareholders (the traditional beneficiaries of outcomes) to other stakeholders.

With negotiation and strategic change comes broader consideration of those involved in that process. As we noted in Chapter 1, stakeholders are critical to strategy. We can consider how stakeholders should be reflected in developing the strategic intent of an organization as well as those who will enjoy the outcomes of that intent. The case of the merger of Hewlett-Packard (HP) with Compaq in 2001 is an illustration of this consideration and of the difficulty in managing intent and outcomes in

Table 4.1 Tregoe and Zimmerman's (1980) nine areas of strategic intent for 'organizations'

Strategic Area focused upon	Definition and actions
Products Offered	Focused on the product mix, look for new ways to improve or extend current product capabilities and achieve higher penetration of current markets
Market Needs	Provides a range of products to fill current or emerging needs of identified markets; develops new products/services; searches for new markets with characteristics similar to the current
Technology	Offers only products/services that emanate from or capitalize on its technical capability; seeks new applications for its technology
Production Capability	Leverages production know-how, processes, systems and equipment; two types: 'commodity' and 'job shop'—former characterized by long runs and scale economies; latter produces a wide range of products that utilize its production know-how
Method of Sale	Establishes primary method for convincing consumers to buy its products and determines products, markets, and geographic scope based on existing channels
Method of Distribution	Leverages strong distribution channels to deliver products, determines product mix, customers, and geographic scope based on existing channels
Natural Resources	Develops products through the use or conservation of natural resources
Size/Growth	Determines the products and markets service based upon the desire to become larger or smaller, may push into unrelated markets if the potential for size/growth exists, often an interim driving force.
Return/Profit	Desires for specific levels of return drive the product and market decisions of this organization, will change market scope in order to achieve its return/profit requirements.

Source: Based on Ice (2007).

organizations (Karnani, 2008). In relation to the three guiding questions we introduced in 4.2.1 above, HP's CEO at the time (Carly Fiorina) considered that the changing external environment necessitated a competitive merger with Compaq, which would enhance shareholder and customer value through efficiency and scale and scope benefits in low-end computing markets. As the investigating Federal Trade Commissioner (FTC) Mozelle W. Thompson noted at the time, when considering the proposed merger from an anti-competitive perspective, this evidence leads me to conclude that the combination—instead of reducing competition by eliminating a 64-bit chip rival—may enhance the merged firm's capabilities and ensure a long-term competitor in the Unix server microprocessor market.

(Fried and Kawamoto, 2002)

However, a significant number of shareholders and other stakeholders, including Walter Hewlett (son of the founder of the company and HP's director), were critical of the merger because it did not address any clear strategic need or encompass any clear shared intent (Fried and Kanellos, 2001). Walter is noted as having stated (Kawamoto, 2002):

We need to recognize that… HP brings no value to low-cost computing and should not be seeking growth in this area by chasing profitless revenues.

Difficulties with achieving this merger, and the subsequent restructuring of the organization in order to implement this strategy (Musil, 2005; Krazit, 2006), resulted in four years of poor results and, ultimately, the dismissal of Carly Fiorina.

While I regret the board and I have differences about how to execute HP's strategy, I respect their decision.

(Fiorina cited by LaMonica, 2005)

The structural changes that Fiorina had implemented following the HP–Compaq merger, which had been brought explicitly into question by market analysts Merrill Lynch near the end of her tenure (LaMonica, 2004), had to be operationally revised by the new HP CEO, Mark Hurd, through 2005 and 2006, using aggressive cost cutting and job layoffs to realize organizational benefits (Krazit, 2006), as well as some reversals of Fiorina's structural developments (Waters, 2006b). There was a general perception, however, that whilst the competitive merger was underpinned by an appropriate and clear strategic intent, its implementation and clarity of outcomes were not (Allison, 2006; Allison and Waters, 2007).

Should strategic leaders need or seek out consensual support, then? This had been a key question in the development and implementation of the HP–Compaq merger (Waters, 2006) and is a much more critical question and activity to pursue than the articulation of the vision of an organization might be, especially when vision and mission statements are often so generic. One solution is proposed by Coyle (2004) through the methodology of a congruence analysis. This requires the strategist to consider corporate intent by establishing the advantages and disadvantages for key stakeholders. In other words, it considers directly the impact of strategic change of intent upon outcomes. The proposed outcomes are evaluated by means of a *gestalt* interpretation, where 'gestalt' means that the strategic manager must consider the overall patterns in the analysis of the major beneficiaries (or losers) in the strategic proposal. We might consider, for example, what a congruence analysis of the Finnish organization

Raisio's corporate strategy in 1997 might have looked like, as they rolled out their Benecol-branded margarine across the globe. Table 4.2 illustrates the strategic relevance and identification of impact factors with the interests of major stakeholders in the environment for Raisio. In this discussion, the active ingredient in Benecol (which reduced cholesterol in the consumer) was a stanol ester extracted from plant materials. This had previously been a waste output from the paper and label manufacturer, United Paper Mills (UPM). The *gestalt* method requires the strategic manager to consider the relative merits and demerits of a given strategic intent for the organization's key stakeholders.

Table 4.2 Congruence analysis for Raisio (mid-1990s Benecol corporate roll-out strategy)

Structured Impact Wheel Factor	RAISIO (Board)	Customers	Employees	Shareholders	Doctors/ health industry
Increase in health concerns	+	++	0	0	++
Drug—food definition?	Unclear	–	–	—	+
Market access	Unclear (follows from above)	++	++	–	+
Recycling of waste pulp and production	+	0	0	+	0
Production costs of stanol ester	—	–	0	–	–
Expense of product	+	—	0	+	–
Spillover to other market segments	++	++	+	+	+

How the ranking of the stakeholder factors in the stakeholder columns above varies:

Unclear—the potential impact on a given stakeholder is not clear prior to this decision being taken

+ there is a likely gain for that stakeholder (interests are aligned)

++ a significant gain for that stakeholder is likely (interests are aligned)

– there is a likely loss for that stakeholder (interests are not aligned)

— a significant loss for that stakeholder is likely (interests are not aligned)

0 there is no likely gain or loss for that stakeholder (interests are not affected for that stakeholder)

In constructing Table 4.2, a structured impact wheel (Figure 4.2) is considered first, from which key primary outcomes are derived in terms of their potential positive or negative impact upon a range of identified stakeholders. Supporting company and market data are drawn from the excellent case discussion presented in Grant (2008b). An impact wheel is a simple analytical method allowing the user to consider

Figure 4.2 PESTLE analysis of adding stanol esters to food

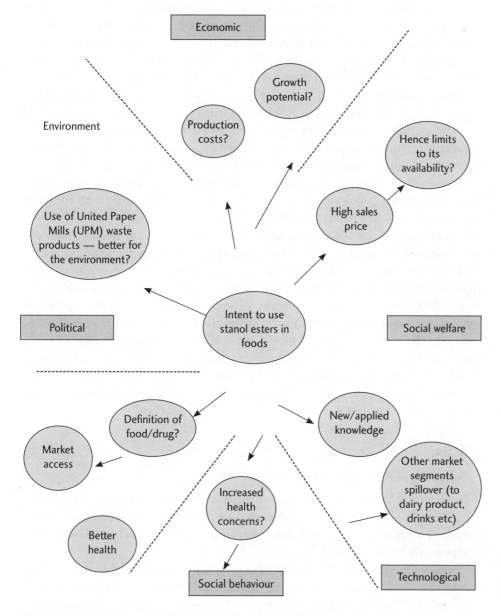

Note: P = Political; E = Economic; ST = Social and Technological; LE = Legal and Environmental; see p. 123.

the consequences of possible future actions, and a structured impact wheel is then explicitly 'structured' by considering specific PESTLE consequences. Hence, in Figure 4.2, consequences of the use of stanol esters in food for a particular health innovation is considered from a range of PESTLE positions. These potential consequences are then considered in terms of their positive or negative impact on identified stakeholders. We will explore PESTLE analysis in more detail below.

Table 4.2 illustrates the *pattern of relative outcomes* (hence it is a *gestalt* interpretation). By inspecting the table, it might be argued that if production costs can be lowered (and hence a lower price potentially be offered to consumers), then only the health industry stakeholders would benefit unequivocally from the proposed corporate strategy. In other words, in Table 4.2, the only column that would then reflect a consistently positive impact (i.e. all consequences would be rated as either positive or netural) would be that for doctors/health industry. This was not the original intention of the strategic managers of Raisio at the time of Benecol's launch in the USA and Europe (where market share and profitability were the intended outcomes). The potential strategic value of the health industry as a driver for some target markets became recognized several years later. As Sten von Hellens (a Raisio spokesperson) was reported as saying in 2000, 'there is evidence in the US that if doctors recommend the product people will buy it... In Europe, we will continue with consumer marketing because it appears to work' (ICIS, 2000).

It is clearly difficult for the strategic manager to consider all the outcomes of a given strategic intent, especially when a given corporate intent might manifest itself as different business strategies that can have unclear implementation concerns (see the HP–Compaq merger discussion). It has also been noted from the Raisio discussion and Table 4.2 that the strategic intention to use stanol ester in foods produced different business strategies in Europe, where the product could be marketed as a food, and the USA, where it was health and medical recommendations, rather than consumer marketing, that dominated. Grant (2008) states that corporate strategy is about determining which industries and markets in those industries your organization wishes to compete within, whilst business strategy considers questions about how your organization will compete in those preferred markets.

---

❶ Stop and think 4.1

Corporate and business strategies

Developing skills in strategic management requires a disciplined approach to language and terminology. Think of three examples of what you might describe as corporate strategy for an organization, and three examples of how that might be achieved by an appropriate business strategy.

Why are these different? What criteria would you use to make this judgement?

In your six examples, which stakeholders in which markets does the stated corporate intent benefit, do you think? Which stakeholder(s) might be losers in their market?

4.4 External analysis

In this section we now consider the development of the external environment and its consequences for the organization. This provides an understanding of appropriate strategic 'futures' in which an organization will be competing. In particular, we can consider futures forecasting models, drawn from political theory (Coyle, 2004), for example. To illustrate how important it is for the strategic manager to consider both emergent and planned strategic intent in light of delivering outcomes for relevant stakeholders, we can consider the approach described by the Field Anomaly Relaxation (FAR) method, as discussed by Coyle (2004). This is a futures-based scenario method that originated in the 1970s and has been applied regularly since then. It allows managers to consider the potential evolution of their competitive organizational environment by assuming that individuals and organizations all exist within 'fields' of interaction. This adopts Lewin's social field theory. These fields are defined as being dynamic, changing with time and the experience of individuals, organizations, and their environments. Thus we can consider future strategic scenarios shaped by individual and collective motives, values, goals, and pressures, so that considerations of what and how competitive factors (as derived from, say, a PESTLE analysis—presented below) might interact to shape future organizational scenarios to higher and higher levels of detail for the organization.

4.4.1 PESTLE analysis

When considering the external forces that drive change, it is useful to group these into categories by factor: political, economic, social and technological, legal and environmental (PEST or PESTLE). It is often useful to identify these as checklist questions for the purpose of analysis as indicated below.

Political

- What impact will government and intra-governmental (EU) directives have on the organization?

- What are the rights and obligations under the law, for the organization and its employees? For example, what is the impact of employment law on HR policy?

- What impact will tax policy, trade, and tariff controls have on the economic, social, and technological aspects of the organization?

- What is the impact of environmental and consumer-protection legislation on the organization?

Economic

- What effect will interest rate changes have on the business?

- How will change initiatives affect labour costs?

- How will change initiatives affect costs for physical resources and plant?
- What is the impact of social, political, and technological factors on finances?
- Is training required and what are the costs?

Social

- What is the impact of the demographic profile on the location of the organization (for example, health and education)?
- What is the impact of the job market, ability, and skills levels?
- What is the impact for social responsibility or governance (consideration of the impact of political, economic, and technological factors on social attitudes)?
- What is the impact of change on social attitudes?

Technological

- What is the impact of technology on work processes (for example, need for job redesign)?
- What is the impact of technology on social processes such as de- or re-skilling, work motivation, job evaluation?
- What is the impact of technological improvement on the business (for example, improved communications or the possibility of remote working)?
- What is the impact of technology on social, economic, and political factors?

Legal

- What are the implications of new legislation for practice? Of possible future legislation?
- What are our responsibilities to our shareholders in the event of new legislation coming into existence?
- What are the implications for governance in relation to employees and other stakeholders?

Environmental

- How can we demonstrate sustainability?
- Are we able to promote our achievements as examples of good practice?
- How progressive should we be and why?
- What concerns do we have about existing practice?

Essentially, the PESTLE analysis seeks to identify the impact of forces from the external environment upon the organization. This is a precondition of problem identification before a planned change strategy can occur. The forces identified by the PESTLE analysis require us to be aware of both the industry environment and the organizational environment.

❗ Stop and think 4.2

The impact of political intervention

If you were an airline manager and the government increased fuel duty, or 'green tax' on air travel, in order to influence consumer attitudes to change, what PESTLE factors would then affect your business? Use the questions in the PESTLE analysis to prioritize these factors and determine your response. Identify which questions are relevant and provide reasons for your decisions.

A PESTLE analysis can clearly identify threats and opportunities to the business caused by external forces for change. These are forces that are usually complex.

The external environment is best considered as consisting of an inner organizational environment surrounded by an external industry environment containing forces shaping change. The key forces in the external environment are:

1. The degree of competition within the industry.
2. The potential for growth.
3. The extent of regulation.
4. Whether the products offered are standard (usually providing low profit margins) or niche products or services.
5. Whether the technological pressures upon the organization are endogenous or exogenous.
6. The extent of the influence of macroeconomic factors.

If we consider these factors (which are stressed by the industrial organizational economics (IOE) approach to strategy—or the 'outside-in' approach mentioned above), then we might argue that the industry environment can be characterized by three broad attributes: the potential for growth; the extent of regulation; whether the products or services are characterized by standard offerings or whether there are opportunities for niche products. These are discussed below.

4.4.2 The nature of competition and potential for growth

The nature of competition and potential for growth are closely related. For example, in young and emergent markets, competition typically is differentiation-focused, supporting premium pricing. As markets mature, costs competition increases and there is limited scope for new market-share acquisition. Strategies of merger and acquisition might become more typical for these market environments. In addition, growth may not mean that an organization wishes to take on more staff or expand its physical environment. Nevertheless these are often a logical consequence of successful development. The reverse is also often the case. Thus, when companies are forced to contract, they often look to reduce costs by cutting staff or selling off less profitable parts of their operation. If we consider the airline industry, for example, we can see how competition and the potential for growth has favoured small, low-cost airlines since the 1970s and been further supported by deregulation of the industry. This has been amplified more recently as all airlines feel the effect of high oil prices, since it is those that are able to invest faster in new technologies, with lower energy demands, that will gain competitive advantage. This has resulted, at present for example, in an industry driven by several dominant pressures for change:

1. No Frills vs 'Premium' service operations—in other words organizations tend to offer either a tailored 'business' service to a smaller range of customers or offer a 'cheap and cheerful' service to a majority of customers. These have been the growth segments over the last decade or so (Fu, Lijesen, and Oum, 2006; Pitfield, 2005).

2. A technological impetus as a driver for growth—as competitors are in conflict about the future growth orientation of the industry—in other words, whether the industry will be one shaped by number of customers/flight or speed of completion of service. In the former camp is Boeing, whilst in the latter is Airbus, with their respective government authorities propping up both organizations. A similar battle was waged in the 1960s, when the former camp won.

3. Increased collaborative formations and alliance operations between airlines in response to price and service quality pressures (Flores-Fillol and Monor-Colonques, 2007)

4.4.3 Extent of regulation

Regulation can prevent a company from entering a marketplace or control competitors in a marketplace (as noted above with the airline industry). An example would focus upon investment funds that, over the years, have been a rich source of income for investment companies. This has led to a situation in which this market is not only competitively overcrowded, but likely to restrict new entrants. The warning is stark. First, in February 2007 a Federal judge in the USA ordered a major investment company, Bear Stearns, to pay $160 million (£82 million) to investors in the Manhattan Investment Fund for failing to alert them to a case of fraud that led to the collapse of the hedge fund. This ruling increased the need for Wall Street to monitor its clients more effectively. It also means that this responsibility is both a moral and legal imperative and a severe brake on potential impropriety (Douglas, 2008).

Another example of direct regulatory control of the external environment of organizations and, as a result, changes to their internal operations, is found in the US Sarbanes–Oxley Act of 2002, which was the direct regulatory response to a number of high-profile accounting scandals in the USA among global organizations. As commented by President Bush (Bush, 2002 cited by Bumiller, 2002) the Act has ensured that 'no boardroom in America is above or beyond the law'. It focuses upon enhancing the responsibilities and reporting requirements of publicly quoted organizations in

America. The Public Company Accounting Oversight Board (PCAOB) was created specifically as a regulatory supervisor, to monitor and validate the implementation and application of the Act. Despite the critics who argue that such additional controls undermine the competitive advantage of US public organizations, there is evidence that the Act is achieving its prescribed goal (Akhigbe, Martin, and Newman, 2008).

4.4.4 Standard offerings or niche products?

Standard products (such as cars, washing machines, microwaves) or standard services (such as fast food) are easy to produce but tend to attract low prices when the market is mature because there are many competitors. They might well have been niche offerings at one time but, as competition increased, profit margins were squeezed. Smarter organizations with managers aware of these difficulties constantly seek some form of differentiation to support added value and a price premium within mature markets (McGrath and MacMillan, 2000). These strategic choices are illustrated in the following case example.

» Case example 4.2

Rolls-Royce's RB–211 aero engine

An example of how a product for the mass market became a profitable niche product is illustrated by Sir John Rose's leadership of Rolls-Royce aero-engines. When Rose joined Rolls-Royce in 1985 the aero-engines market was dominated by two American companies, General Electric and Pratt & Whitney. These companies benefited from Pentagon spending on engine programmes. Their competitive advantage was further assured because they formed an alliance with Boeing, the world's dominant aircraft maker, and with American Airlines, which then accounted for half of the world's aviation activity. In other words, this was a market that appeared impenetrable.

The Rolls-Royce strategy was to build an engine that had technological advantages over its rivals, thus giving customers what they wanted. That meant that Rolls-Royce had to build up its installed base of engines to a point where the revenues from servicing engines insulated it from continual production costs and contractual problems, and then supported innovative, customer-focused development of its aero-engines. Consequently, it is now the Number Two aircraft engine-making company globally. It is Number One, however, on wide-bodied aircraft like the Airbus A380, because of its enhanced reputation with customers achieved through a specific customer focus in the development of its engines. Thus, half of the airlines buying the Airbus A380 chose Rolls-Royce engines. Because of the revenues derived from servicing engines and extensive UK government support in the early 1970s (*Hansard*, 1979), one of its main competitors—Pratt & Whitney—has almost withdrawn from the large airline market. The success of this strategy meant finding a successful »

❯❯revenue stream by developing a niche product that customers wanted. So, what was it that customers wanted?

The answer is that the company made a niche product by recognizing (in the late 1960s and early 1970s) the potential for a future-oriented market driven by cheap air travel but increasingly compromised by the so-called carbon footprint. At this time, mass public awareness of environmental pollution and environmental limits was beginning (with, for example, Rachel Carson's acclaimed book *Silent Spring*—1962—which focused on pesticides and in particular DDT, and Paul and Anne Ehrlich's Malthusian book *The Population Bomb*—1968). This required a new breed of engine that was efficient, quiet, and relatively ecologically friendly. The RB–211 has found over 100 different customers. This is how the engine became a best-seller.

In a similar vein to Rolls-Royce's development of its aero engines, we might also explore the resurgence of Nintendo and their Wii console in the video games industry at the start of this century. From the 1970s through the 1980s, Atari, Nintendo, and Sega were the leading video games-console and game producers. Yet, typical of an industry that required significant cyclical investment to generate increased console specification and game performance, their position was always vulnerable to competitors being able to produce higher-specification games and machines. So, when Sony launched their Playstation in the early 1990s with superior game resolution, speed, and gameplay, Atari had already shifted to software production only, Sega were squeezed out of the market entirely, and Nintendo pushed to the brink of collapse. For both of the latter organizations, technological differences in the format of games sold and the competitive requirement, which required a significant games sales volume (generating positive cash flow) to support market presence, was a major barrier to their strategic success in this market.

❯❯ **Case example 4.3**

Nintendo's development of the Wii console

Prevailing wisdom suggested the market was impenetrable to new or resurgent entrants, with Sony and then Microsoft carving up the high-specification home-gaming sector. However, the sociodemographics of this market had always limited its potential scale to that of traditionally male-oriented gaming formats. By achieving an engagement with a wider demographic, both niche product development could be supported and broader market needs addressed (see again Table 4.1 above). Thus, whilst Nintendo could not compete with incumbent rivals in terms of technological specification, their experience of gameplay through handheld gaming devices supported their deployment of this capability as the key competitive advantage for the Wii console. Hence their competitive success relies not upon graphic realism, but on physical engagement and activity, a trend that Sony and Microsoft are now being forced to follow, to also access a broader market demographic.

> **❶ Stop and think 4.3**
>
> The industry environment
>
> Think of two industries you are familiar with. Consider each of these industries' four attributes: (1) competition within the industry; (2) the potential for growth; (3) the extent of regulation; (4) whether the products or services are characterized by standard offerings or whether there are opportunities for niche products. Then draw up a list of similarities and differences.
>
> Which factors are shaping the development of the industry concerned?

4.4.5 Industrial organizational economics and Five Forces analysis

As mentioned above, one well-known example linking the external environment to the internal environment is Porter's (1980) Five Forces of competition. Whilst not without problems, it does frame a helpful overview of the scope of competitive forces acting upon an organization. The strength of each force depends upon the degree of influence of variables and it is necessary to identify these if at all possible. The difficulty, however, is that the interrelationships of the variables create a complex set of influences that are often hard or impossible to predict with any degree of certainty (the manager at that point may wish to deploy a futures forecasting method such as FAR (which is reviewed shortly) to aid decision making). The overall value of this model lies in its ability to bring critical issues in competitor analysis to the foreground. We now consider the Porter forces in more detail.

The *threat of entry* is determined by political barriers such as licence agreements regulating the conditions for business. Examples of this include care homes for the elderly that require a local authority licence. The economies of scale reflect the optimum balance between cost and quality. Mass markets are more likely to be undermined by situations in which quality rather than unit cost is the main factor. Furthermore, the ability to produce goods will be undermined by poor distribution channels, leaving established companies with a considerable advantage over new entrants. Consumer loyalty depends on the extent to which a brand is well established and is trusted by consumers.

The *bargaining power of suppliers* will determine cost and the extent to which quality standards of materials meet the needs of the company. Some companies create dependency of suppliers. For example, large car companies such as Nissan are able to create exclusivity agreements with their suppliers who, in return, will offer materials at the price agreed with the company. We can see how complex this gets when we consider that the relative bargaining positions of the company and its suppliers determine the cost and quality of the overall finished product. Such agreements are a threat to new entrants. If a new entrant wishes to enter the market for mass-produced goods (for example cars), then it must have considerable resources at its disposal since it will have to obtain even more favourable agreements with its suppliers. If this is also to challenge brand loyalty, then considerable cost advantages must be offered to potential customers.

The *threat of substitutes* depends upon the extent to which a product or service is difficult to copy. For example, it would be difficult to compete with an entrepreneur craftsman with an established reputation selling his/her own unique artwork or furniture without being able to offer some other valued intangible quality to the potential customer. On the other hand, if a product could be produced more cheaply or is perceived to have a higher quality (that is, either tangible or intangible attributes), then the new entrant will have an advantage.

The *bargaining power of buyers* is significant in the sense that in markets that are price-sensitive the company producing the product or service is vulnerable and will easily be undermined by new entrants with a cheaper source of supplies. This factor largely accounts for the success of many developing countries, which have a source of cheap labour and can easily replicate skills of machine processes—essentially mass production (thus reflecting Porter's 1990 model of economic development that focuses upon economies progressing through key stages: production factor, investment growth, innovation growth, and a wealth stage). Where customers are less price-sensitive, as is the case with luxury goods, then a new entrant will have difficulty overcoming brand loyalty. Furthermore, when a company is highly dependent on a limited number of customers in order to sell its products, it is clearly vulnerable to new entrants who can exploit this weakness.

Finally the *intensity of competitive rivalry* is determined by the rate of growth in the industry; the number of competitors; the perceived value of the brand to customers; the degree of under- or overcapacity for products or services; and cost minimization.

This view of the external environment and key competitive drivers, though, struggles to consider cooperation between organizations, the formation of alliances to share resources and capabilities; nor can it easily accommodate the influence of key external sponsors (say governments) for particular organizations or sectors. Thus the five-forces method is then developed towards thinking of factors complementary to strategy development and change, such as organizational structure, the political relationships between actors and agents in organizations, and the political balance in the relationship between the firm and its context. There is a movement away from considering the need to achieve an equilibrium position for the organization in its competitive context, to one of focusing upon differences between organizations and their contexts as reasons for differing competitive advantage positions. The 'outside-in' view (SCP) is then replaced by an 'inside-out' view of competitive strategy. Farjoun (2002), citing Chandler (1962), stresses the implementational issue (our question 3: 'how is strategy used to improve competitive position?') by focusing on the need to consider the relationship between structure and strategy, and that better organizational performance is derived from an internal-process consideration of how organizational assets are organized (i.e. their work structure).

4.4.6 FAR analysis

It was argued previously that PESTLE analysis has limitations. This is particularly the case when the external environment is subject to high levels of turbulence. A more realistic view of an organization's external environment and its change options within this is provided by a FAR analysis, which can be used to support organizational planning. This method is an iterative process: as new scenarios are identified they will add further insight and understanding to the range of possible sectors/factors to consider. The process should be repeated and will converge over a number of iterations to generate more appropriate and more effectively considered scenarios or future stories for an organization's external context.

≫ Case example 4.4

A simple FAR analysis for Wal-Mart

We might consider what a FAR analysis would look like for Wal-Mart using the case materials presented by Grant (2008). A simplified interpretation of Coyle's (2004) methodology might therefore be regarded as a four-step process:

1. Form a view of the future for the industry and its environment (e.g. for Wal-Mart, this might be an increased internationalization of discount retailing). Think of this as considering an imaginative view of the future into which strategic decisions will unfold.
2. Create a language that is appropriate (and memorable) and finely detailed enough to allow the description of how the future outlined in 1. might develop. This identifies the critical uncertainties and their range of possibilities (usually expressed through a ranked and weighted array).
3. Eliminate any clear anomalies.
4. Now consider the possible pathways and routes that survive after the analysis—again usually in the form of a timeline.

Constructing a mind-map or PESTLE analysis will help identify external factors shaping the views of the organization's competitive future context and scope for strategic change. This will encompass the context in which Wal-Mart will be competing and a factor table can then be generated. Such a table can be inspected for the overall pattern of outcomes, to identify what patterns/relationships/issues seem to be contributing to the nature of that future context. Ideally, no more than seven distinct sectors of interest should be identified, which should have clear documentary evidence to validate their tabular position and consideration. From a PESTLE analysis of Wal-Mart, the following key market and industrial factors in the organizational external context may be identified:

1. **D**istribution pressures (economic)
2. US **E**conomic climate (political, economic)

» 3. Lifestyle and **C**ultural development of customers (sociodemographic)
4. Market **A**wareness and understanding (political, sociodemographic)
5. Extent of supplier **I**ntegration and coordination (economics, technological)
6. **T**echnological (and IT) contribution to improved service (technological)

A suitable language for this analysis might therefore be based on the sectors above and generates the acronym **DECAIT.** The factor array for **DECAIT** might look as follows:

D	E	C	A	I	T
Distribution pressures	US **E**conomic climate	Lifestyle and **C**ultural development of customers	Market **A**wareness and understanding	Extent of supplier **I**ntegration and coordination	**T**echnological (and IT) contribution to improved service
D1—significant growth in costs and management of distribution chain	E1—rosy growth	C1—customers increase their strong cost focus	A1—significant development of customer awareness and their needs	I1—increased collaborative relationships at all levels with suppliers	T1—greater convergence of technology informing service
D2—clear growth in costs and management of distribution chain	E2—fair growth	C2—customers maintain a cost focus	A2—improved customer awareness and their needs	I2—sustained collaborative relationships at all levels with suppliers	T2—sustained convergence of technology informing service
D3—no change in costs and management of distribution chain	E3—stagnation	C3—customers weaken in their cost focus	A3—no change in customer awareness and their needs	I3—limited fragmentation of collaborative relationships at all levels with suppliers	T3—weakening convergence of technology informing service
D4—fall in costs and management of distribution chain	E4—recession	C4—customers significantly weaken in their cost focus	A4—relative and competitive weakening in customer awareness and their needs	I4—significant fragmentation of collaborative relationships at all levels with suppliers	
	E5—depression				

We might then test for internal consistency within the sectors in the array, noting that there are a possible 134,596 combinations with this factor/sector array alone, and eliminate those factors that, from a *gestalt* perspective, do not make much 'sense'. That is, E1 with C1 or C2 seem very unlikely combinations. D1 or D2 also seem unlikely to occur concurrently with E4 or E5. The remaining options can be weighted according to their likelihood, based on available data (say on a scale of »

>> 0 to 3), with those combinations of factors and sectors that have high relative scores producing the likely scenarios for the future against which an organization will be competing. Thus, such a considered view of an organizational future can identify how external forces for change might construct the future context and shape the pattern of appropriate strategic choice.

---

❶ Stop and think 4.4

Considering the future context of an organization

Developing a FAR analysis appropriately requires a significant commitment of managerial time, environmental data, and organizational resources. However, it can provide a succinct guide for the changing context of an organization.

To consider this insight, construct a mind-map of key external pressures affecting your organization (or a large organization you know of).

From this mind-map, what factors would you identify and use as the foundation for a FAR analysis?

Why would these be appropriate?

What information would you require to develop your understanding of these factors further?

Do you know where you would find this information?

Being able to answer these questions will continue to help focus your analysis, and the strategic managerial mind, upon relevant and high-priority external factors for an organization, and be aware of the ways they change. We might adopt therefore the entrepreneurial language of McGrath and MacMillan (2000) and state that this is the development of a 'strategic mindset' in the manager.

4.5 Determining a strategic path

In general, we have identified that determining a preferred strategic path, which balances intent and expected outcomes, requires making interrelated organizational choices with trade-offs in competitive positioning, in the context of an uncertain future. Rather than look to the external environment as a stable and predictable context for the strategic manager to work within, therefore, there has been interest in shifting the focus for the strategic manager to internal organizational factors, over which they have more control and flexibility. One recent articulation of this view is called the resource-based view (RBV) approach to strategic thinking. Briefly, this view of strategy formulation seeks to emphasize the uncertainty in competing in the modern globalized environment, by directing the strategic manager to think about how organizational resources (such as capital and staff) can be organized to perform an activity a customer will pay for. This combination of resources allows an organization to have a capability in the market, which underpins an observed competitive market advantage.

The value of combining resources to support a particular strategic intent raises questions of how to value them. Barney's (1991) VRIN (Valuable/Rare/Imperfectly Imitable/Non-substitutable) framework was an early evaluative approach to this problem that seeks to identify, create, and sustain organizational resources that are sufficiently distinctive from those of competitors and have a resistance to imitation, and that can therefore be deployed by the organization to achieve and sustain a market advantage. It may be, for example, that the deployment of those resources is in itself a source of advantage for the organization. Consider, for example, how Marks and Spencer Ltd are known for managing customer complaints and returns. It is therefore part of an 'inside-out' perspective on strategic change.

Thus, originally, the VRIN approach emphasized the view that competitive success can come from organizational differences rather than seeking to deploy a 'market recipe' for commercial success, and tasked strategic managers to identify their organizational resource characteristics comparatively. They then might compile a table, such as Table 4.3, where each resource is scaled comparatively (out of ten).

Overall, whilst it is clear that there remains a very distinctive role for the planning and design of strategy, in response to and in anticipation of external factors shaping the competitive environment of the organization (such as from PESTLE and Five Forces), more varied and, arguably, realistic approaches have been proposed (such as FAR and congruence analysis (see 4.3 above). Whittington's (1993) original framework in Figure 4.1 has therefore underpinned more recent guides to strategic formulation and development, which are discussed below.

Table 4.3 An example of a VRIN table

Resource	Valuable?	Rare?	Imperfectly Imitable?	Non-substitutable?
Physical	8	5	2	4
Reputational	4	7	5	5
Organizational	5	3	7	6
Financial	7	7	8	8
Intellectual	2	7	3	1
Technological	3	8	2	9

4.6 Contemporary strategic formulation and development

We began this chapter by stating that strategy, as practised in most organizations, is underpinned by a specific pathway with clear action outcomes to achieve through a preferred intent. Managers maintain a set of shared assumptions about the importance of understanding the external environment of an organization and how to respond to them, where SWOT analysis, and a view of the organization as being composed of an agreed set of objectives and assumptions through its staff and managers, have played (and continue to play) a key role in that determination. As a teaching framework and series of applied methodologies, this approach remains significant and intuitively appealing. Latterly, there have been more realistic attempts to understand strategic decision making in organizations. The increasingly turbulent external environment of organizations, which began to be a common feature in the 1970s, has driven paradigmatic shifts in the focus of strategic conceptual development and articulated the need to address this environmental complexity, thus shifting the focus of competitive success from that addressed only by an IOE model (Five Forces) to one that also addresses an internal resource orientation. As a result, alternative process-oriented approaches on strategy have emerged in the last two decades, ranging from evolutionary approaches (Nelson and Winter, 1982), chaos theory (Levy, 1994), implementational strategies, addressing the complex inherent 'messiness' of strategy, through to systems approaches (Boulton and Allen, 2007), and strategic implementational and contested-firm issues and intent (Amoore, 2000).

These different focuses for strategic formulation and development have been labelled (Hoskisson, Hitt, and Yiu, 1999 and Farjoun, 2002) as:

1. The SCP paradigm (Structure–Conduct–Performance).
2. The SSP view (Structure–Strategy–Performance).
3. The RBV (resource-based view).
4. The OESP view (Organization–Environment–Strategy–Performance).

From the 1980s onwards, Farjoun (2002) identified a range of emergent concerns that challenged the prevailing mechanistic SCP approaches to strategic management. In the SCP paradigm discussed earlier is a view of strategy (as outside-in) that argues that the competitive advantage of an organization and its positioning are shaped by key external environmental forces, which directly contribute to the organization's performance. There is therefore an assumed causality where the performance of an organization is directly related to its conduct, which is in essence therefore a reflection of key industrial and market factors. Hence, organizational performance is argued to be causally shaped by industrial and market factors. This is the IOE perspective introduced earlier (and identified with authors such as Porter (1980)—the

Five Forces model—and Utterback and Abernathy (1974)—their Industry Life Cycle model). This work, and more, has provided the background for this approach to strategy formulation and intent, and it remains a core analytical methodology. Concerns with this approach focused on implementation and began to become more visible and extend beyond questions of strategy formulation and its static and fragmented nature.

It was noted earlier that the SCP view of the external environment and key competitive drivers struggles to consider cooperation between organizations, nor can it easily accommodate the influence of key external sponsors (say governments) for particular organizations or sectors. Thus, the SSP paradigm shifts the focus of conceptual development in strategic thinking towards consideration of factors complementary to strategy development and change, such as organizational structure, the political relationships between actors and agents in organizations, and the political balance in the relationship between the firm and its context.

Broadly, the third view noted above, the RBV of the organization, develops the strategic focus for the manager upon internal resources of the organization as fundamental to the competitive positioning and success of that organization. Embedded in its core concept of organizational differences (Penrose, 1959; Wernerfelt, 1984) is a position that competitive advantage from strategic formulation, choice, and implementation comes from internal resources and capabilities (the ability to perform a work task), organization, and management. Thus, for example, methods of analysing the value chain of a market activity, and where market opportunities can be exploited or weakness addressed through internal reorganization, emerge from this perspective (Grant, 2008). Whilst it is a powerful perspective, there are concerns, for example, with how and why strategic managers might choose one interpretation of their organization's comparative competitive resources in light of opportunity costs (for other market activities using those organizational resources), and the fit of this judgement with other stakeholders of the organization (Freeman, 1984). If we reconsider the Hewlett-Packard and Compaq case discussed earlier, the articulation and management of Fiorina's strategic intent for a competitive merger was in conflict with the intent of other stakeholders and their preferred outcomes. Mitchell, Agle, and Wood (1997) stress the importance of adopting a fluid view of the relevance of stakeholders for organizations, which is shaped by the urgency of a strategic choice, the power of the stakeholders concerned, and the legitimacy of their efforts to influence the choice of a strategic change and focus. Mitchell, Agle, and Wood use the term 'saliency' to capture how these three contributing factors combine to give a stakeholder in an organization an increasing (or decreasing) influence over strategic decisions made by the organization. Moreover, they also stress that this is dynamic and that the saliency of a given stakeholder will vary over time and context.

Finally, in the fourth focus articulated above, the OESP view takes strategic thinking into the emergent–pluralistic part of Figure 4.1. Broadly, this then considers concerns with how strategies are realized (how they manifest in practice in an uncertain context), what the response of internal change to external and internal pressures is, and the need to consider humanistic influences and sensitivities in strategic formulation and implementation (Farjoun, 2002). The function of time in this model is also important, as it promotes a dynamic processual relationship between internal and external organization factors for change. Strategic intent and strategic outcome are not shaped by a singular, linear or deterministic relationship, despite what the language might suggest.

The progression through these four guiding focuses on strategic formulation and change moves from an explicit consideration of external change factors, to internal change factors and interrelated activities, as the foundation for organizational competitive success. Powell (2002), for example, argues that an organization that possesses a sustainable competitive advantage does not necessarily gain a superior organizational position or performance, clearly forcing us to remember the importance of the management linkage between the intent and the outcome of strategy within a complex external environment. Thus, broadly, as the field has matured, the study and development of strategic management concepts and strategic development have moved towards a more holistic understanding of the focus of the two axes in Figure 4.1 (strategic intent *versus* strategic outcomes).

All these approaches have continued to use the SWOT model as a key design vehicle to help organizations determine appropriate strategic choice and formulation, first by encouraging a design process that seeks to fit internal resource opportunities and potential with external factors of change (see Ice, 2007, for example). Thus strengths and opportunities of the organizational fit with its environment are developed, whilst weaknesses are minimized and potential threats are neutralized. The RBV view then seeks to develop a clear evolutionary fit for an organization, exploiting relevant technical fitness strengths in appropriate market areas (Helfat *et al*, 2006). Farjoun (2002) stresses that this development in strategic thinking (i.e. from SCP to SSP to RBV in particular) has a number of common underpinnings, where for example events in the organizational past have no additional consequence aside from shaping the current environmental context and decisions made about strategies are not considered subsequently.

The OESP view is important in that it is argued to be a challenge to this accepted order of the flow of actions for competitive positioning, where (as discussed above) there is a transition from the 'outside-in' to the 'inside-out' in the consideration of competitive factors within these three focuses. However, all three are responses to the external environment, rather than a consideration of how, and through what mechanisms, the organization might influence those factors. Thus, in the OESP view, there is an explicit consideration of direction of organizational 'posture development'. A final underpinning difference is concerned with the fragmented nature of these three focuses (SCP, SSP, and RBV) on strategic formulation, where they have developed with a narrow attention to the environment, resources, and structure. As a result, considerations of an underpinning theory of the organization, which might be derived from these views, are lacking because of this narrow focus (Phelan and Lewin, 2000). However, the OESP view, along with developments of the RBV of strategy and closer consideration of economic theory, has led to consideration that strategy may yet provide sufficient support for a theory of the firm to be developed (Farjoun, 2002: Phelan and Lewin, 2000). This would provide a powerful conceptual and practical framework for a holistic understanding of organizational competitive and strategic change.

4.7 Summary

In this chapter we have explored external forces for change. We began with an overview of the development of strategic management and how, over a short period of time, this has produced a range of perspectives and ways of thinking for the strategic manager. From that discussion, four dominant approaches have been articulated, which have developed in conjunction with changing external pressures and attempts to respond to the turbulence of the contemporary external environment. Throughout this discussion, the focus has been on:

- identifying key concerns and questions for the strategic manager to consider, which can be derived from the structure of the industry and markets within which the organization competes;
- the impact of a given corporate strategy upon a range of external and internal stakeholders (thus stressing the political aspect inherent in any strategic choice and decision);
- the linkage between a given corporate strategy and resulting business strategies;
- the contingent nature of these concerns and how effective strategic managers need to moderate their engagement with any dominant conceptual perspective so as to limit their risk exposure;
- the need therefore to achieve a balance between planning for the organization and retaining sufficient flexibility to support a sustained evolutionary fit in its competitive environment.

Overall, therefore, engagement and recognition of the nature of drivers for strategic change is a clear requirement for an effective strategic manager.

The purpose of this chapter has been to contextualize the approaches to strategic change in volatile global environments. Managers need to know how to deal with changes forced upon them and, equally, they need to take action before problems emerge—or in order to exploit new opportunities. Managing strategic change is not possible without the ability to understand and analyse factors in both industry and the organizational environments. In the course of this discussion we have identified the importance of a range of simple environmental analysis tools to achieve this. Porter's Five Forces of competition consider important industrial and market structural factors that shape effective competitiveness. The PESTLE analysis helps to identify and analyse the external forces that drive change. A FAR analysis can build upon PESTLE, to help the strategic manager understand the development and evolution of the external competitive environment and the appropriateness (and fit) of a given corporate strategy for that environment. Finally, a congruence analysis then supports an exploration of the potential outcomes of a given corporate strategy for a range of identified strategic stakeholders. A wise manager will attempt to deploy these insights to support, sustain, and potentially lead strategic changes and (re)alignment of the organization's competitive activities in a changing external context.

⊙ Case study

Northern Rock, the business model that led to disaster

On 13 September 2007, Mervyn King, Governor of the Bank of England, addressed the 'Court' that oversees the Bank's affairs. The Court consisted of King, two deputy governors, and sixteen non-executive directors. Some met in the Bank while others were linked by teleconference facilities. They were informed that a big British bank—Northern Rock, a mortgage lender holding £24 billion of ordinary savers' money—was in trouble and plans for a rescue had to be authorized by the Court. Essentially, unless Northern Rock received emergency funding from the Bank of England as 'lender of last resort', it could not continue to operate.

Essentially, the fifth biggest mortgage bank in the UK almost collapsed. Northern Rock had been distinguished by fast growth and low costs. It was also known for its efficient administrative systems. However, in September 2007 it ran out of money. Queues formed outside bank branches and public confidence was destroyed almost overnight. What was unusual was that Northern Rock had a full mortgage book and was financially 'healthy'. Its arrears on residential mortgages were less than half the industry average and yet shares fell immediately by one-fifth. Consequently, its survival prospects became desperate. The Chancellor of the Exchequer, Alistair Darling, assured depositors that the Bank of England would guarantee all deposits.

Institutional investors criticized the Northern Rock Board. Directors were asked to accept responsibility for the crisis they had caused by ignoring obvious warning signs that the business model was very doubtful. They were also criticized for an 'aggressive and lavish remuneration policy'. The Chief Executive was paid £1.3m the previous year. One investor said, 'there is an argument to be made about whether the non-executives sufficiently questioned the business model, given that it was so different to the rest of the market'.[1] A leading fund manager accused the directors of ignoring warnings from the Bank of England and the Financial Services Authority: 'the FSA and the Bank have been saying for some time that short-term borrowing and long-term lending was a very dangerous position to be in. They weren't naming names, but those directors should have known it was aimed at them.'[2]   ⟫

» Despite the assurances that investors' money was safe, extremely long queues formed for three days outside branches throughout the country. Scuffles broke out when branches closed and in some towns police were called out to keep the peace. In the first two days investors withdrew £1.5 billion. Whilst Northern Rock remained solvent, savers feared they might lose their savings and the bank lost credibility.

Facts

In the first six months of 2007, Northern Rock issued one in five new mortgages in the UK. It offered 'generous loans' of up to 125 percent of the value of the proper-ty—to first-time buyers.

The crisis was triggered by UK banks lending money to banks in the United States. A crisis in the US banking system caused by the so-called 'American sub-prime mort-gage meltdown' spilled across the Atlantic. The crisis occurred when US homeowners struggled to pay their mortgages. Consequently, investors who had bought debt, such as the US sub-prime mortgages, saw these asset-securities plummet in value. As a result, banks were caught out and feared that unforeseen problems might emerge in other credit markets. They then stopped lending. Since Northern Rock depended on borrowing from other banks to fund its business, rather on than its own depositors, it ran into trouble. The crisis destroyed the credibility of Northern Rock.

The emergency loan to Northern Rock, underwritten by taxpayers and secured on the bank's assets, reached £16 billion by 20 October and continued to increase by £400 million a day.

The Bank of England, the Treasury, and the Financial Services Authority (regulator) decided to support Northern Rock and a Treasury official said, 'we expected this, but there is no need to panic because it is a solvent institution'. However, the Governor of the Bank of England, Mervyn King, lost credibility by first stating that there would be no bail-out, then reversing that decision.

Northern Rock was hit harder than any other bank by the credit crunch because it relied on money markets, from which it received approximately three-quarters of the funds which it then loaned to borrowers. Other banks, by contrast, relied more on deposits from savers. Advisers were inundated with calls from savers and borrowers who panicked, thus intensifying the crisis.

The financial penalty for Northern Rock's borrowing from the Bank of England is a punitive 7 percent. This makes the bank extremely uncompetitive in comparison to its main competitors.

Northern Rock's business model, which had largely been developed by Adam Applegarth, the young chief executive of Northern Rock,[3] became extremely ques-tionable. Applegarth had joined the bank from university in 1983 as a cashier. At the age of 34 he became an executive director. In 2001, at the age of 38, he became the chief executive. Other executives at Northern Rock are also said to have had limited experience of the City and wider financial markets.   »

» In October 2007 the Board of Directors were humiliated by having to appear before a House of Commons Public Accounts Committee to account for their business model. On 19 October the chairman, Matt Ridley, announced plans to resign. According to *The Sunday Times*, 'the bank said that Dr Ridley and the other directors believed the time was now right for him to go. He had until now been asked to remain while new funding arrangements were put in place and to allow him to appear before the Treasury Select Committee.'[4] Dr Ridley had been a director for over a decade and received an annual salary of £315,000. *The Times* (20 October 2007) reported that 'MPs and trade unions welcomed the resignation. Michael Fallon, a Conservative member of the Treasury Select Committee, said: "Somebody must accept responsibility and it's the head of the organization that honour demands should go. I would hope that he is followed by the chief executive [Adam Applegarth] and in due course by all the non-executive directors."'

The Bank of England Financial Stability Report, published 25 October 2007, called the crisis 'the most severe challenge to the UK financial system for several decades' and stated that the lessons learned from it were that 'banks need to improve their liquidity management, investors need greater scrutiny of clever structured financial products and consumers need to have confidence that the money they put in the bank is backed by a meaningful insurance scheme'.

Finally, questions have been asked about how effectively the Bank of England, the Treasury, and the Financial Services Authority work together. Thus, greater 'stress testing' is necessary in the regulation of banks.

Questions

1. Using an appropriate framework for analysing the external environment, explain the organizational environment in which Northern Rock operated.

2. Undertake a PESTLE analysis to illustrate the various external forces affecting this type of organization.

3. Undertake a SWOT analysis to illustrate what the company should have been aware of.

4. Say why you think Nortern Rock ignored the threats until too late. If it had undertaken scenario planning (such as FAR), would it have spotted this potential outcome in advance?

5. If it had developed an early warning system, what should this have discovered?

6. What suggestion would you make to aid strategic realignment of Northern Rock? (consider structural changes, market positioning, and management changes in particular).

Sources: [1 & 2] *The Guardian*, 'Fall in share price adds to pressure for Northern Rock sell-off', 20 September 2007.
[3] Jeremy Warner's *Outlook*: 'Northern crisis rocks financial system—Bank attacked over Rock rescue', *The Independent*, 15 September 2007.
[4] 'Ten days that shook the City—the first run on a UK bank since 1866 has put the Bank of England in the dock', *The Sunday Times*, 23 September 2007.

■ Study questions

1. Describe the difference between reactive and proactive change.

2. What are external forces for change?

3. What is the purpose of external analysis?

4. What are the four attributes of the industry environment?

5. How would you define the organizational environment?

6. Outline Porter's Five Forces of competition.

7. What tensions are inherent in making strategic choices?

8. Explain the purpose of strategic realignment.

9. Why might internal resources be inadequate in responding to the challenge of external forces?

■ Exercises

Exercise 1
Identify one organization in each of the public, voluntary, and private sectors. Undertake a PESTLE analysis on each, then provide a rationale for the differences you find. Then explain, with examples, how the industry environment affects the organizational environment.

Exercise 2
Choose one organization you have identified in Exercise 1 and develop a framework to conduct a FAR analysis. Be clear as to why you choose your factor headings and make a list of the type and location of information you would need to populate the FAR table. Where possible, are there any clear and obvious anomalies you can eliminate?

Exercise 3
Choose a different organization from that used in Exercise 2 (and from your original list in Exercise 1) and identify a current corporate strategy of that organization. Think about who might be a stakeholder in that corporate strategy and draw up a congruence table. Explain who you feel are the major beneficiaries of that corporate strategy and who you feel are those with most to lose.

Exercise 4
Choose a product and a service. Using Porter's Five Forces of competition, state how you might gain market entry and competitive advantage.

Exercise 5
Consider an organization you are familiar with. Work out how you would develop an early warning system to detect serious problems before they become fatal.

Exercise 6
Identify a suitable organization and undertake an external analysis. Provide a management report by following the instructions below.

1. Introduction—provide a brief overview of the purpose of the external analysis.

2. Begin by providing an industry sector definition. This should include data on:

   a. the nature of the business

   b. changes to the industry sector over the past five years

   c. the main customer profile (including changes) and market situation—whether it is stable, declining, or expanding

   d. the nature of competition, including market share.

      Undertake analyses: PESTLE and SWOT. Use tertiary sources to provide evidence—be clear in always noting your sources. This must be tabulated and followed by a discussion of the critical issues identified. For example, *political analysis* might consider local authority provision for leisure and recreational facilities, in which case a useful tertiary source would be MINTEL. An *economic analysis* might include information from the Family Expenditure Survey, in which case a useful tertiary source might be a TSO publication. A *social analysis* might consider changing demographic patterns, in which case you may wish to use *Social Trends* (TSO). A *technological analysis* might use various official publications such as DTI, CTTI. If in doubt see Table 8 of Jankowicz (1995).

3. From your PESTLE and SWOT analyses, construct a FAR analysis to identify potential future scenarios against which you feel your organization will be competing.

4. Discuss why you feel your organization is, or is not, suitably positioned in the external environment, in light of your findings from (2) and (3).

5. Finally, provide a conclusion that briefly outlines the findings and recommends a course of action.

■ Further reading

Blackden, R. (2007), 'Global stocks tumble as Chinese market falls', *Daily Telegraph*, 28 February 2007, 3. A report on concerns with the Chinese market's growth and potential regulatory changes to control illegal investments.

Choo, C.W. and Bontis, N. (2002), *The Strategic Management of Intellectual Capital and Organizational Knowledge: A Collection of Readings*, New York: Oxford University Press. Very good collection of strategic writings on knowledge management and strategy, presented logically and chronologically, from the key contributors in the field.

Kaplan, R.S. and Norton, D.P. (2000), *The Strategy-Focused Organization: How Balanced Scorecard Companies Thrive in the New Business Environment*, Cambridge, MA: Harvard Business School Press. An important text, from leading authors, that considers the problems of effective implementation of strategy and presents the score card as more than a measurement tool—an integrative tool in organizations.

Kinnunen M. and Korppoo A. (2007), 'Nuclear power in Northern Russia: A case study on future energy security in the Murmansk region', *Energy Policy*, 35(5), 2826–2838.

A contemporary discussion of futures forecasting through a scenario methodology, with a focus on energy viability and security.

Preston P. and Cawley A. (2008), 'Broadband development in the European Union to 2012—a virtuous circle scenario', *Futures*, 40(9), 812–821. A FAR-based scenario analysis of the policy development for broadband in Europe.

Zwicky, F. (1969) *Discovery, Invention, Research*, Toronto: The Macmillan Company. A seminal text in the development of morphological research methods and data analysis.

■ References

Akhigbe, A., Martin, A.D., and Newman, M. (2008), 'Risk Shifts Following Sarbanes–Oxley: Influences of Disclosure and Governance', *Financial Review*, 43(4), 383.

Allison, K. (2006), 'Hewlett-Packard takes soft approach', 15 August ft.com, at <http://www.ft.com/cms/s/2/a1209678–2ca8–11db-9845–0000779e2340.html> accessed June 2009.

Allison, K. and Waters, R. (2007), 'Hewlett-Packard comes back fighting', 30 April ft.com, at <http://www.ft.com/cms/s/0/ba28038a-f6b6–11db-9812–000b5df10621.html> accessed June 2009.

Amoore, L. (2000), 'International Political Economy and the "Contested Firm" ', *New Political Economy*, 5(2), 183–204.

Barney, J.B. (1991), 'Firm Resources and Sustained Competitive Advantage', *Journal of Management*, 17(1), 99–120.

Bawden, T. (2007), 'Screw tightens on a booming industry', *The Times*, 17 February, 59.

Boulton, J. and Allen, P. (2007), 'Complexity perspective', in Jenkins, M. and Ambrosini, V. (eds) (2007), *Advanced Strategic Management*, Basingstoke: Palgrave Macmillan, 215–234.

Bourgeois III, L.J. (1984), 'Strategic management and determinism', *Academy of Management Review*, 9(4), 586–596.

British Quality Foundation (BQF) (2009), several articles on Haier accessed from <http://www.bqf.org.uk/innovation/tag/haier/> and < http://www.inunisono.com/news.asp?id=281&Page=4>, June 2009.

Budworth, D. (2007), 'How to spot the top of the market', *The Sunday Times*, 25 February, 3.

Bumiller, E. (2002), 'Corporate conduct: The President; Bush Signs Bill Aimed at Fraud In Corporations', 31 July, at <http://query.nytimes.com/gst/fullpage.html?res=9C01E0D91E38F932A05754C0A9649C8B63&sec=&spon=&pagewanted=1> accessed March 2009.

Chia, R. and Holt, R. (2006), 'Strategy as practical coping—a Heideggerian perspective', *Organization Studies*, 27(5), 635–655.

Coyle, G. (2004), *Practical strategy: structured tools and techniques*, London: Prentice-Hall.

Cummings, S. (2007), 'Shifting foundations: redrawing strategic management's military heritage', *Critical perspectives on international business*, 3(1), 41–62.

Douglas, M. (2008), 'United States: the year in Bankruptcy: 2007: Part 1', <http://www.mondaq.com/article.asp?articleid=58228>

Farjoun, M. (2002), 'Towards an organic perspective on strategy', *Strategic Management Journal*, 23, 561–594.

Flores-Fillol, R. and Moner-Colonques, R. (2007), 'Strategic formation of airline alliances', *Journal of Transport Economics and Policy*, 41(3), 427.

Forum for the Future (2004), 'Innovation and Sustainability', at <http://www.forumforthefuture.org/files/Innovationforsd.pdf> accessed March 2009.

Freeman, R.E. (1984), *Strategic Management: A stakeholder approach*, Boston, MA: Pitman.

Fried, I. and Kanellos, M. (2001), 'Hewlett family opposes Compaq deal', 6 November CNet news, at <http://news.cnet.com/Hewlett-family-opposes-Compaq-deal/2100-1003_3-275466.html>.

Fried, I. and Kawamoto, D. (2002), 'FTC gives gives HP-Compaq the go ahead', 6 March CNet news, at <http://news.cnet.com/2100-1001-853709.html?tag=txt>.accessed June 2009.

Fu X., Lijesen, M., and Oum T.H. (2006), 'An Analysis of Airport Pricing and Regulation in the Presence of Competition Between Full Service Airlines and Low Cost Carriers', *Journal of Transport Economics*, 40(3), 425.

Grant, R.M. (2008), *Competitive Strategy Analysis*, Sixth edition, Oxford: Blackwell.

—— (2008b), 'Raisio Group and the Benecol Launch', in *Cases to accompany Contemporary Strategy Analysis*, Grant R.M. (ed), Sixth edition, Oxford: Blackwell, 163–184.

—— (2008c), 'Wal-Mart Stores Inc., 2007', in ibid, 57–76.

Hamel, G. and Prahalad, C.K. (2002), 'Competing for the Future' in Henry, J and Mayle, D. (2002), *Managing Innovation and Change*, London: Sage, 23–35.

Hansard (1979), RB–211 Development costs, at <http://hansard.millbanksystems.com/written_answers/1980/may/12/rb211-engine> accessed August 2009.

Helfat, C.E., Peteraf, M.A., Finkelstein, S., Mitchell, W., Singh, H., Teece, D., and Winter S.G. (2006), *Dynamic Capabilities: Understanding Strategic Change in Organizations*, Oxford: Wiley–Blackwell.

Hoskisson, R.E., Hitt, M.A., and Yiu, D. (1999), 'Theory and research in strategic management: Swings of a pendulum', *Journal of Management*, 25(3), 417–456.

Ice, J.W. (2007), 'Strategic intent: a key to business strategy development and culture change', *Organization Development Journal*, 25(4), 169.

ICIS (2000), 'Raisio faces disappointing Benecol Sales', at <http://www.icis.com/Articles/2000/01/31/104470/Raisio-Faces-Disappointing-Benecol-Sales.html> accessed March 2009.

Inunisono (2008), article on Haier accessed from <http://www.inunisono.com/news.asp?id=281&Page=4>, June 2009.

Jackson, S. (2007), 'Military strategy perspective', in Jenkins, M. and Ambrosini, V. (eds) (2007), *Advanced Strategic Management*, Basingstoke: Palgrave Macmillan, 30–47.

Jankowicz, A.D. (1995) *Business Research Projects*, Second edition, London: Chapman & Hall.

Jenkins, M. and Ambrosini, V. (2007), *Advanced Strategic Management*, Basingstoke: Palgrave Macmillan.

Karnani, A.G. (2008), 'Controversy: The essence of strategy', *Business Strategy Review*, 19(4), 28–34.

Kawamoto, D. (2002), 'Walter Hewlett speaks out', 13 March, CNet news at <http://news.cnet.com/2100–1001–858499.html?tag=txt> accessed June 2009.

Krazit, T. (2006), 'HP revels in Fiorina's vision, Hurd's discipline', 28 August CNet news, at <http://news.cnet.com/HP-revels-in-Fiorinas-vision%2C-Hurds-discipline/2100–1003_3–6109896.html?tag=mncol> accessed June 2009.

LaMonica, M. (2004), 'Merrill Lynch to HP—time for a break up', 7 June CNet news, at <http://news.cnet.com/Merrill-Lynch-to-HP-Time-for-a-breakup/2100–1014_3–5227760.html?tag=mncol;txt> accessed June 2009.

—— (2005), 'Fiorina steps down at HP', 9 February. CNet news, at <http://news.cnet.com/Fiorina-steps-down-at-HP/2100–1014_3–5568951.html?tag=mncol> accessed June 2009.

Lawton, T.C. (1995), 'Technology and the new diplomacy: the creation and control of EC industrial policy, with special reference to semiconductors', EUI PhD thesis.

Levy, D. (1994), 'Chaos theory and strategy: Theory, application, and managerial implications', *Strategic Management Journal*, 15(S2), 167–178.

Mantere, S. and Sillince, J.A.A. (2007), 'Strategic intent as a rhetorical device', *Scandinavian Journal of Management*, 23, 406–423.

Martin, M.J.C. (1994), 'Managing innovation in technology based firms', Chichester: Wiley–IEEE.

McGrath, R.C. and MacMillan, I.C. (2000), *The Entrepreneurial Mindset*, Cambridge, MA: Harvard Business School Press.

Mintzberg, H., Ahlstrand, B., and Lampel, J. (1998), *Strategic Safari*, London: Prentice-Hall.

Mitchell, R.K., Agle, B.R., and Wood, D.J. (1997), 'Toward a theory of stakeholder identification and salience: Defining the principle of who and what really counts', *Academy of Management Review*, 22(4), 853–886.

Musil, S. (2005), 'Week in review: Fiorina gets the boot', 11 February CNet news, accessed at <http://news.cnet.com/Week-in-review-Fiorina-gets-the-boot/2100–1083_3–5572068.html?tag=mncol> accessed June 2009.

Nag, R., Hambrick, D.C., and Chen, M.-J. (2007), 'What is strategic management really? Inductive derivation of a consensus definition of the field', *Strategic Management Journal*, 28, 935–955.

Nelson, R.R. and Winter, S.G. (1982), *An Evolutionary Theory of Economic Change*, Cambridge, MA: Belknap Press/Harvard University Press.

Nonaka, I. and Takeuchi, H. (1995), *The Knowledge Creating Company: How Japanese companies created the dynamics of Innovation*, New York: Oxford University Press.

Pascale, R.T. (1988), 'The Honda Effect', in Quinn, J.B., Mintzberg, H., and James, R.M. (1998) (eds), *Strategy Process: Concepts, contexts and cases*, Upper Saddle River, NJ: Prentice Hall, 104–114.

Penrose, E. (1959), *The theory of the growth of the firm*, Oxford: Oxford University Press.

Phelan, S.E. and Lewin, P. (2002), 'Arriving at a strategic theory of the firm', *International Journal of Management Reviews*, 2(4), 305–323.

Phelan, S.E., Ferreira, M., and Salvador, R. (2002), 'The first twenty years of the *Strategic Management Journal*', *Strategic Management Journal*, 23, 1161–1168.

Pitfield, D.E. (2005), 'Some Speculations and Empirical Evidence on the Oligopolistic Behaviour of Competing Low-Cost Airlines', *Journal of Transport Economics and Policy*, 39(3), 379.

Porter, M.E. (1980), *Competitive Strategy Techniques for Analysing Industries and Competitors*, New York: Free Press.

—— (1990), *The Competitive Advantage of Nations*, New York: Free Press.

Powell, T.C. (2002), 'The philosophy of strategy', *Strategic Management Journal*, 23, 873–880.

Rodriguez, A.-R. and Ruiz-Navarro, J. (2004), 'Changes in the Intellectual structure of strategic management research: a bibliometric study of the *Strategic Management Journal*—1980–2000', *Strategic Management Journal*, 25, 981–1004.

Staton-Reinstein, R. (2008), 'The Rights and Wrongs of Strategic Planning', *Security: For Buyers of Products, Systems & Services*, 45(7), 34–36.

Stonehouse, G. (2004), *Global and transnational business strategy and management*, Chichester: Wiley.

Strange, S. (1988), *States and markets*, New York: Blackwell.

Strange, S. and Stopford, J.S. (1991), *Rival States: Rival Firms—competition for world market shares*, Cambridge: Cambridge University Press.

Takahashi, D. (2008), 'XBox 360 defects: An inside history of Microsoft's video games console woes', VentureBeat, at <http://venturebeat.com/2008/09/05/xbox-360-defects-an-inside-history-of-microsofts-video-game-console-woes/> accessed March 2009.

Utterback, J.M. (1996), *Mastering the dynamics of innovation*, Cambridge, MA: Harvard Business School.

Utterback, J.M. and Abernathy, W.J. (1975), 'A dynamic model of process and product innovation', *OMEGA, The International Journal of Management Science*, 3(6), 639–656.

Waters, R. (2006), 'Hurd takes on crucial juggling act at HP', 13 September ft.com, at <http://www.ft.com/cms/s/0/eff0780a-42c3-11db-8dc3-0000779e2340.html?nclick_check=1> accessed June 2009.

—— (2006b), 'HP to scrap Fiorina's global operations unit', 21 June ft.com, at <http://www.ft.com/cms/s/2/9735a936-00c1-11db-8078-0000779e2340.html> accessed June 2009.

Wernerfeld, B. (1984), 'A resource-based view of the firm', *Strategic Management Journal*, 2(5), 171–180.

Whittington, R. (1993), *What is strategy and does it matter?*, London: Routledge.

 Take your learning further: Online Resource Centre
http://www.oxfordtextbooks.co.uk/orc/grieves/

Visit the Online Resource Centre that accompanies this book to enrich your understanding of this chapter. Explore case study updates and answers to questions, test yourself using an interactive flashcard glossary, and keep up to date with the latest developments in the area.

CHAPTER 5

Building and developing competitive advantage

5.1 Introduction

To understand the nature of change, we have so far considered four chapters focused on *Understanding Change*. This chapter brings Part One of this book to a conclusion. So far we have learned a number of things. First, we learned how the four perspectives discussed in Chapter 1 frame the question of change differently. This results in four pathways to change within which different theories prevail. Whilst each perspective provides a useful framework for change, an effective manager needs to understand the strengths and limitations of each position in order to turn valid and reliable knowledge into action. The second point, which was addressed in Chapter 2, is that all interventions have an ethical component and that failure to recognize this leaves us open to the charge of tyrannical omniscience. Chapter 3 addressed the nature of planned change. This suggested that change is often applied mechanistically or through an approach to enhance learning. Yet despite these differences in approach, critics argue that planned change is inevitably aligned with management, and the consequence of this is the tendency to over-simplify complexity through planning. However, whilst planned change is contentious and highly problematic, it would be wrong to assume that change should not be planned. In Chapter 4 we discovered that strategic change focuses predominantly on an analysis of the external environment. In order to complete Part One of this book, we need to add one further point, which is the subject of this chapter. That is, we must learn how to build internal capability and competence. In this chapter we will:

- address the forces for competitive advantage;
- consider the merits and limitations or re-engineering core processes;
- examine high-performance work systems;
- learn why core competencies are critical to the success of the organization;
- investigate how high-performance systems are developed;
- consider whether building and developing competitive advantage is better served by the concept of the learning organization or by organizational learning;
- understand the link between strategic human resource development and strategic HRM as a vehicle for an organization's development.

Where does innovation and change come from? When Peters and Waterman wrote their best-selling text, *In Search of Excellence* in 1984, they provided what they thought was a formula for organizational success. They argued that high-performing organizations such as Apple, Disney, 3M, and Wal-Mart were successful because they were close to their customers and delivered an excellent product or service. These organizations were said to be innovative and to satisfy their customers because they had a passion for excellence. Despite the growth of an Excellence Movement promoting its brand of corporate success, many leading 'excellent' companies began to underperform, raising doubts about their formula for success.

5.2 Building competitive advantage

5.2.1 Forces for competitive advantage

Competitive advantage often appears to possess a 'magical mixture' of strengths to deal with adversity. We can see examples in public and private sector organizations. The performance of race-car teams, football teams, and Olympic teams illustrates this 'magical mixture' of competences. In such teams managers are responsible for motivating their protégés, managing their perceptions, developing complex skills mixes. This is also true in the boardroom and workplace. Another way of saying this is to suggest that exceptional performance and innovation are nurtured from within by developing internal forces of change. Strategy and tactics cannot work in isolation from the processes that generate performance.

> **❶ Stop and think 5.1**
>
> **Identifying processes that make strategy effective**
>
> Think of an example of strategy from any type of organization. Then consider how you would implement this by identifying the key processes required to make the change effective.

There appear to be three forces for change that enable organizations to build competitive advantage. These are:

1. Seeking to discover, experimenting, and developing new opportunities.
2. Designing the organization to exploit strategic advantages.
3. Developing procedures for embedding organizational learning.

Being innovative is a matter of expectation and perception, and appears to occur when people perceive a need to initiate change. For example, people might identify a missed opportunity by spotting a gap in the market. This is reinforced by a will to act and become creative. Innovative practice therefore requires a structure to deliver change. In this regard innovative practice can be encouraged by:

1. Using technology to improve an organization's performance or to enhance knowledge and skills. In other words, technology can enable distinctive competences to be employed effectively to increase market share, develop new markets, or liaise with customers or clients.
2. Developing reward systems to enhance required core competencies that support professional practice.
3. Enhancing or changing value systems to manage expectations and to empower those involved.

Developing imaginative people is what Daft (1998) calls 'corporate entrepreneurship'. Formally, this requires 'creative departments and new venture teams' facilitated by 'idea champions, which go by a variety of names, including advocate, intrapreneur, or change agent' (Daft, 1998 :10). Such champions, accordingly, usually come in two types:

> The *technical or product champion* is the person who generates or adopts and develops an idea for a technological innovation and is devoted to it, even to the extent of risking position or prestige. The *management champion* acts as a supporter and sponsor to shield and promote an idea within the organization. The management champion sees the potential application and has the prestige and authority to get it a fair hearing and to allocate resources to it.
>
> (Daft, 1998: 11)

The twentieth century was the age of mechanization. This was the age that became dominated by the metaphors of modernity or modernism, in which the concept of the machine came to symbolize progress through the application of technology. As a historical epoch the twentieth century had its fair share of turbulence: two world wars, a catastrophic banking crisis at the end of the 1920s, and industrial relations conflicts, but what so far appears to be characteristic of the twenty-first century is the lack of certainty in the application of science and technology as the solution to social problems. What we have learned is that the application of science and technology is not neutral. It is mediated by power. The application of management practice to organizations is also political and we now know enough, at least, to reject the scientific blueprint of scientific management and the certainty that it, along with classical management more generally, offered for the design of organizations. For this reason the twenty-first century appears to be characterized so far by the metaphors of turbulence, unpredictability, just-in-time, and flexibility.

We have seen how strategic management provides an external focus by forcing us to think about powerful forces that impact on the organization. In this chapter we will consider the arguments that suggest that in internal organizational focus is the means to competitive advantage.

As we noted in Chapter 4, Porter's Five Forces of competitive advantage is a tool for identifying industries and organizations that have erected significant barriers to entry into the markets they control. With such control it would be reasonable to assume that to predict high-performing organizations would be relatively easy. However, this does not appear to be the case, as Pfeffer (2002) has pointed out:

> Conventional wisdom then (and even now) would have you begin by selecting the right industries. After all, 'not all industries offer equal opportunity for sustained profitability, and the inherent profitability of its industry is one essential ingredient in determining the profitability of a firm'.
>
> (Pfeffer, 2002: 61, quoting Porter, 1985)

Thus Porter's five competitive forces should enable us to conclude that those that have maximum control of their market should be the highest performers. After all, they can restrict entry to the market with economies of scale, control prices from suppliers, and exact benefits from patent protection. As Pfeffer points out, the reverse is the case. The five top-performing firms from 1972 to 1992 'were characterized by massive competition and horrendous losses, widespread bankruptcy, virtually no barriers to entry' (Pfeffer, 2002: 61):

> The top five stocks, and their percentage returns, were (in reverse order): Plenum Publishing (with a return of 15,689%), Circuit City (a video and appliance retailer: 16,410%), Tyson Foods (a poultry producer: 18,118%), Wal-Mart (a discount chain: 19,807%) and Southwest Airlines (21,775%).

Rather than looking for external factors, the counter-intuitive argument is to look instead for internal forces that drive change. These could include the quality of leadership, the extent to which staff are motivated, the special skills or qualities that employees bring to their organizations. In reality, a complex mixture of these items is responsible for competitive advantage. These are often referred to as core competencies. These are special, unique qualities that an organization possesses at a particular point in time. The following case example illustrates the difficulties experienced by one manager faced with implementing changes required by strategic imperatives constructed by senior managers in the company. It illustrates how executive decisions based on analyses of external forces may not be sufficient to deal with threats from competitors who can compete more effectively on price. A refocusing on quality as a strategic advantage can only work effectively if the company thinks more carefully about its internal forces for change.

» Case example 5.1

The Quality Manager speaks out

The Strategic Planning Committee developed the new vision and mission to lay the foundation for continued growth and success and to provide direction for the future. What the senior team seem to have difficulty understanding is that stating a policy is easy. Everyone recognizes the need for shareholder value but the real issue is how to achieve it. The company's vision is to be the leader in providing the best value in articulated dump-trucks to customers. Of course, providing best value does not mean top-of-the-line products for every customer. Instead, it means providing the right product for each customer. The strategy is aiming to achieve $35 billion in sales and revenue within three years. Nevertheless, with prices not expected to increase, their margin improvement will have to come from cost control. The company must reduce costs by eliminating rework (that is, items that failed quality control tests being remade to meet the customer's specification), negotiate a relaxation of demarcation (that is, union rules governing who is allowed to undertake a particular job), and of overtime rota rules. »

>> As I said, it's one thing stating these objectives but it's another thing achieving them. The company has new challenges ahead in the form of cost pressures, increased competition, growth, and distribution challenges. The strategy is to continually increase shareholder value by aggressively pursuing growth and profit opportunities that leverage their engineering, manufacturing, distribution, information and knowledge management, and financial services expertise. Whilst it is common practice for middle managers to vocally support the strategy implemented by the senior team, the reality on the production line is that continual decisions have to be made in relation to shipping dates and quality control. As quality manager I have to ask myself 'do I ship this to achieve my objective of on-time delivery even though the quality could be better?' Trying to manage a 'right first time' production process into a company where 'firefighting' has been the norm and in which 'getting the job done and out of the door' is paramount provides a curious contradiction. There is little evidence of root-cause analysis of why things are not done 'right first time'. For example, a few of the causes are inventory inaccuracy, with a long list of suppliers who fail to deliver the right quantity and quality at the right time.

We need to change in order to survive and careful strategic planning can address these issues but only by developing and rewarding people, creating the conditions for innovation, encouraging teamwork, and so on. What we lack is an environment that embraces continual learning and improvement. The HR department has arranged several training sessions for employees. Whilst on the course, everyone agrees that a change in working practices is needed, but when they return to their working environment they revert to their old attitudes and practices. This is the trouble with training people from a strategy. To change the mindset we require employees to take control of the problems and identify the solutions. We need to create a culture that pays more attention to the people who manage the process.

5.2.2 Re-engineering the business

One methodology for designing innovation into the business strategy is Business Process Re-engineering (BPR). BPR is based on redesigning processes rather than functions. Because BPR generally requires an organic structure, it challenges vertical bureaucratic management systems. BPR emerged in the writing of Hamel and Prahalad, who challenged managers to:

Look into the faces of your colleagues, and consider their ambitions and fears. Look toward the future, and ponder your company's ability to shape that future in the years and decades to come.

Now ask yourself: do senior managers in my company have a clear and shared understanding of how the industry may be different ten years from now? Is my company's point of view about the future unique among competitors?

(Hamel and Prahalad, 2002: 23)

When Hamel and Prahalad first proposed the idea of BPR they were concerned to address what they saw as managers who were too focused on the urgent and immediate rather than important longer-term business-development opportunities that require detailed attention to the structural architecture of the future. Consequently they raised three questions for managers to answer:

1. What percentage of a manager's time is spent on external rather than internal issues—for example, on understanding the implications of a particular new technology instead of debating corporate overhead allocations?

2. Of this time spent looking outward, how much is spent considering how the world might change in five or ten years rather than worrying about winning the next big contract or responding to a competitor's pricing move?

3. Of the time devoted to looking outward and forward, how much time is spent working with colleagues to build a deeply shared, well-tested perspective on the future as opposed to a personal and idiosyncratic view?

Experience suggested that the time spent looking forward to building a collective view of the future is minimal. Commitment to the new core competencies required for the future is rarely given the attention it deserves since this requires awareness of organizational redesign in order to identify new pioneering product concepts, strategic alliances, development programmes, long-term regulatory initiatives, and so forth. What lies at the heart of these questions is a view that managers are not truly in control of their future because 'the urgent drives out the important' and 'the future is left largely unexplored' with 'the capacity to act, rather than to think and imagine' becoming 'the sole measure of leadership' (Hamel and Prahalad, 2002: 24). The acute admonition of managers failing to build the future is summed up by the remark that:

> any company that is a bystander on the road to the future will watch its structure, values, and skills become progressively less attuned to industry realities. Such a discrepancy between the pace of industrial change and the pace of company change gives rise to the need for organizational transformation.

(Ibid.: 25)

The attempt to get managers to address their futures requires consideration of who the future customers will be, how they will be reached, and who the future competitors are likely to be. BPR can be described as design for innovation but it pays little attention to the dynamics of change and to the core human processes that underlie successful change strategies. Furthermore, it does not pay sufficient attention to identifying the skills or capabilities that will make an organization unique in the future. It is to this last point that we now turn.

5.3 High-performance work systems

5.3.1 The resource-based view of the firm and the identification of internal competencies

What are the high-performance practices? The resource-based view of the firm suggests that 'distinctive human resource practices help to create unique competences that differentiate products and services and, in turn, drive competitiveness' (Cappelli and Crocker-Hefter, 1996). Others, such as Barney (1991a, 1995), argue that sustained competitive advantage results from the acquisition and effective use of bundles of distinctive resources that competitors cannot imitate.

The resource-based view of the firm suggests that organizational performance is influenced by an organization's resources and capabilities (Barney, 1991b; Roos, 1996; Wernerfelt, 1995). This view requires an awareness of how we might redesign to make intangible resources such as experience, knowledge, and skills the source of competitive advantage. One aspect fundamental to this is the related concept of core competencies (Prahalad and Hamel, 1990), which emphasizes that critical social and learned competencies might be the most important intangible assets that can lead to sustainable competitive advantage.

---

❶ Stop and think 5.2

Tangible and intangible competencies

Think of an organization you are familiar with and make a list of the tangible resources (these are, essentially, their material assets). Then identify the intangible resources. Finally state whether you think any of these are unique. Explain your views.

The resource-based view of the firm has therefore influenced the idea of internal competencies, arguing that organizations must develop capability through the application of knowledge and through continuous organizational learning and development in the attempt to produce skills or competencies that are difficult to repeat. An early review of the TQM literature suggested that the key principles of the resource-based view of the firm are related to performance through a customer focus, continuous improvement, and teamwork (Dean and Bowen, 1994). Each of these is implemented through a series of practices, such as collecting customer information and analysing processes, supported by the use of specific quality management techniques such as team building and Pareto analysis. Other writers on TQM add employee involvement and senior management commitment to these in listing the 'basic principles'. The argument is that managers must focus on the future and, in doing so, they must identify the core competencies they require. Others have taken a different road but reached similar conclusions. For example, during the 1980s various researchers in the social and behavioural sciences—particularly work psychologists, organizational sociologists, and some from the OD tradition influenced by contingency theory—investigated a variety of work practices that reduced alienation and improved organizational performance. These included employee involvement and empowerment systems, job redesign, sociotechnical systems, team-focused practices, quality management production systems, self-managed teams, Quality Circles, flatter organizational structures, and flexible technologies. More recently such initiatives have come to be referred to as high-performance work systems (HPWS). The more recent research on these systems focuses on the resource-based view of the firm and the identification of core competencies.

5.3.2 The human aspects of intangible resources

Commitment to an organization appears to have a significant correlation with high performance. A recent study by Whetten and Cameron (2004) indicated that, of 986 firms investigated in their study of major US industries, those that adopted high-commitment practices demonstrated significant benefits compared to those that did not. These included reductions in employee turnover of at least 7 percent, increases in profits of 1 percent per employee, higher stock market valuations, noticeable increases in sales per employee compared to firms that had less effective high-commitment practices. As Sambrook and Roberts (2005) have indicated, other studies of German firms representing ten industrial sectors have produced similar results, leading to the conclusion that effective management is defined by the quality of people-management practices. Using imagination to re-engineer a product in a stable market is very demanding but not impossible, as the following case example illustrates.

❯❯ Case example 5.2

How creative thinking led to improved performance

Spear and Jackson is the UK's oldest tool manufacturer. Its saw division was unprofitable and losing money. Consequently, the company called in consultants who investigated the behaviour of tradesmen in the industry. What they discovered was that joiners, on average, replaced their traditional wood-saws every two to four weeks, but were also very loyal to their preferred brand. This presented a dilemma: how to improve profitability without reducing price? The consultants discovered that three things were important to joiners. These were quality, brand, and price. The difficulty was that price was already low, with a saw selling at £5 and other brands able to compete on price. An approach had to be found to improve the performance of the loss-making part of the business.

A solution emerged when the company's research and development team produced a wood-saw that both made cutting more efficient and accurate, and had a longer life than conventional saws. The product, called the Predator, was therefore launched ❯❯

> ❯❯ at nearly twice the price of the old saw (£9.99) and the intention was to persuade existing and new customers that it was worth paying a lot more for a better product. In order to enhance this innovation the company offered a money-back guarantee to persuade customers of complete satisfaction. Within 16 weeks of the product being launched, the first-year target of 30,000 sales had been exceeded almost seven-fold. That is, 12 months later the company had sold 200,000[1] of its new saws. Furthermore, because demand for the product had been exceptional, a further four product types were added to the Predator range. The example illustrates that price is not the only factor in persuading more customers to buy the product. Innovative ideas were applied to an improved product and this persuaded customers of the advantages. Creativity and imagination were therefore central to product development.
>
> [1] *The Times*, 24 July 2006.

Central to the debate over whether people are critical resources is the view that organizational commitment is at the heart of that process. However, this must be designed into the organization by establishing relevant human resource practices at the strategic level. The recent focus on strategic alignment with HRM has been a fruitful line of research for some. According to Huselid (1995), the argument that strategic HRM can demonstrate efficacy in relation to efficiency and effectiveness is located in Wright and McMahan's (1992) reformulation of Barney's (1991b) resource-based theory of the firm. In this Barney asserts that:

- HR must add value to the firm's production processes.
- The skills the firm seeks must be rare.
- The combined human capital investments of an organization must not be easily imitated.
- A firm's human resources must not be subject to replacement by technological advances or other substitutes if they are to provide a source of sustainable competitive advantage.

❶ Stop and think 5.3

People are critical resources

What argument might be put to support the claim that people are critical resources? Consider (a) ways that people add value to a product or service and (b) how the actions of individuals might damage the reputation of an organization.

This view sees strategic HRM as the critical mediating link between external forces and the outcomes experienced by customers. This is illustrated in Figure 5.1.

Figure 5.1 Strategic HRM as mediator between the external environment and an organization's outputs

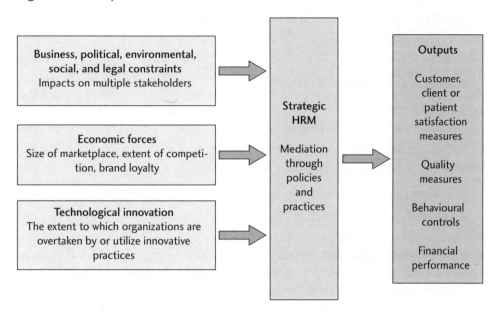

Strategic HRM is seen as a high-performance work practice, which is demonstrated by the resource-based view of the firm, since the 'right' bundles of practices contribute to organizational effectiveness by ensuring that internal competencies provide advantageous strategic positioning. Others, such as Barney (1991a, 1995), argue that sustained competitive advantage results from the acquisition and effective use of bundles of distinctive resources that competitors cannot imitate.

There is a difference between distinctive and reproducible capabilities: the former are characteristics that are difficult to replicate by competitors and the latter can be bought or created by any company with reasonable management skills and financial resources. We might therefore note that, whilst many technical capabilities are reproducible, human capabilities are more dynamic since they reflect 'the capacity of a firm to renew, augment and adapt its core competencies over time' (Teece, Pisano, and Shuen, 1997: 512). This raises a key question about how distinctive capabilities come to exist. Since technical expertise is relatively easy to reproduce, competitive success must result from developing and cultivating core competencies over time. The question then arises as to which are the right bundles of practices to develop.

It has been argued that there are ten core factors that contribute to high performance (Hiltrop, 2005):

1. Reliance on internal recruitment and promotion.
2. Emphasis on teamwork.
3. Strategic career systems.
4. Openness and information sharing.
5. Decentralization and delegation of authority.
6. Concern for people in the management philosophy.
7. Recognition and reward for high performance.
8. Rewards for skills and competencies.
9. Training and development of employees.
10. A longer-term focus in HR decisions.

Hiltrop (2005) has argued that such factors need to be organized by following an organizational capability model proposed by Ulrich and Lake (1990), which establishes internal structures and processes that influence its members to create organization-specific competencies and thus enable the business to adapt to changing customer and strategic needs by:

1. attracting and retaining talent;
2. developing and growing talent;
3. utilizing and mobilizing talent;
4. knowing how to innovate and manage change.

Sustaining this requires ensuring a high consistency between the organization's strategy and HR practices, creating a culture of openness, teamwork, and delegation, building HR capability into the role and mindset of every manager, and by creating opportunities for organizational learning supported by individual coaching and mentoring (Hiltrop, 2005).

5.4 The learning organization or organizational learning?

The focus on internal qualities may result in product or service development, sustainable development, and problem solving, but it is essentially the management of intangible resources that is the key to improvement. The characteristics of the twenty-first century—turbulence, unpredictability, just-in-time, and flexibility—require organizational learning rather than training. This is because organizations need to anticipate change much faster than their twentieth-century counterparts.

5.4.1 The learning organization

Arguments for and against the concept of the learning organization revolve around two central premises:

1. The learning organization is an ideal worth striving for.
2. Systems theory provides a sound theoretical underpinning.

Premise 1 involves a variety of definitions. An early definition of the learning organization suggested that 'learning organizations are characterized by total employee involvement in a process of collaboratively conducted, collectively accountable change directed towards shared values or principles' (Watkins and Marsick 1992: 118). But what does total employee involvement look like? And, for that matter, to what extent can values be shared by all? An alternative approach was suggested by Pedler, Boydell, and Burgoyne, who stated that the learning organization (company) is an 'organization that facilitates the learning of all its members and continually transforms itself' (1991: 1). This comes close to persuading us that it is a worthy goal to which we should subscribe. However, there are two obvious drawbacks with this definition. First is the problem that only certain types of organizations, such as golf clubs, have members. Unless we work in a cooperative, there is little sense in which most people could confirm their egalitarian identity. The second problem is with a recommendation for how we might structure an organization to achieve learning organization status. This raises a dilemma, since it is not possible to answer this conundrum because if we could identify a structure, then we are faced with the criticism levelled at classical management theory. That is, that a blueprint for designing an organization contradicts the principles of continual transformation. More recently, authors such as Garvin (1993) have suggested that the exponents of the learning organization concept need to satisfy three objectives in order to create a tangible result we can subscribe to. These are:

1. A clear definition.
2. Practical operational advice that managers can use.
3. Tools and assessment instruments to measure their achievements.

The difficulty here is that each of these requirements dissolves into subjectivity. That is, for managers to call their organization a learning organization is not something the rest of us would find plausible unless each of these issues were demonstrated incontestably. Even for advocates like Garvin the learning organization concept 'has proved to be elusive'. However plausible it is for consultants to construct concepts such as the learning organization for their clients, when academics do so they require clear, unambiguous definitions that their academic colleagues can test, probe, and contest. When this does not happen we end up with a barren discourse because it does not possess a shared language. Furthermore, without a shared language we end up in a relativistic diatribe. To explore this analogy further, it is like walking with a man in an open field who all of a sudden stops and says that you have now reached his house. Although there are no physical structures to recognize, he then adds that the next time you come this way you will know where to find him. If he means 'find him physically', then you have a problem because it is unlikely you will come upon the exact location a second time. If he means 'find him metaphorically', then he may be referring to a spiritual journey. Either way he expects your perception to match his. Ultimately, the problem we have is one of linguistic relativity; and this is the problem with the learning organization.

The relativity of the concept has been outlined in a recent paper by Jamali and Sidani (2008). This failure to arrive at a consensus is not for lack of effort on the part of empirical researchers. As Jamali and Sidani point out, the 'Complete Learning Organization Benchmark' was a comprehensive diagnostic instrument constructed by Mayo and Lank (1994). This was followed by Rosengarten's (1995) meta-analysis of 30 approaches to developing learning organizations; Nevis, DeBella, and Gould (1995), who sought to understand organizations as learning systems; and Sarala and Sarala's (1996) diagnostic tool for evaluating the learning organization. Watkins and Marsick (1998) identified seven core dimensions of the learning organization, whilst the instrument produced by Pedler, Boydell, and Burgoyne (1997) identified eleven dimensions that were grouped into five categories. Later research by Griego, Geroy, and Wright (2000) refined earlier diagnostic instruments, whilst Armstrong and Foley (2003) produced an instrument that investigated four core dimensions of a learning organization (see Jamali and Sidani (2008) for a full account of these instruments).

Despite this variation in studies seeking to measure the learning organization, there remains a persistent belief that the parameters can be found. This appears to be futile because of the variety of potential intervening variables that can intrude on the realization of the concept. For example, Maria's (2003) study suggests that learning culture impacts on innovation, whilst Dymock's (2003) study of the development of a learning environment is itself based on trust, openness, empowerment, and self-managed teams. This reveals the myriad of interweaving variables and potential barriers. The difficulty of identifying a useful assessment methodology results from the empirical underpinning. Nevertheless, such writers recognize the intangibility of the concept but wish to retain it as a concept that all organizations should strive to endorse. These are mythical templates that 'real organizations could attempt to emulate' (Easterby-Smith, Burgoyne, and Araujo, 1999: 2). In this sense the learning organization is an ideal, 'towards which organizations have to evolve in order to be able to respond to the various pressures' faced by them (Finger and Brand, 1999: 136). Whilst academics may feel slightly uncomfortable with the impenetrable impossibility of defining the learning organization, consultants, in contrast, can make a living from selling intangibility. They do this by focusing on creating a commercially attractive template and presenting it to clients.

Premise 2—that systems theory provides a sound theoretical underpinning—owes much to the work of Senge, who has undoubtedly done more than most to underpin the concept of the learning organization with a rigorous methodology. Paradoxically, there is a tendency in the learning organization literature to present his work as a series of clichéd aphorisms. He might even be guilty of this himself, having made statements to suggest that a learning organization is an organization that 'can create the results it truly desires'. It is a place 'where people continually expand their capacity to create the results they truly desire, where new and expansive patterns of thinking are nurtured, where collective aspiration is set free, and where people are continually learning to see the whole (reality) together' (Senge, 1990: 3).

This academic underpinning owes much to the work of Forester's systems dynamics programme at MIT in the late 1990s (Jackson, 2003). As Jackson points out, Forester's interest was in the ability of complex systems to develop learning potential. This meant that managers needed to learn how complex systems worked. Indeed, we can see the possibilities with flight simulators, since learning is derived from reflecting on our responses to stimuli presented to us. The flight simulator is, of course, a physical structure or environment in which we learn how to fly. Using this analogy enables us to think of organizations similarly: as learning laboratories. The real advantage of systems dynamics lay in the construction of feedback loops to facilitate learning. If, therefore, managers of organizations could learn how to understand their own systems dynamics, then they could understand the complex relationships and underlying properties of their own systems.

Senge's work on reinforcing and balancing feedback loops was subsequently applied to organizational contexts. This appeared to demonstrate the potential to model sophisticated social systems and seemed to account for delays in feedback resulting usually from contradictions in the systems dynamics. In this way, he argued, it was possible to develop archetypes showing regular patterns of behaviour (Jackson, 2003). The learning organization was Senge's attempt to get managers to construct archetypes of behaviour that might have functional and dysfunctional consequences for organizations. This was intended to be a long-term goal and he appeared to criticize simplistic models and frameworks that tended to be applied to complex systems. Managers therefore needed to appreciate the greater complexity inherent in systems dynamics. Thus, he argued that

> the systems viewpoint is generally oriented toward the long-term view. That's why delays and feedback loops are so important. In the short term, you can often ignore them; they're inconsequential. They only come back to haunt you in the long term.

(Senge, 1990: 92)

If we examine the argument that managers and work colleagues should become more knowledgeable in their application of systems theory, then we can see a superficial plausibility in it. Thus, by learning about interrelationships through feedback loops that illustrate causality, we reflect more on the processes of change and, in particular, the time delays it takes to change things. The difficulty with this argument is that we can never be sure of causality. Furthermore, as Senge argues, it takes a long time to recognize the effects of relationships. Clearly, the longer they last, the less certain we can be about intervening variables that obscure causal relationships.

Systems thinking is only one of the five disciplines upon which a learning organization is built. The others are 'personal mastery', 'mental models', 'shared vision', and 'team learning'. Essentially, these appear to be little more than aphorisms designed to put a structure around the systems dynamics. Thus we read that the idea of mental mastery is the formulation of a coherent picture of the results people most desire to attain as individuals, and to learn how to cultivate the tension between vision and reality. In a later book Senge *et al* (1999) illustrate this tension with a diagram of an elastic band. Similarly, mental models are said to reflect enquiry skills enabling reflection. This represents a rather simplified version of Argyris and Schön's (1996) discussion of flawed mental models produced by gaps between espoused theory and theory in use.

The argument that the fifth discipline is the culmination of systems thinking mixed with Organizational Development initiatives reaches its fruition in *The Dance of Change*. Here, Senge *et al* argue that the methodology of the fifth discipline is able to achieve 'profound change'. Unfortunately, the book offers little more than conservative conventional wisdom and fails to reveal any awareness of the real behavioural dynamics of working life. This is because the work is based on a single underlying organic metaphor that is ultimately driven by assumptions of consensus, order, and stability.

Systems theory has led to the view that a sophisticated model can be built and applied. However, whilst Senge has argued for a holistic model of learning to provide feedback loops, this rests upon an assumption that sophisticated modelling will, in itself, bring about a learning system that can be called the learning organization. Unfortunately most systems models are constructed following a predominantly conservative-functionalist approach to conceptualizing their subject matter.

5.4.2 The problem with the learning organization concept

Both premises cited above suggest that the concept of the learning organization appears to be fundamentally flawed. There are a number of reasons for this. The first reason is that there is no practical underpinning framework for a learning organization that we can all agree to. The second reason is that, even if there were a framework, this would constitute a contradiction of continuous innovation and of the very principle of the learning organization. The third reason is the conservative bias underlying the concept.

If this is the ultimate fusion of systems thinking with Organizational Development, then is it the end of the metaphor? Has the underlying discipline of critical social science and ethical values, upon which OD was based, simply become diluted into change aphorisms? Has systems dynamics run its course because it is flawed by the one-dimensional nature of organicism?

The main difficulty with the concept of the learning organization is that it can be an instrument for continual transformation. References in the literature to transforming organizations through learning are naive if all we have to do is guide, influence, and manage these transformations, as Schön implies. This is not simply a theoretical point. Schön's belief that we must invent and develop institutions as learning systems capable of bringing about their own continuing transformation (Schön, 1973: 28) assumes that politics can be managed when wisdom prevails. Unfortunately, empirical evidence suggests the opposite. For example, research by Finger and Brand (1999) reported that it was not possible to transform a bureaucratic organization by learning initiatives alone.

The most critical objection to the learning organization was raised by Salaman and Butler (1994), who state that not only might employees resist organizational learning; the learning organization concept ignores the way that power is exercised, and the behaviours that are rewarded and penalized. Similarly, Weick and Westley (1996) argue that the concepts are contradictory. On the one hand, the concept of organization implies stability, order, and structure, whilst learning, on the other hand, implies disorganization, variety, and change.

If we take this argument to its logical conclusion, we could say that the problem with the learning organization is that it fails to recognize the limitations of its own paradigm. Thus the consensus, inherent in the organic analogy, pretends that the legitimacy of its conceptual language is a universal truth. This discourse depends upon the legitimacy of managerial authority, which is, in turn, a function of maximizing efficiency and effectiveness in the interests of capital. This represents a political interest that raises a much more fundamental problem: for whose interest does the organization exist? For example, voluntary, public sector, and commercial organizations have different motives for their existence. Whilst those who argue for the concept of the learning organization might reject the machine analogy as too controlling, they fail to account for the differences that emerge between organizations, including the most democratic.

The concept of the learning organization ignores the potential 'iron law of oligarchy' outlined by Michels as far back as 1915. For example, how do we deal with the existence of executive and managerial elites who control organizations? Pursuing this point a little further, we might ask how, in a potential scenario that forces managers to reduce labour costs through redundancy, a learning organization would employ the concepts of mental mastery, team learning, or systems thinking to its advantage. The answer, of course, might be to resolve the problem to the mutual satisfaction of all. However, this would require a political decision by management that such a solution favours the interests of the organization. Whilst this is possible, it is by no means inevitable. Owners, managers, employees, shareholders, and stakeholders may often give the appearance of being equivalent but in reality they have different economic interests. The paradox for Senge is that, whilst such different interests could be drawn into his feedback loops, they would contradict the other four concepts of personal mastery. The learning organization concept is naively apolitical, because it assumes that people share the same interests, are not abused by exploitative managers, and are not driven by systems that seek to maximize effort at the expense of rewards.

5.4.3 Organizational learning

In contrast to the learning organization, organizational learning (OL) can be defined. Organizational learning occurs, according to Argyris and Schön (1978; 1996), when individuals within an organization experience a problematic situation and enquire into it on the organization's behalf. A useful way of doing this is to identify barriers to learning in organizations. Organizational learning is based on trust, effective communication, and a sense of collective responsibility (Elliott, Smith, and McGuinness, 2000). Without OL it would not be possible to engage with the creative faculties of individuals, teams, and organizations. Consequently, it would be pointless to engage with the drive to empower individuals in order to maximize their own potential, and thereby the potential to develop the organization from within. Without OL we could not seriously talk about the added value generated by intangible assets and, as a result, management would be back in the darkness of a bygone age when managers followed prescriptive formulae and workers were given blindfolds to constrain the intellect.

Barriers to learning fall within three main categories. These are:

1. *Structural barriers*, such as communication systems, organization structure, and the logistics of operational design.
2. *Cognitive barriers*, such as defensive reasoning.
3. *Social barriers*, such as the methods of working or the relationships between people—although this mainly appears to be between levels of management and the workforce.

Managers should therefore intervene to reduce or eliminate barriers to learning. Structural barriers include an investigation into the effectiveness of systems (managerial, control, technical, political, communication, and human resource systems). Innovation is reduced by bureaucratic procedures when the decision-making process is so time-consuming that it obstructs initiative, or there is little scope for the expression of individuality. The failure to develop new ideas may be related to lack of resources, of expertise, or of empowerment, when people at the lower end of the organization get no involvement until it is too late and ideas appear to be imposed. In one study respondents were asked to identify the statement that most accurately reflected their organization and the extent to which they could relate to a shared vision and mission. They were given two choices: one positive (indicating that they were in control) and the other negative (indicating that the system was in control). Responses were divided evenly. The 50 percent who answered 'it's the system—we have no control' gave three reasons. The first included 'fear', 'threat', and 'discipline', and 'the need to obey' (Grieves, 2006). In such situations, it is not surprising, then, that people saw power and favouritism as a central feature: 'power is centred around a few people—only people with their ear get on'. Furthermore, whilst time can often be seen as a problem—the second reason given: 'it's hectic with people rushing in all directions'—management are occasionally reluctant to discuss major initiatives with the workforce—articulating their reasons such as 'everything was on a need-to-know basis'. Lack of information was the third reason, with employees referring to communications as the 'mushroom model' which resulted in change that was 'forced on employees' and 'done without warning or staff involvement'.

Cognitive barriers should be investigated for attitudes, knowledge, skill, and sensitivity to managing systems and people. The learning environment may also be a limiting factor if it fails to accommodate the relevance of different cognitive styles. The learning environment is an essential component of organizational learning. According to Mumford (1996), human resource professionals who recognize the value of organizational learning should focus on continuous development by identifying how people can work for the long-term success of the organization, know how to develop incremental improvements, and ensure that successes and best practices are embedded in work routines. For Honey and Mumford (1992), diagnosing the interactions that occur in the 'learning environment' requires an examination of four managerial roles:

1. The need to demonstrate enthusiasm for learning through role behaviours.
2. The *provider role*, which seeks to develop opportunities for new learning.
3. The *system builder role* seeks the integration of learning with other systemic processes.
4. The *champion role* seeks to identify change agents who take initiative throughout the organization.

Learning effectiveness depends on the suitability of the environment for learning but should also include the role performance of trainers, instructors, and mentors in creating, sustaining, and encouraging appropriate conditions for learning. The learning environment is therefore significant to the application of technique and to the decision as to the method used in encouraging the development of the learner on a personal journey from ignorance, through to awareness, understanding, commitment, enactment, and reflection (Buckler, 1996). One might argue, therefore, that the essential criteria for effective learning include the environment to facilitate learning, use of the techniques that enable effective learning, and the methods of learning. And, perhaps, we need to think more carefully about the dangers of recruitment and selection criteria in case we end up with a one-dimensional workplace with identical employees.

> **》 Case example 5.3**

How important is diversity to organizational learning?

Advocates of psychometric testing suggest that if we all undertook psychometric tests as part of the recruitment and selection process at work, organizations would be more efficient and effective, because they would be able to identify individuals with personal characteristics best suited to job requirements. Such tests have become very popular and it has been reported that approximately 80 percent of the FTSE Top 100 companies use some form of psychometric testing to recruit staff and to identify suitable candidates for promotion. There are some reasoned arguments in favour of psychometric tests. These are: people with the best personalities are identified for the task and well-balanced people, in particular, are selected for promoted management positions. In theory, this would avoid your worst nightmare: your misanthropic line manager promoted further up the chain of command despite it being common knowledge that he is a megalomaniac with a variety of personality defects. However, there are arguments against. Are such tests in danger of producing typecast performers whose creative flair is reduced because they fit a model of conformity? Consider the case of a gifted mathematician with borderline Asperger's syndrome (autism—defined as a disability) who has underdeveloped social skills. He is not the best of communicators. People known to have Asperger's syndrome include Richard Borcherds, a mathematician who won the Fields Medal in 1998, Bertrand Russell, Alan Turing, Lewis Carroll, Isaac Newton, and Srinivasa Ramanujan. The case of Alan Turing is interesting. Turing worked at the Bletchley Park code-breaking centre during the Second World War. He became renowned for breaking German ciphers and was significant in breaking Enigma. He went on to become the founder of modern computer science. He turned to chemistry and predicted the Belousov–Zhabotinsky reaction, an oscillating chemical reaction that was confirmed in the 1960s.

If any of these people had been subjected to psychometric testing they would possibly have been denied the opportunity to become exemplary individuals, who in turn have helped society by applying their unique talents. There is one simple message for organizational learning: cherish diversity because that is how creativity flourishes.

Social barriers should be investigated for their potential to enhance performance through relationships, motivation, and leadership. One way of doing this is to investigate the gap between corporate ideology and personal mental models. This indicates the degree of commitment. When organizations contain sub-cultures that conflict with strategic objectives, individuals may experience organizational defence routines. For example an early example by Argyris and Schön (1978) sought to demonstrate simple barriers to organizational learning in the form of organizational defence mechanisms. According to Argyris (1993), organizational defence mechanisms are barriers to organizational learning that people put up in stressful situations. Elliott, Smith, and McGuinness (2000) suggest that it is possible to test defensive reasoning by investigating what happens when the conditions that create defensiveness are removed. Research suggests that when individuals work alone under stressful situations they are more likely to display defensiveness when things go wrong (Robinson, 2001). Other examples of defensive reasoning include scapegoating, complacency, clashes of belief systems or ideologies, holding too rigidly to core beliefs, values and assumptions, poor communication (Elliott, Smith, and McGuinness (2000). As Appelbaum and Goransson state: 'Whenever human beings are faced with any issue that contains significant embarrassment or threat, they act in ways that bypass, as best they can, the embarrassment or threat. In order for the bypass to work, it must be covered up' (Appelbaum and Goransson, 1997: 116). Defence routines can be regarded as actions designed to cover up mistakes. The reasons for this include avoidance of embarrassment or avoidance of threat. When individuals resort to such actions they become part of the fabric of everyday life. We often experience defence routines through mixed messages that lead to a range of unintended and counterproductive consequences. Reasons often cited include 'poor change management', 'self-interest', 'blame culture', and 'bullying tactics'.

It is inevitable that managers must confront problems that arise from the interplay of individual behaviours through a concern with group dynamics. From a psychoanalytic perspective it is important to recognize the part that the unconscious and irrational processes play in organizational life. These unconscious processes impact on role effectiveness, group identity, decision making, and political behaviour. They also impact on external relationships with clients and customers (Jaques, 1953; Menzies, 1960; Hirschhorn, 1990). Researchers from this psychoanalytical perspective are concerned to demonstrate dysfunctional behaviours and actions. Following the work of Klein (1975), barriers to learning can be seen to take the form of defensive strategies often related to projection of feelings on to others, denial of aggressive feelings or thoughts, or excessive feelings of hopelessness, depression, or paranoia.

Finally, barriers to learning can be caused by two interrelated factors: organizational culture and communication. As Garavan (1997) points out, authors who include Garvin (1993); McGill, Slocum, and Sei (1992) and Senge (1990) have considered the importance of culture to organizational learning. Although it is difficult to demonstrate how culture affects performance, most authors are agreed that culture is an important determinant of organizational learning and that organizational learning affects performance. Studies of crises have suggested that the relationship between sense making and the development of a safety culture offers important insights into the dynamics of developing effective learning. That is, how to maintain high reliability and/or crisis-preparedness. Bhopal and Chernobyl are cited as examples of barriers to learning, where managers appeared unable to deal with the emotional, informational, and/or cognitive aspects (Elliott, Smith, and McGuinness, 2000). Since culture can be seen as a shared structure of meaning, it is important to identify the barriers to the learning process.

> **❗ Stop and think 5.4**
>
> The learning organization or organizational learning
>
> The discussion so far suggests that the learning organization is a difficult concept to articulate. If you were asked to defend it, what arguments would you make? Once you have done this, defend the argument for organizational learning in preference to the concept of the learning organization.

5.5 Strategic human resource development

Strategic human resource development is central to an organization's progress. It should encourage personal and/or organizational transformations in order to achieve a results-driven approach to change. Gilley, Callahan, and Bierema (2002) argue that 'HRD professionals weaken their organizational image by behaving as though they are in the business of delivering training; their energy is directed toward the number of training courses they deliver and the number of employees they train' (Gilley, Callahan, and Bierema, 2002: 28). Consequently, HRD professionals should not see themselves as attempting to 'fix' employees' shortcomings through remedial training but to develop, cultivate, and nurture their protégés.

This has resulted in the call to challenge activity-based HRD programmes that require HRD practitioners to act as brokers by fitting programmes to the requirements of strategists who are themselves primarily focused on external objectives. This 'clearing house approach' not only 'produces long-term damage to the image and credibility of HRD' (Gilley, Callahan, and Bierema, 2002: 29); it also limits the awareness of developing internal resources as a strategic asset.

By contrast to activity-based HRD programmes, results-driven programmes focus on creating and driving change. Gilley, Callahan, and Bierema (2002) cite several strategies used to develop a proactive approach to developing people as core assets. These are:

1. *Setting strategic direction* by helping business units set long-range strategic goals and develop tactical plans in support of those goals.

2. *Linking learning and change initiatives to business strategy* by ensuring that learning interventions and change initiatives are in concert with business goals and objectives.

3. *Enhancing leadership development* by helping to ensure that current leaders have appropriate leadership and management skills to produce organizational results.

4. *Implementing performance-management systems* that help to improve performance through the use of appropriate development and feedback strategies linked to the compensation-and-rewards system, which include identifying competency maps for all job classifications, performance standards, and evaluation methods used to enhance employee and organizational performance.

5. *Implementing transfer of learning processes* by helping managers instal effective strategies that improve learning transfer.

6. *Assessing organizational effectiveness* by helping leaders determine what their needs are and which services will have the highest organizational impact.

7. *Facilitating and managing change* by helping leaders develop effective plans for implementing change and understanding the human implications of change.

(Gilley, Callahan, and Bierema, 2002: 31)

A results-driven HRD strategy can be said to maximize intellectual capital by ensuring that HRD professionals are equipped with relevant Organizational Development knowledge and skills. Figure 5.2 illustrates how human capital is transformed into social capital, which in turn is transformed into organizational capital. Driving the business through a strategic HRD approach requires a level of sophistication in making change interventions. Awareness of organizational policies and procedures, as well as an ability to analyse and make diagnostic interventions to manage change, describes the current professional status of the HRD professional.

❶ Stop and think 5.5

Intellectual capital and the HRD professional

It has been suggested that HRD professionals should equip themselves with relevant knowledge, skills, and experience in order to develop change interventions. Write down the three headings (knowledge, skills, and experience) and list what you like to acquire over the next year.

Figure 5.2 Knowledge and intellectual capital

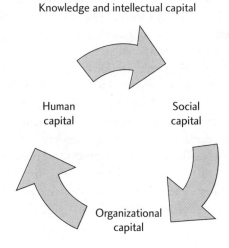

Knowledge and intellectual capital

Human capital

Social capital

Organizational capital

5.6 Summary

In this chapter we have addressed the forces that enable organizations to build competitive advantage by asking how innovation drives change internally. These forces include discovery and experimentation by focusing on internal forces for change rather than leaving everything to external forces of change. Internal forces for change should be constructed so that they exploit strategic advantage by developing procedures for embedding organizational learning. The trigger for change is often a matter of expectation and perception, which occurs when people understand why it is important to achieve a change initiative. Commitment, that is having the will to act, is important as a first step to creativity. We noted that BPR has a useful focus in drawing attention to the need to redesign core processes rather than functions. It also has the merit of challenging vertical bureaucratic management systems. However, whilst BPR can be described as a methodology for innovation, it is restricted to mechanistic change processes and has little to say about the social dynamics of change or about core human processes that underlie successful change strategies. As a result we needed to pay attention to the competencies and capabilities that will make an organization unique. We came to appreciate high-performance work systems by investigating the resource-based view of the firm, which suggests that sustained competitive advantage results from the acquisition and effective use of bundles of distinctive resources that competitors cannot imitate. Studies appear to indicate that high performance is linked to the quality of people-management practices. High-performance organizations focus on people by demonstrating commitment to creating the best place for the best people. This is an example of how strategic HRM becomes the central people strategy underlining organizational change.

We then asked how organizations can anticipate change faster than their twentieth-century counterparts: through the concept of the learning organization, or through the concept of organizational learning? Arguments in favour of the learning organization concept revolve around two central premises: that it is an ideal worth striving for and that systems theory provides a sound theoretical underpinning to create a holistic view of Organizational Development. One major difficulty is the relativity of the concept. If it cannot be defined, then it cannot be measured. In contrast, the concept of organizational learning can be defined. Organizational learning occurs, according to Argyris and Schön, when individuals within an organization experience a problematic situation and enquire into it on the organization's behalf. A useful way of doing this is to identify barriers to learning in organizations. These can be understood by thinking of three types of barrier: structural barriers such as communication systems, organization structure, and the logistics of operational design; cognitive barriers such as defensive reasoning; and social barriers such as work methods or interpersonal relationships.

Finally, strategic human resource development was discussed as a vehicle for an organization's development. The direction from strategic HRM should be articulated through personal and/or organizational transformations. This enables a results-driven approach to change.

⊗ Case study

Fundamental: the company that cares

Background

Fundamental is a company that provides IT business software to clients in the UK. The senior management team is considering opening a new branch in China or India.

The Fundamental motto is 'change through technology'. The managing director of the company requested the HR Department to produce a policy handbook that draws out the values of the company and sets out principles designed for the benefit of employees.

The new booklet states that the company 'respects the rights of the employees and cares about its workforce to the extent that it is engaged in continual personal development'. The company states that employees are the means to improve performance by building and developing competitive advantage through developing a high-performance work system and becoming a learning organization.

As such, they argue, 'there are rewards for high productivity and for participation in company performance schemes'.

Four years ago the company faced an uncertain future. Although things have improved slightly since then, productivity and quality are not keeping pace with demand for business software. Employee turnover has increased significantly, with approximately 65 percent of all part-time staff leaving within a two-year period. Full-time staff with expertise also left. During this time approximately 25 percent of senior technical staff have left the company for career advancement elsewhere. In addition, costs and accidents have increased.

The company now feels it has turned the corner: it has a new building to be proud of; it has recruited and employed an effective workforce; it offers productivity bonuses; it provides employees with a private health scheme. It also offers a good retirement package. Support for this is indicated by a rise in productivity of 18 percent over the past 12 months. Sales are up by 25 percent, and employees' real income has increased by 12 percent, due, in large part, to the bonus and profit-sharing schemes.

The policy handbook claims that five basic principles underlie the company's successful policy. These are:

1. To ensure that all employees are motivated and encouraged to identify opportunities for personal development.
2. To recruit staff who can add to value to the company.
3. To ensure that technology drives change.
4. To ensure that all employees are subject to performance evaluation and monitoring.
5. To create accountability through visibility.   ⊗

❯ The Human Resource Department as an agent of change

The Human Resource Department has engaged in the new process of recruitment and selection. This process is described as 'positive discrimination in order to select the best'. Those who obtain employment can be sure that the company values them. Unfortunately, this means rejecting people who smoke, are clinically obese, have high debts, or participate in high-risk sports. In addition, the company also seeks permission from employees to access various databases, which include:

- Criminal records.
- Credit bankruptcy and mortgage defaults.
- Vehicle licence checks.
- Educational records.
- Curriculum vitae and applications search.

The company believes this is a modern, sophisticated human resource approach because it is able to compare employees' profiles against the national average for physiological, psychological, social, and demographic factors. To support its case, it argues that effective performance management is demonstrated by the way it cares for the well-being of employees and the environment. These are articulated below.

Caring for employees' well-being

Employees are well cared for by the company. Consequently, it administers pulmonary tests each month. It argues that this improves the quality of life for employees. Company doctors who also take regular tests for blood pressure, weight, and diabetes carry out a health profile of each individual. Employees are therefore said to be reassured that their health is regularly monitored and can avoid the inconvenience of going to their local General Practitioner.

The environment

Concern for the well-being of employees extends to the environment. The company provides background music to help eliminate stress; it plays messages to staff throughout the day for the same reason: to relax people. Messages such as 'stay calm', 'help colleagues', and 'remember, the company is our community' are all designed for positive reasons. Employees also receive electronic messages by email. The company argues that this 'thoughtfulness' ensures high morale. Video- and audio-surveillance ensure that staff feel secure.

Performance management

The company monitors over 150 criteria in order to assess employee productivity. These include: keystroke activity; error rate; teams' efficiency and productivity scores; and individual appraisal from line managers.   ❯

❷ Your task

In line with its policy of respecting the rights of the employees and caring for its workforce, the company has decided to embark on an expansion by opening a site in China. In preparation for this development, Fundamental have employed a consultant to identify an appropriate location and consider cultural issues in relation to its current human resource policy. The consultant suggested that he needed to undertake an evaluation of the current situation within Fundamental's existing UK company. It was decided that a survey of opinions was a useful way to gather the views of all employees about the current HR policy.

The survey of attitudes, followed by focus group discussions in the organization, revealed the following negative perceptions about the HR policy. This has surprised management. The survey result is presented in brackets, expressed as a percentage. Focus groups reflect more detailed comments as indicated below.

1. The Use of Technology (72% negative)

The survey revealed that a significant number of employees felt that technology was being used to control their activities. During group discussions the word 'surveillance' was mentioned by different groups to characterize their feelings.

2. Health Monitoring (48% negative)

Discussions revealed some hostility to health monitoring by the company on the grounds of discrimination. One group compared the monitoring of urine and blood samples as a form of 'weeding-out process'. Another group likened the entry-level screening process to 'ethnic cleansing'.

3. Morale (87% negative)

Groups reported an Us and Them attitude despite the appeal to unity by the company. Team morale was described as low. When asked how corporate performance had improved when morale was said to be low, most people stated that initially trust had been given to the new quality programme but after two years doubts were beginning to set in.

4. Communication (83% negative)

This issue appeared to be linked to the previous one. That is, initially the managing director appeared to do the right things. Most areas of change had a 'promising ring' to them. At first, interpersonal communication was emphasized by 'managing by walking about'. However, more recently, the managing director and senior team do not appear to have time for that. In discussion with the consultant, the managing director stated that 'I'm no good at that communications stuff, I'm a hands-on kind of guy. I like to get things done fast and efficiently.'   ❷

❯❯5. Culture Change (58% negative)

Most people in the discussions felt that the organizational culture in respect to motivation was synonymous with manipulation and control. Consequently, some cynicism was expressed about the organization's philosophy and methods.

Using these descriptions of the company, you are required to produce a report that evaluates the problem. This evaluation should be based on your knowledge that the company seeks improvement to performance in building competitive advantage by developing a high-performance work system and becoming a learning organization. What recommendations would you make in relation to:

1. The background issues identified by the survey of attitudes, which appear not to be understood by the HR director and the senior team in the company? State your views on the company handbook and the survey and group discussions.
2. Consider if you would raise any issues about leadership, communication, or morale.
3. Discuss the culture of Fundamental, particularly the link between values, attitudes, and behaviours, and consider the implications for cross-cultural differences—i.e. whether the company would find the Chinese workers more accommodating.
4. Finally, address the ethical issues in relation to the role of the HR Department.

■ Study questions

1. What are the arguments for focusing on internal rather than external forces for change?

2. Why are high-performing work systems future-oriented?

3. How would you distinguish tangible from intangible resources?

4. What is meant by the phrase 'resource-based view of the firm'?

5. Distinguish between distinctive and reproducible capabilities.

6. How do organizations achieve unique competencies?

7. What is strategic HRD? Distinguish between activity-based programmes and results-driven programmes.

8. Is it possible to develop a learning organization? Provide a considered response.

9. What are the merits of organizational learning?

10. What are the barriers to creativity in organizations?

■ Exercises

Exercise 1

Look at Case Example 5.1 and state what you think the problems are. Say how a focus on internal competencies might improve this situation.

Exercise 2

Consider an organization with which you are familiar and identify barriers to learning using structural, cognitive, and social categories.

Exercise 3

Interview two managers and ask them to identify forces in their organization that:

1. seek to discover, experiment and develop new opportunities.

2. are designed to exploit strategic advantages.

3. develop procedures for embedding organizational learning.

4. Compare the results by outlining the similarities and differences.

Exercise 4

One of the arguments put by advocates of strategic HRM is that it is now possible to demonstrate that core processes impact on bottom-line performance (that is, performance that either improves the organization's efficiency, demonstrated through improved financial results, or effectiveness, which is demonstrated through improved customer or client satisfaction). Consider an organization with which you are familiar and, using Figure 5.1 to illustrate your argument, attempt to demonstrate how you might prove this argument. Once you have done this, say what the difficulties might be in persuading the organization's Board of Directors to adopt a development plan to become a high-performance organization.

Exercise 5

Assess an organization using Hiltrop's ten core factors that contribute to high performance and see how well it performs. These were:

- Reliance on internal recruitment and promotion.

- Emphasis on teamwork.

- Strategic career systems.

- Openness and information sharing.

- Decentralization and delegation of authority.

- Concern for people in the management philosophy.

- Recognition and reward for high performance.

- Rewards for skills and competencies.

- Training and development of employees.

- A longer-term focus for HR decisions.

■ Further reading

Armstrong, M. and Baron, A. (2003) *Strategic HRM: The key to improved business performance*, London: Chartered Institute of Personnel and Development. This is a useful text on how HR creates efficiency and effectiveness.

Becker, B.E. and Huselid, M.A. (2001), *The HR Scorecard: Linking People, Strategy, and Performance*, Watertown, MA: Harvard Business School Press. This is a methodology that suggests a strong relationship between HR and performance.

Choo, C.W. and Bontis, N. (2002), *The Strategic Management of Intellectual Capital and Organizational Knowledge*, Oxford: Oxford University Press. Worth reading for the development of intellectual capital.

Clardy, A. (2008), 'The strategic role of Human Resource Development in managing core competencies', *Human Resource Development International*, 11 (2), 183–197. Provides a useful discussion of the role of human resource development (HRD) in developing core competencies. In particular, the literature on strategic HRD is reviewed as a basis for redefining HRD's role in organizational strategy. This focuses on three roles: participating in strategic planning, developing core competencies, and protecting them.

Huselid, M.A. (1995), 'The impact of human resource management practices on turnover, productivity, and corporate financial performance', *Academy of Management Journal*, 38(3), 635–672. Although the book above is more recent, this provides an argument for the link between HR and financial performance.

Taylor, S., Levy, O., Boyacigiller, N.A., and Beechler, S. (2008), 'Employee commitment in MNCs: Impacts of organizational culture, HRM and top management orientations', *The International Journal of Human Resource Management*, 19(4), 501–527. A useful article outlining the effect of top-management team global orientation and 'geocentric orientation'. That is, a study of high adaptability and HRM systems characterized by high-performance work practices related to a multinational organization's culture. The study suggests links that have a direct and significant effect on employee commitment.

Vlachos, I. (2008) 'The effect of human resource practices on organizational performance: evidence from Greece', *The International Journal of Human Resource Management*, 19(1), 74–97. The article presents a study of the impact of human resource management on organizational performance. This is examined through six dimensions: job security, selective hiring, self-managed teams and decentralization of decision making, compensation policy, extensive training, and information sharing.

References

Alvesson, M. and Deetz, S. (1996), 'Critical Theory and Postmodernism, Approaches to Organizational Studies', in Clegg, S., Hardy, C., and Nord, W. (eds), *Handbook of Organization Studies*, London: Sage.

Appelbaum, S.H. and Goransson, L. (1997) 'Transformational and adaptive learning within the learning organization: a framework for research and application', *The Learning Organization* 4(3), 115–128.

Argyris, C. (1993), *Knowledge for Action—A Guide to Overcoming Barriers to Organizational Change*, San Francisco, CA: Jossey-Bass.

Argyris, C. and Schön, D.A. (1978), *Organisational Learning II : Theory, Method, and Practice*, Reading, MA: Addison-Wesley.

—— (1996), *Organisational Learning II*, Reading, MA: Addison-Wesley.

Armstrong, A. and Foley, P. (2003), 'Foundations for a learning organization: organization learning mechanisms', *The Learning Organization*, 10(2), 74–82.

Armstrong, M. and Baron, A. (2003), *Strategic HRM: The key to improved business performance*, London: Chartered Institute of Personnel and Development.

Arthur, J.B. (1994), 'Effects of human resource systems on manufacturing performance and turnover', *Academy of Management Journal*, 37, 670–687.

Barney, J. (1991a), 'Types of competition and the theory of strategy: towards an integrative approach', *Academy of Management Review*, 11(4), 791–800.

—— (1991b), 'Firm resources and sustained competitive advantage', *Journal of Management*, 17, 99–120.

—— (1995), 'Looking inside for competitive advantage', *Academy of Management Executive*, 9(4), 49–61.

Belbin, R.M. (1981), *Management Teams: Why They Succeed or Fail*, Oxford: Butterworth-Heinemann.

Boje, M.D. (1995), 'Stories of the Story-telling Organization: A Postmodern Analysis of Disney as "Tamara-land"', *Academy of Management Journal*, 38(4), 997–1035.

Boje, M.D., Gephard, R.P., and Thatchenkery, T.J. (eds) (1996), *Postmodern Management and Organization Theory*, London: Sage.

Boselie, P., Paauwe, J., and Richardson, R. (2003), 'Human resource management, institutionalization and organizational performance: a comparison of hospitals, hotels and local government', *International Journal of Human Resource Management*, 14, 1407–1429.

Buckler, B. (1996), 'A Learning Process Model to Achieve Continuous Improvement and Innovation', *The Learning Organization*, 3(3), 31–39.

Cappelli, P. and Crocker-Hefter, A. (1996), 'Distinctive Human Resources are Firms' Core Competencies', *Organizational Dynamics*, 3(Winter), 7–22.

Cappelli, P. and Singh, H. (1992), 'Integrating Strategic Human Resources and Strategic Management' in Lewin, D., Mitchell, O.S., and Sherer, P. (eds), *Research frontiers in industry relations and human resources*, Madison, WI: Industrial Relations Research Association, 165–192.

Casey, C. (2002), *Critical Analysis of Organizations, Theory, Practice, Revitalization*, London: Sage.

Colomy, P. (1998), 'Neo-functionalism and neo-institutionalism: human agency and interest in institutional change', *Sociological Forum*, 13(2), 265–300.

Colomy, P. and Rhoades, G. (1994), 'Toward a micro corrective of structural differentiation theory', *Sociological Perspectives*, 37, 547–583.

Cummings, T.G. and Worley, C.G. (1993), *Organizational Development and Change*, Fifth edition, Minneapolis/ St. Paul, MN: West Publishing Company.

Daft, R.L. (1998), *Essentials of Organization Theory and Design*, Cincinnati, OH: South-Western College Publishing.

Dean, J. and Bowen, D. (1994), 'Management theory and total quality: improving research and practice through theory development', *Academy of Management Review*, 19(3), 392–418.

Delaney, J.T., Lewin, D., and Ichniowski, C. (1989), *Human resource policies and practices in American firms*, Washington, DC: US Government Printing Office.

Delany, J. and Huselid, M. (1996), 'The impact of human resource management practices on perceptions of organizational performance', *Academy of Management Journal*, 39(4), 949–969.

Dymock, D. (2003), 'Developing a culture of learning in a changing industrial climate: an Australian case study', *Advances in Developing Human Resources*, 5(2), 182–195.

Easterby-Smith, M., Burgoyne, J., and Araujo, L. (eds) (1999), *Organizational Learning and the Learning Organization*, London: Sage.

Edvinson, L. and Malone, M.S. (1997), *Intellectual Capital: Realizing your company's true value by finding its hidden brainpower*, New York: HarperCollins.

Elliott, D., Smith, D., and McGuinness, M. (2000), 'Exploring The Failure To Learn: Crises And The Barriers To Learning', *Review of Business*, 21(3/4), 17–24.

Etzioni, A. (1975), *A Comparative Analysis of Complex Organizations*, New York: The Free Press.

Fey, C., Björkman, I., and Pavlovskaya, A. (2000), 'The effect of human resource practices on firm performance in Russia', *International Journal of Human Resource Management*, 11(1), 1–18.

Finger, M. and Brand, S.B. (1999), 'The concept of the "learning organization" applied to the transformation of the public sector', in Easterby-Smith, M., Burgoyne, J., and Araujo, L. (eds) *Organizational Learning and the Learning Organization*, London: Sage.

Garavan. T. (1997), 'The learning organization: a review and evaluation', *The Learning Organization*, 4(1),18–29.

Gardiner, P. and Whiting, P. (1997), 'Success factors in learning organizations: an empirical study', *Industrial and Commercial Training*, 29(2), 41–48.

Garvin, D.A. (1993), 'Building a learning organization', *Harvard Business Review*, 71, 78–91.

Gilbert, D. (2006), 'The Idea that Ideas can be Dangerous', in Brockman. J. (ed), *What is your dangerous idea?*, Toronto: Pocket Books, 42.

Gilley, A.M., Callahan, J.L., and Bierema, L.L. (2002), (eds), *Critical Issues in HRD: New Perspectives*, New York: Basic Books.

Greenwood, R., Suddaby, R., and Hinings, C.R. (2002), 'Theorizing change: the role of professional associations in the transformation of institutional fields', *Academy of Management Journal*, 45(1), 58–80.

Griego, O.V., Geroy, G.D., and Wright, P.C. (2000), 'Predictors of learning organizations: a human resource development practitioner's perspective', *The Learning Organization*, 7(1), 5.

Grieves, J. (2006), 'Barriers to learning: conflicts that occur between and within organizational systems', *International Journal of Learning and Intellectual Capital*, 3(1), 86–103.

Guest, D.E. (1987), 'Human resource management and industrial relations', *Journal of Management Studies*, 24(5), 503–521.

—— (1997), 'Human resource management and performance: a review and research agenda', *International Journal of Human Resource Management*, 8(3) 263–276.

Guest, D. and Hoque, K. (1994), 'The Good the Bad and the Ugly: Employment Relations in New Non-Union Workplaces', *Human Resource Management*, 5, 1–14.

Guest, D. and Peccei, R. (1992), 'Measuring Effectiveness: is NHS Personnel Getting It Right?'. *Health Manpower Management*, 18, 33–39.

Hamel, G. and Prahalad, C.K. (2002), 'Competing for the Future' in Henry, J. and Mayle, D. (2002), *Managing Innovation and Change*, London: Sage, 23–35.

Heckman, J.J. (1979), 'Sample selection bias as a specification error', *Econometrica*, 47, 153–161.

Hiltrop, J.M. (2005), 'Creating HR capability in high performance organizations', *Strategic Change*, 14, 121–131.

Hirschhorn, I. (1990), *The Workplace Within*, Boston, MA: MIT Press.

Hoffman, A.J. (1999), 'Institutional evolution and change: environmentalism and the US chemical industry', *Academy of Management Journal*, 42, 351–371.

Honey, P. and Mumford, A. (1992) *The Manual of Learning Styles*, Maidenhead: Peter Honey.

Hoque, K. (1999), 'Human resource management and performance in the UK hotel industry', *British Journal of Industrial Relations*, 37(3), 419–444.

Huang, T.C. (2001), 'The effects of linkage between business and human resource management strategies', *Personnel Review*, 30(2), 132–143.

Humphrey, N. (2006), 'Bertrand Russell's Dangerous Idea', in Brockman, J. (ed), *What is your dangerous idea?* (2006), Toronto: Pocket Books, 63.

Huselid, M.A. (1995), 'The impact of human resource management practices on turnover, productivity, and corporate financial performance', *Academy of Management Journal*, 38(3), 635, 638.

Ichniowski, C., Kochan, T., Levine, D., Olson, C., and Strauss, G. (1996), 'What works at work: overview and assessment', *Industrial Relations*, 35(3), 299–333.

Jackson, M.C. (2003), *Systems Thinking: creative holism for managers*, Chichester: Wiley.

Jackson, S.E. and Schuler, R.S. (1995), 'Understanding human resource management in the context of organizations and their environments', in Spence, J.T., Darley, J.M., and Foss, D.J. (eds), *Annual Review of Psychology 46*, Palo Alto, CA: Annual Reviews, 237–264.

Jamali, D. and Sidani, Y. (2008), 'Learning Organizations: diagnosis and measurement in a developing country context', *The Learning Organization*, 15(1), 58–74.

Jaques, E. (1953), 'On the dynamics of social structure', *Human Relations*, 6(1), 3–24.

Klein, M. (1975), *Envy and Gratitude and Other Works 1945–1963*, London: Virago.

Lawler, E.E., Mohrman, S., and Ledford, G. (1995), *Creating High-performance Organizations*, San Francisco, CA: Jossey-Bass.

Legge, K. (1995), *Human Resource Management. Rhetorics and Realities*, Basingstoke: Macmillan.

MacDuffie, J.P. (1995), 'Human Resource bundles and manufacturing performance: organizational logic and flexible production systems in the world auto industry', *Industrial Labor Relations Review*, 48, 197–221.

Macey, B.A. and Izumi, H. (1993), 'Organizational change, design and work Innovation: analysis of 131 North American Field Studies—1961–1991', in Woodman, R. and Passmore, W. (eds), *Research in organization change and development 7*, Greenwich, CT: J A I Press, 235–313.

Maria, R.F. (2003), 'Innovation and organizational learning culture in the Malaysian public sector', *Advances in Developing Human Resources*, 5(2), 205–214.

Mayo, A. and Lank, E. (1994), *The Power of Learning: A Guide to Gaining Competitive Advantage*, London: IPD.

McGill, M.E., Slocum, J.W., and Sei, D. (1992), 'Management practices in learning organizations', *Organizational Dynamics*, 21, 5–17.

Menzies, L. (1960), 'A case in the functioning of social system as a defence against anxiety', *Human Relations*, 13(2), 95–121.

Mumford, A. (1996), 'Creating a learning environment', *Journal of Professional Human Resource Management*, 4, 26–30.

Murphy, G.D. and Southey, G. (2003), 'High performance work practices: Perceived determinants of adoption and the role of the HR practitioner', *Personnel Review*, 32(1/2), 73–93.

Nevis, E., DeBella, A., and Gould, J. (1995), 'Understanding organizations as learning systems', *Sloan Management Review*, Winter, 73–85.

Newton, K. (1998), 'The high performance workplace: HR based management innovations in Canada', *International Journal of Technology Management*, 16(1/3), 177–192.

Osterman, P. (2000), 'Work Reorganization in an Era of Restructuring: Trends in Diffusion and Effects on Employee Welfare', *Industrial and Labor Relations Review*, 53(2), 179–196.

Pedler, M., Boydell, T., and Burgoyne, J. (1991, 1996, 1997), *The Learning Company. A strategy for sustainable development*, London: McGraw-Hill.

Peters, T.J. and Waterman, R.H. (1982), *In Search of Excellence: Lessons From America's Best Run Companies*, New York: Harper and Row.

Pfeffer, J. (1994), *Competitive Advantage through People*, Cambridge, MA: Harvard Business School Press.

—— (2002), 'Competitive advantage through people', in Henry, J. and Mayle, D. (2002), *Managing Innovation and Change*, London: Sage, 61–73.

Pfeifer, J. and Veiga, J.F. (1999), 'Putting people first for organizational success', *Academy of Management Executive*, 13(2), 37–49.

Pinker, S (2006), 'Introduction' to Brockman, J. (ed), *What is your dangerous idea?*, Toronto: Pocket Books, xvii–xxviii.

Porth, S.J., McCall, J., and Bausch, T.A. (1999), 'Spiritual themes of the learning organization', *Journal of Organizational Change Management*, 12(3), 211–220.

Prahalad, C.K. and Hamel, G. (1990), 'The core competence of the corporation', *Harvard Business Review*, 71–91.

Redman, T. and Mathews, B.P. (1998), 'Service quality and human resource management. A review and research agenda', *Personnel Review*, 27(1), 57–69.

Robinson, V.M.J. (2001), *The International Journal of Educational Management*, 15(2), 58–67.

Roos, J. (1996), *Intellectual performance: exploring an intellectual capital system in small companies*, Israel: Herzlia.

Rosengarten, P. (1995), 'Learning organizations and their characteristics: the case of automotive components suppliers in Britain', Paper presented to the 1995 ECLO Conference, Warwick.

Salaman, G. and Butler, J. (1994), 'Why managers won't learn' in Mabey, C. and Iles, P. (eds) *Managing Learning*, Milton Keynes: The Open University/Routledge, 34–42.

Sambrook, S. and Roberts, C. (2005), 'Corporate entrepreneurship and organizational learning: a review of the literature and the development of a conceptual framework', *Strategic Change*, 14, 141–155.

Sarala, U. and Sarala, A. (1996), *Oppiva, organisaatio—oppimisen, laadun ja Twoottavuuden Yhdistaminen*, Tampere: Tammer-Paino.

Schön, D.A. (1973), *Beyond the Stable State. Public and private learning in a changing society*, Harmondsworth: Penguin.

Senge, P. (1990), *The Fifth Discipline: The art and practice of the learning organization*, New York: Doubleday.

Senge, P., Kleiner, A., Roberts, C., Ross, R., Roth, G., and Smith, B. (1999), *The Dance of Change: the challenges of sustaining momentum in Learning Organizations*, New York: Doubleday/Currency.

Tannenbaum, S. (1997), 'Enhancing continuous learning: diagnostic findings from multiple companies', *Human Resource Management*, 36(4), 437–452.

Teece, D., Pisano, G., and Shuen, A. (1997), 'Dynamic capabilities and strategic management', *Strategic Management Journal*, 18, 509–533.

Timmons, J.A., Smollen, L.E., and Dingee, A.L.M. (1985), *New Venture Creation*, Homewood, IL: Irwin.

Torrance, E.P., *Education and the creative potential*, Minnesota MN: University of Minnesota Press.

Truss, C. (2001), 'Complexities and controversies in linking HRM with organizational outcomes', *Journal of Management Studies*, 38(8), 1–38.

Ulrich, D. and Lake, D. (1990), *Organizational Capability: Competing from the Inside Out*, New York: John Wiley & Sons.

Venkatraman, N. (1989), 'The concept of fit in strategy research: Toward a verbal and statistical correspondence', *Academy of Management Review*, 14, 423–444.

Watkins, K. and Marsick, V.J. (1992), 'Building the learning organization: a new role for human resource developers', *Studies in Continuing Education*, 14(2), 115–129.

—— (1998), *Dimensions of the Learning Organization Questionnaire*, Warwick, RI: Partners for the Learning Organization.

Weick, K.E. and Westley, F. (1996), 'Organizational learning: affirming an oxymoron', in Clegg, S.R., Hardy, C., and Nord, W.R. (eds), *Handbook of organizational studies*. London: Sage.

Wernerfelt, B. (1995), 'The resource-based view of the firm: ten years after'. *Strategic Management Journal*, 16, 171–174.

Whetten, D. and Cameron, K. (2004), *Developing Management Skills*, Upper Saddle River, NJ: Pearson.

Whittington, R. (1993), *What is strategy and does it matter?*, London: Routledge.

Wilkinson, A. and Witcher, B. (1991), 'Quality concerns for managers', *International Journal of Quality & Reliability Management*, 9(2), 64–67.

Wright, P.M. and McMahan, G.C. (1992), 'Theoretical Perspectives for Strategic Human Resource Management', *Journal of Management*, 18(2), 295–320.

 Take your learning further: Online Resource Centre
http://www.oxfordtextbooks.co.uk/orc/grieves/

Visit the Online Resource Centre that accompanies this book to enrich your understanding of this chapter. Explore case study updates and answers to questions, test yourself using an interactive flashcard glossary, and keep up to date with the latest developments in the area.

PART TWO
Implementing change

CHAPTER 6

Culture and change

6.1 Introduction

This chapter describes organizational culture. You will come to appreciate why organizational theorists began to focus on the idea that organizations have cultures.

You will also come to recognize two different perspectives to culture: the *structural-functional perspective*, and the *critical perspective* (what we referred to in Chapter 1 as the *Creativity and Volition: a Critical Theory of Change* perspective). The structural-functional perspective includes three approaches: the 'strong' or corporate culture writers; Organizational Development (OD) writers; cultural climate researchers. The critical perspective rejects the organic analogy of structural functionalism and replaces it with that of the theatre. These two perspectives reflect views that are diametrically opposed to each other. The structural-functional perspective believes that culture is a variable of the organization that can be managed by managers in the interests of efficiency and effectiveness. The critical perspective argues that culture is not a variable and 'is' the organization. But there is one other crucial difference. The structural-functional perspective views culture as the means to provide stability. The critical perspective takes the opposite view and is more likely to see an organization as a dramatic arena in which everything is worked at, roles are played, performances are given, scripts are written, and politics is strategically played out. Rather than undertake cultural analysis, critical theory invites us to engage in organizational analysis.

Once you have understood the two perspectives and various approaches you will need to consider how a manager must come to terms with these apparently irreconcilable perspectives. Or is it possible to be individual by deciding which makes more practical sense to you? This is not an impossible position to take but it is a very difficult one to argue for. To do that you will need to consider the issues in Section 6.6. You may be persuaded that it is more useful to ask how a critical examination of organizational practices can lead to positive organizational change.

At the end of this chapter you will be able to:

- understand why organizational culture emerged;
- identify the structural-functional approach to culture change;
- state what is meant by 'strong' culture;
- define the OD approach to culture;
- understand what is meant by the phrase 'cultural climate';
- critically appraise the value of the structural-functional approach to change;
- recognize why the critical approach to change challenges the assumptions of the structural-functional approach;
- consider how, as an alternative to culture change, it is possible to use knowledge of an organization's culture to develop strategies for organizational change.

6.2 Defining culture

The earliest and most succinct definition of culture is that provided by Edward Tylor in 1891, who argued that culture is

> that complex whole which includes knowledge, belief, art, morals, law, custom, and any other capabilities and habits acquired by man as a member of society.

Tylor was an early anthropologist who used this definition to challenge the ethnocentric views of the late-nineteenth-century adventurers who tended to define other societies as either 'primitive' or 'advanced', depending on the extent of industrialization, urbanization, and 'civilization' they encountered. Tylor's definition challenged this view that culture was a product of a civilized society by arguing that all societies had cultures, which should not be analysed through value judgements. That is, we should not assume that one form is superior to another. They are simply different. But does this argument also apply to organizations?

Organizational sociologists adopted this definition in the first half of the twentieth century, because they were interested in the way that culture could be a cohesive force as people moved from rural community-based structures to societies that were more impersonal and in which the ties that bound people together were not as apparent. This interest in culture as a cohesive force was prominent in Western Europe and in the USA because of the vast movements of people who were uprooted from their local communities and became what Marx called the great urban proletariat. Other parts of the world—China, India, Malaysia, the Gulf States, South America, and Eastern Europe—are experiencing this process of urbanization and industrialization today, and are no doubt struggling with the fears and consequences of cultural change.

Sociologists, as Halmos (1970) pointed out, sought to investigate how personal service professions such as social work, psychiatry, nursing, and teaching were, as Durkheim had suggested, providing a new moral order in society. Others, such as Blauner (1966), were interested in the effects of different work technologies on workers' behaviours and attitudes. Such analyses of working cultures were descriptions of the way people worked, communicated, interacted, were motivated, managed, and controlled.

In the late 1970s management theorists became interested in the concept of organizational culture. The stimulus for this focus was the need to provide an answer to the relative declining economic performance of corporate America and the rise of Japanese methods. What resulted, according to Hickman and Silva (1987), was the decline of the classical and scientific management that had dominated the earlier part of the twentieth century, and the rise of qualitative techniques typified by the Japanese word *kaizen*—which implied teamwork, empowerment, and devolved decision making. In comparison, American business had succeeded well, up to a point, with its emphasis on individualism, impersonal control, and hierarchical supervision. *Kaizen* represented a different approach to work and at its heart was a values-driven belief in working together for the common good.

We can understand the changes in American organizations by visualizing the six eras of management described by Hickman and Silva (1987), who argue that the 'discovery' of culture as a values-driven approach moved organizations closer towards innovation.

Thus the first three periods focused on structure, productivity, and system respectively:

1. The period between 1910 and 1935 was concerned with organizational structure. This was prompted by the sheer volume of economic activity during that period, which encouraged economies of scale, and in turn required hierarchical bureaucratic control and managers to coordinate activity.

2. The period from 1935 to 1955, which was characterized by large economic crises: boom and bust. This included the Great Depression, which began in 1929, the Second World War production of goods and services that expanded the US economy, and the Marshall Plan, which underpinned postwar recovery for many countries.

3. The period between 1955 and 1970 was characterized by the further growth of corporate capitalism and the development of multinational corporations in their pursuit of overseas markets.

The next three periods were characterized by a movement away from scientific management towards qualitative, people-focused issues. This was a slow recognition that people were not just costs. They were also assets or resources to be developed. We can also see the emergence of OD in this period. These qualitative periods reflect a focus on strategy, culture, and innovation respectively:

4. The period from 1970 to 1980 was driven by international competition, which refocused strategy on qualitative criteria.

5. The period between 1980 and 1985 was characterized by the movement towards culture, driven by the failure of the strategic planning approach and the discovery that Japanese companies were more dynamic and quality-focused than American companies.

6. The period from 1985 to date forced a link between culture and new ways of working, such as flatter structures, employee involvement, and innovation.

The 'discovery' of Japanese work practices in the 1980s caused a rush to emulate *kaizen* through new strategies such as employee involvement, empowerment, team working, and quality circles. Human resource management became important as a means to establish qualitative approaches such as participative leadership, motivation, task involvement, and empowerment. The overall consequence was that management studies rediscovered the structural-functional agenda, which placed culture in a prominent position as the corporate glue that binds the other functions together. Paradoxically, whilst sociologists and anthropologists had largely abandoned structural-functional analysis decades before, it was now introduced into management studies. We will explore this in more depth below.

6.3 Culture as a structural-functional component

The structural-functional study of culture began with the functional analysis outlined by Emile Durkheim. In his *Rules of Sociological Method* (1938) Durkheim's analysis required identification of the functions things perform in any structural arrangement. For example, the function of marriage as an institution might be considered as the establishment of rules to order relationships. These rules might be considered as functional if they play a part in establishing order and control. If they do not, perhaps because society changes in some way, then they might malfunction, or even become dysfunctional. Similarly, an organization may consist of various functional components, such as leadership, strategy, communication, management, systems, skills, and so forth. Providing these components work in harmony, they can be regarded as functionally related. That is, they each play a part in the smooth running of the organization.

Functional analyses also require the separation of manifest functions from latent functions. Manifest functions are defined by their purpose, which may include the functions of leadership, strategy, systems, skills, structure. Latent functions are unintended processes, which may be positive or negative. For example, an organization might forbid smoking inside its building. This is a manifest function of its health and safety policy. However, the latent functions of this may be positive (such as people sharing information as they congregate outside in designated areas) or negative (an increase in litter and unproductive time away from the desk). When the unintended consequences are negative, then they are regarded as dysfunctional. For example, an organization's formal human-resources and health-and-safety policies are produced for good functional reasons: to ensure that the organization complies with the law or achieves best practice. If the formal policies in health and safety are subverted by employees who wish to gain bonus payments and by managers who want to achieve targets on time, then, despite those policies being in place, staff motives create a latent dysfunctional problem that was not visualized in advance when the HR team designed their policy. An example of manifest and latent functions is illustrated in the following case example.

⊗ Case example 6.1

Manifest and latent functions in a call centre

Judy was the manager of a call centre dealing with customers' after-sales queries. Over a six-month period she noticed that complaints increased by 34 percent. Over the same period costs rose by six times, compared with the same period the previous year. She called a meeting with supervisors to identify possible reasons for this. What Judy and her team discovered was that the increase in complaints coincided ⊗

> ❯with a 25 percent rise in staff sick leave. This meant the centre had to fill in with temporary and inexperienced staff, which put further pressure on experienced staff, who became overloaded with urgent questions and problems. Two weeks later, at a company meeting, she heard that the company was experiencing a drop in orders for a particular product. She realized that this product generated the majority of complaints for the call centre.
>
> She held a further meeting with her team and identified a distinction between the manifest and the latent functions. That is, the development of the call centre had a clear objective (the manifest function): to help customers resolve difficulties. The latent functions were (1) recruitment (a 15 percent increase in recruitment time); (2) training (a 5 percent increase in training days); (3) supervision (the situation required a 30 percent increase in time spent on close supervision by supervisors). These latent functions were all regarded as dysfunctions, because they had only negative effects on the smooth running of the call centre. In addition, a drop in orders for the product bringing the largest number of complaints was dysfunctional for the marketing department because, despite their best efforts, sales were decreasing because of what they called inverse 'relationship marketing': potential customers being put off a good product because of word-of-mouth reports about the company's poor after-sales service.

The assumptions that lie behind functional analysis are:

1. All organizations operate a principle of equilibrium by balancing inputs and outputs. This means that, like an organism, organizations have needs that must be satisfied.

2. Functional harmony is a normal state that is only disrupted by malfunctions or dysfunctions. If such occur, then the path to normality must be re-established by examining the functional relationships between components, and whether the latent functions support the manifest functions.

3. Culture is a component of an organization that can play a supporting role in achieving, or restoring, equilibrium.

❶ Stop and think 6.1

Consider any organizational function, for example a control system, structure, method of communicating something such as marketing, leadership, or planning. Identify examples of manifest (intended) and latent (unintended) functions. Say how these latent functions emerged and whether they are positive or negative.

6.3.1 Developing strong corporate cultures

In the 1980s a neo-functional argument was promoted by consultants from the 'Excellence Movement'. These writers were less concerned to analyse organizational culture than to promote management advice. The most prominent of these writers were Peters and Waterman (1982), who provided a model for linking the structural components with the cultural component (see their 7S framework in Figure 6.1). They argued that high-performing 'excellent' organizations possess strong corporate cultures. The processes that underlie key functional areas are what really matter, but organizations usually take them for granted. That is, effective core values, positive attitudes, and good working relationships underpin innovation. This is what they mean by 'attention to detail'. As they stated, 'our research told us that any intelligent approach to organizing has to encompass, and treat as interdependent, at least seven variables: structure, strategy, people, management style, systems and procedures, guiding concepts and shared values (i.e., culture) and the present and hoped for corporate strengths and skills' (Peters and Waterman, 1982: 9). This became the 7S framework. Each functional element in the framework was defined by a mnemonic to aim memory. Thus, shared values at the centre represented culture, and other functional areas referred to strategic management (strategy); the way the organizations is organized through a hierarchical or flat structure; the systems used, including health and safety, human resources, financial management, and quality; management style, i.e. the quality of leadership; the number of qualified people (staff); and the levels of experience and training of employees (skills).

They argued that, whilst strategy and structure should be regarded as the hardware of the organization, the other aspects—style, systems, staff (people), skills, and shared values—can be regarded as the 'soft stuff' or supporting mechanisms. Furthermore, they argued that one could easily master the hardware but not the 'soft stuff'. They admonish leaders for ignoring this and urge them to learn how to manage it:

> all that stuff you have been dismissing for so long as the intractable, irrational, intuitive, informal organization can be managed.

(Peters and Waterman, 1982: 11)

We can regard the key cultural processes of excellent companies referred to by Peters and Waterman as having either positive or negative latent functions, because they may support or detract from excellence. They identified eight actions that excellent companies can take:

1. A *bias for action,* which, essentially, suggests that excellent organizations are not paralysed by over-working analysis. The recommendation to 'do it, fix it, try it' is a cliché that could quite easily reflect Action Research.

2. Staying *close to the customer*, which ensures that such companies provide 'unparalleled quality, service and reliability' and in so doing learn from their customers what their needs are.

3. Developing *autonomy and entrepreneurship* by experimenting and being prepared to take risks.

4. Developing *productivity through people,* who, if well managed, are the main source of competitive advantage.

5. Being both *hands-on and value-driven,* so that managers and leaders get involved but demonstrate a commitment through their own personal values and through corporate values.

6. By *sticking to the knitting* or staying within the boundaries of your own knowledge and expertise.

7. Developing a *simple form and lean staff,* which enable both structural effectiveness and efficiency through having just the right number of people.

8. Demonstrating *simultaneous loose–tight properties,* which offer control through delegated authority.

What managers needed to learn was that culture has to be managed, and the famous 7S framework illustrates this cultural alignment.

Other writers from this managerial tradition, such as Deal and Kennedy (1988), articulated the role of culture as a subsystem designed to coordinate the functioning of the organization. Like Peters and Waterman, these writers consider 'excellence' to

Figure 6.1 The 7S framework

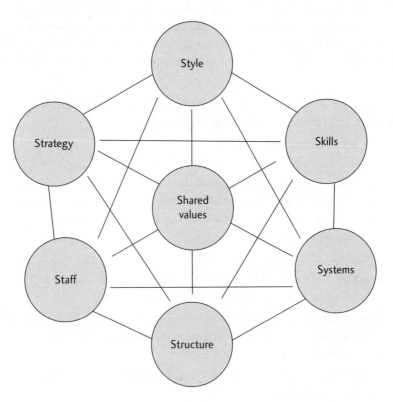

result from a strong culture. Consequently, in the 1980s and 1990s, organizational culture became the route to competitive advantage. This was also the position of researchers like Ouchi and Jaeger (1978), who investigated Japanese work methods. There are common links between these writers. For example:

- A number of these writers are linked to the McKinsey consultancy firm (Tom Peters, Robert Waterman, Allen Kennedy).

- There are clear links with Harvard's Graduate School of Education (Terrence Deal, Richard Pascale, and Anthony Athos).

- There was a circulation of ideas within this small but influential group. For example, as Peters and Waterman pointed out, Pascale and Athos 'assisted us in our concept development' and used this to underpin their work in *The Art of Japanese Management*. Such links were seminal in the development of corporate culture being seen as a vehicle for change towards excellent organizations.

- All of these writers claim that their work is based on research. However, the quality and integrity of their research may be questionable and much of their research is published as little more than aphorisms.

This group of writers on strong corporate culture appeared to have a common purpose: to demonstrate how getting culture right supports innovation. Snyder, for example, argued that 'much attention has been focused on the decline of innovation in American industry, and our concomitant standing in the international marketplace' (Snyder, 1982: 164). Snyder cites two newspaper articles in the footnotes of his article, from *Newsweek*—'Innovation: has America lost its edge?', 4 June 1979—and the second from *Time*—'The Sad State of Innovation', 22 October 1979. Both are examples of anxiety and the search for a solution. Book titles also indicate the anxiety of corporate America in the late 1970s and 1980s. Two popular books were Ouchi's (1981) *Theory Z: How American Business Can Meet the Japanese Challenge*, and Pascale and Athos's (1981) *The Art of Japanese Management*. In this way, organizational culture consulting emerged as a solution to a problem.

6.4 Organizational Development and diagnostic models

Although the corporate culture writers do not provide a methodology, OD writers were more prepared to do so. They also used the organic analogy implicit in the open-systems model but their training in behavioural science—a mixture of work psychology and organizational sociology—meant they were better equipped to provide a structural-functional analysis of an organizational system. For example, Lewis has pointed out that 'OD theory widened to include organizational culture with the interest in culture change' (Lewis, 1996: 13). As a result, in the 1980s culture change became the focus for OD researchers and writers intent on demonstrating that culture change is necessary where greater cohesion is required. A cohesive culture therefore reflects the way that individuals support the goals of the organization and are committed to achieving them. OD models of culture change focused on the importance of integrating the structural components of the organization by engaging the commitment of people. Structural components reflect what has to be done to accomplish the mission. Structural components may include the roles people play, the organization of tasks and people to meet deadlines, and so forth. Commitment, on the other hand, reflects intangible qualities in achieving objectives. In other words, high-performing organizations require their overt practical objectives to be supported by intangible social qualities, which are generally referred to as behaviours but clearly imply positive attitudes and actions valued by the organization. Schein's (1985) example illustrates how cultural integration is seen as a cohesive influence by ensuring that the organization socializes individuals into common cultural elements (a common language, group boundaries, power and status, intimacy and friendship, rewards and punishments, and ideology and religion) that reinforce the structural components of the organization.

Others, such as Bounds *et al*, argue that 'having cultural solutions for internal integration allows people to interact and behave comfortably' because members 'know the rules of the game and can predict and understand what is going on' (Bounds *et al*, 1996: 113). Effective functional adaptation therefore requires conformance between structural components and cultural solutions. Poor conformance is dysfunctional because commitment is lacking.

This integrationist theme is implicit in the structural-functional perspective of culture. The function of the leader is to create a shared value system and identify dysfunctions when they occur. According to Kilman (1982), culture is to the organization what personality is to the individual, a hidden, yet unifying theme that provides meaning, direction, and mobilization. The job for the leader then is to:

- manage the meanings of the workplace by defining, clarifying, negotiating how objectives can be achieved;
- provide direction by demonstrating leadership;
- mobilize commitment by engaging with people.

---

❶ Stop and think 6.2

We have seen how the organic metaphor for culture emerged from structural functionalism. This was adopted in the open-systems literature and applied to organizations. Key assumptions of this metaphor included the ideas of integration and harmony. This required a shared value system. Write down your own ideas for a shared value system by saying what core values you would appeal to. Relate these to a particular type of organization with which you are familiar.

6.4.1 Snyder's diagnostic model

OD writers have tended to use the structural-functional perspective as part of their applied social science vocabulary. The crisis of performance in corporate America during the 1980s therefore created opportunities for OD cultural interventions. As Snyder (1982) argued:

> As recognition of these problems has grown, and the search for solutions increased, managers have found their vocabularies growing by leaps and bounds. Recent additions include such phrases as 'new worker values', 'reindustrialization', 'double digit inflation', and the somewhat mysterious 'paradigm shift'. Perhaps most interesting of all is the phrase 'corporate culture', which many observers believe to explain much of the success of certain Japanese firms and well managed American companies that consistently distinguish themselves in the marketplace, take the lead in technical and managerial innovations, and satisfy the hearts, minds, and pocketbooks of their workers.
>
> **(Snyder, 1982: 164)**

Snyder provides a model consistent with that of OD writers. He argues that, because corporate culture is 'a powerful force in determining the success of mergers and acquisitions, organization development efforts, and the implementation of corporate strategic plans', we need to learn how to achieve the best fit between culture and other functional components. There are two problem situations in which this concept can be employed:

1. Where difficulties emerge with mergers and acquisitions. In such cases, there is a need to align the value systems and the norms of the merged companies. In the most difficult situations these clash, causing disharmony and conflict.

2. When an organization finds that changes in the external environment require it to make internal adjustments. When this happens, it needs to realign its culture with the new vision, mission, and strategic objectives. The need to realign the culture requires changes in values, attitudes, knowledge, and behaviours.

Snyder provides a diagnostic model for analysing and managing cultural change. The model requires identification of dysfunctions and realignment in relation to key elements of culture. These are:

- Strategy and goals.
- Management style.
- Values.
- Human resources.
- Organizational structure.

- Innovation.
- Control systems.
- Bureaucracy.
- Task forces or project teams.
- Customer focus.
- Physical design and use of space.
- External relations, corporate social responsibility, and ethical action.

Managing culture change also requires four competencies related to knowledge acquisition, assessment, and decision making:

1. An understanding of the way that organizational culture affects the organization.
2. An ability to assess the forces that support the status quo as well as those that call for change (using Force Field Analysis).
3. Exercising decisions about the most appropriate changes to make.
4. Knowing the most useful levers to pull to manage culture change.

Methods for understanding an organization's culture include direct observation of the culture by an outsider; survey research using questionnaires and interviews (these may be aimed at past and present employees, as well as knowledgeable outsiders); examination of organizational documents; and direct assessment of the organization's culture by its members. Finally, determining the effects of culture requires two assessments:

1. The compatibility of the organization's strategy and objectives with the culture that supports it.
2. Consideration of how important each aspect of the culture is.

Snyder simplifies this through a matrix that identifies items that are important both to culture and to its compatibility with strategy. The preferred way to undertake this task is to identify the elements of culture that need to be changed. Snyder suggests some cultural characteristics of innovative organizations around which questions might be constructed to fit the matrix. Thus, ideally, innovative organizations should:

- be focused on the extent to which strategic goals are clearly articulated and disseminated through all levels of the organization, and demonstrated by consistent managerial action;
- be driven by a collaborative management style, resulting in action that clearly and consistently communicates values;
- be able to demonstrate a positive HRM and HRD focus;

- be able to ensure that the organization structure is fit for purpose—Snyder echoes Peters and Waterman's 'simultaneous loose–tight controls', and simple structures and lean staff;

- be capable of administering tasks flexibly without undue barriers to development and innovation, having control systems that guide and restrict only under extreme circumstances;

- plan tasks with a bias towards action;

- focus on the processing of information, communication through effective use of task forces and project teams, and staying close to the customer;

- consider the physical design and use of space to reflect ergonomics;

- expect top management to devote substantial time to external relations, and to corporate social responsibility and ethical action.

6.4.2 A Force Field Analysis: deciding on the most appropriate changes

The response to each of these questions should be placed into the matrix and examined to see if it is highly important or not. Follow Exercise 2 at the end of this chapter if you wish to undertake this task now. A Force Field Analysis (FFA) must be undertaken, followed by decisions about which forces to change.

Snyder's work provides us with the potential advantage of realigning the culture to the new demands of the situation. The methodology has the benefit of combining organizational diagnosis with cultural analysis using FFA to guide the outcome to a decision. In this way we can explore the structural-functional aspects of the organization. The model is one of the best-known examples of OD applying behavioural science to organizational problems. The purpose is to help managers think through the issues before they embark on cultural change. It should not go unnoticed that the elements of culture identified by Snyder are similar to the Peters and Waterman 7S framework. The advantage is that Snyder provides a model to analyse and manage cultural change. The structural-functional view is a neat analysis of cultural change but it deals with complexity by organizing it into specific parameters.

> **❗ Stop and think 6.3**
>
> Turn each element of Snyder's list of key elements of organizational culture into a question to see how you might apply it to an organization you are familiar with. Do some imaginative thinking and write down potential responses to your questions.

Organizational Development writers seek to establish a culture-change model that requires values that:

1. support and satisfy the organization's primary needs, such as profit maximization, or to provide a service valued by customers;

2. enable people to work cooperatively. This requires work structures and compliance procedures that enable people to work effectively;

3. drive positive behaviours to support an organization's core functions: to provide products or services efficiently and effectively.

6.4.3 Cultural climate

The corporate culture and OD writers view culture as a structural component of an organizational system. In contrast, those who research cultural climate are interested in something more pragmatic: measuring the attitudes of people towards their organization. These researchers tend to focus on the same issues as the corporate culture and OD writers, but seek to extend the debate on culture by turning the intangible qualities of culture into a tangible artefact. They do this through questionnaires designed to test the 'health' of an organization's climate. In this way, a snapshot of attitudes at a particular time can be achieved. This enables researchers to measure responses to questions, which can be done with different workgroups or entire organizations. Attitudes to work are then assessed to see how problems are perceived and to identify their potential causes. Researchers are interested in assessing the extent to which attitudes and behaviours support the core functions of the organization. According to Rousseau (1988), cultural climate is central to influencing the perceptions and behaviour of a workforce. Cultural climate is often referred to as 'an intervening variable' between the context of an organization and the behaviour of its members. For this reason, it is important to 'understand how employees experience their organizations' (Patterson *et al*, 2005: 379). This work by Patterson *et al* has indicated that affective components at the individual level of analysis influence perceptions about meaning and commitment.

The constructs used for measuring cultural climate tend to change as a result of the interests of the researchers. Early definitions tended to focus on four dimensions. These are illustrated in the work of Campbell *et al* (1970) as:

- Individual autonomy.
- Degree of structure imposed on the situation.
- Reward orientation.
- Consideration, warmth, and support.

Other writers have added more dimensions, which include role stress and lack of harmony; job challenge and autonomy; leadership facilitation and support; and workgroup cooperation, friendliness, and warmth (James and Sells, 1981;

James and James, 1989; James and McIntyre, 1996). This list, as Patterson *et al* (2005) inform us, has grown to include leader's psychological distance, managerial trust and consideration, communication flow, open-mindedness, risk orientation, service quality, and equity.

In their attempt to consolidate this field of concepts, Patterson *et al* (2005) have adapted the Competing Values Model of Quinn and Rohrbaugh (1983). Consequently, they have developed a methodological instrument—the Cultural Climate Measure (CCM)—to measure climate.

One difficulty is the confusion that arises from the distinction between cultural climate and culture. A solution is proposed by Schneider (1990), who limits climate to the interaction between processes, behaviours, and patterned responses to organizational situations. Schneider recommends the following technique:

1. Identify the issues, processes, and events that affect employees.

2. State the consequences (behavioural outcomes) of the issues, processes, and events that affect employees.

3. Determine the main influences between processes, events, and behavioural outcomes as they become patterns of habitual activity.

Organizational culture, by contrast, 'comes to light when employees are asked why these patterns exist', to which responses generally refer to shared values, common assumptions, and patterns of belief held by organizational members (Patterson *et al*, 2005: 382). Investigating cultural climate has the benefit of identifying specific concerns people have that are likely to affect performance. These concerns might relate to leadership style, organizational structure, communication, quality management methods, health and safety, innovation and creativity, ethics and sustainability, and so on (see Verbos *et al,* 2007). Investigating cultural climate avoids the problems of finding a 'perfect' model that can identify all relevant variables and processes.

---

❶ Stop and think 6.4

It has been argued that organizational climate can be measured. If you were to measure an organization's climate, what questions do you feel would reveal important attitudes in the workplace? Consider a service, such as a hotel, and write questions you feel you would ask employees.

As mentioned above, the structural-functional perspective views culture as a component of an organization, so, since its organic metaphor is shared by the cultural climate researchers, we can identify five main assumptions of this perspective that are contentious and alert us to be careful if we apply it to cultural change. These assumptions include:

1. The open-systems model, which assumes that if cohesion, integration, and consensus are not achieved, then an organization will display dysfunctional features. But why should these characteristics represent equilibrium, the normal state for an organization?

2. The view that organizational culture integrates personal commitment with organizational needs. This assumption is problematic because what motivates individuals is subject to many factors, which include age, whether people perceive equity in the rewards distributed for the effort they invest, trust in leadership, and so on.

3. The idea of culture as a discrete component or variable interrelating with other component parts. We can easily argue the reverse, that the culture of an organization represents everything that happens in that organization. Rather than being a mere component, it is, in fact, more an embracing descriptive concept.

4. The view that culture can be successfully managed. The difficulty with this assumption is the view that organizational culture is a tool that can be employed to achieve greater efficiency. Imagine, for example, a merger of two organizations with very different cultures. The possibility that these cultures can be reconstructed into a new culture is by no means certain. Indeed, it might be agued that the very intangibility of culture makes it impossible to manage.

5. The view that a weak culture is dysfunctional. It could be argued, however, that the concept of weak culture depends upon one's perspective. What exactly does 'weak' mean? Does it really mean that, when the shares of an excellent company drop significantly on the stock market, the culture is becoming weak? Was this the case with some of the so-called excellent companies such as IBM, Apple, Disney, 3M, Wal-Mart?

6.5 The critical perspective

We have seen how the structural-functional perspective on culture creates three main arguments:

1. That strong cultures can be identified and represent excellent performance.

2. That culture is an analytic tool that can be used for Organizational Development.

3. That cultural climate can be measured.

We also noted that the work of the strong corporate culture writers, the OD writers, and the cultural climate researchers rests on a number of assumptions that are problematic. Accordingly, the five concluding assumptions stated above have been challenged by Critical Theorists. Critical Theorists are therefore more interested in understanding reality as a symbolic universe. We will explore this further below.

6.5.1 Culture as a symbolic universe

Recent summaries of the critical perspective on change management, such as those of Brewis (cited in Knights and Willmott, 2007), Carnall (2007), and Rickards and Clark (2006), focus on the symbolic quality of culture. The differences between the critical approaches are less important than their objection to the idea of managing culture through an organic metaphor. That objection finds a shared understanding in the phenomenology of social interaction articulated in the sociological approach of Berger and Luckmann, who point out that 'man occupies a peculiar position in the animal kingdom. Unlike other higher mammals, he has no species-specific environment, no environment firmly structured by his own instinctual organization' (Berger and Luckmann, 1976: 65). What enables us to break free and continually restructure our social worlds is our unique ability to construct symbolic universes. Thus:

> Symbolic universes are social products with a history. If one is to understand their meaning, one has to understand the history of their production. This is all the more important because these products of human consciousness, by their very nature, present themselves as full blown and inevitable totalities.
>
> (Berger and Luckmann, 1976: 115).

An organization is therefore a symbolic universe. Its external appearance and the actions people take in its name are symbolic acts. An organization is therefore a dramatic arena in which people orient their actions symbolically, revealing or masking their true intentions. Seen this way, culture is not a variable that can be managed. Culture is everything done in the name of the organization. As Smircich (1983) and Brewis (2007) point out, one moves from viewing culture as a component part, or something that an organization 'has', to something that an organization 'is'.

Table 6.1 Two perspectives on organizational culture

Structural-functional perspective	Critical perspective
Culture is a structural variable. This view rests on the assumptions inherent in the organic analogy. This analogy creates a series of oppositions such as strong/weak culture; functional/dysfunctional. Culture is central to this by enabling better integration.	The concept of culture is synonymous with organization. One therefore engages in organizational analysis rather than cultural analysis. We should identify situational facts by viewing organizations as analogous to theatres.
Culture is a potential tool to improve performance by developing shared values.	Organizations are social constructs of power. They are controlled by individuals or elite groups who define reality for others.
A strong culture should be integrated through unitary interests.	Organizations reflect a plurality of interests. Organizational analysis should examine the similarities and differences between people.

A useful visual comparison can be made between the two perspectives identified so far. Table 6.1 illustrates these.

The differences between the two perspectives are significant. The structural-functional perspective views culture as a potentially useful tool to be used to improve performance, whilst the critical perspective rejects this premise. Therefore, writers from the critical perspective argue that, since culture is synonymous with organization, then we should talk about organizational analysis and not cultural analysis. The following case example illustrates how the idea of a strong corporate culture is not always synonymous with effectiveness.

❯❯ Case example 6.2

The macho culture behind the world's toxic debt

What do Freddie Mac, Fannie Mae, Northern Rock, and Lehman Brothers have in common? The answer is, they can all be regarded as strong corporate cultures driven hard by their leaders, with corporate values designed to enhance financial performance. Also, they briefly shared similar successful growth strategies based on 'mortgage securitization'. This is a process in which mortgage retail lenders (banks and building societies) make loans, take a fee, then sell the mortgage to an investment bank. The bank then bundles thousands of mortgages together and issues bonds based on that bundle of loans. For at least ten years these corporate cultures were seen as successful models to be emulated by others. The idea of mortgage securitization was originally created in 1983 and was known as 'collateralized mortgage obligation' or CMO. However, it wasn't until Michael Osinski, who worked as a computer strategist for Lehman Brothers, created a software model that enabled intricate networks of bonds to be created, based on homeowners' payments, that an imaginative system for exploiting the market and its customers was created. As Osinski stated, in 1988, 'I began a thirteen-year effort to streamline the process of securitizing home mortgages. As well as other forms of debt... lenders had gone nuts with property'. What made Osinski's software solution 'perfect' was that the American government, through Freddie Mac and Fannie Mae, absorbed the default risk. By 1988 CMOs had an annual output of $94 billion. According to Osinski, 'this was the era described in the popular book *Liar's Poker*. Wall Street guys felt cool and funny; people who were getting ripped off were dumb, ugly and deserved it. I got a $50,000 bonus cheque, a 50 percent dollop on top of my salary. Peanuts to the traders, but the easiest work I had ever done.'[1]

The cultures that support such financial institutions can be described as strong corporate cultures obsessed with excellence. But that version of excellence does not include stakeholders. Nor does it wish to be restricted by governance or compliance procedures. The values that underpin these cultures not only are aggressive, but also see customers as dupes or simpletons to be exploited by traders. As Osinski points ❯❯

> out, 'the next month, after I pocketed my $100,000 bonus I left Lehman Brothers for Kidder Peabody, which was the number one underwriter of CMOs... Working with another programmer I wrote a new mortgage-backed system that enabled investors to choose the combinations of yield and risk that they wanted by slicing and dicing bonds to create new bonds. It was endlessly versatile and flexible': a proverbial 'money tree' in institutions populated by 30-year-old millionaires.

The software provided by Osinski was often referred to as the 'grinder'. This butcher's analogy suggests that a percentage of offal was placed into the grinder with pieces of sirloin (further analogy suggesting better-quality products) to provide some 'real dog food'. To the rest of us that is a euphemism for 'toxic assets', another grammatical contradiction to describe the underlying problem of the first banking crisis of the twenty-first century.

[1] 'The Man who blew up Wall Street', *The Sunday Times*, 5 April 2009.

Thus the terms used by structural functionalism, such as the 'health' and 'vitality' of the organism, are very restrictive. If one pursues instead the idea of drama, we get a different picture, in which corporate greed nearly destroys the system it created and the costs have to be borne by the taxpayer. Seen as drama, the language changes from the idea of strong macho cultures to little more than behavioural games of self-aggrandizement and exploitation of unwitting customers and clients.

❶ Stop and think 6.5

You have now read two different perspectives on organizational culture. How do you think you would approach the subject? Write down what you think are the advantages and disadvantages of each. Finally, say how you would apply the concept of culture to an organization.

6.6 Using knowledge of culture to manage change

Despite its sophistication in analysing organizational culture, there is a problem with the critical perspective. That is, it does not seek to engage in cultural change because it is intended to examine, analyse, and criticize organizational practices, including management, leadership, and ethics. Whilst it provides a rich source of analysis and critique, it is not a means for developing or changing an organization's culture.

Critical analysis cannot lead culture change but it can lead to organizational change. It is well to ask how a critical examination of an organization's activities can lead to positive organizational change. But then, of course, we have to ask the question 'positive for whom?' Whilst we can include the organization's purpose, which it intends to achieve efficiently and effectively, we cannot assume that a particular managerial view is definitive. An examination of any current business-related newspaper will reveal that some shareholders are not happy with certain business leaders, that some leaders have risked the reputations of their organizations, their brands, and the working lives of many employees through poor business models, unethical practices, or political manipulation. One of the difficulties of functional analysis was the over-emphasis on cohesion with no explanation of who benefits from this. For example, one group in an organization (directors) might benefit disproportionately from rewards such as wages, pensions, and severance packages, compared to other groups of employees. Similarly, a manager might receive performance-related pay whilst other workers do not receive anything for their part in the success of the organization. It is also the case that many executive directors benefit despite their mistakes. See the case example below.

≫ Case example 6.3

Between the Rock and a hard place

Adam Applegarth is the man that the media have charged with wrecking Northern Rock. He is now regarded as acting unethically because, just prior to the crisis, he sold £2.6m of shares in the company when he was able to get a good price on the stock market. He is said to have urged investors and employees at the same time to buy more shares, in full knowledge of the impending crisis. This was seen as the height of hypocrisy.[1] Northern Rock ended up with a 'liquidity problem' and asked the Bank of England for help. Northern Rock was Britain's first big victim of the sub-prime crisis, which was portrayed as an 'act of God' similar to 'a freak flood'. In reality, it resulted from poor decision making and an unsound business model. Yet Applegarth received an 'enormous bonus, awarded for the very strategy that landed Northern Rock in the mire'.[2]

[1&2] *The Sunday Times*, 18 November 2007.
Additional sources:
'The bosses who broke Britain: Another bank bailout and a fall in the pound—The Sunday Times reports on who's to blame and the prospects for recovery', The Sunday Times, 25 January 2009.
'The tide is turned [sic], but for how long?', *The Times*, 19 September 2007.

If those who adopt a critical perspective argue that culture cannot be managed because it 'is' the organization and is not a variable of the organization, then we can easily reach a managerial *impasse*. When managing cultural change is thwarted by problems, then perhaps we can use a skilful, critical-analytical approach to change social practices rather than culture per se. The alternative to the structural-functional view of culture change is to recognize that cultural analysis proceeds by opening up the possibility of behavioural change. It does this by encouraging a collaborative approach to managing change through education, mentoring, and coaching.

This is what Lewin had in mind with his technique of Force Field Analysis. His concern was therefore to illustrate how change at the individual or group level can only proceed by identifying how the behaviours of those who hold them are motivated to change. To encourage this he suggested a three-stage heuristic device to unfreeze, change, and refreeze behaviours and attitudes. In other words, motivation itself is not enough if bad habits keep pulling us back to repeat old ways. Behavioural change then proceeds by experimenting with new ways of doing things and acquiring new habits, attitudes, and mental models. This is illustrated in Table 6.2, in which Lewin's (1951) model of behavioural change is refined by Schein (1964). This involves a seven-step process of change:

1. Inactivity.
2. Denial.
3. Frustration.
4. Acceptance.
5. Testing.
6. Application.
7. Integration.

These steps fit into Lewin's three conditions as illustrated in Table 6.2.

Table 6.2 Schein's (1964) reworking of Lewin's three-stage model of individual and group change

Condition	Characteristic
Unfreezing (stages 1–4) - Inactivity - Denial - Frustration - Acceptance	Awareness of the need to change behaviours is informed by the benefits. Thus existing attitudes begin to 'thaw out' and a readiness to change emerges
Movement to change (stages 5–6) - Testing - Application	Experimentation with and implementation of: - new behaviours - new systems - new processes
Re-freezing (stage 7) - Integration	New ways to become comfortable The benefits of change are observed Rewards are instrumental in refreezing new behaviours

Table 6.3 Facilitating behaviour change

Unfreeze	Establish commitment and motivation
	Educate, coach, or mentor
	Define objectives
	Ensure time, information, and resources are committed
	Identify the barriers and forces for change through Force Field Analysis
	Communicate the agreed drivers to change
Facilitate movement to change	Identify concerns of all involved
	Identify appropriate interventions
	Allocate responsibility
	Monitor progress
	Implement knowledge and skills development
Re-freeze	Provide regular feedback
	Provide appropriate rewards
	Ensure that appropriate support networks are established
	Systematize new behaviours

Managing change is therefore the responsibility of management. Organizational analysis proceeds by recognizing a shared organizational problem and engaging people who are motivated to solve it though a three-stage process of unfreezing, facilitating movement, and refreezing. Taking each stage in turn, we can identify what leaders can do to facilitate behaviour change (Table 6.3).

The difficulty is that those who manage organizations may never be aware that they have responsibilities to their staff, in which case, they will never move to the unfreezing stage, because they are not aware of the need to change. Such people will never discover what managers can do to facilitate positive proactive change because they are more concerned to control the behaviour of people than to develop their human resources. But this illustrates that critical organizational analysis must go beyond the interests of the leader or manager in controlling a limited number of variables that focus simply on functional alignment.

6.7 Summary

We began by defining the first modern concept of culture, as articulated by Edward Tylor in 1891 to describe societies as cultural entities. Culture, for the first time, was viewed as a 'complex whole' rather than an attribute of society. The debate about organizational culture reflects this simple argument. The application of organizational culture as an influential variable to improve organizational performance emerged in the late 1970s as a response to the difficult economic climate in the USA. The search for a new way of working was influenced by Japanese work practices. Organizational writers, particularly Harvard professors, adopted the structural-functional perspective and promoted strong corporate culture and positive cultural climate as a key variable to achieve functional integration. Organizational Development researchers and writers such as Schein and Snyder created models for OD cultural interventions and proposed cultural intervention strategies. Managers were urged to develop 'strong' corporate cultures. Cultural-climate researchers sought to measure attitudes of people towards their organization. Despite limiting their approach to surveys of attitudes, they tended to extend the debate by examining the intangible qualities of culture.

Critics of the structural-functional perspective claim that the organic analogy leads to inappropriate analyses. In keeping with Tylor's original definition of culture as 'a complex whole', they challenged the view that culture was a variable to be managed. The critical perspective values the importance of critique as a virtue in itself. Whereas the structural-functional perspective sought to promote efficiency and effectiveness by developing the health of the organization, the critical perspective challenges this by asking critical questions such as 'healthy for whom?', 'who makes decisions and why?', 'what are the motives?', 'is this practice ethical?', and so on. In other words, the assumption that harmony and integration are essential objectives is seen as problematic because organizations are political coalitions.

We are left with two straightforward arguments. The structural-functional view of culture change provides a simple approach by arguing that cultural integration is necessary, that consensus is required, and that this is actually achievable. Against this, the critical perspective argues that culture is an analytical device that enables the observer to raise difficult questions about practice. As an analytical device, culture is not a management tool. It is better seen as an unfolding drama in which different actors play out their roles, make demands upon each other, act out displays of status, manage things, negotiate, and compete with other organizations. Critical theorists present us with a managerial problem. They do not seek cultural change because they are not interested in organizational performance. This raises a crucial question: do they have any advice to offer to management scholars? Their response is that it is more useful to ask how a critical examination of organizational activities can lead to positive organizational change. These activities include challenging the perceptions of reality by questioning why things happen the way they do. The difficulty is that critical theorists raise bigger questions than many managers are equipped or prepared to deal with. Nevertheless, what we discover with the arguments for culture change is the sophistication of the arguments for cultural analysis. The type of analysis we make will also require reflection about the critical issues. Consequently, we are also forced to confront the ethical issues identified in Chapter 2 and we are reminded, in particular, that an intervention is also a political act of change. The ultimate questions we must satisfy ourselves with are whether our analytical framework is objective, and how culture change benefits the organization. Does it benefit employees, wider stakeholder groups, and management?

⭐ **Case study**

Organizational culture in a primary school

My first teaching post as a newly qualified teacher (NQT) was in a large primary school in the suburbs of a large town. The head teacher, as tends to be the norm within larger schools, was a manager rather than a teacher: he believed that his job was to oversee the smooth running of the school. In practice, the idea of smooth running meant control of pupils and staff. He did not participate in any form of teaching. His symbolic role was evident in school assemblies and in his observations of teachers in the classroom. In this way control was demonstrated. The roles of the head and his deputy head were markedly different from the same role I had observed in many other schools, either as part of my teaching practice or through the succession of schools in which I had taught as a supply teacher.

The deputy head had a visible presence throughout the school because she would wander into classes and observe teaching unannounced. This was primarily focused on the four newly qualified teachers, myself included. Part of the requirement of the NQT process was a full-year induction period in which the NQT would be observed. I had learned at university and in teaching practice that this was supposed to be a positive mentoring experience, designed to offer advice from an experienced teacher. This job position allowed my first two terms of the induction period to be completed, and was my first opportunity to work on a daily basis within a whole school community. This was my first full-time job, and was temporary to cover the maternity leave of an existing member of staff. I was full of enthusiasm, commitment, and optimism. I was passionate about teaching; I gained just as much satisfaction from studying the topics as my pupils did. Being with my pupils was inspiring, testing, and rewarding. However, my own personal confidence was shattered early on.

The culture of the school highlighted a clear division between the separate year groups. For example, the two teachers and teaching assistants from Year One would sit together in the staff room. This would be the same for other year groups. Each year group felt undervalued but assumed that the other groups had something they did not. I first experienced this in the nursery. The nursery operated as a separate area from the main school building. Logistically, this is simply because nursery workers do not have a play time and thus their dinner times differ slightly from those of the rest of the school. But in this school, the nursery staff openly expressed that they didn't enjoy sitting in the staff room. They felt that they didn't know anyone and felt uncomfortable. This was despite weekly staff meetings. The whole atmosphere was divisive. This attitude of 'them' and 'us' existed throughout the school. It was worse, though, in the lower Key Stage One infant years, and the older Key Stage Two junior years. Neither the head nor the deputy tried to break down these barriers, because they always sat elsewhere.

Strange as it seems, both the head and the deputy head appeared to find it difficult to relate to children. Perhaps this accounts for their controlling behaviour. »

❯❯ The head's leadership could only be described as remote, possibly because he had a continuous cycle of meetings with educational representatives and with the many heads of neighbouring 'clustering' schools. Success rates and quality marks were the key criteria. Some information from the heads' meetings would be brought to the rest of the school staff in monthly meetings, where key dates were noted in diaries, and new schemes and guidance would be briefly discussed. The deputy had day-to-day management responsibility for staff but she never attempted to develop relationships between people. Neither appeared to show interest in the children by simply taking the time to talk to them. But they were proud of their achievements, which revolved around their performance targets, which were solely focused on Year Five and Six classes.

As a young teacher I found some of the staff in this school very unapproachable. This appeared to reflect the controlling influence of management within the school.

The deputy head had never been one for words—in fact, I couldn't really remember her actually speaking to me from the day I got the job. When she passed me in the dinner hall she sort of smiled nervously in my direction. It wasn't in any way comforting and was without comment. She came across as someone who did not feel comfortable with small talk or interacting with staff. Her first formal introduction to me occurred, not as an induction process—I never had one of those—but as an abrupt intervention in my class during the first week. On another occasion I had tried to get acknowledgement from one of the Year Six teachers. She ignored me repeatedly, even when I stood beside her in her own classroom. This particular teacher deputized for the deputy head and received increased pay to do this. She was unapproachable. Other teachers cautioned me to be careful because she was married to the head. This raised questions of nepotism, since she appeared to have achieved this position without the job being advertised, and without any other teachers being made aware that there was a promoted position on offer. She was also the trade union leader—a position that seemed to be a conflict of interest.

Throughout the school, the children were not encouraged to express opinions outside the topics they were covering within the school day. The other teachers I provided cover for were obsessive about putting coloured pencils in the correct place, marking style, about how much was covered in each session. I noticed, however, that these teachers were also paid frequent visits by the deputy head. In this way, good practice was equated with control.

The experience taught me early on that training does not prepare you for dealing with micro-management, poor interpersonal relationships, and obsessive control over children's imagination and expression. I have left that school now and I have seen similar examples elsewhere. Since then, the schools I've chosen to return to for supply work I admire and respect, because they are managed by people who are more inspirational and who care about the futures of their pupils. These schools by contrast value staff. I am now much happier because I have discovered that there are ❯❯

❱some enlightened leaders and managers who support their staff and who do actually make a difference.

Questions

1. There is an implied link between leadership, culture, and motivation. Outline why this is the case.

2. In order to corroborate the views stated, how would you investigate the culture of this school?

3. Your investigation revealed that this view of the school's culture was held by other teachers. Therefore you decided to make an intervention on behalf of the Local Education Authority. Using Table 6.3, draw up an action plan to improve the culture of the school.

■ Study questions

1. Define organizational culture as precisely as you can.

2. Say what organizational culture has to do with organizational change.

3. What is meant by the phrase 'strong culture'?

4. Explain the meaning of the structural-functional thesis.

5. Outline Snyder's methodology.

6. State how critical analysis differs from functional analysis of culture.

7. What is meant by cultural climate and how does this differ from culture?

8. Why are emotions, politics, leadership, and ethics worthy of cultural analysis?

9. What might happen to an organization if it fails to operate ethically?

10. It might be said that culture is the invisible membrane that surrounds all other activities in an organization. The problem is that if it were simply the glue that held everything together, then it would be a conservative force. What arguments can you put for making culture a progressive force for change?

■ Exercises

Exercise 1
Consider two organizations, one with a strong culture and another with a weak culture. Then list the attributes that cause these different cultures. When you have done this, say why you would consider one as positive and the other negative in relation to organizational performance.

Exercise 2

Ascertain the cultural fit of your organization.

Step one

Using Snyder's cultural fit methodology, ask how your organization would answer the following questions. Once you have a response to each question, you should ask (a) how important each response is and (b) whether each response is compatible with the organization's strategy.

Questions:

- Are the strategy and goals that result from this analysis clearly articulated and disseminated through all levels of the organization?
- Are the strategy and goals demonstrated by consistent managerial action?
- Does the management style result in appropriate positive behavioural outcomes?
- Does management style communicate values?
- Can the organization demonstrate a strategic human resources focus in relation to (a) policies, (b) training, and (c) personal development?
- Is the organization's structure appropriate to meet its strategic objectives?
- Are there any unnecessary barriers to development and innovation?
- Are control systems there simply to guide people or do they restrict innovation?
- Are tasks planned with a bias to action or restricted by bureaucracy?
- Is information and communication effectively managed through task forces or project teams?
- Is the organization close to the customer?
- Does the physical design and use of space reflect the needs of those who use it in terms of functionality? That is, does form follow function?
- Does senior management devote sufficient time to external relations and to corporate social responsibility and ethical action?

Step two

Having answered these questions, you need to undertake a Force Field Analysis. To do this, decide what needs to be changed and state why. You will need to identify which are positive and can be enhanced further, then decide which are barriers to change or potential barriers to change and must be minimized.

Step three

The final step is to identify what levers of culture change you would employ. Snyder recommends the following courses of action:

- Ignore it.
- Attempt to strengthen it.
- Manage around it.

- Change the organization's objectives, strategies, systems, etc. where they are incompatible with the culture.

- Attempt to change the culture pattern.

Exercise 3

The phenomenological perspective perceives organizational reality to be characterized by flux and uncertainty rather than by consensus and dysfunction. Consider an organization you are familiar with and illustrate this through the various unfolding dramas that take place. To undertake this task you must:

- *Identify examples of staging.* What are the forums in which events are enacted? How are events staged—what are the physical arrangements? How are agendas organized and why? Are props used in any particular way?

- *Who are the main actors?* How do they define their version of reality? Do they appeal to reason, to emotions, do they use commands, humour, or appeals to support their points?

- *What scripts are performed?* What motives are stated? Can you think of other possibilities that are not revealed to the audience? What types of pairing between people occur, and who challenges the definitions and why? Why do some things not get challenged?

Finally, although an apparent consensus may be achieved and recorded, does this reflect reality? Is there a gap between the front-stage and the back-stage performances?

Exercise 4

Identify an organization's climate by describing the processes and events that affect employees' attitudes. Identify and state what the behavioural outcomes are. Finally, state the consequences for individual autonomy; degree of structure imposed on the situation; reward orientation; consideration, warmth, and support; role stress; job challenge and autonomy; leadership facilitation and support; workgroup cooperation, friendliness, and warmth.

Exercise 5

In an organization known to you, identify the drivers of ethical practice and say how effectively they are achieved. State whether you consider these to be fully embedded in the culture of the organization.

■ Further reading

Bate, P. (1995), *Strategies for Cultural Change*, Oxford: Butterworth-Heinemann. A good critical discussion of culture and particularly the 'happy atom' of Peters and Waterman. Bate provides a good critique of the 'strong corporate cultures' approach.

Brewis, J. (2007), 'Culture', in Knights, D. and Willmott, H. (eds), *Introducing Organizational behaviour and management*, London: Thomson Learning. Very good example of critical discourse.

Beugelsdijk, S., Slangen, A., and van Herpen, M. (2002), 'Shapes of organizational change: The case of Heineken', *Journal of Organizational Change Management*, 15(3), 311–326. A good example of change strategies at this company based on changes in leadership.

Lewis, D. (1996), 'The organizational culture saga—from OD to TQM: a critical review of the literature (Part One)', *Leadership and Organizational Development Journal*, 17(1), 12–19. Although this review is dated, Lewis still provides a very good survey of the literature.

Peters, T.J. and Waterman, R.H. (1982), *In Search of Excellence: Lessons From America's Best Run Companies*, New York: Harper and Row. A classic of the Excellence Movement and, of course, the source of much critique for the 7S framework and culture as a variable within this.

Schein, E.H. (1984), 'Coming to a new awareness of organizational culture', *Sloan Management Review*, 25, 3–16. Schein is seen as the foremost exponent of culture from an OD perspective.

Snyder, R.C. (1982; 1985), 'To Improve Innovation, Manage Corporate Culture', in Bennis, W.G. *et al*, *The Planning Change*, Fort Worth, TX: Holt, Rinehart and Winston, 164–171. This is the most methodical text to deal with cultural integration from a structural-functional perspective.

■ References

Berger, H.S. and Luckmann, T. (1976), *The Social Construction of Reality*, Harmondsworth: Penguin.

Blauner R. (1966), *Alienation and Freedom*, Chicago, IL: University of Chicago Press.

Bounds, G., Yorks, L., Adams, M., and Ranney, G. (1996), *Beyond Total Quality Management: toward the emerging paradigm*, New York: McGraw Hill.

Brewis, J. (2007), 'Culture', in Knights, D. and Willmott, H. (eds), *Introducing Organizational behaviour and management*. London: Thomson Learning, 344–374.

Campbell, J.P., Dunnette, M.D., Lawler, E.E., and Weick, K.E. (1970), *Managerial behavior, performance, and effectiveness*. New York: McGraw Hill.

Carnall, C. (2007), *Managing Change in Organizations*, Fifth edition, Harlow: Prentice-Hall.

Deal, T. and Kennedy, A. (1988), *Corporate Cultures: The Rites and Rituals of Corporate Life*, Harmondsworth: Penguin.

Durkhein, E. (1938), *The Rules of Sociological Method*, New York: The Free Press.

Halmos, P. (1970), *The Personal Service Society*, London: Constable.

Hickman, C.R. and Silva, M.A. (1987), *The Future 500: Creating Tomorrow's Organizations Today*, London: Unwin Hyman.

James, L.A. and James, L.R. (1989), 'Integrating work environment perceptions: explorations into the measurement of meaning', *Journal of Applied Psychology*, 74, 739–751.

James, L.R. and McIntyre, M.D. (1996), 'Perceptions of organizational climate', in Murphy, K.R. (ed), *Individual differences and behavior in organizations*, San Francisco, CA: Jossey-Bass, 416–450.

James, L.R. and Sells, S.B. (1981), 'Psychological climate: theoretical perspectives and empirical research', in Magnusson, D. (ed), *Toward a psychology of situations: An interactional perspective*, Hillsdale, NJ: Erlbaum, 275–292.

Kilman, R.H. (1982), 'Getting Control of the Corporate Culture', *Managing*, 3, 11–17.

Knights, D. and Willmott, H. (2007), *Introducing Organizational behaviour and management*, London: Thomson Learning.

Lewin, K. (1951), *Field Theory in Social Science*, New York: Harper and Row.

Lewis, D. (1996), 'The organizational culture saga—from OD to TQM: a critical review of the literature (Part One)', *Leadership and Organizational Development Journal* 17(1), 12–19.

Ouchi, W.G. (1981), *Theory Z. How American Business Can Meet the Japanese Challenge*, Reading, MA: Addison-Wesley.

Ouchi, W.G. and Jaeger, A.M. (1978), 'Type Z organization: stability in the midst of mobility', *Academy of Management Review*, April, 305–314.

Pascale, R.T. and Athos, A.G. (1981), *The Art of Japanese Management*, New York: Simon & Schuster.

Patterson, M.G., West, M.A., Shackleton, V.V.J., Dawson, J.F., Lawthom, R., Maitlis, S., Robinson, D.L., and Wallace, A.M. (2005), 'Validating the cultural climate measure: links to managerial practices, productivity and innovation', *Journal of Organizational Behavior*, 26, 379–408.

Peters, T.J. and Waterman, R.H. (1982), *In Search of Excellence: Lessons From America's Best Run Companies*, New York: Harper and Row.

Quinn, R.E. and Rohrbaugh, J. (1983), 'A spatial model of effectiveness criteria: toward a competing values approach to organizational analysis', *Management Science*, 29, 363–377.

Rickards, T. and Clark, M. (2006), *Dilemmas of Leadership*, London: Routledge.

Rousseau, D.M. (1988), 'The construction of climate in organizational research', in Cooper, C.L. and Robertson, I.T. (eds), *International review of industrial and organizational psychology* (Vol. 3, 139–158), New York: Wiley.

Schein, E.H. (1964), 'The Mechanism of Change', in Bennis, W., Schein, E., Steels, F., and Berlew, D. (eds), *Interpersonal Dynamics*, Homewood, IL: Dorsey Press.

—— (1983), 'The Role of the Founder in Creating Organizational Culture', *Organizational Dynamics*, Summer, 13–28.

—— (1984), 'Coming To A New Awareness Of Organizational Culture', *Sloan Management Review*, 25, 3–16.

Schein, E.H. (1985), *Organizational Culture and Leadership*, San Francisco, CA: Jossey-Bass.

Schneider, B. (1983), 'An interactionist perspective on organizational effectiveness', in Cummings, L.L., Hillsdale, B.M., and Peterson, M.F. (eds), *Handbook of organizational culture and climate*, Thousand Oaks, CA: Sage, xvii–xxi.

—— (1990), 'The climate for service: an application of the climate construct', in Schneider (ed), *Cultural climate and culture*, San Francisco, CA: Jossey-Bass, 383–412.

Smircich, L. (1983), 'Concepts of culture and organizational analysis', *Administrative Science Quarterly*, 28(2), 339–358.

Snyder, R.C. (1982; 1985), 'To Improve Innovation, Manage Corporate Culture', in Bennis, W.G. *et al*, *The Planning Change*, Fort Worth, TX: Holt, Rinehart and Winston, 164–171.

Tylor, E.B. (1891), *Primitive Culture*, London: John Murray.

Verbos, A.K., Gerard, J.A., Forshey, P.R., Harding, C.S., and Miller, J.S. (2007), 'The Positive Ethical Organization: Enacting a Living Code of Ethics and Ethical Organizational Identity', *Journal of Business Ethics*, 76, 17–33.

Wehrfritz, G., Kinetz, E, and Kent, J. (2008), 'Lured into Bondage', *Newsweek*, 21–28 April, 29–32.

 Take your learning further: Online Resource Centre
http://www.oxfordtextbooks.co.uk/orc/grieves/

Visit the Online Resource Centre that accompanies this book to enrich your understanding of this chapter. Explore case study updates and answers to questions, test yourself using an interactive flashcard glossary, and keep up to date with the latest developments in the area.

CHAPTER 7

Power, control, and organizational change

7.1 Introduction

In this chapter we are particularly interested in the exercise of power and its relationship to organizational change. If we define power as 'the potential ability to influence behaviour, to change the course of events, to overcome resistance, and to get people to do things that they would not otherwise do' (Pfeffer, 1993: 204–5), then we are interested in understanding the theories that lie behind the use, or abuse, of power. Power can be exercised in a variety of ways that will have a significant impact on how organizational change is perceived. We need to be aware that, when we intervene in an organization, we are engaging in a political intervention that has ethical consequences. Furthermore, the perspectives introduced in Chapter 1 encourage us to learn the art of organizational change, which requires an understanding of the assumptions that underlie one's own strategic role in the process of change. Thus, whether people are compelled to comply, or compliance is by voluntary agreement, depends upon the approach we take. You will learn to appreciate that power and control are interwoven into almost all areas of organizational life.

There are four main themes to this chapter. First is the recognition that organizational change is itself an intervention. Second, you will understand how structural theories inform change. Third, you will discover that paradigms and ideology may assist or restrict change. Finally, you will discover that power affects the way people perceive change through the psychodynamics of power and conflict.

By the end of this chapter you will:

- understand the nature of power;
- appreciate issues related to organizational change as a political intervention;
- understand structural theories of change;
- recognize assumptions that underpin the use of power in change situations;
- understand behaviour theories related to change;
- distinguish between paradigms and ideologies and consider how different ideologies may present opportunities or barriers to change;
- understand how the exercise of managerial power may lead to unethical practice;
- appreciate the psychodynamics of power;
- appreciate how the use or abuse of power may affect the mental life of the organization.

7.2 Organizational change as a political intervention

The concept of planned change is linked to the Organizational Development (OD) tradition and, in particular, to its seminal development phase in the 1980s. OD writers seek to create helpful interventions that are based on the open-systems model. Whilst the model is useful, it carries potential dangers when those who use it forget it is an analogy. Where this happens, the open-systems model can be criticized for its assumptions of cohesion, integration, and consensus. Some writers have gone much further, suggesting that organizational change itself is, at its worst, tyrannical and, at its best, a force seeking to control events and people.

Adopting a critical discourse, McKendall has argued that not only does organizational change involve the desire to control things to the advantage of management, but that planned change itself is ethically unsound because it reduces personal freedom:

> There is power in change; a great deal of power. But the power of planned change does not reside solely in the escalation of organizational productivity or in the improvement of less than optimal conditions. Neither does it reside exclusively in progress, innovation, nor increased efficiency. There is another side to planned organizational change. In addition to these often cited benefits of change, planned organizational change is a powerful management tool because the very dynamics of planned change subsume human freedom and thereby induce conformity and compliance with management's wishes throughout the organization.

(McKendall, 1993: 94)

McKendall argues that organizational change inevitably involves 'an element of domination' and this occurs in at least one of four ways. These are:

1. Creating conditions of uncertainty and ambiguity.
2. Disbanding groups and altering the nature of the informal organization.
3. Reinforcement of the position and rights of management.
4. Causing the entrenchment of management purposes.

This line of reasoning suggests that, despite the best intentions of the OD writers and consultants to act honourably, humanely, and ethically, all change efforts involve an attempt to increase managerial control. Thus, organizational change involves an 'increase in the power of management, and it occurs whether or not management consciously intends it' (McKendall, 1993: 94). Although McKendall does acknowledge the expressed intentions of the OD tradition to pursue strategies that increase openness, develop opportunities to enable people to make informed choices, and encourage autonomy, individual freedom, and self-esteem through concern with the human processes, she nevertheless argues that organizational change efforts focus on a limited set of values:

> Most authors do not consider the questions of freedom or autonomy; instead organizational change theorists concentrate on goals such as organizational effectiveness, organizational health, organizational efficiency, and goal attainment.

(McKendall, 1993: 95)

Other critical writers have argued that interventions often involve an unequal distribution of power. For example, Kelman and Warwick (1978) state that change agents sometimes fail to recognize situational and structural factors that enhance their power, or 'ethical ambiguity' that emerges in the control exercised. They also suggest that planned change is inevitably manipulative. Brimm (1972) argues that organizational change efforts are controlling because they seek to influence the 'misdirected'.

This argument is not uncommon, but if we are to find a way out of the *impasse* that would paralyse an ethical approach to managing change, we must confront three assumptions that lie behind this argument. These are:

1. The assumption that employees are the only stakeholders in an organization.

2. The assumption that planned change is inevitably top-down, so either results in deliberate manipulation or is simply a misguided managerial prerogative to manage at all costs.

3. The assumed equation of organizational change with inevitable loss of freedom for employees.

It would be useful to consider these in turn. First, it is too easy to assume that employees are the only stakeholders in an organization. Consider, for example, an environment in which a nuclear power station malfunctions, creating a dangerous situation for local communities and for the national interest. If that situation had been caused by employees who failed to follow correct safety procedures, then other stakeholders would have the right to demand compliance. Similarly, if a chief constable wished to change police officers' arrest procedures to deal with errors of judgement arising from the existence of a 'van culture' in which stereotypes are circulated and never confronted, then such a programme would be undertaken in the public interest. Thus, many situations involve judgements about a balance of power. Consider, for example, the objectives of a public sector organization such as social services, which has a duty to protect children from the activities of paedophiles. It is necessary at all times to be clear about whom the objectives are designed to help.

Second, planning change does not inevitably suggest that it must be undertaken in a top-down manner. Internal change may well be driven by a variety of employees and for numerous reasons. We can also reverse the argument and suggest that many employees might want to see change develop, but such initiatives can become stifled by poor communication channels, or by blocking attitudes and tactics of middle managers. In other words, innovation is not always the prerogative of management and should be encouraged throughout the organization.

The third problem, that organizational change inevitably means a loss of freedom for employees, is based on an assumed zero-sum game played between management and employees. If people perceive that organizational change brings some improvement to their working lives and economic prospects, then this provides a clear reason for intervening.

Figure 7.1 Managing the politics of organizational change requires harmony between organizational and employee needs, to achieve mutual autonomy

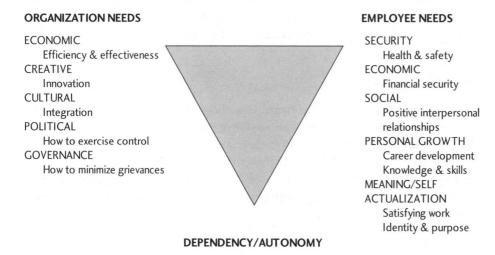

ORGANIZATION NEEDS

ECONOMIC
  Efficiency & effectiveness
CREATIVE
  Innovation
CULTURAL
  Integration
POLITICAL
  How to exercise control
GOVERNANCE
  How to minimize grievances

EMPLOYEE NEEDS

SECURITY
  Health & safety
ECONOMIC
  Financial security
SOCIAL
  Positive interpersonal
  relationships
PERSONAL GROWTH
  Career development
  Knowledge & skills
MEANING/SELF
ACTUALIZATION
  Satisfying work
  Identity & purpose

DEPENDENCY/AUTONOMY

Each set of needs can be expressed positively (increasing autonomy)
or negatively (decreasing autonomy)

How can we align the interests of organizations with the politics of planned change? Figure 7.1 provides a useful solution to this dilemma. This illustrates that we need to reconcile the organization's needs with those of employees. In order to avoid a zero-sum game between these interests, we have to think about the relative dependency/autonomy that will be gained or lost. Thus, if the organization gains at the expense of employees, then there will be an absolute increase in employee dependency. On the other hand, if employees win and the organization loses, then they will achieve an absolute increase in autonomy. However, if a mutual compromise can be found, then there will be a relative increase or growth in autonomy for both parties.

The organization's needs and the individual's needs require a delicate balance. As Etzioni points out:

> Nowhere is the strain between the organization's needs and the participant's needs—between effectiveness, efficiency and satisfaction—more evident than in the area of organizational control. In part, the two sets of needs support each other. An increase in the income of a corporation might allow it to increase the wages and salaries it pays; an increase in the prestige of a school might increase the prestige of the teachers who work there. To the degree that the two sets of needs are compatible, little control is necessary. The participants will tend to do what is best for the organization in order to gratify their own needs, and the organization in seeking to serve its needs will serve theirs.

(Etzioni, 1964: 58)

Such meshing of needs is never complete, because a 'corporation's profit might grow, but wages may not increase. Thus an organization must make deliberate efforts to reward those who conform to its regulations and orders and to penalize those who do not'. A successful political strategy is therefore 'largely dependent on its ability to maintain control of its participants' (Etzioni, 1964: 58).

---

❶ Stop and think 7.1

Draw two columns on a sheet of paper. One should be headed *'needs that do not change'*. The second should be headed *'needs that change over time'*. Under each heading write a list of five things that an organization might expect of its employees. Then, again in each column, write a list of things that individuals might expect of their employer. When you have completed your lists, count how many expectations are permanent and how many change with time. Finally, explain how power relationships might influence the outcomes.

If we superimpose the political character of change—that is, whether it is top-down or bottom-up—upon the intended harmony of organizational and individual interests, we arrive at the final formulation as illustrated in Figure 7.2. The type of approach taken will depend upon two things: whether you consider control to be neutral (as structural-functional analysis assumes) or political (as suggested by stakeholder theory and critical theory). Thus, you might ask which stakeholders' interests are being served. Or whose motives are served?

Figure 7.2 Balancing political interests when planning change

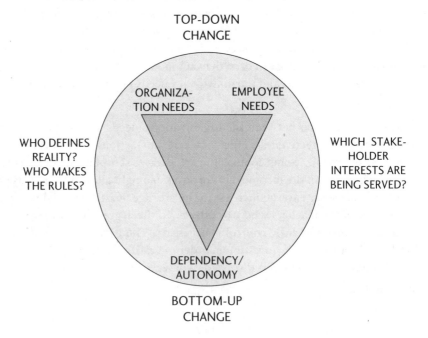

7.2.1 The use of power to influence change

There are many practices that may not be legally defined as unethical but that may result from collusion between subordinates and others who hold positions of power. Often such examples are not perceived as controversial and tend to be rationalized by means of situational expediency. These are related to the five main sources of power articulated by French and Raven (1968) and involve the relative perceptions of the manager and subordinates. The examples below indicate how this can occur when an individual makes decisions that are informed by perceptions and situational circumstances that constrain reflective judgement.

1. *Reward power* is seen to legitimize actions when a subordinate perceives the manager has the ability and resources to obtain rewards for compliance with directives. These often take the form of pay, promotion, praise, recognition, and the granting of various privileges. Whilst this is quite a natural process, it can give rise to a conflict of interest when the motives of a subordinate are informed by personal gain and those of the manager seek to achieve instrumental objectives.

2. *Coercive power* might not legitimize actions taken to conform in the eyes of subordinates, but it does explain how collusion is sometimes related to perceived fear of punishment. This may be extremely subtle, of course, since the perception of punishment might be related to desired personal objectives or rewards such as promotion, or an increase in pay. Abuse occurs when holders exercise power in such a way that subordinates fear that non-compliance may lead to the allocation of undesirable tasks or to lost opportunities for career progress.

3. *Legitimate power* reflects the assumptions of subordinates that a power holder, as manager or supervisor, has a right to expect compliance with a particular course of action. This is fairly typical of the positional power that exists within bureaucratic structures. Unless subordinates are extremely knowledgeable about their own rights in relation to a particular manager's legitimate right to command obedience, they are likely to be drawn along by the situation.

4. *Referent power* occurs when a particular manager exercises influence for charismatic reasons or because of personal attributes perceived to be desirable by subordinates. In situations where a conflict of interest may occur, collusion in a course of action might result because subordinates are over-zealous in their pursuit of particular objectives while failing to reflect on the consequences of their actions. This may often be the motive for *group-think*, the consequences of which can be disastrous for an organization.

5. *Expert power* develops when a leader is perceived to have a special knowledge, expertise, or degree of competence in a given area. In such cases subordinates and, indeed, other stakeholders are likely to defer to the expertise of a particular individual and alternative judgements and information can be overlooked.

(Modified from French and Raven, 1968)

Because individuals often seek to achieve organizational objectives, their tendency to ignore conflicting value systems can create value dilemmas and ethical conflicts of interest. Many people report conflict of interest in their work. Examples often cited in relation to overt practices include bribes, gifts, slush funds, concealing information from customers, shareholders, or more generally from the marketplace, engaging in price fixing, and so on. We can regard these examples as institutionalized practices, but there are also examples where ethical problems emerge because of workplace pressures to achieve results.

How people come to rationalize their judgements is partly explained by the exercise of power, but it is also informed by the belief that actions are neither illegal nor unethical. This is illustrated by Gellerman (1986), who argues that four commonly held rationalizations that lead to ethical misconduct are held by managers. These are:

1. The belief that the activity is within reasonable ethical and legal limits—that it is not 'really' illegal or immoral.

2. A belief that the activity is in the individual's or the corporation's best interests—that the individual should somehow be expected to undertake the activity.

3. A believe that the activity is 'safe', because it will never be found out when publicized: the classic crime-and-punishment issue of discovery.

4. A belief that, because the activity helps the company, the company will condone it and even protect the person who engages in it.

(Gellerman, 1986)

---

❶ Stop and think 7.2

Try to identify two examples of corporate misconduct that fit one of the four rationalizations described by Gellerman.

Although many organizations inform employees about organizational values, rules, and guidelines, or abide by professional codes of practice, change agents must consider the consequence of their interventions. There are some dilemmas to confront here.

The first major dilemma is the extent to which the pursuit of humanistic values is contradicted or compromised by the desire to achieve organizational effectiveness or efficiency. As Cummings and Worley argue, 'more practitioners are experiencing situations in which there is conflict between employees' needs for greater meaning and the organization's need for more effective and efficient use of its resources' (Cummings and Worley, 1997: 57). As a result, it is important to identify any areas of potential concern at the point of agreeing a contract with the client system. It should be clear, therefore, that any contract must make it transparent that organizational efficiency and effectiveness will depend upon improvement through the organization's employees. This has not always been the case, as where more programmed approaches to change management (for example, TQM, BPR) have sometimes adopted instrumental and formulaic approaches to their interventions.

The second dilemma is related to a conflict of values that change agents are likely to face in relation to the different perspectives of stakeholder groups. This inevitably means that different stakeholders will need to be consulted and their views explored in order to arrive at a workable intervention strategy. The difficulty is that each group of stakeholders may defend its own territory, giving rise to potential conflicts of values.

A third dilemma relates to technical ability. In other words, a change agent who fails to act with sensitivity to the needs of the client system and who fails to possess sufficient knowledge and skill at underpinning behavioural issues is acting unethically. Thus the ability to analyse a problem situation and to diagnose a potential solution requires an awareness of the variety of intervention strategies appropriate to the nature of the problem identified.

7.3 Structural theories and political change

7.3.1 Political strategies of organizations

At a structural level theorists argue that organizations should be designed, managed, and coordinated in such a way as to maximize political expediency. This means that, depending upon the purpose for which the organization exists, there will be a suitable political strategy. Table 7.1 illustrates the relationship between organization purpose and strategy.

Table 7.1 The relationship between organization purpose and strategy

Type of organization	Purpose	Strategy
Political organizations	To win power and exercise ideas and authority.	To mobilize supporters, influence the mass media, engage and challenge alternative views.
Charitable organizations and trusts	To promote the interests of the organization.	To inform, educate, raise profile, and obtain donations from the public.
Public limited company	To provide effective governance.	To develop, promote, and manage initiatives that will benefit the public. To inform the public about the way their money is spent, and demonstrate transparency.
Social weighting	To make a profit for shareholders by selling a product or service.	To be competitive in the marketplace by innovating and managing costs.

We could extend these examples *ad infinitum* but the point is to illustrate that each requires a different political strategy to achieve its objectives. What you may have noticed is that, whilst each strategy is relatively clear, the success of a strategy depends upon a form of engagement. Thus, political organizations have to engage with their potential electorate; charitable organizations and trusts have to appeal to emotional sensitivities or prick the conscience of the general public; local authorities have to focus on the message they wish to send to the local population about governance; and public limited companies have to make a profit, but achieving that will require a balance of motivational influences and persuasion in order to energize employees to compete effectively with other organizations. Some form of engagement therefore lies behind each strategy. We generally do not notice this, because engagement describes processes that make the strategy possible.

Each strategy is the result of political debate that has emerged over many centuries and we can crystallize this by examining how and why these strategies have emerged. Essentially there are four types of theory derived from the concerns of political theorists about the role of the state. Each reflects an argument about how best to manage people and is just as applicable to the management of contemporary organizations. These are:

1. *Force theories,* which argue that a strong guiding hand is necessary to give leadership, direction, and control. Examples include Rousseau's concept of the 'general will', in which the state was required to make laws, regardless of the different views and wishes of the people. Other examples were provided by Machiavelli—decisive action and the use of force are fundamental to success in achieving outcomes, at least under certain conditions in which conflict and political upheaval are evident— and Hobbes—the state (Leviathan) is necessary and the interests of the ruler have to prevail in order to ensure that order and stability are maintained.

2. *Elite theories*, which argue that all organizations contain ruling elites and followers. Elite theories emerged out of the arguments of force theories and argue that an uneven distribution of power is simply an inevitable fact of life. Those in power may have more influence over decision making but, even in elective government, not all power resides in the official representatives. Various experts, lobbies, and powerful groups exert different forms of political power. What characterizes elites is that they may be closed, or restricted, to certain groups of people. Closed elites will only permit a privileged group to enter. This is the case with political totalitarian regimes such as China, Burma, or North Korea, and with political/religious societies such as Iran. However, such elites can also exist in democratic societies, where they are more likely to be characterized as open elites, since entry to the privileged group is possible, based on influence in the form of money, position, political power, and cultural capital that enables the cultivation of social networks.

3. *Consent theories,* which form the basis of contractual relations between governments and the governed or, for our purposes, between the organization and its employees. Such theories are diametrically opposed to force theories. These

emerged, largely, from the political writing of Locke. Consent theories stress that the state should be the servant of the people and not their master.

4. *Conflict theories*, which stem from the writings of Marx, who argued that change emerges as a result of conflicts between different economic classes. Power is used by the dominant class over the others. Classes could be defined by their relationship to the means of production, so, in a capitalist society, we can distinguish between owners and workers. According to this view, those who own organizations need to control and exploit those who work in them in order to make profit. Capitalism inevitably requires coercion, which may take many subtle forms, such as persuasion, rhetoric, and ideology. Owners maximize their interests by exploiting others, which results in continual struggles between the different interests that each class holds. Conflict is therefore an inevitable instrument of change.

We find variations of these arguments today in most organizations. For example, in some public limited companies it would not be unusual to find variations of force theories suggesting that there is no scope for individuals to exercise their views, since this is the prerogative of management. Similarly, elite theories today suggest that power elites emerge to take control of political institutions (Mills, 1956; Dahl, 1963). Michels's 'iron law of oligarchy' (1949) suggests that elites in modern organizations are inevitable because of:

- the role that organizational structure plays in the unequal distribution of decision making and the concentration of power in limited hands;
- reliance on expertise, which concentrates power in the hands of certain groups, particularly in a knowledge economy;
- the need to rely on professional administrators who are able to exert their own influence over decision making.

But other, simplistic elite arguments exist, such as the view that those who get to the top of organizations are naturally gifted people whose traits and talents propel them into leadership positions. A variant of this argument is that people who rise to exercise power do so because they have control needs that seek to maximize their own political ambitions over others.

We will also find examples of consent theory. These are reflected in the move to a more participative form of human resource relationship that replaced the industrial relations conflicts of the past. Thus, because modern organizations are required by legislation to operate according to legal–rational principles (for example, to comply with health and safety, employment contracts, disability, ethnic, and gender rights), contractual relations form the basis of agreements between the organization and the employee. Consent theories have largely been responsible for the recognition that participation, involvement, and transparency require a pluralistic concept of power.

It can be argued that conflict theories are demonstrated by conflict in global capital, which causes continual and relentless pressure on companies to produce goods faster and more cheaply. This inevitably forces greater control over employees and seeks to extract greater value from their efforts, often by using technology to replace people. Table 7.2 illustrates three positions on the use of power that can be observed in the management of change.

Table 7.2 Three positions on the use of power

	Force theory and elite theory imply unitarism	Consent theory implies pluralism	Conflict theory implies a continuous dialectic between two opposing interests
Characteristics	All organizations contain ruling elites and followers. Leaders have unilateral authority to manage. Despite differences, all members should unite behind a common purpose or strategy.	An organization is composed of different interests, which may conflict. Leaders should demonstrate participative management.	Organizations are composed of two groups: employees who produce goods and services, and those who own organizations.
Whose interests are at stake?	Elites may have a closed or restricted membership. In democratic societies, organizational elites are more likely to be open, yet reflect specific social backgrounds.	Recognizes that there are very often opposed interests based on economic, social, political, and cognitive differences.	Seeks to identify the underlying motives for change and link these to the economic system of employer or employee interests.
Who runs organizations?	Organizations are controlled by oligarchies and must be managed with absolute authority. Force must be used when required. Leaders assume that everyone shares the same unitary interests.	Accepts the possibility that organizations may be run by elites, but not the idea that there is one simple group of followers, because modern society generates diverse views.	Owners run organizations and employ managers to resolve conflicts. Concepts such as participative management or empowerment are simply ideological devices to mask the real economic differences between ownership and the exploitation of labour.
Is conflict inevitable?	Conflict is not unusual and, in the last resort, will be controlled by force.	Conflict is dysfunctional if it is not resolved by rational debate. When this occurs, the services of a third party may be used to arbitrate.	Conflict is inevitable and is the driving force for change.

7.3.2 Assumptions about the use of power in organizational change

As a result of the three positions on the use of power that can be observed in the management of change today (Table 7.2), debate revolves around three assumptions that drive organizational change. These are unitarism, pluralism, and conflict. These are discussed below.

1. *Unitarism* emerged from force theories and elite theories and describes a form of political governance in which power is centralized. In organizations we can see that a unitary system of management expects that decision making is centralized. A further defining characteristic has emerged from the desire to manage industrial relations through the human resources function. Thus, HR strategy is predicated on the view that all employees share the goals of the organization and will be committed to these. The overarching assumption is that the authority structure, in which management makes the decisions, is accepted by all. If conflict occurs, it is seen to be dysfunctional because the system is not working properly. As Green (1987: 6) has argued, 'the approach may be viewed as paternalistic whereby the firm itself is best able to look after the interests of employees'. This view of organizations tends to be seen as impractical, because it refuses to recognize that conflict is a normal characteristic of differences in economic and social status, as well as in ideas and values. Indeed, conflict may be healthy for an organization if it generates progressive change.

2. *Pluralism* emerged from consent theories. The pluralistic argument is that modern organizations are complex and contain different interests, just like society, whose views and differences must be accommodated in order to achieve a psychological contract in which people are motivated to perform effectively and efficiently. Thus, effective change is seen to result from involving employees in the decision-making process. Those supporting a pluralist argument for organizational change would argue that it is important to reconcile the differences between various groups. It therefore follows that participative management is a feature of this approach.

3. *Conflict* is the driving force for organizational change because competition is a necessary feature of capitalism. As a result, nations and organizations compete for scarce resources and this forces change. At an organizational level, organizations structure inequality so that differential benefits are obtained by particular groups of people. This inequality gives rise to disenchantment and conflict emerges. As a result, managers are used to resolve these conflicts. Organizational change can therefore be described as revolutionary rather than evolutionary.

One is likely to adopt one of the approaches to managing change illustrated in Table 7.2. Unitarism is a form of political governance in which power is centralized. It emerged from force theories and elite theories.

Morgan appears to take the position that a manager's place is to resolve conflict. Thus, he argues that 'the pluralist manager is, after all, not politically neutral. He or she recognizes the politics of organization and accepts his or her role as an organizational power broker and conflict manager'. Such managers therefore 'use conflict as a means of promoting desired ends…' (Morgan, 1993: 215–16). But he goes further, arguing that a pluralist perspective enables change to be managed by using conflict to the advantage of the organization rather than eliminating it. Instead of seeing conflict as dysfunctional, as the unitarist approach does, pluralism recognizes the possibility that conflict can be used in a productive way. Morgan gives some practical reasons why conflict can be an advantage. These include using conflict as:

- a challenge to apathy;
- a source of innovation;
- resolving the problem of groupthink;
- using difference to stimulate change.

To Morgan, one of the most important skills of the pluralist manager is 'to find ways of maintaining just the right level of conflict' (Morgan, 1993: 216). On the one hand, 'too much conflict can immobilize an organization by channelling the efforts of members into unproductive activities', whilst too little 'may encourage complacency and lethargy'.

Conflict theorists, like the critical perspective generally, take a less conciliatory position and argue that Morgan simply provides solutions designed to paper over the cracks. They are more likely to ask how power is used and abused.

❶ Stop and think 7.3

Attempt to find examples that fall into each of the perspectives on power illustrated in Table 7.2. Once you have done this, consider which you feel best reflects the evidence you would use to justify your case.

7.4 Paradigms and ideology

We can note the difference between researchers interested in the structural properties of systems and those who are interested in behavioural dynamics. Thus, whilst conflict theorists would argue that organizational rationality is viewed as a series of devices to persuade or coerce employees to maximize efficiency, they still subscribe to the possibility of objective rationality. By contrast, researchers interested in dynamic human processes rather than systemic properties can point out that objective rationality is a myth caused by two sets of dynamics—dominant coalitions and bounded rationality. Innovation may well be the product of a fertile mind but it can be stifled by subtle political processes.

The enemy of innovation may be the mindset within ourselves. For Pascale (1990), conflict is a productive force when it is used to 'disturb equilibrium' and challenge the conventional wisdom. Pascale's observation reflects not only his own experience but that of Kuhn's (1970) famous text on *The Structure of Scientific Revolutions*. Where Kuhn used the more precise term of paradigm, others have used the terms 'mindset', 'worldview' or 'mental model', and 'ideology' to reflect how a way of thinking restricts the pursuit of knowledge. These other definitions tend to confuse the issue. For this reason, we will stick with the terms paradigm, a shared view containing a number of assumptions, and ideology, an internally coherent set of ideas designed to persuade people of a particular worldview.

Kuhn's use of the term paradigm refers to the way science proceeds in a disjointed manner. This is because old paradigms outlive their usefulness when they no longer provide satisfactory scientific explanations. A new paradigm emerges and this resembles a leap of faith by scientists willing to explore new forms of enquiry unhindered by the old rules. Organizational analysis has been profoundly influenced by the concept of the paradigm as an analytic frame of reference. However, whereas Kuhn's definition affected the philosophy of science by outlining the process of factual knowledge accumulation through problem solving, the definition derived from Burrell and Morgan (1979) refers to the assumptions and knowledge claims that lie behind an analytical perspective in explaining the social world. Burrell and Morgan classify paradigms in four categories:

1. *Functionalism* (objective regulation), which assumes that human action is based on rational action and that this can be understood by testing hypotheses through quantitative measurement.

2. *Interpretative Paradigm* (subjective regulation), which seeks to understand how humans derive meaning from their actions.

3. *Radical Humanist Paradigm* (subjective radical change), which suggests that, as social actors, people experience barriers that constrain their potential.

4. *Radical Structuralist Paradigm* (objective radical change), which views conflict as the driving force of social change.

Although one can argue that these paradigms are incommensurate (that is, if you accept one paradigm then you must reject the truth claims of the others), Burrell and Morgan in fact argue for an analytical plurality. Their main aim is to resist the domination of the structural-functional perspective. We can see the dominance of this paradigm in the concept of management control.

Management control comes in a number of forms, which we can regard as administrative, technical, or managerial. Administrative control can best be understood as the controls put in place to accomplish a task. Similarly, technical controls are constructed to ensure that people comply with an agreed method, and these are monitored by quality systems. Whilst inappropriate administrative and technical controls can adversely affect innovation, it is managerial control that has the greatest impact. This is because, unlike machines, people bring creativity and uncertainty to the workplace and, whilst creativity can be cultivated and encouraged, it can also be stifled. The physical and psychological environment created by a manager is therefore a central aspect of this.

The structural-functional perspective focuses on the management need to control technical and social processes (unitarism). If we employ the other paradigms, we come to different conclusions. For example, the interpretative paradigm is interested in how the linguistic construct of 'control' is defined and whether it is shared or contested. Thus actors other than management will often give different interpretations of how control is constructed and applied. The radical humanist paradigm is more concerned to identify the barriers that result from the way that management control is applied. Finally, the radical structuralist paradigm adopts the quasi-objective approach of structural functionalism but argues that conflict rather than consensus is the driving force of all social change. Therefore this paradigm argues that control is continually contested and that this dialectic process leads to change. One can see therefore that management is not a neutral process. Organizational rationality changes with the paradigm one adopts.

7.4.1 Dominant coalitions and bounded rationality

It is perfectly possible to accept that, whilst organizations are not neutral enterprises, ownership does not inevitably have to suggest that employers are consciously exploiting employees. An economic system might well be unfair by favouring those people with capital and disadvantaging those without, but individuals' motives should not be confused with systemic properties. As Bacharach and Lawler (1980: 67) point out:

> Organizations are neither the rational, harmonious entities celebrated in managerial theory nor the arenas of apocalyptic class conflict projected by Marxists. Rather it may be argued, a more suitable notion lies somewhere between those two—a concept of organizations as politically negotiated orders.

As we noted in Chapter 1, the multiple constituencies perspective forces us to recognize the conscious interests of different groups as they are played out through the concept of political negotiation. However, we need to understand that interest groups are not passive constituencies. Each constituency has its own motives. In this respect, Bacharach and Lawler identify five assumptions underlying the dynamics of political engagement in organizations:

1. Organizations are best conceptualized as political bargaining systems.
2. Specific decision-making spheres are the primary arenas for bargaining and conflict in organizations.

3. Within the decision spheres, most organizational politics involves the efforts of actors to mobilize interest groups and coalitions for the sake of influencing the decisions of those in authority.

4. Interest groups merge into coalitions and select tactics to achieve their common objectives.

5. The formation of coalitions and coalition alliances will depend on the nature of the organizational structure and on the distribution and control of organizational resources.

Coalitions are composed of interest groups that emerge to advance a strategy for their own interests. Thus they seek to influence those who hold formal positions of authority. Their tactics may be either covert or overt. Managers are part of this process because they are likely to belong to various coalitions. There are two related concepts that help us to understand the process. These are:

1. The role of management as the *dominant coalition*. This was identified by Cyert and March (1963).

2. The process of decision making that emerges referred to as *bounded rationality* (March and Simon, 1958).

The dominant coalition is useful because it explains a paradoxical relationship between systemic needs and individual needs. For example, an organization's primary needs are to achieve efficiency and effectiveness, whilst individual needs are grouped around personal goals. Coalitions therefore form around these different interests. As a result, a process of bargaining emerges between members of the firm's dominant coalition, which facilitates a temporary consensus. This, however, is usually vague, with metaphorical allusions. The dominant coalition achieves compromises that might not satisfy each party entirely but result in temporary harmony. The dominant coalition should therefore be seen as an informal decision-making mechanism that exposes the myth of objective rationality in making decisions through formal instruments of policy. For example, on the surface, a meeting to decide a strategic objective might appear orderly and follow procedures and protocols. Below the surface one can often detect behavioural strategies that may not be fully aligned with the agreed objectives.

Observation of organizational politics therefore suggests that the idea of rational decision making is a myth. Instead, we can think of decision making as an imperfect process resulting from argument, debate, and conflict. Bounded rationality also challenges the myth of objective rationality because:

> objective rationality... would imply that the behaving subject moulds all his behaviour into an integrated pattern by (a) viewing the behaviour alternatives prior to a decision in panoramic fashion, (b) considering the whole complex of consequences that would follow on each choice, and (c) with a system of values as criterion singling out one from the whole set of alternatives.

(Thomas, 2003, quoting Simon, 1947)

In this extract Simon is pointing out that no individual can be in complete command of the situational facts. Furthermore, we cannot fully appreciate the consequences of potential alternatives. Because rational choice is therefore constrained, managers simplify complexity while acting as if they were in full control of all rational choices: they work with satisfactory rather than perfect solutions to problems. Simon calls these satisficing solutions, in contrast to the ideal, which he refers to as optimizing solutions. What emerges are managerial routines for making similar, and potentially dangerous, decisions in future. We can explore the twin processes of the dominant coalition and bounded rationally by looking at Case example 7.1.

7.4.2 Ideological control within organizations

Elite theorists argue that organizations become oligarchies by virtue of the need to create hierarchies. Conflict theorists extend this argument by claiming that not only do oligarchies reflect class differences in relation to the means of production, but they also become justified by ideologies that serve to legitimize the use of power. Despite the theoretical differences, we need to explore how oligarchies affect change. One way to do this is to identify ideological differences within or between organizations. Whilst we can use the term ideology to refer simply to a set of ideas, it is more useful for our purpose to view it as a dominant logic required and expected within an organization. For example, in Chapter 6 we noted that strong culture advocates argue that a culture can be the dominant force for change, providing it is driven by the values of a strong individual or management group. However, there is an alternative way to view this. A

Figure 7.3 Harrison's ideological orientations of an organization's character

Power Orientation	Role Orientation
The power-oriented organization is competitive and jealous of its territory. Some modern conglomerates project images of power ideology. They buy and sell organizations and people as commodities, in apparent disregard of human values and the general welfare.	An organization that is role-oriented aspires to be as rational and orderly as possible. In contrast to the wilful autocracy of the power-oriented organization, there is a preoccupation with legality, legitimacy, and responsibility.
Task Orientation	**Person Orientation**
In the organization that is task-oriented, achievement of a super-ordinate goal is the highest value. Nothing is permitted to get in the way of accomplishing the task. If established authority impedes achievement it is swept away.	Unlike the other three types, the person-oriented organization exists primarily to serve the needs of its members. The organization itself is a device through which the members can meet needs that they could not otherwise satisfy by themselves.

strong culture can be driven by a well-meaning paternalist but it can just as easily be driven by a neurotic megalomaniac or by an oligarchy that may negatively influence the cultural psychodynamics of the organization. We can therefore regard an ideology as a belief system. Harrison (1972) (see Figure 7.3) provides a useful example.

Harrison suggests that organizations develop ideologies from the dominant leaders who control them. This may also be true of different operational units within a single organization. We can therefore imagine how the four types of *power*, *role*, *task* and *person* orientation can lead to the creation of a dominant coalition, which might also be an oligarchy. We can also imagine how a particular type of bounded rationality might emerge within each type. To understand this, read the following case example.

❯❯ Case example 7.1

Understanding your organization's character

During the commissioning and start-up stages of a US chemical plant in Europe, it became apparent that the Americans and local nationals involved had rather different ideas about decision making and commitment to decisions. Consider the approach of each group:

The Americans tended to operate within what I shall later describe as a task-oriented ideology. In problem-solving meetings they believed that everyone who had relevant ideas or information should contribute to the debates and that, in reaching a decision, the greatest weight should be given to the best-informed and most knowledgeable people. They strove, moreover, for a clear-cut decision; and once the decision was made, they usually were committed to it even if they did not completely agree with it. Some of the nationals, however, came to the project from very authoritarian organizations and tended to operate from a power-oriented ideological base (this will also be described later). Each individual seemed to be trying to exert as much control as possible and to accept as little influence from others as he could. If he was in a position of authority, he seemed to ignore the ideas of juniors and the advice of staff experts. If he was not in a position of authority, he kept rather quiet in meetings and seemed almost happy when there was an unclear decision or no decision at all. He could then proceed the way he had wanted to all along.

The task-oriented people regarded the foregoing behavior as uncooperative and, sometimes, as devious or dishonest. The power-oriented people, however, interpreted the task-oriented individuals' emphasis on communication and cooperation as evidence of softness and fear of taking responsibility.

Each group was engaging in what it regarded as normal and appropriate practice and tended to regard the other as difficult to work with or just plain wrong. The fact that the differences were ideological was dimly realized only by the more thoughtful participants. The remainder tended to react to each other as wrongheaded individuals rather than as adherents to a self-consistent and internally logical way of thinking and explaining their organizational world.

Source: Harrison (1972), 150–151.

Extending this point about the way bounded rationality works, we can note Pascale's example of General Motors in the 1980s, in which senior managers invoked an ideology that inhibited employees from expressing their views or using initiative that might challenge the prevailing mindset. As a result, employees became initiated into 'learned helplessness', which was communicated partly through social routines that taught managers how to be compliant if they valued their careers. Pascale (1990) argues that a variety of factors inhibit or promote the opportunity for innovative change; these include:

- Whether an elite group or a single point of view dominates decision making.

- Whether employees are encouraged to challenge the status quo.

- The process through which new members become socialized into the organization's norms, prejudices, and practices.

- The extent to which data are suppressed or cultivated in some way.

- The extent to which reward systems appear to be fair.

- The extent to which genuine empowerment occurs.

When a paradigm is expressed ideologically, routines are played out. If these routines seek to control imagination and critical thinking, then they undermine confidence or initiative. Tactics of ideological control include:

- Humiliation, which has the effect of closing down free expression of ideas.

- Overloading employees with detail and pressing deadlines that prevent effective performance.

- Sanitizing topics and presenting limited options.

- Resorting to subterfuge.

- Creating dichotomies that simplify complexity into good or bad alternatives.

Examples of similar tactics are illustrated in the following case example, which illustrates how one (positive) paradigm is replaced by another (negative) paradigm. It also illustrates how ideology is used to persuade people of the legitimacy of the paradigm.

» Case example 7.2

When a star performer is placed in an iron cage

Star had been an iconoclastic company renowned for its innovation in the pigments industry. As is usually the case, innovative and small, fast-growing companies become the targets for takeover by larger, and sometimes more lethargic, companies looking to increase their own performance by taking over a rising star. It is usually hoped that the rising star may become a cash cow for the new parent.   »

>> Unfortunately for Star, the parent company 'Iron Cage' installed a managing director from its own ranks in order to coordinate quality assurance systems and achieve cultural integration with the corporation. In practice, this meant overlaying heavy bureaucratic structures on an innovative star. The employees of Star considered the irony of this takeover. This was seen to be analogous to placing a cast-iron harness on a thoroughbred racehorse.

A second problem perceived by employees was the ethics of change. That is, most felt that the decision-making process was coercive: changes to working practices had to be accepted under pretence of inevitability. All Star's managers disagreed with the language of change that was used. They were told that they were part of a much bigger corporate enterprise now and had to be integrated into its ways. One way of doing this was to replace the entire top team of managers with senior managers from the new corporate elite. In addition, quality systems provided the bureaucratic structure that the corporate parent thought Star required to complete its transformation.

Two years after the takeover Star managers felt intensely negative. Their feelings were emotional and expressed elliptically using euphemisms. This language illustrated how they had been worn down by the dominance of the new ideology. They reported that, because the change intervention failed to involve Star employees, it stifled their creativity. Organizational change was therefore seen as politically coercive and dictatorial.

The relationship between language and power was expressed subtly. For example, euphemisms were used to avoid open conflict but this suppressed their feelings. They referred to the 'new elite' or 'cadre' who 'give the impression that they walk on water'. The takeover was seen as 'ethnic cleansing'. They felt alienated by 'the top cats' and the relentless pace of the 'top man who was driven by short-termism'. References to a 'siege mentality' and to a sense of 'us and them' prevailed. This ran counter to the previous progressive approach of the company prior to the takeover. The motives of the new elite were seen to be short-term because 'the top cats want their elevation to the board of directors'. As a result everything was said to be 'systems-driven'. Decision making was defined as 'propose and tell'. The plant manager, pigments manager, and research and development manager, amongst others, stated that the new political structure of the organization was keeping them 'stifled and chained down'. This resulted in a decrease in experimentation (essential to a progressive niche-market chemical company) with new ideas and product development. The training manager reported that company loyalty had been abandoned because people were finding it difficult to commit themselves, stating that 'five years ago it was my company. Now, it's just the company I work for. The dynamics were radically altered because the new senior team think strategy is just flow diagrams and their plans have no reference to people.'

Seven years after the takeover, Star moved from a highly profitable company to an underperforming company. Iron Cage itself was eventually broken up and sold off.

This case example illustrates how the very people at the heart of a previously successful business were alienated. Although employees of this company found the content of change difficult to comprehend (we need to understand that these are employees responsible for its previous success, most of whom were professionals with PhDs), it was the way that change was managed that caused a process of disillusionment. Why do some people manage the politics of change so badly?

Morgan (1993) informs us that there are basically five behavioural strategies that we can all adopt. These are:

1. *Avoidance of the problem or situation* because we do not want to deal with the difficult consequences. This sometimes occurs because we procrastinate and put off a decision to a later time.

2. *Compromising* by negotiating or dealing with a situation to satisfy each party.

3. *Competing*, because of the challenge that rivalry offers and its enhancement of personal ego and power, largely due to the win/lose mentality meaning the submission of an opponent.

4. *Accommodating, complying or submitting* to the other party.

5. *Collaboration*, which requires searching for a solution that will enhance the outcomes for both parties.

A manager responsible for change will use one or more of these strategies. However, when the ultimate outcome of a change programme is business improvement, then we need to recognize that we require the willing cooperation, motivation, and expertise of those best able to achieve this: employees. We can devise some simple questions for deciding which route to take. These are:

1. Is the cooperation of others required and does this require me to call on their motivation, knowledge, and expertise in the interests of the business? Alternatively, if I were to force change upon people, are there any potential negative consequences that are likely to impact upon the business?

2. What type of psychological contract would maximize business outcomes? Being coercive would require a win/lose strategy. In this case you must be certain of winning, and convinced that those who lose will not be less motivated. Adopting a utilitarian strategy carries the expectation that only limited motivation is required because people get paid to come to work. Finally, adopting a values-driven strategy assumes that a high degree of cooperation is required because innovation depends upon strategic human resources. These are expressed in Figure 7.4.

We can see from Figure 7.4 that if the response to question 1 is 'yes', then we must collaborate or compromise. Collaborating is the preferred response since it will seek collective solutions to problems. It has the advantage of confronting

Figure 7.4 Political strategies for managing change

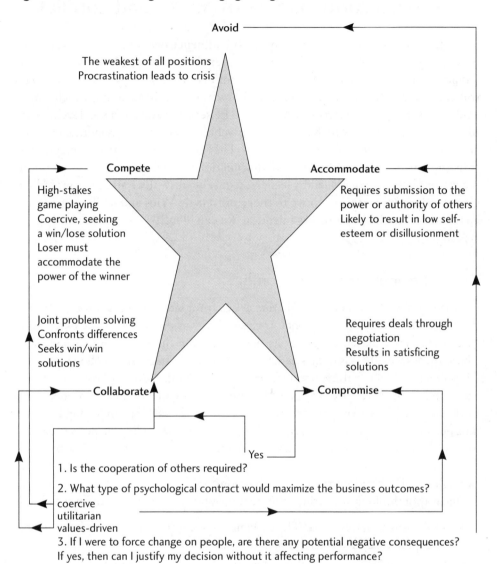

Avoid

The weakest of all positions
Procrastination leads to crisis

Compete

High-stakes
game playing
Coercive, seeking
a win/lose solution
Loser must
accommodate the
power of the winner

Joint problem solving
Confronts differences
Seeks win/win
solutions

Collaborate

Accommodate

Requires submission to the
power or authority of others
Likely to result in low self-
esteem or disillusionment

Requires deals through
negotiation
Results in satisficing
solutions

Compromise

Yes

1. Is the cooperation of others required?

2. What type of psychological contract would maximize the business outcomes?
coercive
utilitarian
values-driven

3. If I were to force change on people, are there any potential negative consequences?
If yes, then can I justify my decision without it affecting performance?

differences and sharing ideas. Compromising is more likely to result from the utilitarian position typical of the wage/effort bargain. Thus, accommodation results from a win/lose power relationship or from a cultural climate in which open dialogue is not practised. Being competitive is likely to alienate people and will have a negative impact on performance. Finally, avoidance is the weakest of all positions and has a negative impact on one's reputation as a change manager.

7.5 The psychodynamics of power and conflict

We noted above that ideology has a powerful influence over the way people experience organizations. We can extend this argument by illustrating how the psychodynamics of power and conflict can become influential. There are three main ways this can occur. The first is through social psychological behaviours, which can be explained through Transactional Analysis. The second is through the development of dysfunctional traits, which cause deep psychological tensions resulting in a concern for the mental life of the organization. The third extends neuroses by referring to pathological cultures that display dysfunctional tendencies because emotions are manipulated or controlled by leaders. Consequently, if we add the four ideologies identified by Harrison above to those of Kets de Vries and Miller (1984) discussed below in the neurotic organization, we can identify at least nine ideological typologies.

7.5.1 The amplification of conflict

One useful way of analysing conflict that arises from interactions is through the way people communicate. Transactional Analysis (TA) was developed by the psychiatrist Eric Berne. TA is based on positions that arise from three different personalities. These are described as ego states, labelled as *child, adult,* and *parent.* Following Berne, it is possible to identify the ego state from the words used, the tone of voice, from gestures, and from attitudes of the people communicating in a particular context. This has been a useful tool for psychotherapy but it is equally useful in understanding how interpersonal communication creates either clear understanding or perceptual distortions by mixing inappropriate emotional and cognitive messages. We learn these ego states during primary and secondary processes of socialization: in the family and through social institutions such as organizations.

One way of thinking about these different ego states is to consider them as follows:

- Adult—rational discourse. The exchange of ideas in which two or more people attempt to reach a balanced conclusion.

- Parent—offers two possibilities. First, the *critical parent* who lays down standards, or rules to control situations, behaviours, and attitudes. This is recognized by the orders and command statements communicated. We often see this when people resort to electronic forms of communication such as email. Second, the *nurturing parent* is recognized by the degree of consideration given in the communication.

- Child—can be subdivided into the *spontaneous child,* the *intuitive child,* and the *adapted child.* This last category can be further subdivided into *compliant child* or *rebellious child.* These various ego states illustrate how we have internalized ways of coping in relation to the parent state.

Whilst the balance between these states will vary from individual to individual, it is interesting that those who control the discourse in organizations will achieve either a parallel transaction—for example, adult to adult—or a crossed and dysfunctional transaction such as parent to child, or parent to adult, or adult to parent. If a senior manager expressed commands rather than made requests, then s/he would adopt a critical-parent ego state. Such an individual is likely to be authoritarian and inconsiderate of the feelings of others.

In organizations, TA can be used to investigate the positions people adapt to a situation. In a parallel transaction, the discourse progresses by obtaining an appropriate response. But each response is a demonstration of power. For example, we could see how an adult-to-adult transaction is empowering because it seeks equal participation. In a crossed transaction we encounter inappropriate and sometimes difficult statements and responses. Even silence can be seen as a response either of dependency or of the refusal to engage. For example, a manager who adopts the critical-parent state seeks to assert authority and control.

---

❶ Stop and think 7.4

What type of transaction is taking place and why?

The new senior manager introduced himself and proceeded to outline his business strategy to the assembled staff, who had been asked to come and listen to the 'very important announcement'. After he had outlined his plans, he stated:

'You are either with me or you're out of here. Who's with me?' he demanded.

At that point, the room, full of people, fell into an embarrassing silence.

7.5.2 The mental life of the organization

As we have observed above, the potential to amplify conflict is a real issue for change leaders. Other writers have suggested the similarity of organizations to families. Furthermore, some psychologists and psychoanalysts have argued that, just as families can be dysfunctional, so can organizations.

Leadership can have its dark side. Some leaders either inherently possess or develop personality traits such as narcissism and omnipotence that make them feel invincible. This can be the source of their success but it can also be the cause of their downfall. Morgan (2004) reminds us of Miller's (1990) Icarus paradox by pointing out that the Greek mythological character, Icarus, flew so close to the sun with his artificial wax wings that the wings melted. Because strategic leaders are so powerful, their once-compelling visions can become seriously flawed. Many of us, however, experience this to a lesser extent with things we take for granted. This can work in negative as well as positive ways. For example, we might be reminded what love is only when we lose it. We might discover sanity when we become less compulsive about success. Whatever form this takes, we are dealing with unconscious mental processes. Thus, in a similar way to how socialization may repress individuality, organizations can repress creativity and energy.

Horney (1957) has pointed out that, although many people become obsessive about something, they do not have to be prisoners of their unconscious minds. Her studies of neurotic individuals influenced the humanistic psychology of Maslow and Rogers. Her argument is that neurotic symptoms, or 'rackets', are symptomatic of unresolved deeper conflicts. This may result in practical difficulties but they also produce deep psychological tensions such as anxieties, depression, inertia, detachment, overdependence, and indecision. The individual is usually blind to these traits. Such pressures can lead to a divided personality. Whereas Freud believed that a person's inner conflicts result from instinctual drives that are challenged by the conventions, rules, and regulations of a 'civilized' society, Horney argued that inner conflicts result from our desires. She identified three basic neurotic traits:

1. Moving towards people.

2. Moving against people.

3. Moving away from people.

Moving towards people is a trait that a person develops because of specific feelings of isolation or fear. People adopt strategies to cope with this. Such traits appear in childhood. The need to win over the affection of others may be founded upon a sense of isolation and the need to feel more secure. In its early stages, this trait seeks a resolution. Consequently, individuals will experience anxiety or conflicts and may display episodes of temper; they usually develop a coping strategy more commonly associated with passivity in order to win approval. Over time such coping tactics become more sophisticated. In adults, the needs for association and approval manifest in other ways through deeper relationships. These needs can appear to be compulsive. Thus, the relationship may not be based on genuine interest or love but on the need to win approval. Although Horney is concerned with childhood as the seminal experiences we all encounter, we can consider how organizations may cause us to display certain conflicts such as anxiety, depression, anger, a sense of exploitation, and so on. As a result, we adopt strategies to cope. But those strategies will be played out in relation to the emotional experiences we had as children. At meetings, for example, we may withdraw both physically and mentally, or feel a sudden rush of anger in response to someone who has been tactless, but the ultimate coping strategy for this type of person is to resolve the inner conflict by being less assertive, and more subservient by subjecting themselves to the perceived greater power of others.

Moving against people is an act of hostility born of a hostile family environment. Individuals learn to cope through fighting and rebelling against the demands placed upon them. They distrust the people close to them. As adults, such people assume the world is hostile because they filter all potential and real experiences through their own perceptions of distrust. In an organizational setting, for example, this ideology or way of perceiving relationships with others is similar to McGregor's Theory X manager, who makes decisions to control people because they cannot be trusted. The workplace is basically perceived as a hostile environment with a superficial veneer of polite, fair-minded relationships. This remains the case, providing that other subservient people know their place and submit to the authority of managers and leaders. This trait finds its resolution in strategies designed to control others, but is manifested as a type of learned selfishness and belief in 'every man for himself'. Characteristically, such people dislike weakness in themselves and others. They strive for recognition as successful individuals and they have a high need for prestige. Control is a device to avoid trusting people. It is likely that, in extreme cases, such traits develop into the exploitation of others.

Moving away from people is a trait that develops because of childhood experiences that cause such individuals to distance themselves from family and close relationships. This occurs because such people feel too close to those around them and, consequently, attempt to create distance from their family. The coping strategy is to retreat into a secret world. Over time they develop neurotic tendencies such as detachment from others. Such individuals may demonstrate superficial engagement with others, providing that such relationships do not intrude into their inner circle. They also display tendencies such as superiority, isolation, and a fear of being required to join others. In an organizational setting, teamwork relationships are difficult and these individuals perform better when they have a specific individual task to perform. They may perform well as 'completer finishers', to use Belbin's term, but they are not team players. This is only unhealthy when it becomes a compulsive behaviour: when neurosis predominates and removes freedom to decide whether to seek isolation in time of stress. Then, neurosis removes free will, forcing individuals to develop a pattern of behaviour that involves excessive isolation.

The three neurotic traits described above are, of course, extreme examples. Many of us, from time to time, experience such inner conflicts. As Horney argues, we do not need to be prisoners of our own subconscious drives. We can reflect upon them and learn to resolve such conflicts. The central point for us to note here is that, as Horney argued, the competitive spirit of modern civilization is fertile ground for neuroses; organizational life is potentially one of the most competitive arenas for many of us. Such arenas can cause good people to become disillusioned and withdraw. We will examine this below.

❶ Stop and think 7.5

To what extent do you think we can refer to the mental life of the organization? Think of five ways that the use or abuse of power in organizations could affect our emotional feelings or psychological attitudes.

7.5.3 The neurotic organization

As we have seen, neurosis means the development of compulsive tendencies. It is believed that self-reflection may assist in minimizing the effects of these behaviour traits. However, some individuals might not have the means, or the inclination, to be self-reflective. If such people are in positions of power, they may create structures that other people are expected to emulate in order to enhance their careers. The idea that organizations can display neurotic tendencies has been articulated by Kets de Vries and Miller (1984). Organizations can display dysfunctional tendencies when emotions are manipulated or controlled by leaders who have pathological traits. Thus Kets de Vries and Miller argue that neurosis develops when a particular style becomes predominant. In such situations organizations begin to display characteristic behaviour patterns. Behaviours and attitudes become rigid and distorted. These, in turn, influence the perceptions of employees towards objectives. In particular, the neurotic style of the senior executive influences the way the organization functions through the way it is structured, by the approach to strategy, and particularly through the culture.

Kets de Vries and Miller argue that the relationship between leaders and organizational pathology is demonstrated more clearly in small, centralized firms or departments with a single leader, or where a unified group is able to influence decision making. They describe five specific neurotic organizational profiles. These are illustrated in Table 7.3 and are described as 'paranoid', 'compulsive', 'dramatic', 'depressive', and 'schizoid'.

Each type is caused by a particular leadership style. What we need to note at this point is that whilst leaders create opportunities, they can also generate unnecessary risks. Furthermore, the ideologies generated by chief executives create shared fantasies for groups within the organization. Following the psychodynamic work of Kets de Vries and Miller (1984), some organizations can be regarded as 'sick' because they demonstrate dysfunctional behavioural characteristics.

The *paranoid* organization obsessively monitors the external environment for the schemes and plan of competitors, but this is characterized by an unreasonable lack of trust. Even partnership and alliances are viewed in a Machiavellian way. Control is exercised by means of a complex management information system designed to analyse the dangers of the outside world. This in itself is less of a problem than its recourse to the demanding procedures expected of employees to detail everything through reports. One symptom is its obsession with meetings as a feedback mechanism to control information rather than to share ideas.

The *compulsive* organization is obsessed with formal control mechanisms to control the inner working of the organization. Invariably this involves people processes. Rules, policies, and procedures are constructed to deal with *minutiae* including dress codes, external relationships, and corporate instructions about communicating external relationships. Thus behaviour is circumscribed for almost every eventuality. Relationships are viewed in power terms, between authority and dominance on one hand and functional role and submission on the other.

Table 7.3 Neurotic styles of individuals and organizations

Dysfunctional characteristics	• Suspicion • Mistrust • Hyper-alertness	• Perfectionism • Seeking submission • Inability to relax	• Self-dramatization • Narcissistic preoccupation	• Feeling worthless • Loss of motivation	• Detachment • Estrangement • Indifference
Core fantasy	• Cannot trust anyone	• Must control	• Want to impress	• Hopeless	• Doesn't matter
Dangers	• Seeking and finding suspicions confirmed	• Inward orientation • Indecision	• Superficiality	• Pessimism	• Frustration with emotional isolation
Organizational focus and structure	• Organizational intelligence • Control structure	• Information systems for formal control • Standardization	• Bold new ventures • Growth • Primitive structure	• Formal routines • Hierarchy without leadership	• Political playground for sub-top
Decision making	• Redundant analyses	• Carefully planned uncertainty reduction	• Based on hunch, instinct, etc. • Unreflective	• Tribal battles among sub-top vie for approval by 'leader'	• Tribal battles among sub-top vie for approval by 'leader'
Power	• Centralized with top management	• Top management and corporate staff	• Narcissistic leader	• Leadership vacuum	• Leadership vacuum • Shifting coalition
Strategy	• Risk averse: – reactive – diversification	• Planned in detail • Long-term theme	• Anything that moves • Corporate wild growth	• Aimless • Too busy with petty stuff	• Product of individual goals, power, and politicking
Change	• 'Muddling through' • Fear of 'leaks'	• Too rigid for the process of change	• In defiance of failure, leader fails to bend	• Meaningful change does not occur	• Small, incremental • Often obstructed

Source: Kets de Vries and Miller (1984).

In an interesting case study indicating how an organization moved from one form of neurosis (paranoid) to another (dramatic), Kersten (2007) points out that what characterizes a *dramatic* neurosis is its narcissism. That is, such an organization is 'so enamoured with its own story and so fully believes in its own reality, morality and promises that it begins to place itself outside of the rules and regulations that govern the rest of the world' (Kersten, 2007: 67). Consequently, such organizations perform grand dramas because they believe in myths of their own making. Consequently, they create 'false and incomplete information', which causes them to become 'dangerously uninhibited' (Kets de Vries and Miller, 1984). Dramatic organizations are impulsive and dangerously hyperactive.

The *depressive* organization is apathetic. It is conservative and lacks self-confidence. Its communication style is passive. It is highly routinized and does not require employees to demonstrate initiative. Such organizations exist in the public and private sectors but they continue to exist in the latter only because their environment is relatively stable.

Finally, the *schizoid* organization is distrustful and demonstrates detachment and indifference. People feel estranged from one another and leadership is in constant doubt about which proposal to adopt. Consequently, plans get implemented in a half-hearted way. Actions depend on the mood of the leader or senior manager. Leadership is therefore inconsistent.

The examples given above are all reifications. That is, in reality an organization cannot have a life of its own. Instead, what we feel and experience is a product of relationships in which some people have more power than others. Whether this power is used well or badly depends upon the leaders and those who are required to conform to their requests. When power is used badly, it is dysfunctional for the organization in the long run because it creates a pattern of behaviour that may be pathological. In this section we have explored ways in which unresolved conflicts in attitudes, values, and needs create deep psychological personal tensions. Sometimes these are expressed as deeply hurtful remarks caused by crossed transactions. On other occasions they may become the predominant ideology pervading the organization.

❯❯ Case example 7.3

Delusions of grandeur? The case of a compulsive, dramatic, and paranoid leader

Conrad Black (Lord Black of Crossharbour) was a Canadian and the son of a wealthy brewery magnate who gained British citizenship. He was famous for his unusual business strategies, 'for his arrogance, and for bringing legal actions against anyone who challenged him'.[1] Black was a millionaire newspaper tycoon who was said to have it all: Hollinger, the international media empire that once controlled The Daily Telegraph newspaper group. He owned prestigious newspapers such as *The Daily Telegraph*, the *Melbourne Age* and *Sydney Morning Herald*, and had a financial stake in more ❯❯

» than 500 newspapers. He appeared to become obsessed by his own invincibility, which ultimately became his downfall.

In July 2007, Black was convicted on three charges of fraud and one charge of obstructing justice. At his trial he faced a fine of $1m (£492,000) and a 35-year jail sentence. He was fortunate to escape a more serious charge of tax evasion, and was cleared of eight other charges, which included racketeering. Had he been charged with these offences he could have received a 100-year prison sentence. He was eventually convicted of 'defrauding investors of honest services by embezzling millions of dollars in phoney "non-compete" clauses attached to the sale of newspapers at his Hollinger media empire'.[2]

The prosecution informed the court that he scorned shareholders, regulators, and the law. He was described as arrogant and he refused to pay back non-compete fees of $7.2m paid under a November 2003 agreement, and admit that they were 'not properly authorized on behalf of the company'.[3] Flouting the law in this way was compounded by his 'underhand attempt' to sell the Telegraph Group to the Barclay twins, and his closest business partner of 36 years, David Radler, provided evidence to the court that Lord Black was intimately involved in the scheme to defraud Hollinger International. He stated that Lord Black instructed him to siphon off millions of dollars in 'off-the-books' payments negotiated with other companies.[3]

A report of the trial indicated that Black had not envisaged this outcome. Instead, he had stated that he would win in three stages: 'stage one is the adulations of joy at the so-called downfall. Stage two is the big battle… and then stage three is where I win'. Black was 'convinced that he has a special relationship with God, and always believed in his invincibility'. Furthermore, 'he was inspired by a strange mixture of heroes, which included Alexander the Great, Napoleon and General MacArthur, Churchill, Nixon, Franklin Roosevelt, and Maurice Duplessis, the dictatorial leader of mid-20th-century Quebec. Black had a picture of Al Capone on the wall of Hollinger International's New York boardroom and would jokingly point him out to visitors as "our chief shareholder"'.[3]

[1] Case study of Lord Black cited in Tricker, B. (2008), *Corporate Governance*, Oxford: Oxford University Press.
[2] Clarke, A., 'Supreme court to hear Conrad Black appeal', available at <http://www.guardian.co.uk>, 19 May 2009.
[3] Silvester, C., 'Fall of an arrogant fraud: What really brought down the empire of Conrad Black?', *The Independent*, 15 July 2007.

As a final analytical framework for analysing power in organizations, it would be useful to combine the types of power identified by French and Raven earlier in the chapter with the frameworks from Harrison (Figure 7.3) and Kets de Vries and Miller (Table 7.3). Table 7.4 illustrates this combined framework. It should be remembered, however, that any framework is simply a guide or model for thinking about issues. The real analytical ability lies with the knowledge, experience, and skills of the analyst. Most complex organizations will display a variety of these characteristics.

Table 7.4 Analytical framework for observing organizational power

Harrison's description of ideologies / French and Raven's types of Power	Power Ideology	Role Ideology	Task Ideology	Person Ideology
Reward Power	Characterized by differential rewards which are likely to depend on motives of powerful individual. Look for signs that grant privileges to certain individuals, relationships.	Rewards based on role performance.	Rewards based on collaborative effort.	Rewards based on peer evaluation.
Coercive Power	Punishment results from an unsatisfactory result. Attributions based on assumptions of personality rather than circumstances. In transactional terms, language style is likely to be 'controlling parent'.	Coercion results from failing to follow the rules.	Group's coercion and sanctions.	Coercion results in exclusion from professional group, usually because the profession is brought into disrepute.
Legitimate Power	Legitimacy is idiosyncratic. Rules are often made to fit a situational need and may be made retrospectively to suit certain interests.	Behaviour and actions are based on rule following.	Legitimacy is based on what the group deems acceptable to accomplish the task.	Behaviour and actions based on professional code of conduct.

Table 7.4 Analytical framework for observing organizational power (cont.)

Referent Power	Personality is dominant force, although in transactional terms nurturing rather than controlling parent may be language style if coercion is not evident.	Rules restrict excesses of personality becoming dominant.	Key individuals likely to drive motivation.	The knowledge and status of a renowned professional motivates others.
Expert Power	Based on the control of knowledge and information. Only those who need to know are informed.	Expertise is based on role performance. Competencies are clearly defined by work standards.	Group's performance is based on the balance required for the team. As the task changes, new skills and knowledge will be sought.	Professional standards and code of ethics prevail to guide. However, expertise will be based on a mixture of knowledge, skills, and experience.
Organizational Dysfunctions	Obsessive, compulsive behaviour. Emotional conflicts likely. Overconfidence in own ability. Potential for any of the neurotic characteristics likely.	Over-reliance on rules at the expense of client or customer needs. Suppression of emotion can lead to dissatisfaction or demoralization.	Performance norms suggest that group dynamics are underdeveloped. Emotions have not been addressed; feelings have not been brought out or explored before moving on to the task.	Overconfidence in own ability. Potential for any of the neurotic characteristics likely.

Source: Kets de Vries and Miller (1984)

7.6 Summary

We began by defining power as 'the potential ability to influence behaviour, to change the course of events, to overcome resistance, and to get people to do things that they would not otherwise do'. We encountered four main strands in the description of power control and organizational change. Firstly, we discovered that organizational change is itself an intervention. We encountered critical arguments that suggested that change interventions were merely an exercise in managerial control. Whilst this may be true, there was a counter-argument to suggest that not all situations are exploitative.

Secondly, we encountered structural theories of organizational change that form the basis of all assumptions about the way change is introduced. It is important to begin by recognizing that organizations serve a variety of purposes and that it is the nature of their political engagement that drives their strategies. However, the nature of that strategic engagement reflects an argument about how best to manage people: by force, by consent, or, in a view characterized by conflict theory that does not accept either of these alternatives, such discourse is a product of capitalism, which contains its own logic of exploitation. Consideration of these issues should help you arrive at your own appreciation of change interventions, particularly in relation to the driving assumptions behind a particular leader's intervention style. These assumptions were referred to as unitarism, pluralism, or conflict.

Thirdly, the discussion of paradigms and ideology helps us to see how creative thinking might be advanced or restricted. You will have reflected on the nature of managerial control, that is, whether it is simply a technical and neutral process, or is informed by the emergence of dominant coalitions. You will also have noted how the ideology can be used as a control mechanism by managers trapped by their own limitations.

Finally, that power affects us all was explained by the psychodynamics of power and conflict. We can each recognize how conflict can be amplified by the way words are used. Transactional Analysis helps us to understand this. We should also recognize that organizations are arenas in which complex interactions are played out, and where motives may reflect deep psychological traits. We considered three unhealthy neurotic traits, which, from time to time, some of us may exhibit. The important issue, then, is not whether you recognize this but what you do about it. The final section could have been posed as a question: can organizations be neurotic? The answer, having considered the chapter, is likely to be that this will depend upon the way a manager exercises control: whether s/he exploits and alienates people. But the point about the concept of the paranoid organization is simply to reflect on the dominant tendencies: paranoid, compulsive, dramatic narcissism, depressive, or schizoid. These each reflect a style that a leader is ultimately responsible for.

⭐ Case study

Leadership, ethical misconduct, and the exercise of power in a multinational company

You are the human resources director of a multinational electronics company and you have been alerted to rumours that a major international newspaper is investigating your company's agreements with certain national governments. Having read of rumours in the morning newspaper you are struck by a particular paragraph »

❯ suggesting that allegations of corporate misconduct are rife. The report is a sudden shock and makes you reflect on a variety of worrying comments you had previously ignored. The particular paragraph referring to 'the gilded palace where women and fresh fruit were available in equal measure' worries you because you know where this is and you know of the African dictator who has been the cause of many difficult relationships with your company, which eventually secured a large contract to build a telecommunications centre in his country.

You realize you must investigate the situation quickly before you become consumed by it. Your role as a guardian of corporate governance and ethical behaviour is potentially undermined by certain phrases in the newspaper report, such as 'slush fund', 'greasing the palms of dictators', and 'corporate misconduct'. Consequently, you decide to do a little scouting in the hope that your raised awareness is proved to be unfounded. As you leave your office to speak with the communications director, you hear chatter from the office grapevine, which seems to suggest a wider awareness of the article you have just read. You ask yourself a number of questions. Why would these people be talking about the article? Have I been the only one not to know what's going on? Are these rumours true? Then you realize that you will be at the centre of any formal inquiry. On that basis you decide to act quickly. Unfortunately, the communications director confirms your worst suspicions and this raises your anxiety level to near-fever pitch.

You begin trying to analyse the problem by identifying the signs and symptoms of the case. You start with the finance director, who tells you that there are some financial irregularities, but that payments generally appear to be 'above board'.

'What do you mean, that irregularities appear above board?' you ask.

'Well', he states, 'there is a maze of transactions which have not gone through normal channels.'

When you ask what this means he replies that 'if you want to win contracts with African dictators, then you have to be prepared to be a little unorthodox in your dealings'.

'What does that mean?' you ask, in alarm. His behaviour is awkward. He avoids eye contact and his speech is carefully punctuated with difficult pauses. He states that, last month, a number of police officers had visited the company, as well as the homes of one or two executives, because an anonymous informant had indicated that there were irregularities in payments, and a number of bank accounts that led to further accounts in Switzerland. You ask whether he is referring to legitimate, albeit irregular or unusual, payments, or whether he means money laundering. He states that 'they believe it's money laundering'. The finance manager, who is also sitting in on the meeting, states that 'even if the reports were true, and I'm not saying they are, the Swiss would never reveal any details of accounts they hold. What I'm saying is that it's a storm in a teacup.'

You feel uncomfortable about the contradictions you have just heard and decide to investigate company records. These records reveal that the company has been ❯

»cited in bribery cases in the past, before you joined the company. Six years earlier, the company had been indicted in a corruption scandal for a contract of over £30 million. Despite being the highest bidder, the company won the contract. A Serbian business contact had later admitted that your company had paid him £300,000 for ensuring that a rival bid was not considered. The records indicate various 'commissions', which go through a variety of bank accounts in Europe (including Swiss accounts) to the Virgin Islands, then back to Europe again. Although you are no financial expert, you know enough to recognize unorthodox practice and you have one simple question: 'why is this such of a maze of transactions?'

The following day, you receive an anonymous note in your in-tray, listing names of company officials and deals they have made. You then receive a phone call from the chief executive requesting your presence at an impromptu meeting he is holding. The meeting confirms the initial scouting enquiry you made yesterday; he confirms that six executives have been arrested and are making 'full and frank statements' to the police. Two other managers at the meeting comment that 'I'm afraid it's been like the Wild West' and 'there have been systematic irregularities'. After you express astonishment that, as head of HR, you had been kept out of the loop, the CE states that your role is to 'put things right' by reviewing working practices.

The following morning, you visit three of the managers who have been helping police with their enquiries, who tell you that, in the electronics industry, it is normal practice to offer inducements to obtain contracts. One says, 'Look, what you HR people don't understand is that everyone is doing it. It's a very competitive marketplace. If you don't, you lose the contract.' The others say that it is a matter of 'personal development'. When you explore this puzzling remark further, they say that 'your career depends upon it' and that 'pay and promotion were offered as an inducement'. One manager stated that, six months after he joined the company, he was told that 'his career depended on the contracts he won and he was provided with the means to entertain clients'. Another stated that he was persuaded by the fact that his career would come to nothing unless he complied with his line manager's expectations. 'After all,' he said, 'you people require performance appraisals to be undertaken by line managers. What do you expect?'

When you return to the office you decide to interview five other executives who have not been as successful in their careers. That is, they receive far less remuneration and no performance-related pay, and their careers have been headlined with lesser contracts. You know two of these people well and had always assumed that their line managers' reports were a clear indication that, after very promising starts with the company, they had never reached their full potential. Now you begin to wonder. One of them tells you that 'four years ago, when I joined the company, I was riding on the crest of a wave, but then my prospects crashed after I refused to wine and dine some of the world's worst dictators. What I was being asked to do conflicted with my personal values.' Another says that he was on the fast track until he pointed out that what he was expected to do contradicted company policy. He refers you to »

❯the corporate values statement about 'transparency, trust, and honesty in all commercial transactions'. The third executive says that he became disillusioned with the large gap between the publicly stated values of the company and what he had been asked to do.

'What was that?' you asked,

'Offer inducements, that is, bribes in my language, to people in exchange for contracts. There is a culture of hypocrisy pervading the company,' he states.

'What a mess,' you say to yourself. 'How do I make sense of all this and how do I make recommendations to the Board of Directors?' You decide that the real issue is one of governance. In order to come to a clear assessment, and make recommendations for change, you decide to undertake a diagnostic evaluation. This is the task you set yourself.

Task

Undertake a diagnostic evaluation of power, values, compliance, leadership, and morale.

1. Using the French and Raven typology, decide how power was exercised.
2. Why does there appear to be a gap between the espoused values of the company and the practices that led to the current problem? In particular, is there evidence of defensive reasoning in the rationalizations you have heard people use to justify their actions?
3. Identify compliance systems and procedures that give you cause for concern.
4. Can you identify any relationship between leadership and morale?

When you have undertaken this evaluation, write a report to the Board of Directors recommending organizational change to control the abuse of power, develop coherent values, develop effective compliance systems and procedures, and establish responsible leadership.

■ Study questions

1. Explain the different sources of power as articulated by French and Raven. You should provide examples from organizations known to you.

2. How might the pursuit of humanistic values be perceived as a political intervention?

3. What is a pluralistic approach to managing change?

4. Argue the case that all forms of knowledge are ideological.

5. Why could a mindset trap critical thinking?

6. In Case Example 7.2, why did senior managers feel alienated?

7. Is it possible to manage change without conflict? Provide reasons for your response.

8. Do you think that McKendall is correct in arguing that organizational change inevitably involves 'an element of domination'?

9. Some organizational psychologists and psychoanalysts argue that organizations can be dysfunctional. What are the merits of this argument?

10. What is a paranoid organization? Is it really possible to diagnose a real organization in this way?

■ Exercises

1. Write a list outlining how individuals and groups within organizations might be seen as dysfunctional. This should also apply to managers and leaders. You will need to provide an *informed* view on the subject of dysfunctional employees. Your response will need to explore your considered views on motivation, group processes, effective management, and leadership. You must be aware that who does the defining is critical to this. Finally, you must propose an answer to the questions 'is it possible to give an objective account of dysfunctional employees, and if so, how?' and 'how do you know your examples could be held up to objective scrutiny?'

2. Managing organizational politics requires ground rules. Write what you would consider to be an effective policy for each of the following eight factors from the Times 100 Best Companies. These factors are:

   a. Leadership: how employees would like to feel about the head of the company and senior managers.

   b. Well-being: how staff feel about stress, pressure, and the balance between their work and home duties.

   c. My manager: how employees would like to be treated by their immediate boss and their day-to-day managers.

   d. My team: people's feelings about their immediate colleagues—in particular, are the team processes managed effectively? Is decision making effective?

   e. Fair deal: how happy employees are with their pay and benefits. This should include consideration of who receives performance-related pay, if appropriate.

   f. Giving something back: to what extent companies are thought by their staff to put back into society in general, and the local community in particular.

   g. My company: positive feelings about the company.

   h. Personal growth: the extent to which people feel they are developed, stretched, and challenged by their work.

3. Using Harrison's typology in Figure 7.3, consider how there may be gaps between espoused values and actual work practices. Think about how you might measure the gap between what an organization formally claims and what people actually do. Using your organization or university, test this framework. For each of the headings ask the following questions:

a. How are rewards distributed and how do people perceive this process?

b. Are there any examples of coercive or manipulative behaviour? If so, how does this work?

c. Is behaviour rule-guided to the extent that actions are perceived to be legitimate?

d. At an individual level, how is power exercised: is it shared, collegiate, formal or interpersonal?

e. How is expertise defined and regarded?

f. Is information shared or selectively distributed?

Once you have the information you require, consider how the answers fit the typology. You may use this in conjunction with the activity in Exercise 4 below.

4. Using Table 7.2 as a guide, see if you can give your an organization a clean bill of health. Use the headings and the criteria to draw up a list of questions that you could put to individuals. Make sure these are skilfully written. You can use this activity in conjunction with the one in Exercise 3 above.

■ Further reading

Burrell, G. and Morgan, G. (1979), *Sociological Paradigms and Organizational Analysis*, Oxford: Heinemann. This is a classic text, often cited for its reference to epistemology. The real question posed is whether paradigms are commensurate in social sciences.

Doz, Y.L. and Kosonen, M. (2007), 'The New Deal at the Top', *Harvard Business Review* (June), 98–104. Provides an interesting account of the power associated with traditional delegated leadership roles in large companies. Such leaders, the authors argue, are often 'semi-autonomous feudal barons, using considerable discretion to achieve their goals'. The authors provide an interesting new approach that students may find useful.

Harrison, R. (1972), 'Understanding Your Organization's Character', *Harvard Business Review*, 50(3), 119–128; reprinted in Harrison, R. (1996), *The Collected Papers of Roger Harrison*, Maidenhead, Berks: McGraw-Hill. This is a useful text from a well-known OD consultant. It provides a series of papers on OD written throughout his career but this one is useful in characterizing ideology.

Kets de Vries, M.F.R. and Miller, D. (1984), *The Neurotic Organization, Diagnosing and Changing Counterproductive Styles of Management*, London: Jossey-Bass. Provides a provocative idea that neuroses can be caused by leaders who create a culture reflecting their style.

Kersten, A. (2007), 'Fantastic performance and neurotic fantasy: A case-based exploration of psychodynamic development', *Tamara Journal*, 6(1), 65–82. This is an interesting argument that organizations stage their own grand dramas and come to believe in the myths they make.

Moore, F. (2006), 'Strategy, power and negotiation: social control and expatriate managers in a German multinational corporation', *International Journal of Human Resource Management*, 17(3), 399–413. Students interested in qualitative accounts of power (through Symbolic Interactionism) will find this illuminating for its account of the negotiated order of expatriate staff in the London office of a German multinational bank.

Morgan, G. (2004), *Images of Organisation*, London: Sage. Morgan's book has now become a classic text. Although he raises critical questions and provides an excellent framework that is easy to remember, he tends to fall back on a managerialist approach to organizations.

Sun, Y. and Wen, K. (2007), 'Environmental Challengers for Foreign R&D in China', *Asia Pacific Business Review*, 13(3), 425–449. For students interested in the power relationship between companies looking to locate to China and cultural expectations of the host country, this account explores how 'the power relationship, on the one hand, is affected by a company's capability and its potential to exert influence in the global market. On the other hand, it is affected by their experience, presence and technology in the host country in particular.'

■ References

Bacharach, S. and Lawler, E.B.J. (1980), *Power and politics in organizations*, San Francisco, CA: Jossey-Bass.

Brimm, M. (1972), 'When is a Change not a Change?', *Journal of Applied Behavioural Science*, 8, 102–107.

Burrell, G. and Morgan, G. (1979), *Sociological Paradigms and Organizational Analysis*, Oxford: Heinemann.

Cummings, T.G. and Worley, C.G. (1997), *Organization and Change*, Minneapolis/St. Paul, MN: West.

Cyert, R.M. and March, J.G. (1963), *A Behavioral Theory of the Firm*, Englewood Cliffs, NJ: Prentice-Hall.

Dahl, R.A. (1963), *Modern Political Analysis*, Englewood Cliffs, NJ: Prentice-Hall.

Etzioni, A. (1964), *Modern Organizations*, Englewood Cliffs, NJ: Prentice-Hall.

French, J.R.P. and Raven, B.H. (1968), 'The Bases of Social Power', in Cartwright, D. (ed), *Studies in Social Power*, Ann Arbor, MI: Institute for Social Research, University of Michigan Press, 150–167.

Gellerman, S.W. (1986), 'Why "good" managers make bad ethical choices', *Harvard Business Review*, July–August, 85–90.

Green, G.D. (1987), *Industrial Relations*, Second edition, London: Pitman.

Harrison, R. (1972), 'Understanding Your Organization's Character', *Harvard Business Review*, 50(3), 119–128; reprinted in Harrison, R. (1996), *The Collected Papers of Roger Harrison*, Maidenhead, Berks: McGraw-Hill.

Horney, K. (1957), *Our Inner Conflicts*, London: Routledge & Kegan Paul.

Kelman, H. and Warwick, D. (1978), 'The Ethics of Social Intervention: Goals, Means and Consequences', in Zaltman, G. (ed), *Processes and Phenomena of Social Change*, New York: Wiley.

Kersten, A. (2007), 'Fantastic performance and neurotic fantasy: A case-based exploration of psychodynamic development', *Tamara Journal*, 6(1).

Kets de Vries, M.F.R. and Miller, D. (1984), *The Neurotic Organization, Diagnosing and Changing Counterproductive Styles of Management*, London: Jossey-Bass.

Kuhn, T.S. (1970), *The Structure of Scientific Revolutions*, Chicago, IL: University of Chicago Press.

March, J.C. and Simon, H.A. (1958), *Organizations*, New York: Wiley.

McKendall, M. (1993), 'The Tyranny of Change: Organizational Development Revisited', *Journal of Business Ethics*, 12, 93–104.

Michels, R. (1949), *Political Parties*, Glencoe, NY: The Free Press.

Miller, D. (1990), *The Icarus Paradox*, New York: Harper Business.

Mills, C.W. (1956), *The Power Elite*, New York: Oxford University Press.

Morgan, G. (1993), 'Organizations as Political Systems', in Mabey, C, and Mayon-White, W. (eds), *Managing Change*, Second edition, Milton Keynes: Open University Press, 212–217.

—— (2004), *Images of Organisation*, London: Sage.

Pascale, R. (1990), *Managing on the Edge*, Harmondsworth: Penguin.

Pfeffer, J. (1993), 'Understanding Power in Organizations', in Mabey, C, and Mayon-White, W. (eds), *Managing Change*, Second edition, Milton Keynes: Open University Press, 201–206.

Silvester, C. (2007) 'Fall of an arrogant fraud: What really brought down the empire of Conrad Black?', *The Independent*, 15 July.

Simon, H.A. (1947), *Adminstrative Behaviour*, New York: The Free Press.

Thomas, A.B. (2003), *Controversies in Management*, London: Routledge.

 Take your learning further: Online Resource Centre
http://www.oxfordtextbooks.co.uk/orc/grieves/

Visit the Online Resource Centre that accompanies this book to enrich your understanding of this chapter. Explore case study updates and answers to questions, test yourself using an interactive flashcard glossary, and keep up to date with the latest developments in the area.

CHAPTER 8

Leading change

8.1 Introduction—the problem with management

In this chapter we will learn to appreciate how subtle the process of leading change is. The first hurdle to deal with is being able to define 'leadership', because this term is often used interchangeably with the term 'management'. We also need to dispel the myth that there is a universal definition of leadership. The study of great leaders will not help us to understand the issues that contemporary leaders must deal with. Instead, we need to see the idea of leading change within an organizational context that is itself located in a particular historical epoch. We begin with studies of behavioural styles because these help us to understand what we can learn about the relationship between tasks and people. But within the behavioural style approaches we also discover the importance of the situation as a determinant of a leader's style. Furthermore, motivational issues are important, because it is argued that leaders can identify challenging pathways to goals and valued rewards.

A second main theme to consider is the emergence of strategic leadership and the role of the leader as strategic architect and tactician. What we encounter here is a view that a strategic leader is responsible for the design and implementation of an organization's strategy. As a tactician, the strategic leader was required to learn from military tactics. We can learn much from this even if it is by criticizing some of the assumptions that lie behind such arguments. We should also note a very useful critique of planned change in the form of logical incrementalism—the view that change does not occur in linear stages. But there is a further argument that strategic leadership should be considered more as an art than a science.

The third main theme to consider is leadership attributes. Contemporary research suggests that, whilst we will find little in the idea of leadership traits, we can note that the perceptions of followers are important. By focusing on leader attributes we can investigate what personal and situational qualities people find most important in a leader. Furthermore, how important is self-esteem, or should we train leaders by encouraging self-efficacy whereby they acquire cognitive, social, linguistic, and/or physical skills appropriate for the role they perform? We might also ask under what conditions we can apply the concept of servant leadership. As you will have noticed in the previous chapter, leadership is inextricably linked to the cultural psychodynamics of an organization. We therefore touch upon this again with the concept of the narcissistic leader, which is related to leadership attributes through the concept of self-esteem.

The concept of transformational leadership extends the idea of servant leadership. What we need to consider here is the type of strategic engagements we require. Furthermore, we might ask whether, if strategic leadership can empower people, developing human capital can lead to competitive advantage.

We conclude the study of leading change by considering results-based leadership in an attempt to draw the various strands together. Once we have an appreciation of the issues involved in leading change, we need to act as a catalyst and mobilize people.

This chapter is therefore designed to enable you to think clearly about leadership but, most importantly, its purpose is to challenge the idea that there is a simple formula.

In this chapter we will:

- Compare and contrast the concepts of 'management' and 'leadership'.
- Examine behavioural research into leadership.
- Look at the emergence of strategic leadership.
- Consider contemporary research into leadership attributes.
- Explore the concept of transformational leadership.
- Assess results-based leadership.

8.2 Management and leadership

Following Knights and Willmott (2007: 266), we can identify 'three common meanings of management'. These are:

1. Management as a discipline.
2. Management as a function.
3. Management as a social group or elite.

Management as a discipline can be regarded as a set of practices used to maximize the efficiency and effectiveness of people at work. In other words, as a discipline it has the specific and universal objective of maximizing output in the most economical way in the interests of shareholders. The second use of the word management, as a function, recognizes that a group of people called managers have responsibility for planning, coordinating, and executing the way that work is undertaken within the workplace. The third definition, management as a social group, suggests that managers are a distinct social category and acquire not just managerial expertise but also a privileged status in their own organizations. Each of these definitions suggests that power is used in a particular way. In the first, it is used as a form of ideology that implies that there is a dominant logic associated with commerce and business. In the second, it implies that those with the right knowledge, training, and skill have the 'right' to manage others. In the third definition, managers' power rests in their elevated social status, which confers upon them greater financial and material rewards than upon others, irrespective of effort.

We can extend this third category by arguing that power elites are composed of people who come from select social strata. For example, as we might observe in the post-Soviet economies, elites emerged from the old power structures of communist oligarchs. In the West, by contrast, the power elite may seem more open but it still comprises a relatively small group of people. For example, in British society there are very strong interconnections between schools, universities, clubs, and social pastimes. Business elites are dominated by public-school-educated men who graduated from Oxford or Cambridge and usually qualified as accountants. A survey of those in control of Britain's companies reveals the top ten schools, universities, pastimes, and clubs time and time again. Half of the 15,000 company directors surveyed for *The Sunday Times* by Hemscott, a London information firm (*Sunday Times* Survey, 14 October 2001) had a public-school (private) education. Of those, Etonians led the field by a significant margin, and Oxford and Cambridge Universities were significantly ahead of London, Nottingham, and Glasgow (the next three in the list). Whilst leaders are generally regarded as being different from managers, we need to recognize that they belong to managerial and power elites.

---

❶ Stop and think 8.1

Identify a particular organizational setting and describe how management might be seen as (a) a discipline, (b) a function, and (c) a social group.

8.3 Behavioural research into leadership

8.3.1 Behavioural Styles of leadership

Although early research into leadership assumed that genetic traits could be identified and potential leaders discovered, it became apparent that the behavioural style of a leader could be influenced through experience, personal development, mentoring, and training. It also became apparent that different organizational contexts contain contingencies that determine how a leader should learn to use different leadership styles to enhance performance. The Behavioural Styles perspective on leadership sought to build profiles of effective leader behaviours. A leadership style is viewed as a general pattern of behaviour that favours either tasks or people in decision-making activities.

Behavioural Styles research emerged during the Second World War in an attempt to identify effective leaders. As Kreitner, Kinicki, and Buelens (2002: 454) have pointed out, 'it was a response to the seeming inability of trait theory to explain leadership effectiveness and to the Human Relations Movement'. Leader Behaviour became the main focus precisely because it was believed that how a leader behaved had a major impact on followers. Researchers therefore began to investigate how different behavioural styles had an impact on leadership.

Prominent Behavioural Styles studies are now well documented; they include the Ohio State studies (see Fleishmann, 1974); the University of Michigan studies (see Likert, 1961); and Blake and Mouton's (1964) managerial grid. The Ohio State studies focused on two determinants of leadership: *'consideration or concern for member's needs'* and *'initiating structure'*, which reflected the way that a leader organizes his or her staff and defines the task. Despite exhaustive studies, the researchers concluded that there is no best style of leadership. The most important conclusion is that effectiveness in achieving a task results from situational factors such as how much control was required, the degree of judgement required, the skills required, and so forth.

Although no best leadership style was found to exist for all situations, at least the discovery that leadership style depended on situational factors became a critical focus for research. Like the Ohio State studies, the University of Michigan studies identified the behavioural differences of effective leaders. Essentially, they tend to:

- be employee-centred, supporting and developing employees;
- use group supervision in preference to individual control;
- set high performance goals.

One of the best-known examples of the Behavioural Styles approach is Blake and Mouton's (1964) managerial grid. This is a tool constructed on two axes to find how a manager constructs a relationship between task and relationship focuses:

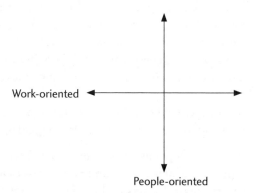

The most effective style was considered to be high performance in both work-oriented and people-oriented focuses. The grid provides a visual metaphor for understanding the relationship between concerns for people and for performance, and how this interaction influences the choice of leadership style.

The Behavioural Styles perspective on leadership makes a meaningful attempt to balance the opposing forces of the social and technical aspects of management, but this balance depends upon the extent to which followers prefer a particular style. The difficulty is that the Behavioural Styles approach does not account for the diversity of effective leader behaviours we are likely to encounter in different situations.

8.3.2 Research into context and contingencies

A second criticism of Behavioural Styles emerged from situational theorists, who argued that different contingencies affect both how a leader's style will be accepted by followers, and the efficiency and effectiveness by which each task will be measured. The main contingencies are:

1. The type of *task* performed and, particularly, whether it is highly structured or requires the creative imagination of people for its resolution. For example, a bureaucratic task is highly structured, in comparison to one in an advertising agency. The bureaucratic task is designed this way because of the high predictability and repeatability of the operation. The task in the advertising agency is not predictable and requires a different creative output for each client.

2. The nature of the *technology* and, particularly, the extent to which the technology enables the task to be structured or requires the application of technical expertise. For example, a computer program might require a task to be highly structured because the people operating it are each required to follow the same sequence of steps from beginning to end.

3. The nature of the *environment*, which requires careful appreciation in designing how the task will be structured and supported by technology. For example, a call centre will be designed as a large open-plan office, so that information is accessible to a number of people, and many people can easily be supervised. In contrast, if academics, or students in a library, were required to work in such circumstances, then creativity and thoughtful reflection would diminish. Appropriate design therefore requires an appreciation of all three elements (task, technology, and environment), but requires, in particular, awareness that *form follows function*. That is, that design should be based on the function for which the environment is intended.

Situational theorists such as Fiedler (1967: 29) argue that the leader's degree of control and influence are important but that these also depend upon situation:

> the performance of a leader depends on two interrelated factors: the degree to which the situation gives the leader control and influence—that is, the likelihood that [the leader] can successfully accomplish the job; and the leader's basic motivation—that is, whether [the leader's] self-esteem depends primarily on accomplishing the task or on having close supportive relations with others.

A leader may not have as much authority to make strategic decisions as s/he would like. In such a situation the ability to control or influence followers is limited by personal influence. Conversely, a strategic leader may be responsible for thousands of people in many different countries, but might have to depend on the ability of local managers to engage with and motivate employees with very different cultural expectations. The degree to which leaders have situational control depends upon three critical variables:

1. *Leader–follower relations.* Leaders who have good relations with their followers create dependable employees who can be relied upon to achieve their objectives.

2. *Task structure.* More structured jobs—that is those with clear guidelines—give the leader more formal control over people.

3. *Position power.* A formally recognized position in the hierarchy is important, but a leader is able to gain greater psychological compliance through careful consideration of rewards and punishment.

As Kreitner, Kinicki, and Buelens (2002: 460) have noted, a leader's situational control has been demonstrated to be extremely relevant. However, two meta-analyses (Narayanan, Menon, and Spector, 1999; Lackman and Weaver, 1998) argue that some refinement is needed to Fiedler's model of situational control, since not all situations in his model could be replicated.

8.3.3 Path–Goal theory

Situational research has illustrated the importance of contingencies in order to take researchers beyond Behaviour Styles of leadership and the investigation of followers' preferences for a particular leadership style. However, there are factors other than situational contingencies. The most obvious is related to the motivational calculus. An example of this is the Path–Goal theory, which is derived from research into leadership styles, employee characteristics, environmental factors, and employee attitudes and behaviour. The model, proposed by House (1971) (see Figure 8.1), is based on the Expectancy theory of motivation. That is, that motivation involves a trade-off between the amount of effort required to obtain a reward and the likelihood of being successful in achieving the outcome. Path–Goal theory takes this further by arguing that a leader can influence this motivational calculus by identifying challenging pathways to goals and valued rewards.

The Path-Goal theory consists of four interrelated elements:

1. *Leadership styles*: in particular situations, followers accept a particular style. Styles range from being directive, to supportive, to participative, to achievement-oriented. For example, being directive is accepted by followers in certain situations where time is limited and the leader is known to have valuable expertise or trusted judgement. At the other end of the spectrum, achievement orientation is expected of a leader when, for example, a team shares objectives in winning or performing at a certain level.

2. *Employee characteristics*: whether an employee has the required skills and experience to achieve the task (task ability), given the perceived *locus* of control (that is, whether followers perceive the situation or themselves to be the main determinant of change); or the extent to which employees have achievement needs. Finally, employees' needs for structured information will depend upon the complications of the task and their experience.

3. *Employee attitudes and behaviour*: the extent of job satisfaction, whether a leader is accepted by employees, and whether employees are motivated by intrinsic rewards (job satisfaction) or extrinsic ones (outside the workplace and for which pay is the only compensation).

4. *Environmental factors*: the nature of the task, the authority system, and the workgroup. For example, a task may be simple or complicated. Authority may be based on acceptance of roles, or devolved from the leader. Consequently, the workgroup may be no more than a collection of individuals performing a task, or may be a self-managed team.

Figure 8.1 Path–Goal theory

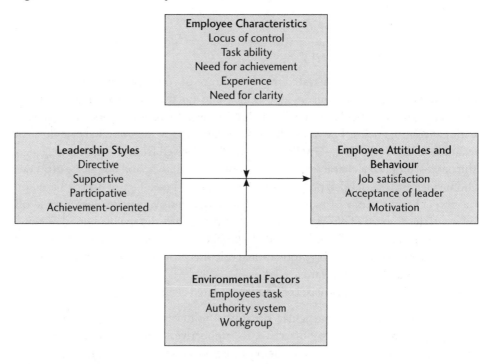

---

❶ Stop and Think 8.2

Consider a situation in which you or someone you know has had to influence the direction of change. Using the Path–Goal theory, evaluate the extent to which there was congruence between leadership style, employee characteristics, employee attitudes, and environmental factors. When you have considered these issues, say whether the change was (a) very successful; (b) marginally successful; or (c) unsuccessful. Your answer to this should reflect the motivational calculus. That is, to what extent did people believe they could achieve the outcome given the effort required? Finally, you might ask whether the leader influenced motivation by identifying challenging pathways to goals and valued rewards. If not, what might s/he have done?

A careful study of one's own behavioural style, and how to improve or modify it to suit the context, is a theme of the Behavioural Styles approach. Various contingencies affect how a leader's style will be accepted by followers. As Fiedler (1967) pointed out, the leader's degree of control and influence over a situation is important. Behavioural research revealed other factors such as the importance of an individual's and team's motivational calculus. We note, in particular, that Path–Goal theory suggests that a leader can influence the motivational calculus by identifying challenging pathways to goals and valued rewards.

8.4 Strategic leadership

8.4.1 The leader as strategic architect

The concept of strategic management was put forward in the 1980s. The doctrine of strategic leadership in business can be traced back to Selznick (1957), who viewed the strategic leader as the strategist responsible for developing a 'distinctive competence' by aligning the 'internal state' of the organization with its 'external expectations'. Selznick argued that the strategic leader was responsible for building policy into the organization's social structure. This was referred to later as 'implementation'. The idea of the strategic leader gained currency in the 1960s with the Design School of strategy, which focused on assessments of the external and internal situations. A good example is the use of SWOT (strengths, weaknesses, opportunities, threats) analysis to assess the character of the environments.

The Design School of strategy took strategic leadership seriously, as Mintzberg, Ahlstrand, and Lampel (1998) inform us. It is this perspective, more than any other, that has fashioned the cult of the strategic leader as the architect of the organization. By stressing the need for a conceptual framework, it laid the foundation for exploring what leaders do. The Design School of strategy recognized that the chief executive officer (CEO) has a role to play in strategy formulation. The CEO is the senior strategist who sits at the apex of the organization. Leadership became a matter of making internal and external appraisals of strengths, weaknesses, opportunities, and threats, within the organization's context.

The job of the leader was to tailor the fit between the demands of the external environment and the internal capabilities required within the organization. Examples of the demands driven by the external environment include changing customer preferences, population trends, and demographic change, political changes through legislation, economic changes such as interest rate movements, the impact of global demand for products or services, threats from competitors (or developing the quality of products and services better, faster, or more effectively than competitors), and consideration of the supply chain. These have been summed up by the acronyms PEST (political, economic, social, and technical factors) or BPEST (business political, economic, social and technical factors) analysis, although in Chapter 4 we suggest that PESTLE (political, economic, sociodemographic, technological, legal, and environmental) is a more helpful acronym nowadays.

Leaders were therefore the strategic architects of change by developing and implementing strategy. The essence of good strategy was simplicity and the essence of the good strategist was to bring about simplicity in the face of complexity. A good example of this, as Andrews (1971) informs us, was the need for simple diagnosis, followed by prescription and action. Central to this distinction 'is the associated premise that structure must follow strategy' (Mintzberg, Ahlstrand, and Lampel, 1998: 32). The development of the Strategic Planning School in the 1970s added further to the leader's role by arguing the need for objective setting and undertaking an external audit followed by an internal audit.

Critics of Strategic Planning have argued that it was a discipline founded on inadequate analysis typified by the so-called 'laundry-list' approach (PEST(LE), SWOT, and a variety of other matrices). This failure to gather detailed data for diagnosis and analysis was said to result in an over-simplified strategy. According to Mintzberg, strategic leadership became over-reliant on the new layer of planners who used planning matrices to determine strategy. This process meant that planners and executives 'made no real effort to search for, or analyze, an array of strategic alternatives before making decisions'; consequently, 'companies all too often adopted strategies by default rather than by choice' (Wilson, 1994: 13). As a result, other critical qualitative factors, such as the culture of the organization, were ignored. Mintzberg, Ahlstrand, and Lampel summed this up by arguing that

> the belief that strategic managers and their planning systems can be detached from the subject of their efforts is predicated on one fundamental assumption: that they can be informed in a formal way. The messy world of random noise, gossip, inference, impression, and fact must be reduced to firm data, hardened and aggregated so that they can be supplied regularly in digestible form. In other words, systems must do it, whether they go by the name of (reading back over the years) 'information technology,' 'strategic information systems,' 'expert systems,' 'total systems,' or just plain so-called 'management information systems' (MIS). Unfortunately, the hard data on which such systems depend often proves to have a decidedly soft underbelly.

(Mintzberg, Ahlstrand, and Lampel, 1998: 69)

This suggests that hard statistical information, as the only important source of 'real' data, is illusory. Hard data may be viewed as objective but are in fact 'limited in scope' precisely because they lack 'richness' and often fail 'to encompass important non-economic and non-quantitative factors'. Furthermore, 'much hard information is too aggregated for effective use in strategy making'. This is clearly problematic for strategic leadership because too much information comes too late and is often unreliable. The art of effective leadership is lost in a morass of often incomprehensible data, thus reducing speedy and effective action.

8.4.2 Competitive Strategy: the strategic leader as tactician

During the 1980s the concept of strategic management was adopted because of the increasing influence of economics. Porter (1980) widened the scope for analysis by looking beyond the organization, and to strategic leadership in particular. Strategic leadership was equated with military campaigns and with writings of sometimes ancient sages such as Sun-Tzu, who lived around 400 BC. Competitive and tactical strategy became the developmental focus of a newly emerging view of strategic management. Thus the tactics, cunning, and guile advocated by Sun-Tzu became simplistic maxims for leadership. Competitive strategy found its voice by echoing the use of ploys and deceptions such as 'when capable feign incapacity; when active, inactivity', to be found in *The Art of War*. As Mintzberg, Ahlstrand, and Lampel (1998) point out, 'he [Sun-Tzu] devoted a good deal of attention to specific position strategies' that were suitable metaphors for the new strategy game.

Other military tacticians such as von Clausewitz were adopted by strategic management. Von Clausewitz was a Prussian army officer who had been taken prisoner by Napoleon. After observing Napoleon's tactics first hand he wrote his famous text *On War* between 1815 and his death in 1831. In its wake, strategic leadership became equated with strategies from Napoleon and infused by metaphors such as 'open-ended', 'fluid', 'creative campaign', and 'tactical manoeuvring'.

The Competitive Strategy approach also adopted the tactical metaphors of Niccolò Machiavelli's sixteenth-century text *The Prince*. Machiavelli's descriptions of Cesare Borgia's use of cunning and deception as tactics were cited as tactics for contemporary turbulent times. For example, it is easy to cite Machiavelli ('in order to enter a country, one needs the goodwill of the inhabitants') to support tactics for the politics of globalization.

Central to Machiavelli's account is the idea of effective leadership and followers' behaviour. In *The Prince* we learn that people will resist change if their customs are challenged or overturned. Therefore the leader should be as 'cunning as the fox' and as 'brave as the lion'. That is, he should use strategies appropriate to the circumstances. Furthermore, Machiavelli argued that mercenaries and auxiliaries should be avoided because they are motivated only by money, which suggests for leaders that, where possible, modern organizations should remunerate, cultivate, and develop their own staff properly in order to gain commitment and retain their own competencies.

In encouraging parallels with military strategy, the Competitive Strategy approach draws a number of dangerous and over-simplistic analogies. First, any analogy with military tactics is dangerous. Capitalism requires trust in order for cooperation and competition to develop within a framework of rules. The military campaigning analogy leaves little room for ethical social responsibility. Second, the analogy with military tactics ignores the fact that, in war, the art of politics has broken down. Military tactics represent dysfunctional rather than normal situations: most of the examples represent societies in turmoil where cooperation is not evident. Third, simplistic interpretations are often made of historical and political knowledge. For example, the impression given is that Machiavelli's preference was for duplicity, which is in fact far from the truth, and interpretations are based on only one of his books because it is the best known. The reality is that competitive strategy requires checks and balances, not ruthless tactical campaigning.

8.4.3 Logical incrementalism: what the leader really needs to know about change

A great deal of criticism has been made of the attempt to lead strategic change in a neat, logical, linear sequence from strategic analysis of the external environment, via internal analysis of competencies, to future-oriented change actions. Indeed, it could be argued that a majority of corporate descriptions of how change was achieved often underplayed the importance of hidden process. What we often read, therefore, is little more than a mythological presentation of events as they were remembered afterwards. The empirical case studies undertaken by Quinn (1978; 1980), for example, illustrate that 'when well-managed major organizations make significant changes in strategy, the approaches they use frequently bear little resemblance to the rational–analytical systems so often touted in the planning literature' (Quinn, 1978: 7). In addition to an important academic point about how strategy really emerges, there is also an important methodological point to be made. For example, if we were to ask senior executives from ten organizations to complete a questionnaire stating how strategy emerges, we would be likely to get a retrospective gloss of the processes they were involved in. In many respects this is not unlike the competitive strategist misrepresenting historical reality by looking at events and ignoring processes because processes are not available for observation. What is likely to happen is that processes become events in the minds of observers.

Because people remember more of an event that triggers a course of action than they do of the subtle processes that led to the events themselves, they misjudge (misdiagnose) the causes of changes and construct inappropriate solutions (intervention strategies). Thus, events become quantified and sequenced.

> ❶ Stop and think 8.3
>
> Think back to a situation you encountered some years ago that appeared to have a profound effect on you. Write briefly what happened. When you have done this, think through the subtle processes that may have contributed to this change. Consider, for example, the various people involved and their potential motives, their actions and reactions. Consider also what you learned about yourself and how this changed your own thinking. What you will discover is that there are many potential outcomes that could have resulted, and trying to explain why this outcome occurred is very difficult to state categorically. In the end, you are left with assumptions about the event, because not all the processes were obvious to you at the time.

In contrast, if we were to take the time and trouble to observe the flow of processes and events leading to strategic decisions, then a greater subtlety would emerge. Qualitative data are often more revealing, but they require a greater level of situational knowledge. Quinn's point is that the Strategic Planning approach, which requires leaders to move through a sequence of analyses, underemphasizes qualitative factors because they are difficult to capture.

As a solution, Quinn calls for us to engage in 'logical incrementalism'. This is a conscious and purposeful approach requiring empirical observation of processes. Most importantly, it requires testing new ideas in a circular process rather than a linear one:

> The full strategy is rarely written down in any one place. The processes used to arrive at the total strategy are typically fragmented, evolutionary, and largely intuitive. Although one can usually find embedded in these fragments some very refined pieces of formal strategic analysis, the real strategy tends to evolve as internal decisions and external events flow together to create a new, widely shared consensus for action among key members of the top management team. Far from being an abrogation of good management practice, the rationale behind this kind of strategy formulation is so powerful that it perhaps provides the normative model for strategic decision making—rather than the step-by-step 'formal systems planning' approach so often espoused.
>
> (Quinn, 1978: 7)

At first it may appear that there is no role for a strategic leader, but this is not the case. The recognition of what really occurs allows the leader to develop a strategy for managing this process because, 'properly managed, it allows the executive to bind together the contributions of rational systematic analyses, political and power theories, and organizational Behaviour concepts'. Furthermore, it 'helps the executive achieve cohesion and identity with new directions…' because it enables the management of power relationships, individual needs, and assessment of informational and analytical inputs, in order to decide on the most appropriate course of action. His observations reveal that able executives

> artfully blend formal analysis, behavioural techniques, and power politics to bring about cohesive, step-by-step movement toward ends which initially are broadly conceived, but which are then constantly refined and reshaped as new information appears. Their integrating methodology can best be described as 'logical incrementalism'.
>
> (Quinn, 1980: 3).

If consciously designed, this process can enable a manager to become an effective change agent who can incrementally:

- improve the quality of information utilized in corporate strategic decisions;
- manage the various needs and sequencing of subsystems through which decisions tend to be made;

- deal with the personal resistance and political pressures any important strategic change encounters;
- build the organizational awareness, understanding, and psychological commitment needed for effective implementation;
- decrease the uncertainty surrounding decisions by allowing for interactive learning between the enterprise and its various environments;
- improve the quality of the strategic decisions themselves by systematically involving those with most specific knowledge; obtaining the participation of those who must carry out the decisions; and, avoid premature closure which could lead the decision in improper directions.

Because it is unlikely that any one individual can oversee strategic change sequentially, through a series of well-defined steps, the role of the strategic leader is to build the capacity of change agents within the organization. This will require such people to be aware that developing most strategies requires numerous feedback loops back to earlier stages 'as unexpected issues, or new data dictate' (Quinn, 1980: 4).

» Case example 8.1

Managing strategic change: comparing the Strategic Planning approach to logical incrementalism

The Strategic Planning approach to managing change

The main elements include:

1. Analysing the internal situation for its strengths, weaknesses, competencies, problems.
2. Projecting current product lines, profits, sales, and investment needs into the future.
3. Analysing selected external environments and opponents' actions for opportunities and threats.
4. Establishing broad goals as targets for subordinate groups' plans.
5. Identifying the gap between expected and desired results.
6. Communicating planning assumptions to the divisions.
7. Requesting proposed plans from subordinate groups with more specific target goals, resource needs, and supporting action plans.
8. Requesting, developing, and considering special studies of alternatives, contingencies, or longer-term opportunities.
9. Reviewing and approving divisional plans for corporate needs.   »

⊗ 10. Developing long-term budgets related to plans.

11. Implementing plans.

12. Monitoring and evaluating performance against plans and against budgets.

While this approach is excellent for some purposes, it tends to focus unduly on measurable quantitative factors and to under-emphasize the vital qualitative, organizational, and power-behavioural factors which so often determine strategic success in one situation versus another. In practice, such planning is just one building block in a continuous stream of events that really determine corporate strategy.

Source: Quinn (1978).

Logical incrementalism

Following Quinn's research into how senior executives in large companies develop strategy, it is clear that, whilst they may begin with a plan, circumstances force change and strategy formation becomes 'fragmented', 'evolutionary', and 'intuitive'. He states that 'executives do consciously manage individual steps proactively, but it is doubt-ful that any one person guides a major strategic change sequentially through all the steps. Developing most strategies requires numerous loops back to earlier stages as unexpected issues or new data dictate. Or decision times become compressed and require short-circuiting leaps forward as crises occur' (Quinn, 1980: 4). Given time and careful observation, certain patterns emerge in the successful management of strategic change in large organizations. The following actions reflect the summation of observations of senior executives in large corporations.

Logical incrementalism is evidenced by the way strategic leaders:

1. Create awareness and commitment incrementally because 'most strategic issues emerge in vague or undefined terms'.

2. Are effective change managers who actively develop informal networks to get objective information.

3. Seem to consciously generate and consider a broad array of alternatives by amplifying understanding and awareness rather than relying on 'satisficing' (that is, accepting good enough or barely satisfactory compromise solutions).

4. Build credibility through visible actions and legitimize new viewpoints before reaching new strategic decisions.

5. Make tactical shifts and develop partial solutions which often encounter little opposition.

6. Broaden political support and understanding to achieve sufficient momentum. This can be undertaken in a variety of ways such as through committees, task forces, retreats, and so forth.   ⊗

> » 7. Overcome opposition by recognizing that there is a variety of legitimate views that need to be explored. Thus, 'wise executives do not want to alienate people'.
>
>   8. Structure flexibility through building buffers, slacks, and activists because 'there are too many uncertainties in the total environment for managers to program or control'.
>
> *Source:* Quinn (1980).

The dominant tendency of strategic leadership today takes the form of SWOT, PESTLE, and competitor analyses. The development of the Strategic Planning School in the 1970s added further to the leader's role by arguing the need for objective setting. Yet, whilst this is the job of the CEO, over-reliance on sterile statistical evidence is problematic. In the 1980s the focus broadened to include leadership tactics and, whilst the focus on tactics emphasized the need for strategic leadership, it had the unfortunate consequence of over-emphasizing parallels with military strategy. However, perhaps the most important contribution of strategic management was the critique of change as a neat linear sequence. Logical incrementalism forcefully argued that leaders ignored hidden processes vital to success or failure. The strategic management view of leadership moved from the use of relatively unsophisticated quantitative techniques to a qualitative approach that requires leaders to develop their skills and fine-tune their art.

8.5 Leadership attributes

In the early twentieth century, it was commonly believed that leaders are born rather than made. It was widely assumed that certain people possess traits that make them what they are. This widespread belief was partly responsible for pseudo-scientific studies like phrenology, which looked for physical traits that predispose people to evil, or to commit crimes. Similarly, it was assumed that it would be possible to find genetic traits for leadership. Prior to the Second World War, various studies attempted to identify leadership traits, and some were identified. In 1948, Stogdill attempted to summarize these studies. This was also repeated by Mann in 1959. Stogdill's review suggested that five traits distinguish leaders from followers:

1. Intelligence.
2. Dominance.
3. Self-confidence.
4. The amount of energy and activity expended.
5. Task focus, relevance, and knowledge.

Unfortunately, Stodhill concluded that these five traits do not accurately predict which individuals became leaders in organizations. This was also supported by the work of Mann, who identified seven categories of personality traits from the literature. In particular, he found that, whilst intelligence was the best predictor of leadership, all correlations between positive traits and leadership were weak. Despite the lack of evidence for a positive correlation between particular personality traits and leadership, the traits approach has received more recent attention.

8.5.1 Contemporary trait research

In the early twentieth century, trait theory research into leadership—the idea that individuals possessed inherited traits—ran into many difficulties. Firstly, it was unable to separate genetic ability from circumstance, situation, family background, opportunity, and privilege. A further difficulty was the problem of cultural relativity. Thus, the individual regarded as a great leader by one society might not be appreciated by another. For example, Genghis Khan may have been considered as a great leader by his followers, but his enemies were more likely to regard him as a tyrant. A third difficulty is situational relativity. For example, trait theorists could not account for why an effective leader in one situation (politics) might not be an effective leader in another (business) situation. A further difficulty is explaining historical relativity, because being an effective leader in one historical epoch might not mean that such an individual could be as effective in another very different historical epoch. Such questions, therefore, force us to look at the extent to which context or situation is important. We also need to understand whether the needs of followers are important. This, of course, will depend upon the number of stakeholder groups the leader needs to influence. Famous historical leaders often have only one group of stakeholders (followers) to consider, whereas business leaders have multiple stakeholder interests to deal with. Finally, we may also need to know the extent to which different types of knowledge, skill, and experience are important in order to lead a group of people. We can therefore conclude that the qualities that characterize a good leader cannot be reduced to a simple set of personality characteristics or traits.

A more interesting set of questions relates to whether leadership ability could be developed. As a result of behavioural research we discovered that many factors are important, including self-awareness and learning. We can therefore ask 'what circumstances might encourage an individual's potential to demonstrate leadership?' and also 'what skill does a person already possess?', or 'what are the barriers to developing potential leadership ability?' What we have learned from the history of leadership studies is that effective leaders can change their behavioural style in response to the situation they are dealing with. We know this from studies of behavioural styles and from situations or contingent factors.

In 1986, Lord, De Vader, and Alliger re-analysed Mann's data using more recent statistical techniques. They concluded that people hold perceptual 'prototypes' of what they believe constitutes leadership. These are essentially one's mental representation of the traits and behaviours possessed by leaders. This novel way of looking at traits indicated that these are intrinsically bound up with the perceptions of followers. In other words, one might be more likely to believe that an individual possesses effective leadership traits when that person exhibits behaviours consistent with one's prototypes (perceptions guided by personal values).

---

❶ Stop and think 8.4

What leadership qualities do you admire most? Write a list of as many as you can think of, without evaluating them. When you have done that, group them under a few headings, as makes sense to you. For example, integrity and honesty would go together. Now consider two people you work with or have previously worked with, who match some of these qualities. Identify what is missing in each case. Now say how you think these qualities emerged. Are they innate, were they encouraged, are they the result of experience, or do they result from knowledge?

Finally, say why you recognize these qualities to be important. Is it because you possess similar innate qualities, or is it because of the life experiences you personally have had that enable you to judge others against them?

Later research confirmed that, whilst traits may not be objective or positive indicators of a person's ability, the perceptions of followers play a very important part in attributing qualities to a leader. This is particularly the case with gender and ethnicity. Work by Hall, Workman, and Marchioro (1998) suggests that the perceptions we have of an individual leader are related to gender differences. Thus, people who hold strong stereotypes of associations between masculinity and leadership are more likely to find that such traits are demonstrated by men than by women. Conversely, people who are less rigid in associating masculinity with leadership are more likely to perceive leadership traits as not gender-specific.

Other researchers sought to address ethnic or cross-cultural differences. For example, Kouzes and Posner (1995) asked 20,000 people from different nationalities: 'what values (personal traits or characteristics) do you look for and admire in your superiors?' Four traits were identified as common across cultures: (1) honesty, (2) looking forward, (3) inspiring others, and (4) competence. Such research indicates that followers want to be led by people with specific behavioural attributes. This later research on traits has nevertheless departed significantly from the original approaches. For instance, it recognizes that an individual may inherit certain traits, although these are undoubtedly influenced by social relationships. This results in discussions of personality and character.

8.5.2 Personality and character

A good example of how personality and character result from a complex mixture of inherited characteristics and social control can be understood by considering the concept of self-esteem. Self-esteem can be regarded as one's personal feeling of self-worth. The concept is therefore associated with positive or negative self-images. These can relate to whether we feel happy with things like our own body image; comfortable with our own ability to communicate with others; or that people generally like us, or not. Self-esteem can be measured by questionnaires that seek agreement or disagreement with both positive and negative statements. Those who agree with the positive statements and disagree with the negative statements have high self-esteem. They perceive themselves as 'worthwhile, capable, and acceptable. People with low self-esteem view themselves in negative terms. They do not feel good about themselves and are hampered by self-doubts' (Kreitner, Kinicki, and Buelens, 2002: 120).

As Kreitner, Kinicki, and Buelens (2002) point out, high self-esteem is not always a positive thing. Thus, whilst people with high self-esteem might handle failure better than those with low self-esteem, in some circumstances people with high self-esteem become egotistical and boastful when faced with pressure situations (Bandura, 1989). In situations where leaders exaggerate their own abilities above those of their peers, the consequences for collaboration may be negative. Therefore, whilst high self-esteem may be positive, this depends upon other inherited attributes, such as creativity, intelligence, and persistence. Many of these are cultivated and nurtured through socialization. Conversely, the informal learning situations through which people develop personality and character may result in destructive and anti-social behaviour. Self-esteem may well be associated with the individualist cultures that have developed in the West since the beginning of the twentieth century. It might also be related to cultural differences between organizations. For example, the following case example suggests that the expectations of subordinates are related to context.

> ## » Case example 8.2

Character and its consequences

Jeremy came from a military background, which appeared to suit his personality. He was obsessed by rules and regulations. His first act on becoming our new leader was to demonstrate his efficiency with the budget by inviting everyone for a corporate lunch. He provided the cheapest option available: packed lunch in a bag. It is not difficult to excuse a first example with a new leader. One can put it down to uncertainty about procedures.

As time went on, a pattern of behaviour emerged and his character began to impose itself. For example, we came to learn that Jeremy always talked over other people in order to get his point across. He never complimented actions of subordinates and he failed to develop people. Jeremy also dreamed of controlling things in more efficient ways. One of these dreams was to introduce an online mood meter so that when staff came into the office in the morning, they could indicate whether they were happy, sad, angry, or frustrated. Unfortunately for him, his subordinates refused to register their moods on a daily basis. Of course, they did not formally complain but, as is the case with most forms of subtle resistance to change, they just ignored the meter »

> ❯ as well as the repeated emails he sent to engage them. If Jeremy had demonstrated any form of charisma, then the story might have been different. As a consequence of Jeremy's leadership, subordinates constantly watched out for unsuspected consequences. This was largely because he chose to define reality for his staff. He never used the word 'team' but preferred instead to refer to 'his staff' in the possessive. He often stated, for example, that 'any problems caused by his staff would be dealt with'. Despite the flaws in Jeremy's character, 'his staff' undertook their daily tasks remarkably well. This was largely because they were realistic and understood what had to be done despite his appeals to his personal ideology or his preferred definition of reality. One of the things that he brought into the organization as a result of his military background was a clear distinction between management and the line, that is, between leaders and subordinates. This explains why the concept of teamwork was always difficult and only functioned where people knew their place. Whilst it is true to say that Jeremy's subordinates are not inspired by his qualities, his character does, at least, have a positive aspect. His words and his actions are retold to others as a form of humour and as a kind of displacement activity.

Perhaps a more useful way of identifying those people with leader potential, or developing people to become leaders, is by encouraging self-efficacy. This can be regarded as the way we each make judgements about the chances of successfully achieving a task. Self-efficacy is a process of learning what knowledge, skills, and experience to apply to particular situations. In other words, self-efficacy can be regarded as the gradual acquisition of complex cognitive, social, linguistic, and/or physical skills through experience (Gist, 1987). For example, Kreitner, Kinicki, and Buelens (2002) report that 1995 research by Diener and Diener using a sample of 13,118 students from 31 countries illustrates a strong correlation between self-esteem and life satisfaction in individualistic cultures (e.g. USA, Canada, New Zealand, Netherlands) and a moderate positive correlation in collectivist cultures (e.g. Korea, Kenya, Japan). It would therefore appear that individualistic cultures are based on strong societal institutions that socialize people to strive and achieve as individuals and, conversely, collectivist cultures socialize people to focus more on responsibility for communal or collective duties. These issues may be important for leaders of trans-national organizations because they affect the way that values are understood, and suggest that motivations may be different from those the leader is familiar with.

Personality is defined as 'the combination of stable physical and mental characteristics that give the individual his or her identity' (McCrae, 1993). Personality traits can be regarded as the product of both genetic and environmental influences. Although there has been a variety of standardized personality tests over the years, the most common tests of personality have included:

1. Eysenck's seven pairs of traits based on extraversion or introversion.
2. The 'Big Five'—neuroticism, extraversion, openness to experience, agreeableness, and conscientiousness—often used to describe dimensions of personality.

Figure 8.2 Psychometric methods

Psychometric methods offer organizations a way to improve the quality of selection and promotion decisions by systematically collecting information about candidates.
TYPICAL TESTS INCLUDE:
16PF and MYERS-BRIGGS

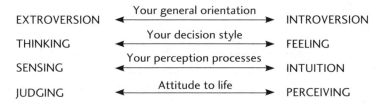

EXTROVERSION	Your general orientation	INTROVERSION
THINKING	Your decision style	FEELING
SENSING	Your perception processes	INTUITION
JUDGING	Attitude to life	PERCEIVING

Correlates: Personality type, Occupations and Management/Leadership Style

3. The Myers–Briggs test (see Figure 8.2), based on 16 personality types and used for problem solving and decision making in groups. This seeks a complementary mix of different personality types and fits people into behaviour types rather than traits, because the aim is to organize people around complementary behaviour patterns.

The Big Five test, for example, determines personality by aggregating scores that reveal each dimension of personality in relation to how positively or negatively a person scores on each scale.

Character is seen as an attribute of leaders. Scholars who choose to investigate character tend to argue that 'character is revealed in the moral and ethical choices we make' and to 'act with character is to show virtue' (Sarrros, Cooper, and Hartican, 2006: 683). Furthermore, character and virtue are said to be related to 'the ethical qualities of persons', and 'with what we view as good, or excellent, or praiseworthy about them' (Tjeltveit, 2003: 400). Authors who see character as an essential attribute of leadership focus on the concept of authenticity. Thus the central attribute of a leader is his or her consistency in applying moral standards to organizational life. As a result, such people are known for their integrity and for their ability to apply a moral compass (Bass and Steidlmeier, 1999) to their decisions.

There is a danger, however, that the attributes that have been identified look like vague generalized qualities. For example, Kirkpatrick and Locke (1991) argued that character contained six leadership traits (drive; the desire to lead; honesty and integrity; self-confidence; cognitive ability; and knowledge of the business). Similarly, Gergen (2001) argued that character, vision, and political capacity are three essential traits for leadership, and Tait's (1996) investigation of 18 UK business leaders argued that character consisted of honesty, fairness, compassion, humility, and being one's own person. As, Sarrros, Cooper, and Hartican (2006) suggest, many of these character attributes are reconstructed in Barker and Coy's (2003) seven attributes:

1. Humility.

2. Courage.

3. Integrity.

4. Compassion.

5. Humour.

6. Passion.

7. Wisdom.

This raises a very important question: does this type of research take us back to the difficulty that early twentieth-century research faced in attempting to identify scientific universal qualities? Indeed, are such researchers not simply reinventing a square wheel that is no use to anyone embarking on the leadership journey? In order to test this, Sarros, Cooper, and Hartican (2006) constructed a Virtuous Leadership Scale (VLS). They produced definitions for each of the Barker and Coy attributes and constructed a rating scale. The definitions were:

1. Humility is the quality of being humble, or having a modest sense of one's own significance.

2. Courage is setting a direction for the long term and taking people along without being hampered by fear.

3. Integrity is consistently adhering to a moral or ethical code or standard. A person with integrity consistently chooses to do the right thing when faced with alternative choices.

4. Compassion is concern for the suffering or welfare of others; providing aid or showing mercy for others.

5. Humour is the ability to invoke laughter or see the funny side of a painful predicament.

6. Passion is having a source of energy or enthusiasm from one's soul that enables that person to produce extraordinary results.

7. Wisdom is possessing experience and knowledge, together with the power of applying them critically or practically.

Sarros, Cooper, and Hartican (2006) used a 'convenience sample' of 238 respondents, conducted electronically through the Australian Management Character Survey (AMCS). This was distributed via the national Australian Institute of Management (AIM). They concluded that:

Our findings reveal that Australian managers report integrity as a key character attribute. Coincidentally, integrity is the trait most cited by executives as important to ethical leadership... The second highest character attribute was humour... Because the sample was Australian managers, and research indicates that Australian managers generally have a laconic sense of humour as part of their leadership make-up... this finding may not be replicated in studies of managers in the UK or the USA, for example... However, the study did isolate statistically significant differences among sub-groups on specific character attributes. Females scored higher on compassion than males.

(Sarros, Cooper, and Hartican, 2006: 691)

Although leadership attributes are a more recent reworking of trait theory, this categorization reaches very different conclusions, dispelling the myth of fixed genetic characteristics. Thus, whilst trait theory in leadership was a failure—correlations between positive traits and leadership were weak—more recent research suggests that followers are more likely to believe that an individual is an effective leader if he or she exhibits behaviours consistent with their own internal images (or 'prototypes'). Such prototypes or mental images may be quite varied, but they are likely to be influenced by variables such as national culture differences, gender, age, and experience. Congruence between a leader's behaviour and followers' preferred perceptions positively affects motivation. A focus on the attributes a leader requires is useful because it reminds us that interpersonal qualities are important, particularly when engaging with followers. We can also see that leaders can develop themselves through learning, and appreciate the interpersonal qualities required for a particular type of role. Developing a measured appreciation of self-esteem is important. We have seen how leaders can be overconfident, possessing excessive self-esteem. Thus, we discovered that it might be more useful to train leaders by encouraging self-efficacy. If self-efficacy can be regarded as the gradual acquisition of complex cognitive, social, linguistic, and/or physical skills through experience, then we need to focus on how leaders make judgements. This is what the idea of servant leadership describes. Servant leadership recognizes the importance of shared interests. Its purpose is to share power; build community and cultivate authenticity in leadership, with the leader being described as the first among equals.

8.5.3 Narcissistic leaders

Narcissism can be described as an intense personal motivational need to have one's assumed superiority reaffirmed by others. Classically, this is a form of self-admiration that the individual requires to have continuously reaffirmed. This was discussed in Chapter 7, where narcisism was viewed as a personal trait that desires power and control, which in turn affects others. We have seen some examples of narcissistic leadership exhibited at the head of corporate financial institutions. Although self-esteem is linked with traits of narcissistic leaders, it is a contorted internalized version. Emmons (1987) links four factors to the narcissistic leader:

1. *Exploitativeness/Entitlement,* which is internalized as a need to get respect believed due.

2. *Leadership/Authority*, internalized as a need to be the centre of attention.

3. *Superiority/Arrogance*, internalized as 'I am better than others'.

4. *Self-absorption/Self-admiration*, internalized as a preoccupation with 'how extraordinary and special I am'.

Personality theorists suggest that narcissism is traceable to a combination of genetic factors and early parental relations (Millon, 1981; Livesley *et al*, 1993), and is linked to biased self-esteem (Emmons, 1984; Morf and Rhodewalt, 1993; John and Robins, 1994) and 'affective intensity' or mood swings (Emmons, 1987) following criticism (Rhodewalt, Madrian, and Cheney, 1998). Individuals who score high in narcissism 'react to negative feedback with more anger and aggression than do individuals low in narcissism' (Chatterjee and Hambrick, 2007).

Because CEOs influence the cultural psychodynamics of an organization (see Chapter 7), researchers are interested in how personalities manifest in organizational outcomes. For example, whilst narcissistic leaders have high power needs, which appears to help their career advancement, they appear likely to make 'flawed decisions' due to their 'arrogance, sense of entitlement, and especially a continuous need for affirmation' (Chatterjee and Hambrick, 2007: 354). Because these features are absent from self-esteem, they come to characterize narcissism. Such leaders may be highly successful, but equally it is these features that may lead to their downfall (see the following case example).

❯❯ Case example 8.3

Narcissistic leadership or just bad luck?

Three chief executives of British banks have been largely responsible for £500bn of taxpayers' money having to be spent bailing out their banks after extraordinary tales of mismanagement. Who are they?

- Adam Applegarth, former Northern Rock CE, in 2007.
- Andy Hornby, adored by the City until he took over HBOS.
- Sir Fred Goodwin descended from hero status when the Royal Bank of Scotland (RBS) shares crashed by two-thirds overnight and suffered the biggest loss (of £28bn) ever recorded by a company in Britain.

Goodwin, Hornby, and Applegarth are now discredited. What do they have in common? Goodwin was said to be 'autocratic and fearsomely controlling'.[1] He pursued an ambitious expansion strategy that began with the purchase of National Westminster Bank, then Churchill Insurance, then a stake in the Bank of China. He was reported to have said that 'he had turned RBS into a "sausage machine", making loans, packaging them up into complex securities, and selling them on so that it could make more loans'.[2] In 2007 he bought the Dutch bank ABN–Amro for £50bn. As a result, RBS's assets and liabilities mushroomed.   ❯❯

> ≫ Applegarth increased Northern Rock's lending from £42bn to £113bn between the end of 2003 and the summer of 2007. An employee with whom he had an affair somehow managed to buy five homes using loans from the bank, despite earning just £30,000 a year.[2]
>
> Like Goodwin and Applegarth, Hornby used depositors' money, and 'had an air of invincibility'.[2] These qualities have been cited as evidence that they do not appear to consider themselves accountable to the public.
>
> [1] 'The Sunday Times report on who's to blame and the prospects for recovery', The Sunday Times, 25 January 2009.
> [2] Simon Hattenstone, 'Sir Fred, just say sorry', The Guardian, 24 January 2009.

8.5.4 Servant leadership

Servant leadership is a description of a particular type of leadership, where the leader focuses on the interests of the followers. The purpose of servant leadership is to share power, build community, and cultivate authenticity in leadership. The concept was introduced to the leadership literature by Greenleaf (1977). For Greenleaf, the servant leader is a visionary thinker who recognizes the importance of a shared vision. To encourage this, it is necessary to cultivate the development and empowerment of followers. The leader is therefore the first among equals:

> The servant leader is servant first... It begins with the natural feeling that one wants to serve... first. Then, conscious choice brings one to aspire to lead... The difference manifests itself in the care taken by the servant—first to make sure that other people's highest-priority needs are being served. The best test and the most difficult to administer is: Do those served grow as persons? Do they, while being served, become healthier, wiser, freer, more autonomous, [and] more likely themselves to become servants? And what is the effect on the least privileged in society[?] [W]ill they benefit or, at least, not be further deprived?

(Greenleaf, 1977: 13–14)

According to Washington, Sutton, and Field (2006: 701), the 'primary motivation for servant leadership is the desire to effectively serve followers in order to accomplish shared goals'. The concept of servant leadership carries implications of social justice on the one hand, and the pragmatic desire for motivation and self-managed work performance among followers. We can see how this concept might be used by specific types of leader, such as a trade union leader or the senior partner in a profession. However, it may be more difficult to see how different interest groups, such as shareholders and employees, might be persuaded. Nevertheless, this has been recommended as a useful theory for organizational leadership. Levering and Moskowitz

(2000), for example, report that a number of key American companies have adopted this approach.

In the attempt to identify the attributes of servant leadership, Washington, Sutton, and Field (2006) have attempted to provide the structural foundations for a model to support the theory. The traits shared by both this kind of leader and their followers tested and confirmed four hypotheses. Washington, Sutton, and Field's study of 126 supervisors and 283 employees confirmed that followers' perceptions of their leaders' values were critical in respect of:

- empathy, when leaders visibly appreciated followers and demonstrated a duty of care;
- integrity, to ensure that trust dominates over fear;
- competence, which (as Greenleaf suggested) is necessary to inspire confidence in the leader's skills, knowledge, and abilities;
- agreeableness, because both the agreeable individual and the servant leader emphasize altruism and support for others.

---

❶ Stop and think 8.5

Many situations today require a team approach to managing change. However, some situations lend themselves better than others to this approach. Write two lists headed (a) situations that require servant leadership and (b) situations that would not work with servant leadership. When you have done this, provide reasons for each situation listed.

8.6 Transformational leadership

The relationship between leaders and followers has been explored in the section above dealing with attributes of leaders. The extent to which people are empowered, and whether leadership is shared or distributed, were seen to be important. These occur when leadership requires teamwork to achieve results, which is particularly critical in situations where cooperation is high and task-structured routine is low. For example, in highly routine situations (bureaucracies, assembly tasks, or service tasks such as McDonalds) mechanistic approaches require little leadership flair unless the task or market situation changes dramatically, because such tasks are clearly defined. However, when tasks are not, then a greater level of initiative is required by many people. Such fluid situations require an empowered approach to leadership.

The concept of transformational leadership reflects an attempt to illustrate this type of engagement in organizations. It captures the idea that strategic change and development must stimulate followers as much as leaders. It also reflects the idea that enhanced performance can result only from teamwork: the imaginations of all the people involved in the pursuit of a task or goal. In other words, if human capital is the key to competitive advantage, then an appropriate leadership style is required.

The term transformational leadership first emerged in a very different context. It was first used in 1973 by the sociologist Jim Downton in his book *Rebel Leadership: Commitment and Charisma in the Revolutionary Process*, where he referred to a leadership style as a form of collaborative engagement with interesting dynamics. Thus it occurred in situations where leaders and followers raised each other's performance through motivation and moral commitment. The concept was developed further by James MacGregor Burns in 1978 when he contrasted the term transformational leadership with transactional leadership (this is leadership that is little more than an exchange relationship between reward and effort. No effort is made to develop, nurture or motivate employees). Like Downton, Burns's interests were different from those of the advocates of effective business and management techniques. He was interested in how successful political leaders engage with followers in what he called 'transforming leadership'. He states:

> transforming leadership… occurs when one or more persons engage with others in such a way that leaders and followers raise one another to higher levels of motivation and morality. Their purposes, which might have started out as separate but related, as in the case of transactional leadership, become fused. Power bases are linked not as counterweights but as mutual support for common purpose. Various names are used for such leadership, some of them derisory: elevating, mobilizing, inspiring, exalting, uplifting, preaching, exhorting, evangelizing. The relationship can be moralistic, of course. But transforming leadership ultimately becomes moral in that it raises the level of human conduct and ethical aspiration of both leader and led, and thus it has a transforming effect on both.

(Goethals, Sorenson, and Burns, 2004: 20)

The concept was further elaborated by Bass (1998), who described the impact that transformational leadership had on followers. Respect, trust, admiration, and loyalty reflect the motives for commitment of followers.

Bass qualified transformational leadership by articulating four core dimensions. These are:

1. *Idealized influence* (or charisma) reflects a high degree of conviction so that followers are able to identify with the aims of the leader. Charisma is clearly an emotional relationship that appeals to followers, but it also reflects shared values.

2. *Inspirational motivation* reflects the manner in which the leader articulates a vision that appeals to followers. Inspirational motivation challenges followers to attain higher standards. Followers are motivated by a strong sense of purpose. A leader must possess very effective communication skills in order to create a compelling sense of direction.

3. *Intellectual stimulation* describes how the leader challenges assumptions and takes calculated risks. Followers are stimulated by the ideas generated and by the empowered approach to personal and organizational development.

4. *Individual consideration* describes the way the leader attends to followers' needs. Leadership requires the will to act as a mentor to others. Patience and time to coach others is critical to empowering and developing people. The ability to listen and engage followers at an interpersonal level demonstrates commitment.

❶ Stop and think 8.6

If you were to take on leadership responsibility for a group of people, what challenges would you set if you followed the criteria set out by Bass? Apply these to an existing scenario.

While transformational leadership can be applied to most organizational situations, the emergence and effectiveness of such leadership may be facilitated by some contexts and inhibited by others (Krishnan, 2005). As Krishnan points out, 'Waldman *et al* (2001) found that CEO charismatic leadership enhanced performance only under conditions of perceived environmental uncertainty' and Shamir and Howell (1999) argued that 'charismatic leaders are more likely to emerge and be effective when the tasks of organizational members are challenging and complex and require individual and group initiative, responsibility, creativity, and intense effort; and when performance goals are ambiguous and extrinsic rewards cannot be strongly linked to performance' (Krishnan, 2005: 443). There appears to be some justification for such findings, since Burns had also indicated that transformational leadership requires a leader to expose contradictions between the articulation of values and practice itself. The concept of transformational leadership extends the idea of servant leadership, since it focuses on the type of engagement required to achieve a given task. In particular, it links strategic change to empowerment and team relationships. It moves us in the direction of recognizing that human capital is the key to competitive advantage.

8.7 Results-based leadership

Consult the internet and you will find leadership development programmes that claim that participants will:

- 'master leadership';
- develop 'individuals' capacity for creating vibrant organizations';
- 'enhance the creative potential of employees';
- 'discover and confront limitations and blind spots', and so on.

In such programmes, it is common to find that the concept of leadership relates to many other areas, which include the use of power; the importance of integrity and authenticity; the leader's role in developing a positive organizational climate; complexity management; encouraging innovation; and so on. This leads to confusion, as Ulrich, Zenger, and Smallwood (1999) point out:

> Pinpointing the very concept of leadership felt akin to grappling with a ghost, because no two people saw the same thing or defined it in the same way. Leadership development programs that we experienced were amorphous. Sponsors complained that their programme did not produce any noticeable change in the attendees' leadership Behaviour. At one point, we purchased over 30 books with leader or leadership in the title to add to the extensive library each of us had collected. Some told inspirational stories of a leader's successes. Others shared secrets of what leaders believed accounted for their achievements. But all had a common dimension. They focussed inward and concluded with a 'wish list' of attributes possessed by successful leaders... The more we pondered leadership as merely a bundle of attributes, the more we concluded that the solitary focus on inner attributes of the leader left something important and obvious out of the leadership equation.

> **(Ulrich, Zenger, and Smallwood 1999: xii)**

Ulrich, Zenger, and Smallwood are critical of approaches that simply list attributes but fail to qualify them in any meaningful way. Consequently, they suggest that a useful way of thinking about organizational leadership is to begin by grouping them into three categories. These are related to personal qualities ('what leaders are'), knowledge and capability ('what leaders know'), and behavioural style ('what leaders do'). Another way of remembering these headings is to think of them as character, knowledge, and action. These are illustrated in Figure 8.3.

Figure 8.3 Ulrich, Zenger, and Smallwood's organizational leadership categories

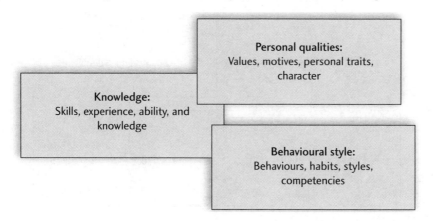

The objective of organizational leadership is to:

1. Set a direction for the future by creating a vision that, ideally, encapsulates unique capabilities.

2. Mobilize commitment by engaging with individuals and teams in performing a task.

3. Engender capability by building the structures and teams to support the direction of change.

By understanding the importance of leadership attributes, individuals learn what it is they need to develop, for example, which personal qualities they need to work on, what type of knowledge they require, which is the most important behavioural style to employ in a given situation. In reality it is only through simulation and practical experience that these can be developed. In other words, to know what attributes are required is one thing, but to deploy them successfully is another.

The main difficulty with listing generic attributes is that individuals believe they either have these qualities or will acquire them; but context changes everything. What may look like a good set of attributes today might not be so suitable in the future; as the context changes, so the mix of attributes will also need to change. A further difficulty with generic models of leadership attributes is the over-emphasis on qualities for CEOs. This is not helpful for others who have to lead in other ways.

In order to move away from what may appear to look like a shopping-list mentality, Ulrich, Zenger, and Smallwood suggest that leaders should focus on results. This means being clear about what needs to be done and providing a clear plan of action for others to follow. In this way, achievements can be measured against goals. Thus, leadership related to results means those results the leader deems necessary. A balance is therefore struck between the cost to change and the advantages gained from doing so. This can also be inverted: the costs of not changing and the disadvantages of doing nothing. This is illustrated in Figure 8.4.

Figure 8.4 Results matrix

The cost of change	Advantages gained
The cost of not changing	Disadvantages of doing nothing

Leaders need to focus on results by thinking about the costs, and advantages or disadvantages. We can ask 'how much will this change cost us?' but knowing whether the change is beneficial depends upon the perceived advantages to be gained. A more complete picture emerges only when we ask the contrary questions: 'what are the costs of not changing?' and 'what are the potential disadvantages?'

8.7.1 Using a balanced scorecard

A balanced scorecard is a method for developing an organization by identifying and satisfying stakeholders. This can also be regarded as stakeholder analysis. You can find detailed discussion of this in Freedman (1985); Kaplan and Norton (1993; 1996).

Developing the idea of stakeholder analysis and linking it with leadership competencies and results, Ulrich, Zenger, and Smallwood (1999) argue that leaders should be results-focused, identifying the needs of four key stakeholder groups: employees, organization, customers, and investors. In this way, the leader has to work out where compromises may have to be made. The type of questions we might ask include:

1. In relation to the organization, what results or outcomes do we want to achieve, and how does this relate to the critical success factors?

2. In relation to investors, we want to know some basic things, such as: how can we attract more investment? or what results will investors be happy with? or what will be the consequences if we take a particular course of action?

3. In relation to employees, we might ask what performance targets we can achieve. How many employees are required to complete this task to get the results we need? What is the extent of employee commitment and do we need to improve it?

4. In relation to customer results, we might ask who our key customers are, and what they require. How effectively do we meet their deadlines? Do we monitor customer feedback effectively?

Finally, by combining results with attributes or competencies, we can achieve a more effective and balanced approach to leadership. The following case example illustrates the difficulty of not involving stakeholders when leading a change initiative.

» Case example 8.4

Devising strategy with stakeholder needs in mind?

Background

EMI has a long and distinguished history. However, like other companies in the music business, its sales have declined dramatically. In 2007 EMI was bought for £3.2bn by »

>> Terra Firma, a private equity group that sought to transform its fortunes. Tony Wadsworth, who had been the Chief Executive of EMI(UK) for 25 years, was replaced by Guy Hands. In order to make the company more efficient, Terra Firma expects to make EMI 'leaner and fitter' by cutting the workforce worldwide by approximately 1,500 to 2,000 staff and by restructuring the company. Hands has stated that 'we have spent a long time looking intensely at EMI and the problems faced by its recorded music division which, like the rest of the music industry, has been struggling to respond to the challenges posed by a digital environment'. Consequently, 'we believe we have devised a new revolutionary structure for the group that will improve every area of the business. In short it will make EMI's music more valuable for the company and its artists alike.'*

The problem with the industry is that it has suffered severely from piracy and, more recently, because legitimate but relatively cheap downloads do not offset the fall in CD sales. The internet has given consumers more control and record companies less. Bands themselves now make more of their money through touring than through record sales, which passes by record companies like EMI. This also means that artists have become more powerful. Consequently, EMI will need to reshape its business by developing new relationships with stakeholders—managers, staff, and artists—in order to keep up with the changing nature of the music industry.

EMI was the label that promoted bands like the Beatles, Pink Floyd, David Bowie, Queen, Radiohead, Coldplay, Kylie Minogue, Robbie Williams, and Lily Allen. Radiohead have now left EMI, describing the new management as acting like 'a confused bull in a china shop', and 'Robbie Williams has gone on strike and has refused to deliver his new album... Tim Clark publicly stated that Robbie "would not release another EMI record until the management's plans became clearer"'.*

The attempt to reposition EMI labels to ensure they are 'completely focused' on finding and developing artists remains a core aspiration of Guy Hands and the new EMI Board. Despite this aspiration, the Terra Firma takeover of EMI appears to raise questions about the difficulties of dealing with stakeholders who have a good deal of power and influence over their collective market situation.

Source: *Katie Allen and Richard Wray, 'EMI confirms thousands of job losses', guardian.co.uk, 15 January 2008.

8.7.2 What the leader needs to do when managing change

Managing change and mobilizing people are critical to this idea of linking specific attributes to results. We can organize our thoughts about this as follows.

1. *Establishing the catalyst for change.* This means not changing things without diagnosing the need to change. The catalyst for change will be one of three things: a dysfunction within the organization, factors external to the organization's environment, or the need to innovate. A clear diagnosis and accurate problem definition are essential.

2. *Who is responsible for leading change?* As well as individuals, this might include a steering group, which may take responsibility for the planning, implementation, and monitoring of change. Alternatively, specific individuals might be identified to champion the change. Clearly, such people, as leaders in their own right, need to demonstrate their own personal qualities or character, their own applied knowledge, and their behavioural style in order to take action.

3. *Communicating a shared need to change.* Everyone in the organization needs to understand why change is necessary. This means communicating the reasons for change, how it will affect them, and what is expected of them. It is important not to lose sight of the need to communicate enthusiasm, and to articulate how the outcome will benefit the different stakeholders.

4. *Establishing the vision.* All visions require a mission. This is essentially a method for implementing the vision. However, behind each mission lies the need for critical success factors (CSFs): key objectives that need to be accomplished. The CSFs usually require changes in behaviour, and might also require changes in attitudes. Because of this, it is important to be aware of Lewin's concerns about the difficulties of behavioural change. Although you will find references to Lewin elsewhere in this book, you should note that his three-stage model for managing personal and group change requires unfreezing current attitudes and behaviours, moving these on by identifying changes, and finally refreezing these by practising them until they become habits.

5. *Mobilizing commitment.* Having clear ideas about change is one thing, but it is quite another to achieve it. Achieving the vision requires mobilizing the commitment of everyone in the organization affected by it. Mobilizing commitment is really about two things: the need to establish commitment; and building coalitions. In this way change has a higher chance of success.

6. *Defining systems, structures, and resources to achieve the result.* Change is likely to require some change to operating systems. That is, doing things differently, changing behaviours, and acquiring new habits require a new procedural approach or system. This might involve changes to the quality system, or to the financial and other management systems. Changing systems often requires changes to the way people's activities are structured, which might involve establishing teams to develop core processes, for example. Finally, resources—human and physical—must be allocated.

7. *The need to monitor progress.* To know the extent of progress always requires measurement of something. The leader or steering group therefore needs to monitor how things are developing, identifying which CSFs have been achieved by the deadline set, and making adjustments where required. For example, a task might prove more complicated than when it was first considered.

8. *Planning for unintended consequences.* No leader or steering group can plan for everything in advance. There are always unintended consequences, some

favourable, others not. This means planning for Murphy's Law—'if anything can go wrong, it will'. This is because we are dealing with complexity, and with any action there is always a number of possible outcomes that we never plan for. For example, if five people decide to plan for a task that will take five days to complete, it is unlikely that they will consider the possibility that all five members might fall ill the next day. If two members fall ill, then the decision to extend the deadline will depend upon the extent of the expertise of the remaining team members. Whilst it is not always possible to plan for all contingencies, leadership is required in order to exercise judgement in relation to the most preferred outcome, given the new situation.

Results-based leadership can appear mechanistic and, indeed, would be without an appreciation of the other leadership research and arguments discussed throughout this chapter. One really needs to consider this concept only after a thorough reading and understanding of the previous sections. But once you have done this, you will understand why sensitivity to qualitative issues is important. Results-based leadership should be regarded as an attempt to merge the various strands of behavioural research, strategic leadership, leadership attributes, and transformational leadership, by arguing that leaders should focus on results. Results-based leadership suggests using a balanced scorecard approach to identify and satisfy stakeholder needs. When these needs have been analysed, the leader needs to manage change by acting as a catalyst and by mobilizing people.

8.8 Summary

We began this chapter by comparing two terms that are often used interchangeably: management and leadership. What we have discovered is that leadership should be seen in its own organizational context. It is therefore a mistake to look for universal criteria. The study of great leaders will not help. What will help is the careful study of one's own behavioural style and how to improve or modify it to suit the context. We also noted that different contingencies such as the type of task performed, the nature of the technology, the nature of the organization's environment, and the design of its internal environment all affect how a leader's style will be accepted by followers. As Fiedler pointed out, these determine the leader's degree of control and influence over a situation. Behavioural studies have revealed that there are other factors involved beyond situational contingencies. We noted the importance of individual and team motivational calculus. Thus, the relationship between the Path–Goal theory and Expectancy theory suggests that a comparison of the amount of effort required to obtain a reward with the likelihood of being successful in achieving the outcome is critical. Path–Goal theory suggests that a leader can influence the motivational calculus by identifying challenging pathways to goals and valued rewards.

The emergence of strategic leadership is a more recent development. The idea of the strategic leader was developed in the 1960s by the Design School of strategy, which focused on assessing an organization's external and internal situations. This is still a dominant tendency today in the form of SWOT, PESTLE, and competitor analyses. The development of the Strategic Planning School in the 1970s added further to the leader's role, by arguing the need for objective setting; and yet, whilst this is the job of the CEO, over-reliance on sterile statistical evidence is problematic. In the 1980s strategic leadership was refocused by Porter's book on *Competitive Strategy*. Whilst the focus on tactics emphasized the need for strategic leadership, it had the unfortunate consequence of over-emphasizing parallels with military strategy. One of the greatest contributions of strategic management was the criticism of the view of change as a neat linear sequence from strategic analysis of the external environment, via internal analysis of competencies, to future-oriented change actions. Logical incrementalism forcefully argued that the majority of corporate descriptions of how change has been achieved ignore hidden processes that might lead to success or failure. In essence, the strategic management view of leadership moved from a relatively unsophisticated quantitative approach to one that viewed leadership as a qualitative art.

Analysis of leadership attributes is a more recent reworking of trait theory. Thus, whilst theorists' attempts to find an authoritative list of leadership traits was a failure—correlations between positive traits and leadership were weak—more recent research suggests that followers are more likely to believe that an individual is an effective leader if he or she exhibits behaviours consistent with their own internal images (or 'prototypes'). If there is congruence between a leader's behaviour and followers' preferred perceptions, then a positive motivational relationship may be established between leader and follower. A focus on the attributes a leader requires is useful because it reminds us that interpersonal qualities are important, particularly when engaging with followers. Developing a measured appreciation of self-esteem is important. We have seen how leaders can be over-confident, possessing excessive self-esteem, and that it might be more useful to train leaders by encouraging self-efficacy. If self-efficacy can be regarded as the gradual acquisition of complex cognitive, social, linguistic, and/or physical skills through experience, then we need to focus on how leaders make judgements. The section on narcissistic leadership alerts us to the characteristic that may well propel high achievers into positions of power. Whilst narcissistic traits may have some advantages, we need to be mindful of the high risks, and the doubtful decisions leaders having them are likely to make.

If leadership attributes analysts began by focusing on the congruence of followers' prototypes with the abilities of a leader, then we might conclude that leaders can learn much by doing the reverse: by building relationships. This is what servant leadership describes. Servant leadership recognizes the importance of shared interests. Its purpose is to share power; build community, and cultivate authenticity in leadership, with the leader being described as the first among equals.

The concept of transformational leadership extends the idea of servant leadership by focusing on the type of engagement required to achieve a given task. In particular, it links strategic change to empowerment and team relationships. It moves us in the direction of recognizing that human capital is the key to competitive advantage.

Finally, results-based leadership seeks to balance personal qualities with appropriate knowledge and behavioural style. A balance is therefore struck between the cost of making change and the advantages gained from doing so; and an awareness developed of the costs of not changing and the disadvantages of doing nothing. One way of striking this balance is by using a balanced scorecard, which seeks to identify and then satisfy stakeholder needs. We noted that leaders can focus on results by identifying the needs of four key stakeholder groups—employees, organization, customers, and investors. When these needs have been analysed, the leader needs to manage change by acting as a catalyst and by mobilizing people, and can use the balanced scorecard to measure progress.

⭐ Case study

Leading change: the case of Sir Clive Woodward

In 2003 Sir Clive Woodward brought English Rugby its most notable team triumph for decades by returning from Australia with the World Cup. Woodward's success was achieved by applying best-practice business methods. So much so, that the book he published afterwards—*Winning!*—became a bestseller in the British business community. Its message was that leadership was about passion, commitment to excellence, and attention to detail. He once stated that leading his team to victory was 'no different from running Tesco or British Rail'.

Apart from winning 21 caps for England, Woodward had been a salesman for Xerox. He had also run his own computer-leasing business in Maidenhead. His experience in sport and business led him to the conclusion that the qualities of top leaders and the techniques of effective leadership are the same in both environments:

> There's a complete parallel. Running a successful company you need the same skills as you do to run a successful sports team.

First day in the job as England coach

Going to work on his first day as England coach was an emotional experience. He recalled:

> It's not a match day so the place is empty, but even in its apparent silence Twickenham hums with energy. As a player, this place filled me with pride and brought out my best. Just walking on to the pitch in 1980 with the English rose on my chest, I felt physically larger, stronger. Here I am, seventeen years later. I wonder will it be the same? I'm the England coach now. Will I feel the same raw anticipation and excitement? Driving around the massive stadium to the administration building, I'm struck by the heritage of this great institution. Some 130 years of history and expectations leave a legacy. In my head I hear ❯❯

» the chattering voices of a long line of coaches who have come before me. 'Do you think he has it?' I hear them ask. 'Is he up to the job?'

Creating a professional attitude begins at the top. When he entered his new workplace Sir Clive discovered that it was a cheery organization that had previously been managed in a rather unprofessional way, as the following extract illustrates:

Pulling into the car park… all the numbered spaces are full, so I turn into the one marked 'visitor', gather up my phone and briefcase, and head for the entrance. A cheerful receptionist finishes her call and looks up from her computer screen.

'Hello. How can I help?' she asks with a smile.

'Hi, I'm Clive Woodward.'

'And you're here to see… ?' Another smile.

'I'm here to see Don Rutherford.' Don is director of rugby for the Rugby Football Union.

'I wasn't informed of any visitors. Do you have an appointment?' she asks, her face turning quizzical. 'Just one minute, please,' and before I can say anything she has the phone to her ear.

'I have a Mr Woodward in reception for Mr Rutherford. He doesn't have an appointment.' Then, after a slight pause, 'Yes… right… oh, of course. Okay, thanks for that.'

She turns back to me. 'I'm very sorry, Mr Woodward…'

'Please call me Clive.'

'Of course, Mr Woodward. Mr Rutherford will be right down to see you.'

It's not yet 9am and I guess this wasn't the welcome I was expecting from my new employers. Perhaps I was meant to start next Monday? How odd. Sitting in the faded lounge I notice a few rugby magazines that are months out of date. Friday's paper is draped across the chair opposite. The room is stark and bare. There are no pictures of rugby players to be seen anywhere. Nothing to indicate this is the home of English rugby, save the obvious presence of the stadium over my shoulder.

After 15 minutes, Don Rutherford comes down the stairs into reception. I've known Don for years. He had been at the helm of England rugby for more than two decades. He is highly respected by most in the game, including me. I am pleased to see him. 'Clive. We didn't expect you. What are you doing here?' Maybe Don had his wires crossed as well. After all, he had been responsible for finalizing my contract.

'I'm here to start work. Normally I'd be in by 7am, but it's only day one, so I thought I'd give you all a bit of time. I'd like to settle into my office, you know, and get things started.'   »

>> 'Oh… but you're the coach. We thought you'd work from home and go out to the players and the clubs. What do you need an office for?' Clunk.

The penny dropped. After 17 years in business I thought I was a pretty sharp negotiator, only to suddenly realize I had completely forgotten to discuss the most obvious of necessities in my contract: an office and a phone.

'Don, I'm the full-time coach now. I need to work from an office at Twickenham, not at home. Could I meet my secretary and we'll sort out the office later?'

'A secretary? What for? Your place is out on the pitch with the players. Why would you need a secretary?' Looking back, I realize Don wasn't being deliberately difficult. He was in uncharted territory. I was the first professional coach in the RFU's history. The previous coach, Jack Rowell, had several businesses to run while doing the job, and so needed a hands-on director like Don just to get the job done. It was how things were run for decades, perhaps forever.

'I've come here to do a job, Don. Most mornings except match days I'll be here to work. To start I'll need an office, phone, a computer and a secretary…'

'But we don't have an office prepared for you,' Don says.

'Then I'll just start work here in reception until one is ready. I have a mobile phone and several calls to make. Let's just stop all this and get on with it.'

Sir Clive Woodward is the most successful leader the England Rugby team had. He is driven by passion and energy to win. One of the most important aspects of success is to cultivate people's basic desire to enjoy their job and be challenged in the process. This begins with a working environment where people learn and progress and develop a little more each day. In order to develop as a team, the players needed to trust their leader:

I was itching to apply my ideas to the England set-up. But I'd have to tread carefully with this team. Without their trust, we'd get nowhere. The group of players I could hear coming into the room now to take their seats included some who had just been through a tough Lions tour to South Africa. They were returning only to find wild speculation in the press about whether or not they'd even have a coach in the lead-up to what was billed as the toughest series of autumn internationals in England's history.

Once they could trust the coach, they could be challenged. With such engagement comes commitment. Once this had been established, Woodward stretched the team with advice from experts and experiences from other areas of life. For example, he brought in a specialist to conduct eye workouts to improve the players' peripheral vision and reaction times. He used the Royal Marines' training camp to sharpen their ability to make quick decisions, and to develop team spirit and leadership skills. He also analysed players' psychological responses to competitive situations with the aid of >>

❯ technology that monitored positioning and work rate during a match. Whilst he claims that being a rugby player is like any business, one thing appears to be important in his approach as a leader: balancing the routine with innovation. The routine requires players to 'train, talk to people, go to the gym', whilst innovations reflected 'leading developments in world sport'. The players' response was positive: they enjoyed the challenge and performed accordingly.

Questions

1. Describe the context and contingencies that were changed by Sir Clive Woodward. Consider task, technology, and environment.

2. How did he establish effective leader–player relations?

3. Apply Path–Goal theory to illustrate the motivational calculus, the challenging pathways to goals, and the valued rewards he developed.

4. How did Sir Clive Woodward encourage self-efficacy?

5. Bass qualified transformational leadership by articulating four core dimensions. Do any of these apply to Sir Clive Woodward?

■ Study questions

1. Compare and contrast the terms 'management' and 'leadership'.

2. What contingencies or situational factors are likely to affect leadership style?

3. What are the implications of the Path–Goal theory of leadership?

4. What is the main criticism of Strategic Planning, and why should a leader be cautious about this approach?

5. Explain what is meant by logical incrementalism.

6. What are leadership attributes?

7. Under what circumstances is servant leadership appropriate?

8. Compare and contrast the terms 'transformational' and 'transactional leadership'.

9. What is meant by results-based leadership?

10. Should any plan for change ignore or involve stakeholder interests?

■ Exercises

Exercise 1

Think of a sport, an event, an expedition, a task, a performance, or an organizational activity that requires leadership. Take a sheet of paper and at the top write your chosen example. Then draw a line down the middle and write two headings: on the left 'leadership', on the right 'management'. Then state which aspects of your example fall under each heading. Finally, consider why you have defined them as such. You should find that you have described the functions of leadership and management. What you should discover is that both terms are distinct but also functionally interrelated.

Exercise 2

Identify a particular organizational setting and construct a method to investigate as many aspects of the Behavioural Styles approach as possible. Develop a methodological instrument to include probing questions and observations. Once you have constructed this instrument, ask your tutor or supervisor to assess it critically. Then test it out, once in the setting for which it was designed, and once in a setting for which it was not designed. When you have done this, compare and contrast the results.

Exercise 3

Consider someone you believe demonstrates leadership attributes. Then rank your perception against the five traits of (a) intelligence, (b) dominance, (c) self-confidence, (d) the amount of energy and activity expended, and (e) task-focus, relevance, and knowledge. Score 1 as very high and 5 as very low for each. When you have done this, consider how much of the leader's behaviour was bound up with your perception of effective leadership. Finally, consider whether you have looked for any negative or contradictory habits or behaviours. If you did not do this, then attempt to do it now. Reach a balanced conclusion about the merits of trait theory.

Exercise 4

Identify someone you know who has leadership responsibility for a change situation. Refer to each of the core dimensions of transformational leadership—idealized influence, inspirational motivation, intellectual stimulation, individual consideration—and rate the abilities of the leader on a scale of 1 (high) to 5 (low). When you have done this, imagine that you have to provide feedback, and state what advice you would give to that person.

Exercise 5

Consider a change issue in an organization you are familiar with. Identify the needs of the key stakeholder groups. For example, employees; the organization; customers; investors. Now consider how much attention you would give to each in order to address their needs.

■ Further reading

Bass, B.M. (1998), *Transformational Leadership: Industrial, Military, and Educational Impact*, Mahwah, NJ: Lawrence Erlbaum Associates. The classic refinement to the ideas of Burns on transformational leadership.

Burpitt, W. (2009), 'Exploration versus Exploitation: Leadership and the Paradox of Administration', *Journal of Behavioral and Applied Management*, 10(2), 227–246. A useful account of the effectiveness of transformational versus transactional leadership in responding to disruptive environmental change.

Chatterjee, A. and Hambrick, D.C. (2007), 'It's All about Me: Narcissistic Chief Executive Officers and Their Effects on Company Strategy and Performance', *Administrative Science Quarterly*, 52, 351–386. Students interested in the relationship between leadership and narcissism will find this study of 111 CEOs in the computer hardware and software industries interesting, not just because it shows that CEOs demonstrate self-aggrandizement through 'strategic dynamism and grandiosity, as well as the number and size of acquisitions' they make also demonstrate 'extreme and fluctuating organizational performance'. Is it any surprise that their bold actions with big wins or big losses are 'generally no better or worse than firms with non-narcissistic CEOs'?

Marks, M.L. (2007), 'A framework for facilitating adaptation to organizational transition', *Journal of Organizational Change Management*, 20(5), 721–739. A useful account of leadership and organizational transformations in which the author proposes a framework for 'facilitating adaptation to organizational transition, to both overcome the undesirable consequences of transitions and to accelerate achievement of the transition's strategic objectives'.

Mintzberg, H., Ahlstrand, B., and Lampel, J. (1998), *Strategic Safari*, London: Prentice-Hall. An excellent historical account of the changing schools of business strategy.

Rickards, T. and Clark, M. (2006), *Dilemmas of leadership*, London: Routledge. A text about leadership, useful for its breadth and diversity.

Ulrich, D., Zenger, J., and Smallwood, N. (1999), *Results based leadership*, Cambridge, MA: Harvard Business School Press. A useful and very readable account.

Woodward, C. (2005), *Winning*, London: Hodder Paperbacks. An excellent example of English rugby's route to success in the 2003 Rugby World Cup. This is of interest to managers and sports leaders alike, because Sir Clive had been a successful businessman before he became an international rugby coach.

■ References

Andrews, K.R. (1971), *The Concept of Corporate Strategy*, Homewood, IL: Irwin.

Bandura, A. (1989), 'Regulation of Cognitive Processes through Perceived Self-Efficacy', *Developmental Psychology* (September), 729–735.

Barker, C. and Coy, R. (2003), *The 7 Heavenly Virtues of Leadership*, Management Today Series, Sydney: McGraw-Hill.

Bass, B.M. (1998), *Transformational Leadership: Industrial, Military, and Educational Impact*, Mahwah, NJ: Lawrence Erlbaum Associates.

Bass, B.M. and Steidlmeier, P. (1999), 'Ethics, character, and authentic transformational leadership behaviour', *Leadership Quarterly*, 10(2), 181–217.

Blake, R. and Mouton, J. (1964), *The Managerial Grid: The Key to Leadership Excellence*, Houston, TX: Gulf Publishing Co.

Burns, J.M. (1978), *Leadership*, New York: Harper & Row.

Chatterjee, A. and Hambrick, D.C. (2007), 'It's All about Me: Narcissistic Chief Executive Officers and Their Effects on Company Strategy and Performance', *Administrative Science Quarterly*, 52, 351–386.

Eagly, A.H. and Karau, S.J. (1991), 'Gender and the Emergence of Leaders: A Meta-Analysis', *Journal of Personality and Social Psychology*, May, 685–710.

Emmons, R. (1981), 'Relationship between narcissism and sensation seeking', *Psychological Reports*, 48, 247–250.

—— (1984), 'Factor analysis and construct validity of the narcissistic personality inventory', *Journal of Personality Assessment*, 48, 291–300.

—— (1987) 'Narcissism: Theory and measurement,' *Journal of Personality and Social Psychology*, 52, 11–17.

Fiedler, F.E. (1967) *A Theory of Leadership Effectiveness*, Maidenhead: McGraw-Hill.

Fleishman, E.A. (1974) 'Leadership Climate, Human Relations Training and Supervisory Behaviour', in Fleishman, E.A. and Bass, A.R. (1974), *Studies in Personnel and Industrial Psychology*, Third edition, Homewood, IL: Dorsey.

Foti, R.J., Fraser, S.L., and Lord, R.G. (1982), 'Effects of Leadership Labels and Prototypes on Perceptions of Political Leaders', *Journal of Applied Psychology* (June), 326–333.

Freedman, E. (1985), *Strategic Management: A Stakeholder Approach*, Boston, MA: Pitman.

Gergen, D. (2001), 'Character of leadership', *Executive Excellence*, 18, 5–7.

Gist, M.E. (1987), 'Self-Efficacy: Implications for Organizational Behaviour and Human Resource Management', *Academy of Management Review*, (July), 472–485.

Goethals, G.R., Sorenson, G.J., and Burns, J.M. (2004), *Encyclopedia of Leadership*, London: Sage.

Greenleaf, R.K. (1977), *Servant Leadership: A Journey into the Nature of Legitimate Power and Greatness*, Mahwah, NJ: Paulist Press.

Hall, R.J., Workman, J.W., and Marchioro, C.A. (1998), 'Sex, Task, and Behavioural Flexibility Effects on Leadership Perceptions', *Organizational Behaviour and Human Decision Processes* (April), 1–32.

House, R.J. (1971), 'A Path–Goal Theory of Leadership Effectiveness', *Administrative Science Quarterly*, 16, September, 321–338.

John, O.P. and Robins, R. (1994) 'Accuracy and bias in self-perception: Individual differences in self-enhancement and the role of narcissism', *Journal of Personality and Social Psychology*, 66, 206–219.

Kaplan, R. and Norton, D. (1993), 'Putting the Balanced Scorecard to Work', *Harvard Business Review*, September–October, 134–147.

—— (1996), 'Using the Balanced Scorecard as a Strategic Management System', *Harvard Business Review*, January–February, 75–87.

Kinicki, A.J., Horn, P.W., Trost, M.R., and Wade, K.J. (1995), 'Effects of Category Prototypes on Performance-Rating Accuracy', *Journal of Applied Psychology* (June), 354–370.

Kirkpatrick, S. and Locke, E. (1991), 'Leadership: do traits matter?', *Academy of Management Executive*, 5(2), 48–60.

Knights, D. and Willmott, H. (2007), *Introducing Organizational Behaviour and Management*, London: Thomson Learning.

Kreitner, R., Kinicki, A., and Buelens, M. (2002), *Organizational Behaviour*, Second European edition, Maidenhead: McGraw-Hill.

Kouzes, J.M. and Posner, B.Z. (1995), *The Leadership Challenge*, San Francisco, CA: Jossey-Bass.

Krishnan, V.R. (2005), 'Transformational leadership and outcomes: role of relationship duration', *Leadership & Organization Development Journal*, 26(5/6), 442–457.

Lackman, M.E. and Weaver, S.L. (1998), 'The Sense of Control as a Moderator of Social Class Differences in Health and Wellbeing', *Journal of Personality and Social Psychology*, (March), 763–773.

Levering, R. and Moskowitz, M. (2000), 'The 100 best companies to work for in America', *Fortune*, 141(1), 82–110.

Likert, R. (1961), *New Patterns of Management*, New York: McGraw-Hill.

Livesley, W.J., Jang, K.L., Jackson, D.N., and Vernon, P.A. (1993), 'Genetic and environmental contributions to dimensions of personality disorder', *American Journal of Psychiatry*, 150, 1826–1831.

Lord, R.G., De Vader, C.L., and Alliger, G.M. (1986), 'A Meta-Analysis of the Relation between Personality Traits and Leadership Perceptions: An Application of Validity Generalization Procedures', *Journal of Applied Psychology* (August), 402–410.

Mann, R.D. (1959) 'A Review of the Relationship between Personality and Performance in Small Groups', *Psychological Bulletin*, July, 241–270.

McCrae, R.R. (1993), 'Moderated Analyses of Longitudinal Personality Stability', *Journal of Personality and Social Psychology* (September), 577–585.

Millon, T. (1981), *Disorders of Personality*, New York: Wiley.

Mintzberg, H., Ahlstrand, B., and Lampel, J. (1998), *Strategic Safari*, London: Prentice-Hall.

Morf, C.C. and Rhodewalt, F. (1993) 'Narcissism and self-evaluation maintenance: Explorations in object relations', *Personality and Social Psychology Bulletin*, 19, 668–676.

Narayanan, L., Menon, S., and Spector, P.E. (1999), 'Stress in the Workplace: a comparison of Gender and Occupations', *Journal of Organizational Behaviour*, (August), 63–73.

Phillips, J.S. and Lord, R.G. (1982), 'Schematic Information Processing and Perceptions of Leadership in Problem-Solving Groups', *Journal of Applied Psychology* (August), 486–492.

Porter, M.E. (1980), *Competitive Strategy: techniques for analysing industries and competitors*, New York: Free Press.

Quinn, J.B. (1978), 'Strategic Change: Logical Incrementalism', *Sloan Management Review*, 20(1) (Fall), 7–21.

—— (1980), 'Managing Strategic Change', *Sloan Management Review*, 21(4) (Summer), 3–20.

Rhodewalt, F.J., Madrian, C., and Cheney, S. (1998) 'Narcissism, self-knowledge, organization, and emotional reactivity: The effect of daily experiences on self-esteem and affect', *Personality and Social Psychology Bulletin*, 24, 75–87.

Sarros, J.C., Cooper, B.K., and Hartican, A.M. (2006), 'Leadership and character', *Leadership & Organization Development Journal*, 27(8), 682–699.

Selznick, P. (1957), *Leadership in Administration: A sociological interpretation*, Evanston, IL: Row, Peterson.

Shamir, B. and Howell, J.M. (1999), 'Organizational and contextual influences on the emergence and effectiveness of charismatic leadership', *Leadership Quarterly*, 10(2), 257–283.

Shelly, R.K. and Munroe, P.T. (1999), 'Do Women Engage in Less Task Behaviour Than Men?', *Sociological Perspectives*, Spring, 49–67.

Steiner, R. (*Sunday Times* survey, 14 October 2001).

Stogdill, R.M. (1948) 'Personal Factors Associated with Leadership: A Survey of the Literature', *Journal of Psychology*, 35–71.

Tait, R. (1996), 'The attributes of leadership', *Leadership & Organization Development Journal*, 17(1), 27–31.

Tjeltveit, A.C. (2003), 'Implicit virtues, divergent goods, multiple communities', *American Behavioural Scientist*, 47(4), 395–414.

Ulrich, D., Zenger, J., and Smallwood, N. (1999), *Results based leadership*, Cambridge, MA: Harvard Business School Press.

Waldman, D.A., Ramirez, G.G., House, R.J., and Puranam, P. (2001), 'Does leadership matter? CEO leadership attributes and profitability under conditions of perceived environmental uncertainty', *Academy of Management Journal*, 44, 134–143.

Washington, R.R., Sutton, C.D., and Field, H.S. (2006), 'Individual differences in servant leadership: the roles of values and personality', *Leadership & Organization Development Journal*, 27(8), 700–716.

Wilson, I. (1994), 'Strategic Planning Isn't Dead—It Changed', *Long Range Planning*, 27(4), 12–24.

Woodward, C. (2005), *Winning*, London: Hodder Paperbacks.

Take your learning further: Online Resource Centre
http://www.oxfordtextbooks.co.uk/orc/grieves/

Visit the Online Resource Centre that accompanies this book to enrich your understanding of this chapter. Explore case study updates and answers to questions, test yourself using an interactive flashcard glossary, and keep up to date with the latest developments in the area.

CHAPTER 9

Diagnosing organizations

9.1 Introduction

In Chapter 1, we identified four perspectives—the structural-functional perspective, the multiple constituencies perspective, Organizational Development, Creativity and Volition: a Critical Theory of Change—that provide frameworks for interpretation and therefore analysis of organizations. The difference between analysis and diagnosis is subtle. For example, the structural-functional perspective will provide an analysis of input, outputs, and internal processes; the multiple constituencies perspective will assist in identifying the power of different stakeholder groups and the organization's responsibility to each of them (governance); Organizational Development will analyse the effectiveness of organizational functions such as leadership, communication, culture, motivation, and values; while Creativity and Volition: a Critical Theory of Change challenges the previous perspectives by forcing us to question the motives behind change. Organizational diagnosis, in contrast, is problem-focused, concerned with defined problems or dysfunctions. This chapter therefore seeks to illustrate how organizational diagnosis requires an ability to analyse problem situations.

In this chapter we will:

- Discover the importance of organizational diagnosis.
- Consider Action Research and process consultation.
- Learn how to construct a diagnostic map.
- Use framing to analyse an organizational problem.
- Understand the relevance of the client system.
- Learn to use a method for defining and presenting a problem statement to the client.
- Discover the difference between manifest and latent problems.

9.2 Defining a problem

This chapter is not intended to be a do-it-yourself guide to organizational diagnosis. It has quite a different, if no less important, purpose: to show the reader how to be clear about the nature of the problem facing an organization, then know what interventions to make in order to resolve the problem. An organizational problem is always defined in relation to a change perspective. To understand this you may wish to look at the Case Example—Shakespeare's *Henry V*—in the final section of this chapter. If we view a complex problem simplistically (that is, through a single analytical frame of reference) when other analytical frames may be required, then we end up with a poor diagnosis of the problem. As we noted in Chapter 2, the problem with the Ford Pinto was defined simplistically. That is, it was defined exclusively as a technical problem. Inevitably the solution failed because it did not diagnose the underlying (latent) issues, so was therefore inappropriate, and eventually led to a major court case, which Ford lost. Diagnosis should not have proceeded by limiting the frame of reference to a structural-functional perspective only. Some obvious questions were overlooked (Anand, Ashfoith, and Joshi, 2005; Butterfield, Klebe Trevino, and Weaver, 2000), such as:

- What is the nature of the technical problem?
- Are there any ethical issues to consider?

- Are there any learning issues in relation to management processes?
- Are there any political issues that prevent an open solution to the problem?

9.2.1 Manifest and latent problems

It is important to distinguish between *manifest* and *latent problems* and to determine the problem focus. A manifest problem is one defined by someone in the organization, usually a person close to the problem who has direct experience of it. The difficulty is that, because a manifest problem is simply a manifestation of something problematic occurring within the organization, it might not be the root cause of the problem. In other words, we need to distinguish cause from effect. Manifest problems are therefore issues that emerge and are spotted, whereas the root cause is referred to as the latent problem.

---

❶ Stop and think 9.1

Think of a current manifest problem you are experiencing or identify one you previously experienced. Then answer the following questions.

- Who defined the problem and why was it defined this way?
- How complex is the manifest problem? That is, does it involve:

  A. technical issues?

  B. ethical issues?

  C. stakeholder issues?

- How contentious is the defined problem—would other stakeholders see it the same way?
- How accurate is the information?
- Can you separate facts from opinions?
- Do the facts contradict the organization's policies?
- How much is opinion and how much is fact?
- Is there any evidence of interpersonal or interdepartmental conflict?
- Is there any evidence of leadership difficulties?
- Is there any evidence of stress or anxiety?

Once you have answered these questions you will be able to decide whether you have sufficient knowledge of the problem, or need to obtain further information.

In this stop and think activity, you will have noted that you have to make decisions about whether you have enough information about the problem, or will need to search for more. The difficulty for an organization's managers and members is identifying whether they have enough information about a problem. This is what Harrison refers to as the consultant's dilemma:

> The level at which an individual or group is willing and ready to invest energy and resources is probably always determined partly by a realistic assessment of the problems and partly by a defensive need to avoid confrontation and significant change.
>
> **(Harrison, 1995: 26)**

An OD consultant is aware that manifest problems are likely to be caused by much deeper issues. The consultant's dilemma, therefore, is being faced, on the one hand, with the decision to lead the client into 'areas which are threatening, unfamiliar and dependency provoking…', whilst 'being guided by the client's own understanding of his problems and his willingness to invest resources in particular kinds of relatively familiar and unthreatening strategies'. For Harrison, time is critical to the decision. Thus, where time permits:

> this dilemma is ideally dealt with by intervening first at a level where there is good support from the norms, power structure and felt needs of organization members. The consultant can then, over a period of time, develop trust, sophistication and support within the organization to explore deeper levels at which particularly important forces may be operating.
>
> **(Ibid.)**

Deeper levels of enquiry require greater knowledge and skills in dealing with behavioural issues; and this is precisely the dilemma that Harrison presents us with. Deeper interventions involve latent problems. These are underlying problems that give rise to manifest problems. If we use a physical analogy of a volcano, then what we see on the surface is perhaps relatively little—a small amount of smoke, perhaps. Seismologists, however, may be able to detect movements in the earth's tectonic plates because they are able to apply knowledge and experience to the problem. Imagine, then, if the seismologists became concerned about a potential increase in volcanic activity. Should they immediately tell the media, local people living nearby, or local government? The simple answer is similar to Harrison's organizational dilemma. It all depends upon time and knowledge of the parameters they are working with. The parameters then require an analysis of symptoms and signs.

9.2.2 Symptoms and signs

One of the difficulties with managing change is the temptation to think of manifest problems as the cause of the difficulty experienced. For example, we might receive complaints from customers and see the complaints as the problem; or feel the effects of stress at work and treat stress as the problem. In reality the root causes of such problems often lie much deeper. The purpose of organizational diagnosis, therefore, is to establish whether there is a problem, to identify who defines it this way and why, and to clarify the relation between cause and effect.

When anything goes wrong with an organization, this is usually signalled to you by symptoms and signs. These are not the same. In a medical sense, doctors make a distinction between symptoms and signs mainly because they can reliably assess signs but they have to take a patient's word for the symptoms he or she is experiencing. Consequently doctors can only guess at the severity of an illness. The following stop and think activity illustrates both symptoms and signs. Symptoms are what you experience internally, but they are not always visible. Symptoms therefore require the patient to communicate the problem clearly to the doctor. Conversely, the doctor's judgement requires a clear interpretation of what is communicated. Problems of communication and perception may become barriers to a clear diagnosis. However, the doctor may be assisted in his or her observation by signs. Signs are visible and objective external indicators that the patient might not be aware of until it is too late. On the other hand, the doctor may be very concerned about signs s/he is able to observe.

---

❶ Stop and think 9.2

Septicaemia
In older children and adults the symptoms and signs of septicaemia may occur together with those of meningitis. From the following list, can you distinguish signs from symptoms?
Symptom or sign?
Fever (possibly with cold hands and feet)
Chills
Pain in legs or arms
Unusual skin colour or pale complexion
Pain in abdomen or chest
Breathing problems or rapid breathing
Diarrhoea
Nausea or vomiting
Sore muscles or joints
Drowsiness
Confusion
Behaviour changes—may be irritable or restless
Rash

Analysing symptoms and signs in an organization is similar to the doctor–patient relationship. Diagnosing a problem consists of a similar distinction between symptoms and signs. Symptoms can be regarded as manifestations of something that might be dysfunctional within the organization. For example, a high turnover of staff in an organization may be symptomatic of a deeper problem: the wages being low, or the place psychologically uncomfortable. Low wages provide an example of a single cause but discomfort may be due to a mixture of leadership and cultural factors. If managers consider that too many staff are leaving, resulting in a high cost because of the amount of retraining required, they might decide to analyse the situation in order to identify the cause. As in the doctor–patient relationship, symptoms require careful judgement to ensure that what is communicated is accurate. Signs, on the other hand, are visible because they are recorded or documented. Symptoms can be made objective by using attitude surveys to investigate complex issues. By doing this, we encounter deeper levels of information that might lead to deeper interventions. Perhaps a better way of stating this is to begin with the distinction between facts and perceptions. You may find it useful to consider the following stop and think activity.

---

❶ Stop and think 9.3

Organizational symptoms or signs?

	Symptom or sign?	*Simple or complex?*
Morale		
Absenteeism		
Leadership		
Turnover of staff		
Happy staff		
Loss of sales		
Customer complaints		

We can see that absenteeism can be regarded as a simple indicator of a potential underlying problem, because records will exist and we can make a simple count of the extent to which people are absent. This is also the case with turnover of staff, loss of sales, and possibly customer complaints, because all should be recorded. However, morale, leadership, and happiness are complex indicators of underlying problems because we require further information to confirm them. An example of how external signs sometimes contradict the insider's perception of reality is illustrated in the following case example.

❯❯ Case example 9.1

Britain's weather forecasters beaten by amateurs

On 15 October 1987, Britain's TV weather forecasts predicted strong winds, but nothing more. The BBC's TV weather forecaster, commenting on a viewer's report of a hurricane on the way, said 'don't worry, there isn't'. ❯❯

> ≫ That night southern England was struck by the storm of the century. Winds gusting to 150 miles per hour (185 kilometres per hour) tore down 15 million trees and caused 19 deaths and over £1 bn of damage. In the public outcry that followed, a major question recurred: why was there no accurate warning?
>
> The answer was simple: to the insiders of the Meteorological Office the evidence was not overwhelming. External signs were indicated by members of the public but were added to the other evidence available, and the overall picture found was inconclusive. Consequently, the forecasters made the wrong judgement.

Apart from the need to check for external signs, the case example above illustrates another feature of diagnosis. That is, like weather forecasting, organizational analysis is not an exact science. It relies on judgement, which in turn is based on experience, knowledge, and skill.

9.3 Action Research and process consultation

The term 'Action Research' was first used by Lewin in 1944 to describe the process of joint collaboration through which the knowledge and experiences of an organization's members are combined in order to jointly identify and solve problems. Process consultation refers to a procedure used by the consultant or facilitator to engage with the client system in order to make Action Research possible. When Schein (1997) formulated the concept of process consultation he contrasted it with the 'expert' role because he was attempting to construct a 'clinical' model, which starts with the needs of the client system. This process is said to be client-driven because it involves the researcher in the client's issues, rather than involving the client in the researcher's issues.

In Chapter 3 we compared the planning model with the Action Research model of enquiry. Both models identify diagnosis at an early stage. The Action Research model, however, adopts a two-stage approach to this, illustrated in Figure 3.5 above. Step three requires a preliminary diagnosis once data are gathered on the problem. Step five requires a joint diagnosis with the key individuals or stakeholders. The Action Research model is a (heuristic) device designed to discover problems or experiment by observing action. This dual process combines the knowledge and expertise of the organization's members with the behavioural knowledge and expertise of the internal or external consultant. Thus a joint diagnostic relationship is formed to enable the gathering and analysis of data. Action Research and process consultation emphasize the need to teach clients how to diagnose problems and prescribe interventions for themselves rather than taking a pre-packaged, 'off-the-shelf' approach to change.

> **!** Stop and think 9.4
>
> What is meant by 'client'?
>
> Six basic types of client have been identified by Schein (1997). These are:
> 1. *Contact clients*—the individual(s) who first contact the consultant with a request, question, or issue.
> 2. *Intermediate clients*—the individuals or groups that get involved in various interviews, meetings, and other activities as the project evolves.
> 3. *Primary clients*—the individual(s) who ultimately 'own' the problem or issue being worked on; they are typically also the ones who pay the consulting bills, or whose budget covers the consultation project.
> 4. *Unwitting clients*—members of the organization or client system above, below, and laterally related to the primary clients, who will be affected by interventions but are not aware of this.
> 5. *Indirect clients*—members of the organization who are aware that they will be affected by the interventions but are unknown to the consultant, and who may feel either positive or negative about these effects.
> 6. *Ultimate clients*—the community, the total organization, an occupational group, or any other group that the consultant cares about and whose welfare must be considered in any intervention that the consultant makes.

Consultants must consider how they classify clients. This is usually based on the nature of the problem being addressed, but related to the level at which they are working. Problems can be identified by level, as illustrated in Table 9.1.

Process consultation requires that:

1. A helping relationship is established between the consultant and the client system.

2. An investigation proceeds through diagnostic evaluation rather than by taking the word of the primary client.

3. Internal and external consultants work within the boundaries of their knowledge and experience.

4. Every action is considered an intervention.

5. The client system must always 'own' the problem and be involved in all stages of its resolution.

> **!** Stop and think 9.5
>
> Identify a problem situation you have experienced or are currently engaged with and consider how you would deal with the dilemma below.
>
> Process consultation requires that a helping relationship is established between the consultant and the client system, and that a diagnostic evaluation is required. However, this may be challenging if you appear to be confronting the knowledge and experience of the primary client.

Table 9.1 Types of relationship

Levels / Types of relationship	Individual level	Group or team	Organizational	Inter-organizational
Intrapersonal	Working with one individual whose needs are related to counselling, coaching, mentoring and training.			Working with groups outside the organization to identify and develop inter-organizational benefits such as strategic alliances or joint ventures.
Interpersonal	Attending to individual needs such as leadership development, enhancing presentation skills, improving competence.	Inter-group (between different groups); working with relationships between people, working with informal groups or networks, or with team dynamics.	Intra-group (within group); working to coordinate organizational units in keeping with organizational aims and objectives.	Working at a societal or trans-global level with the wider national or international community in resolve difficulties pertaining to the health of larger systems such as the ecosystem or international trade. These usually take the form of projects.
Organizational	Strategic attention focused on senior managers with key responsibilities. Coaching, mentoring or dialogue is required.	Strategic attention needs to focus on goals, roles, and composition of team members, as well as group dynamics.	Working with problems or issues that affect everyone, such as the mission, strategy, and welfare of the whole client system.	Strategic organizational alliances are required to resolve problems.

The implications that flow from this are that the consultant should never accept the initial formulation of 'the problem' as described by the primary client. This is because the primary client is the first point of contact, perhaps the managing director or a training manager, who has a manifest problem to discuss with you. A wider diagnostic reading of the situation is therefore required and it is important to understand different views of the problem. It is therefore important to involve a cross-section of people in the diagnosis and intervention through Action Research.

9.4 Phases of diagnostic interventions

Most diagnostic models are based on the original Action Research model developed by Lewin (1946) and informed by the later writings of French (1969) and Schein (1988). The consulting cycle is regarded as a series of phases that the consultant should work through from beginning to end. The phases are considered to be both a pragmatic and an ethical guide to defining organizational problems, leading to an effective intervention. An example is illustrated in Figure 9.1 (see also Phillips and Shaw, 1989).

Schein (1988) argues that the consultant, as analyst, should be careful not to identify with the individual who requests the invitation. Although this individual may be the primary client, the consultant must suspend judgement about his or her definition of the problem. Consequently, the consultant should explore the problem by obtaining views from the wider client system. The wider **client system** can be regarded as any part of the organization that is likely to be affected by the intervention. One therefore cannot simply assume that the problem defined by the primary client is an objective statement of fact, no matter how convincing this appears at first.

Defining the problem therefore begins with a statement from the primary client, followed by further preliminary investigations to establish whether the initial problem statement is accurate. By undertaking a wider preliminary investigation, other points

Figure 9.1 Phases of diagnostic interventions

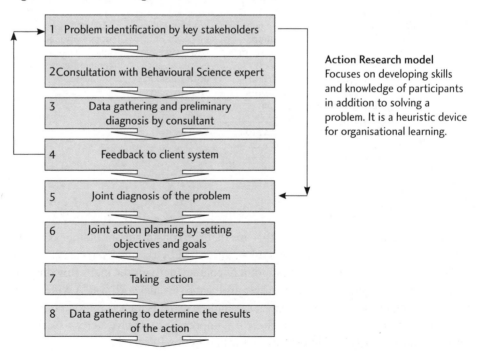

Action Research model
Focuses on developing skills and knowledge of participants in addition to solving a problem. It is a heuristic device for organisational learning.

of view can be identified in order to triangulate perceptions. Problems can have a single cause, or might have a series of interconnections that make it difficult to identify a particular aspect of the situation. Because the organizational systems we seek to investigate are complex, it is often the case that networks of relationships need to be identified.

Defining the problem should proceed with a clear statement of the issue(s). The initial contact statement should be regarded as the manifest problem. However, as we noted above, we need to test out our assumptions with the wider client system, in which case we may discover that the root cause of the problem is not that initially stated. Consequently, we have to distinguish between the manifest problem and the latent problem. Once we have made this distinction, we must decide if the latent problem is a malfunction or a dysfunction (that is, something that has gone wrong, a deviation from expectations), or a developmental issue, such as quality improvement. The next step is to establish the evidence for the problem statement. Essentially we need to know how much is based on fact, and how much on inference.

❗ Stop and think 9.6

Identify an organizational problem and proceed through each of the stages below.

1. Defining the problem should proceed with a clear statement of the issue(s).

2. The initial contact statement should be regarded as the manifest problem.

3. Distinguish between the manifest problem and the latent problems. Are they the same or different? Can you detect any underlying issues?

4. Ask yourself, 'to what extent are we dealing with facts or perceptions?'

What does this suggest? Is it a simple procedural problem, or a matter of control systems such as financial, quality, or health and safety? Or does it involve other layers of the map—for example, power, control, culture, ethics, leadership, job redesign, and so forth? This should be followed by the level of analysis—individual, group, organizational, as discussed in Chapter 2. The next stage requires a decision about the most appropriate methods of data collection. In reality, judgements are always a compromise between the resources at our disposal—that is, time, money, access to key individuals or stakeholder groups—and knowing the most effective methodology for the analysis if resources are not an issue. We need to know if the analysis requires statistical, documentary, content analysis data, or data from individual interviews, focus group meetings, observations, linguistic analysis, or group dynamics/interaction analysis. Finally, we need to present our findings in the form of graphs, figures, tables. We might need to demonstrate our findings through a Pareto analysis, a cause-and-effect analysis, a hard or soft systems diagram (for higher levels of complexity), or a frequency table. See Table 9.2 for the process of defining and presenting the problem to the client.

Table 9.2 A method for defining and presenting the problem to the client

How is the problem defined?	1. What are the manifest problems? Why are they defined as such?
Preliminary latent or underlying issues	2. Are there any potential latent or underlying problems that need to be investigated at this stage? For example, is the root cause likely to be different from the problem outlined? If so, what other issues are in need of preliminary investigation?
Hypothesis	3. Construct a clear statement or hypothesis for investigation
Malfunction, dysfunction, or development opportunity?	4. Is this a malfunction, a dysfunction or is it a developmental issue (searching for an improvement)?
What is the evidence?	5. How sound is the evidence? What are the facts and what are the inferences? How much of it is perception?
Latent or underlying issues	6. What latent or underlying issues does the situation suggest (power, control, culture ethics, leadership, motivation, job design, process improvement, etc.) that the primary client may not have considered?
Stakeholder concerns	7. Is there any evidence from the wider client system that causes a redefinition of the problem?
What level of analysis is required?	8. Individual, group, organizational.
Framing the analysis	9. What perspectives and frames are suggested by point 6 above?
What methods of data collection are required?	10. Statistical, documentary, content analysis, interviews, observations, linguistic analysis, group dynamics/ interaction analysis, other.
How will the findings be demonstrated?	11. Graphs, figures, tables, Pareto analysis, cause-and-effect analysis, soft systems diagrams, observation sheets, interaction frequency, etc.

9.5 The art of organizational diagnosis

In the introduction to his book, Morgan (1986) suggests that effective professionals in all walks of life develop the art of reading situations. Although we often assume this to be an intuitive process, it is, in fact, an acquired skill. As he points out:

> If we take a closer look at the processes used… we find that this kind of mystique and power is often based on an ability to develop deep appreciations of the situations being addressed. Skilled readers develop the knack of reading situations with various scenarios in mind, and of forging actions that seem appropriate to the readings thus obtained.

(Morgan, 1986: 11)

For Morgan, the images we use to gain insights into situations are derived from metaphors, and these illustrate two things. First, we can analyse organizations from various perspectives in order to understand more clearly what is happening to them and taking place within them. Second, we can use metaphors in a prescriptive way in order to recommend changes (i.e. to redefine and develop specific characteristics within the organization) with the aim either of improving organizational effectiveness, or of enhancing the quality of life experienced by employees.

9.5.1 Constructing a diagnostic map

Metaphors therefore aid organizational diagnosis by providing clients with data, interpretations and recommendations. Morgan (1986; 2004) recommends that we do two things:

1. Make a diagnostic reading of a situation.
2. Follow the diagnostic reading with a critical evaluation of that reading.

A diagnostic reading begins with the use of a metaphor. The way a metaphor works in language is critical to this process. To understand this, we need to see a metaphor as a mental image that cross-fertilizes one construct with another. This is provocative, because it challenges assumptions. For example, if we see an organization as a machine, we might ask a number of questions, but two should illustrate this. First, does this organization need to be bureaucratic in order to pursue its objectives? Second, should every department be controlled in the same way (machine-like)? If we then adopt another metaphor, this time culture, we might come to an imaginative insight by asking further questions. Once again, although we might have a wide range of questions, two should illustrate this:

- What do we need to control—just systems such as finance, quality, health and safety (in a machine-like way), or the actions of people also (cultural)?
- Are there any contradictions between the culture of the organization and its control systems?

The cross-fertilization created by metaphors enables us to create a diagnostic reading and a critical evaluation. The metaphors used to reframe organizations challenge managers to think of them as multiple realities. The most important aspect of a metaphor, following Tsoukas, is its ability to prescribe meaning rather than describe it: 'Metaphors, similes and analogies, more than literal assertions, do not simply describe an external reality; they also help constitute that reality and prescribe how it ought to be viewed and evaluated' (Tsoukas, 1991: 570).

An example of this is the eight metaphors Morgan uses to construct a diagnostic map of the organization. These are:

1. *Machine*, which suggests the need to control things (bureaucracy, scientific management, classical structural-functional emphasis on design). The machine metaphor provides a recipe to control and coordinate.

2. *Organism,* which suggests the management of throughputs using the open-systems model. The metaphor helps us to understand the importance of organizational needs, and provides us with the ability to identify dysfunction within a system.

3. *Learning,* which suggests self-regulation and collective organizational learning.

4. *Culture,* which suggests values, social rules, and relationships.

5. *Political systems,* which suggests the use of power and control. The organization as a political system helps us to understand that organizations are never neutral entities, and are composed of interest groups that engage in tactics for position and resources.

6. *Psychic prisons,* which suggests that organizations can put up barriers to performance. The metaphor allows us to see organizations comprising unconscious needs that result from structures, control communication, and leadership.

7. *Flux and change,* which suggests that organizational change may result from wider change and conflict.

8. *Instruments of domination,* which suggests that organizations can be destructive to the people within them, to society, and to their environment.

❗ Stop and think 9.7

Compare and contrast two of Morgan's metaphors by applying them to the same organization, and examine how each enables you to analyse a different aspect of the organization.

To follow Morgan, an effective consultant or change agent should be a person possessing diagnostic skills. A useful way to see this is to begin with a map. As with our example of a weather forecast, a change agent needs to be able to identify changing patterns. Sticking with this analogy a little longer will help us to see the point better. In conventional map-making, all the information that has been gathered must be analysed in order to turn it into a map. The map is made for a particular purpose—for traffic, for tunnels or sewers, walkers, and so on—the function of which is to guide particular users. Maps can be exact representations drawn to scale, or they can be conceptual, as with the London Underground map. If we think of a map as representing data, then we can identify different representational systems. For example, Morgan's organic metaphor (which is, of course, more commonly referred to as the open-systems model) will allow us to investigate dysfunctions within the system and identify the system's (or sub-system's) needs or deficiencies. We might seek to overlay a second frame (hence a machine model) upon the first in order to identify the effectiveness of control systems. This, in turn, might require a third frame (culture) in order to identify and improve cultural characteristics such as corporate values, ethics, behaviours, and attitudes. This in turn might force us to think about being more proactive in the future, by implementing collective learning solutions leading to a fourth frame. What we have done here is to take the basic problem and expose it to critical analysis. In order to move towards a viable intervention, an investigation of the wider client system has revealed that it was necessary to overlay the initial problem with a series of maps or frames. These are like transparent layers that enable us to obtain a more complete picture of the problem, leading to a potential solution.

Organizational maps can be constructed around the systems in operation. Generally these are related to control functions such as HRM/HRD, finance, production, technology, environmental management, and quality systems. Unlike the single map of the aerial cartographer, organizational maps can be multi-dimensional. We can draw maps for all organizational control systems by identifying the objectives of each system and the activities that result from those objectives. The main purpose of such systems, of course, is to ensure that actions are planned in a systematic manner. All existing systems will contain explicit or informal rules about how deviations or problems can be identified and dealt with as a matter of course. That is to say, they should identify procedures for taking corrective action. Any organizational system should, therefore, identify its:

- purpose;
- actions;
- procedures for corrective action.

Airports are examples of systems that have developed extremely sophisticated procedures for processing passengers and their luggage in maximum comfort. If we regard this as their main purpose, then we can identify the actions they take. An airport's prime function is to ensure that passengers can move freely through its corridors, either inwardly on to aircraft or outwardly at the end of their journey, with the least possible disruption for the passenger. With increasing size and complexity of airports, potential problems multiply. As more people travel through an airport, more space is needed, and everything takes longer. Whilst the various systems are designed to make mass air travel quicker and more pleasurable, malfunctions do occur. Although airports have procedures for taking corrective action in the event of an emergency, even the most sophisticated systems can become dysfunctional when corrective actions contradict the main purpose or objectives of the business. The following case example illustrates how, as systems grow, the purpose of the system becomes less clear. As a result, procedures for taking corrective action become fuzzy.

>> **Case example 9.2**

Dysfunctional thinking at King's Cross station

On 18 November 1987, a fire began at about 19:30 GMT in a machine room under a wooden escalator at King's Cross Underground station. Thirty-one people died in an accident that was thought to have begun from a discarded match. Forensic scientists identified the initial fire as having started near step 48, and been carried up the steps by the moving escalator, where it spread to other locations, notably plywood skirting board which was impregnated with oil and grease. The flames ignited a rubber dressguard and balustrades coated with yacht varnish, and moved on to the treads and risers. Hot gases used up the oxygen from the air and thick black smoke began to suffocate passengers.

The disaster was the most serious accident in London Underground's history. The following report illustrates what happened.

In 1987, most of the escalators on the Underground system were made of wood and so presented a fire risk. Between 1980 and [19]87, 13 serious fires were reported in stations. One at Oxford Circus resulted in the introduction of an experimental ban on smoking in February 1985. However, the ban may have contributed to the King's Cross fire, since it led to passengers lighting cigarettes as they left the [platforms for the] escalator. Investigators later found evidence of several small fires that had burnt out beneath the escalators at King's Cross. It was concluded that a lighted match that fell onto the machinery beneath the escalator had ignited the fire.

Staff cuts across the Underground in the 1980s had diminished the frequency of routine cleaning in stations. At King's Cross, this caused dangerous levels of grease, dust and debris to gather in the undercarriages of the escalators. On 18 November 1987, that highly flammable accumulation beneath the Piccadilly Line escalator caught fire. The flames first burnt low down in the escalator trench, rather than burning upwards. They burned for some time, fuelled by the dirt and grease, building up a significant heat and power. Since the flames were not visible, the strength and size of the blaze were underestimated.[1]

Dysfunctional processes

The primary purpose of London Underground is to transport passengers into and around the capital city. However, it has a secondary purpose—to secure the safety of passengers—which becomes paramount in the event of an emergency. Unfortunately, this latter purpose was fuzzy. As a result, staff were not trained in passenger-safety procedures.

The problem was exacerbated by a series of dysfunctional processes. For example, when the alarm was raised by a passenger at approximately 19:30, a member of the Underground staff went to inspect the area, as required by a procedure from the Rule Book of London Underground. As he was not normally based at King's Cross station, he had not received any fire training for that location. He was unclear   >>

>> about the actions he should take. Consequently he failed to inform the station manager or the station controller. In any case, there were no procedures for corrective action, because there was no evacuation plan. By chance, two police officers with radios were present, but their radios did not function below ground. One officer ran to the surface to call the London Fire Brigade at 19:34. Further time was lost in alerting station management and staff. The police officers started to evacuate passengers from the lower levels of the station by way of the Victoria Line escalator and through the tube lines. They had no knowledge of the geography of the station and believed they had chosen the quickest and only way for passengers to reach the surface in safety. The first London Fire Brigade personnel reached the tube lines at 19:43. However, an explosion or 'flashover' occurred and all areas filled with dense black smoke.

The relationship between London Regional Transport (LRT) and London Underground was confusing. For example, LRT believed that all operational matters, including safety, were matters for the operating company. Conversely, although financial controls were strictly monitored by LRT, safety was not. LRT appeared unaware of their corporate responsibilities.

Procedures for corrective action were also undermined by the roles and responsibilities of key personnel. For example, specialist safety staff held mainly junior positions and were concerned solely with the safety of staff, not passengers. These cultural assumptions were a product of division directors. For example, the operations director responsible for the safe operation of the railway system viewed his responsibilities as running trains rather than the safety of lifts and escalators. Evidence suggested that management within London Underground had not perceived the need for emergency plans for evacuation in case of fire, nor had they complied with the 1985 total ban on smoking within London Underground. Managers held the view that fires were inevitable on the oldest and most extensive underground system in the world. London Underground was proud of its reputation as a professional railway company. Unhappily its staff were lulled into a false sense of security by the fact that no previous escalator fire had caused a death. Consequently, coordination of health and safety within London Underground was unknown, as safety became a divisional matter with each director believing he was responsible for safety in his division only.

The myth perpetuated was that the Underground system was just trains running on tracks below ground. Consequently, the facilities above ground were outside the perceived system. This was consolidated by the fact that, since no one had been killed in earlier fires, it was believed that both passengers and staff acted as fire detectors and there would be sufficient time to evacuate passengers. Consequently, there was no staff training in fire drill or evacuation procedures. Nor could they appreciate the problems of smoke, since the fire policy was based on fire prevention rather than scenario testing.

---

[1] Available at <http://www.20thcenturylondon.org.uk/server.php?show=conInformationRecord.110>.

9.5.2 Frames and diagnosis

When we consider the metaphors suggested by Morgan, what we need to appreciate is that, when a skilled organizational analyst reaches a judgement, this will be based on his or her organizational knowledge and experience. Each component of this knowledge and experience refers to different theories and their limitations. We can regard each component as a reference point or 'frame' that indicates how theories, and therefore judgements, shape diagnostic analysis. Figure 9.2 illustrates the increased level of complexity when additional diagnostic frames are added.

Bolman and Deal (1991) provide a model for reframing organizations. This can be seen as an alternative categorization to that of Morgan. They suggest four frames, which they refer to as structural, human resource, symbolic, and political. Others, such as Schön and Rein (1994), Harrison and Shirom (1999), and Grieves (2003), have argued for the need to challenge organizational complacency by reframing existing

Figure 9.2 Diagnostic frames

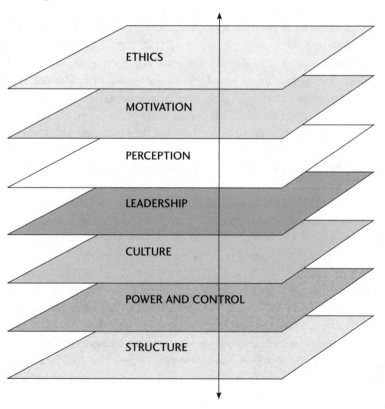

assumptions, belief, value systems, and activities. In addition to theories, frames will also be based on broader reference schemes, such as paradigms (see Chapter 7) or perspectives (see Chapter 1). We can illustrate how each perspective identified in Chapter 1 would deal with the same problem as follows. The structural-functional perspective would search for a more suitable structural change in order to re-establish harmony. The multiple constituencies perspective would search for a change strategy that satisfies (the most dominant) stakeholders. The OD perspective would search for the underlying behavioural issues that underlie the structural problem. Finally, the Critical perspective would investigate the motives of the other three—particularly in relation to performance, efficiency, and effectiveness.

Diagnostic frames therefore inform one's judgement about the nature and potential cause of a problem. The frame, either explicitly or implicitly, will suggest how the problem is to be understood. Figure 9.3 illustrates that the four perspectives introduced in Chapter 1 may be used to help choose from potential diagnostic frames that lead to change pathways, and on to four intervention categories described by Cummings and Worley (1993) and introduced in Chapter 3.

To clarify how this works, as we discussed in Chapter 3, the structural-functional perspective gives rise to empirical–rational strategies for change. The multiple constituencies perspective and OD give rise to normative re-educative strategies for change, whilst the fourth perspective—Creativity and Volition: a Critical Theory of Change—forces us to think about processual or emergent issues that affect the change process. These lead to change pathways.

Framing the analysis is, therefore, the prelude to an intervention. However, as we have seen, analysis is never neutral. Figure 9.3 illustrates that the perspectives and the frames of analysis are essentially the building blocks that lead to the diagnostic reading and the critical analysis that Morgan referred to.

9.6 Complexifying simplicity

Finally, it is wise to end this chapter with a cautionary note on the dangers of using models of change for diagnostic purposes. They should be used with care. We might use the phrase 'complexifying simplicity' to reverse the often-used phrase 'simplifying complexity'. This is because, when it comes to organizational analysis and diagnosis, we must be cautious about assuming that there are simple 'levers of change', or easy 'change strategies'. The reason for stating this is that there is no easy short-cut to the acquisition of knowledge or the development of skill applied through experience over time. We must remember that diagnosis relies on understanding theories and concepts. Therefore we must be clear about these theories and concepts before we apply any conceptual model. If we reverse this process and use a model without understanding the issues that lie behind it, then our quick fix is likely to end up with unknown and potentially dysfunctional consequences. For this reason managers and consultants should take care to avoid the knee-jerk reaction provided by the quick fix.

In Chapter 3 we noted that normative re-educative models of change require a higher degree of reflexivity than rational–empirical models. The Action Research model focuses on developing the skills and knowledge of participants in addition to solving a problem. This is a heuristic device for organizational learning designed to develop the organization's capacity to learn by enhancing knowledge, skills, and experience. However, we also noted that managers and consultants must rely on the judgement of a behavioural science expert, or take the time and trouble to understand the implications of their actions on the behaviour of staff. In order that managers and consultants can make systematic diagnoses when they are faced with complex situations, they require a methodology.

In Figure 9.3 we can see how the four perspectives lead to an understanding of the diagnostic frames. This means that there is a variety of ways in which an understanding can be achieved. As we have seen, there are different interpretations of cultural analysis and political analysis, just as there are of task-related activities. For example, someone using the structural-functional perspective will produce a different type of cultural analysis to that of a Critical Theorist. The former will attempt to identify functional relationships or dysfunctions. The latter will criticize this, arguing that this approach is misguided for many reasons, including the mistaken assumption that culture is a variable that can be manipulated to the advantage of management. The same is true of leadership. In order to appreciate this, we can see how there might be different interpretations of leadership. The following case example questions how we arrive at interpretations of reality.

This case example illustrates the problem we began with in Chapter 1. That is, multiple interpretations result from the application of different perspectives. There are, therefore, different pathways to change. Those able to engage in effective analysis and diagnosis are aware of this before they make a choice of model or metaphor.

9.7 Summary

This chapter has focused on organizational diagnosis. We began with a distinction between symptoms and signs. Symptoms reflect awareness within the organization that some aspect is malfunctioning. That is, someone is aware of a problem, although the cause may not be immediately apparent. In contrast, signs are external. They reflect an outsider's awareness of a problem, which might not be detected by those in

Figure 9.3 Framing the analysis

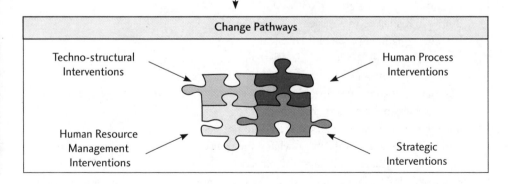

Perspectives

Structural-functionalist

Creativity and
Volition/
Critical Theory

Multiple
constituencies

Organizational
Development

Diagnostic Frames

Culture

Power &
Control

Leadership

Ethics

Motivation

Structure

Learning

Perception

Change Pathways

Techno-structural
Interventions

Human Process
Interventions

Human Resource
Management
Interventions

Strategic
Interventions

❯❯ Case example 9.3

Shakespeare's *Henry V*

Shakespeare's play *Henry V* was written in 1599. It is famous for Henry's speech to soldiers awaiting battle at Agincourt in 1415, which many trainers use as a good example of leadership. They use it to inspire, to motivate, and to develop articulate transformational leaders. The speech is full of rhetoric and hyperbole, to stir pride and motivate the troops. It may be used as an example of transformational leadership because it demonstrates how Henry plucks victory out of potential defeat. Henry encourages his troops as follows:

> This day is called the feast of Crispian:
> He that outlives this day, and comes safe home,
> Will stand a-tip-toe when the day is named,
> And rouse him at the name of Crispian.
> He that shall live this day, and see old age,
> Will yearly on the vigil feast his neighbours,
> And say 'To-morrow is Saint Crispian.'
> Then will he strip his sleeve and show his scars.
> And say 'These wounds I had on Crispian's day.'
> Old men forget: yet all shall be forgot,
> But he'll remember with advantages
> What feats he did that day: then shall our names,
> Familiar in his mouth as household words
> Harry the king, Bedford and Exeter,
> Warwick and Talbot, Salisbury and Gloucester,
> Be in their flowing cups freshly remember'd.
> This story shall the good man teach his son;
> And Crispin Crispian shall ne'er go by,
> From this day to the ending of the world,
> But we in it shall be rememberéd;
> We few, we happy few, we band of brothers;
> For he to-day that sheds his blood with me
> Shall be my brother; be he ne'er so vile,
> This day shall gentle his condition:
> And gentlemen in England now a-bed
> Shall think themselves accursed they were not here,
> And hold their manhoods cheap whiles any speaks
> That fought with us upon Saint Crispin's day.

This is heroic leadership at its best; it gives the impression that there are universal qualities to leadership. But, as we argued in Chapter 8, this idea is a myth and we can always find alternative examples. Thus, a structural-functional perspective may see ❯❯

❯❯ Henry's speech as culturally integrationist—the desire to build a strong culture and achieve success. It will therefore measure this by criterion of functional fit—it was the right speech at the right time for the purpose for which it was intended. Similarly, the strategist familiar with Porter's *Competitive Strategy* will reinforce this perspective by referring to the Machiavellian tactics used by Henry, who combined the appearance of sincerity with the use of deceit and ultimate force to achieve his objectives—the subjection of France to his rule.

Conversely, from a multiple constituencies perspective, then, it could be suggested that, whilst Henry was victorious in battle, the French were killed in their thousands, and prisoners were slaughtered at his request. But this led to his being unable in the long run to persuade the French of his legitimacy to their throne. He therefore failed to find a satisfactory compromise, by exercising a win–lose strategy against the French. The Organizational Development perspective would agree with the structural-functional perspective in its search for cultural integration, but it would agree also with the multiple constituencies perspective that any successful change strategy requires the involvement of all stakeholders in the interests of effective governance.

The perspective—Creativity and Volition: a Critical Theory of Change—would find Henry's actions highly partisan, driven by his own personal motives. Critical theorists would also see his strategy as unethical, because Henry endorsed rape and pillage of the people of the fortress Harfleur. Consequently, they would challenge the strategic objectives further and argue that Henry was a war criminal who massacred prisoners in defiance of existing conventions. Furthermore, the facts rather than the myth appear to support the argument that he used power to seek his own advancement at the expense of his friends. He executed Falstaff and his companion Bardolph. He 'turned on his beloved advisers and comrades-in-arms, Harry and Thomas Percy, at the Battle of Shrewsbury in 1403. Later, he would disavow his old tutor and long time ally, Henry Beaufort, in a dispute with the Pope over papal authority in England' and in the 'most notorious case' Henry burned Sir John Oldcastle, a battlefield friend, to death. Ultimately, he was a heretic who failed to earn a king's right to power by being virtuous.[1] The critical theorist would therefore be forced to investigate Henry's personal characteristics, which may suggest paranoia or neurosis (as we discovered in Chapter 7). Finally, a postmodern scholar (also operating from within this perspective) might argue that there is no ultimate reality, only multiple versions of reality constructed for different motives, and Henry himself constructed this myth to secure a place in history.

[1] Fernandez-Armesto, Felipe (2009), Professorial Fellow of Queen Mary, University of London, and a member of the Faculty of Modern History, University of Oxford. Available from <http://www.bbc.co.uk/history/british /middle_ages/henry_v_01.shtml>.

the organization itself. Sometimes insiders appear to be blind to problems. Becoming a skilled practitioner of organizational diagnosis is rather like an apprenticeship. The ability of managers or consultants to diagnose problems depends upon their ability to acquire craft knowledge. Action Research is a process of joint collaboration to help participants develop their understanding of problems, and to apply interventions. It is made possible through process consultation. This process is consistent with Schein's 'clinical' model, designed to identify the needs of the client system, and involves a joint diagnostic relationship that will lead to constructing a diagnostic map.

⭐ Case study 1

Analysing manifest and latent problems in Powersmart

The senior team of Powersmart, a nuclear generating facility, had received the results of a survey into staff attitudes to a change management programme introduced over the previous six months. Because of the findings, the senior team requested that an external consultant address what they considered a clearly defined problem. The senior team defined the problem as 'lack of motivation caused by poor teamwork practices'. The training manager, Tom Glazier, who represented the senior team in discussion with the consultant, requested that the consultant draw up a plan of action for teamwork training in order that all individuals in the organization should know how to perform effectively in their tasks and be motivated as a result. John Knox, the consultant, stated that before he could agree terms of reference he needed to undertake some preliminary investigation of the wider client system. This required three days' work with a representative sample of employees. The sample was approximately 33 people representing all occupational groups, out of 100 staff. The training manager was eventually persuaded of the importance of undertaking appropriate and reliable analysis, although he was confident that his definition of the problem would be borne out by further investigation. In addition, John Knox requested company documents relating to the survey of change management practice previously carried out. He decided to undertake observations by participating in meetings, and to undertake interviews with key individuals such as managers, team leaders, and team members. Following these, he also undertook focus group discussions in order to qualify his own interpretation of the data.

The documentary evidence

Company documents included corporate feedback on the survey results (produced by a national HR consultancy company) to staff. The feedback stated:

> just over half of you took the opportunity to take part in the recent staff survey. This level of response provides a representative picture of your views and shows a number of strengths on which to build for the future. However, there are some areas where improvements could be made. The results are summarized below and provide a fair and unbiased account of your views about Powersmart.   ≫

» Staff Survey

Percentage satisfied with:
Those who find work interesting—46%
Those who find work challenging—61%
Satisfaction with pay—65%
Opportunity to use skills and abilities—39%
Job security—27%
Accomplishing something worthwhile—46%
Opportunity for career development—15%
Feedback on your performance—23%

Percentage who agreed
Feel proud to work for the company—38%
Feel that good performance is recognized—28%
Feel that good performance is not rewarded—56%
Felt they were involved in the preparation of their department's business plan—31%
Felt their work was relevant to the business plan—57%
Felt they were encouraged to be cost-conscious—64%

Views of immediate supervisor
Gives me credit if I have done a good job—38%
Encourages me to work as a team member—42%
Provides clear objectives—32%

The history of the company

After two days of discussions and observations with staff, John Knox made a series of notes about the impressions he had gained. The notes reflected the following issues.

Powersmart had been privatized out of the state-controlled authority. Consequently there had been a legacy of hierarchical command structures with bureaucratic rules and regulations. Although the culture had remained largely mechanistic, attempts to change it occurred in 2010 through the concept of *'fitness for purpose'*.

In January 2010 head office forced Powersmart to develop a change strategy. This required the reorganization and reduction of staff. Previous change had left staff feeling uncertain about the benefits of a long-term future in a 'flatter' and 'leaner' organization. The current change strategy appeared to leave team members feeling that their *psychological contract* had changed for the worse. There was also a degree of confusion and uncertainty about the aims and objectives of corporate strategy.

John Knox consulted the staff survey and had a further discussion with Tom Glazier to clarify the facts. These were corroborated as follows: »

>> 1. Unlike standard commercial firms, Powersmart was effectively two organizations bundled into one. It had two principal objectives. First, because it had previously been a government agency, it was charged with the task of observing statutory obligations in relation to safety. Second, it was now required to act entrepreneurially in order to operate as a commercial company.

2. Powersmart had decided to create 'an integrated team of managers' who were responsible for both functions simultaneously.

3. All parties agreed that the two sets of objectives resulted in some tension. However, they disagreed about the extent of the tension. The senior team argued that any difficulty managing the objectives would be resolved by effective teamwork. Middle managers and supervisors argued that they simply passed instructions down in a functional manner, and that the objectives for each week were defined for themselves and their teams. Team members were maintenance engineers. They described Powersmart as containing two sub-cultures: one that applied legislative and operational measures governing safety, and the other that was commercially focused and needed to increase profits and control expenditure.

When John Knox asked the technicians to express their views about their experience, they described this as 'operating like submariners, continually submerged on patrol, under the ocean but with no real idea where they were going since only the captain knew the true course'. They stated that 'communication relied on rumour, was drip-fed although they did get the occasional peek through the periscope'. Extending the nautical metaphor, the team members stated that 'as crew, we would like to see the charts in order to know where we are really sailing'.

Manifest and latent problems

John Knox was faced with contradictory information. On one hand, the senior management team had provided a clear and unambiguous statement of the manifest problem. On the other hand, investigations of the wider client system appeared to indicate that the true cause of the situation lay in a number of latent problems, which included leadership skills, inadequate communication of information, ineffective teamwork, poor morale, and distrust of the company's motives.

Consequently, John decided that if he provided what the senior team requested, the problem they sought to address would not be resolved and tensions would remain in the management system. Indeed, they might be exacerbated. He therefore opted for a simple yet pragmatic method to be used in the focus groups in order to get a clearer snapshot of these issues.

Task

Make a list of what you think John will discover.

⊛ **Case study 2**

Dysfunctional thinking at King's Cross station: part 2

Read Case Example 9.2 again, and ask yourself 'how could a company, whose sole purpose was to transport passengers into and around the capital city, not have considered the safety of passengers between leaving the train and surfacing at ground level?'

The cultural assumptions perpetrated the myth that the underground system was just trains running on tracks below ground with facilities above ground being out of the sphere of visibility. The unions involved mirrored this thinking, assuming safety of their members was their main concern.

Questions

1. What is a dysfunctional process?

2. Explain the sequence of the unintended unfolding processes that led to disaster in this case.

3. Could anything have been done to eliminate them?

4. Draw a poster-sized map of the safety system you would put in place and illustrate the critical processes you would redesign.

5. What formal rules would you create to guide future decision making?

The map will apply analytical frames or concepts, such as Morgan's metaphors, to provide participants with a multi-layered approach to complex problems. We ended with a note of caution, by arguing that we cannot reduce complexity simply by applying models. Thus, whilst Morgan's metaphors may serve as models to guide our judgement, they do not replace knowledge, skill, and experience: after applying the metaphors, where we take them rests upon our competence.

■ Study questions

1. What is organizational diagnosis and how would you distinguish it from analysis?

2. Describe the art of diagnosis by stating what you regard as the knowledge, skills, and experience you would like to acquire to make you a competent practitioner of change.

3. What do the terms 'Action Research' and 'process consultation' refer to?

4. What does reframing an organizational problem mean?

5. What is meant by a diagnostic frame and why would it be informed by a change perspective?

6. Why is analysis never neutral?

7. What does Morgan mean when he states that 'images or metaphors only create partial ways of seeing'?

8. Explain how each of the metaphors described by Morgan might provide a focus for analysis.

9. Why is it necessary to triangulate perceptions of the client system?

10. Distinguish between manifest and latent problems.

■ Exercises

Exercise 1
Draw a conceptual map of any control system—such as financial control, quality control, or health and safety—for an organization you are familiar with. Identify the functions, actions, and procedures for corrective action in the event of deviations from expectations. Then do the same for the cultural system, followed by the political system. Once you have done this, explain which is the easiest and why the others are more difficult to outline.

Exercise 2
Considering the consultant's dilemma described at the beginning of this chapter, and using the analogy of a volcano, say why presenting the problem to a manager may be difficult. Base this on your knowledge of an organizational problem you have previously encountered.

Exercise 3
Think of a potential problem at the organizational level. Illustrate the importance of triangulation by stating how different interpretations might be given by (a) a senior manager, (b) a team leader, and (c) a shop-floor employee.

Exercise 4
Using Table 9.2, diagnose a problem.

■ Further reading

Cummings, T.G. and Worley, C.G. (2004), *Organisational Development and Change*, Fifth edition, Minneapolis/St. Paul, MN: West. This is a classic text. It is restricted to OD and does not consider alternative approaches, but it is recommended as a useful source for understanding OD practice.

Harrison, M. and Shirom, A. (1999), *Organizational diagnosis and assessment: bridging theory and practice*, London: Sage. This is a very useful and detailed text on the subject of analysis and diagnosis. It is recommended for readers who require more depth to their thinking about diagnostic skills.

Jackson, N. and Carter, P. (2000), *Rethinking Organisational Behaviour*, London: FT/Prentice-Hall. This text is recommended as an example of critical thinking. It provides alternative viewpoints and its strength is its use of a critical approach to concepts in organizational behaviour. It is therefore highly original in what it seeks to achieve.

Morgan, G. (2004), *Images of Organisation*, London: Sage. Morgan's book is now becoming a classic text. Although Morgan raises critical questions and provides an excellent framework that is easy to remember, he tends to fall back on a managerialist approach to organizations.

Schein, E.H. (1995), 'Process consultation, action research and clinical inquiry: are they the same?', *Journal of Managerial Psychology*, 10(6), 14–20. This gives a good account of Schein's definition of process consultation and considers the clinical model as applied to organizational analysis.

■ References

Anand, V., Ashfoith, B.E., and Joshi, M. (2005), 'Business as usual: the acceptance and perpetuation of corruption in organizations', *Academy of Management Executive*, 19(4), 9–23.

Bolman, L.G. and Deal, T. (1991), *Reframing organizations: artistry, choice and leadership*, San Francisco, CA: Jossey-Bass.

Burrell, G. and Morgan, G. (1982), *Sociological Paradigms and Organisational Analysis*, Aldershot: Gower.

Butterfield, K.D., Klebe Trevino L., and Weaver G.R. (2000), 'Moral awareness in business organizations: influences of issue-related and social context factors', *Human Relations*, 53, 981.

Cummings, T.G. and Worley, C.G. (1993), *Organizational Development and Change*, Fifth edition, Minneapolis/St. Paul, MN: West Publishing.

French, W.L. (1969), 'Organization Development: objectives, assumptions and strategies', *California Management Review*, 12, 23–39.

Goffman, E. (1959), *The Presentation of Self in Everyday Life*, Garden City, NY: Doubleday.

—— (1969), *Strategic Interaction*, Philadelphia, PA: University of Pennsylvania Press.

Grieves, J. (2003), *Strategic Human Resource Development*, London: Sage.

Harrison, M. and Shirom, A. (1999), *Organizational diagnosis and assessment: bridging theory and practice*, London: Sage.

Harrison, R. (1995), 'Choosing the Depth of Organizational Intervention', in Harrison, R., *The Collected Papers of Roger Harrison*, Maidenhead, Berks: McGraw-Hill, 13–65.

Hochschild, A. (1983), *The Managed Heart: Commercialization of Human Feeling*, Berkeley, CA: University of California Press.

Lewin, K. (1946), 'Action research and minority problems', *Journal of Social Issues*, 2.

Likert, R. and Likert, J.G. (1976), *New Ways of Managing Conflict*, New York: McGraw-Hill.

Mann, S. (1997) 'Emotional labour in organizations', *Leadership & Organization Development Journal*, 18(1), 4–14.

Morgan, G. (1986), *Images of Organisation*, London: Sage; (2004), Second edition, London: Sage.

Phillips, K. and Shaw, P. (1989), *A Consultancy Approach for Trainers*, Aldershot: Gower.

Schein, E.H. (1988), *Process Consultation: its role in Organization Development*, Reading, MA Addison-Wesley.

—— (1997), 'The concept of "client" from a process consultation perspective, A guide for change agents', *Journal of Organizational Change Management*, 10(3), 202–217.

Schön, D. and Rein, M. (1994), *Frame reflection: towards the resolution of intractable controversies*. New York: Basic Books.

Thompson, P. and McHugh, D. (1995), *Work Organisations: A Critical Introduction*, London: Macmillan.

Tsoukas, H. (1991), 'Missing Link: A Transformational View of Metaphors in Organizational Science', *Academy of Management Review*, 16(3), 566–585.

Weihrich, H., Seidenfuss, K. U., and Goebel, V. (1996), 'Managing vocational training as a joint venture— can the German approach of co-operative education serve as a model for the United States and other countries?', *European Business Review*, 96(1), 31–40.

 Take your learning further: Online Resource Centre
http://www.oxfordtextbooks.co.uk/orc/grieves/

Visit the Online Resource Centre that accompanies this book to enrich your understanding of this chapter. Explore case study updates and answers to questions, test yourself using an interactive flashcard glossary, and keep up to date with the latest developments in the area.

CHAPTER 10

Change models

10.1 Introduction

It will be useful to begin this chapter with a note of caution. As indicated in the previous chapter, models should not be used as a substitute for careful analysis. Nor should they be used as a replacement for experience, knowledge, and skills. Nevertheless, there is an argument to suggest that models can be used as a guide to direct attention to areas that need to be managed and changed. Organizational change is one of the predominant themes to have affected management in the twenty-first century. In this book we have considered various themes that, directly or indirectly, have implied models that are sometimes used to influence the design of change initiatives. This chapter therefore provides a variety of models that may help you to think through the issues a little more clearly. Each of the headings is related to chapters you will have read, where you can go for greater depth.

We begin by considering the difference between strategic change and personal change. They are similar, and you can see this in the process. However, the content is different. With strategic organizational change you would need to understand the four pathways illustrated in Figure 1.1 in Chapter 1. This is effectively the model that drives this book and you should be familiar with the arguments related to it. In other words, the implications of Figure 10.1 are related to the context of pathways to change. Personal and group-related change, on the other hand, focuses on personal pathways using the Path–Goal model.

Section 10.3 is related to *cultural change*. As noted in Chapter 6, the structural-functional approach provides models of change such as the 7S framework and Snyder's OD approach. This is supplemented here by reference to Tichy's change levers and influencing the cultural climate. Section 10.4 presents a rationale for

Figure 10.1 Defining strategic change

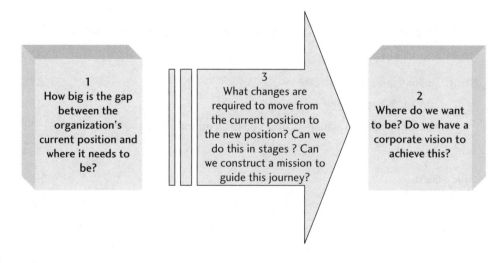

assessing the *readiness for change*, by finding out how much you know and deciding what you need to know before implementing change. Section 10.5 is related to Chapter 9. The focus here, however, is simple: to consider in greater depth the relationship between compliance and culture, since this is a theme that has emerged at regular intervals throughout the book. Section 10.6 explains the classic Deming cycle and the balanced scorecard, both of which are used throughout organizations to implement and measure. Section 10.7 is linked to Chapter 5, and particularly to the resource-based theory of the firm. It therefore sets out a framework for that purpose. Section 10.8 enables you to think about personal and group-related change. This is exactly what Lewin was interested in. Section 10.9 provides a model of creativity and section 10.10 concludes with a useful strategy for building an ethical climate.

By the end of this chapter you will:

- Have considered the merits and disadvantages of applying a model to change.
- Have learnt how to apply models to change situations.
- Be able to recognize how you might apply models to the three levels of change: individual, group, and organizational.
- **Be ready to reflect on how you might refer back to the themes and issues throughout the chapters, so as to learn more about some of the models that might be used in organizational change.**

---

❶ Stop and think 10.1

What changes have you experienced in the last year? Consider changes at an individual level, a group level, and finally at an organizational level. Make a list of these changes and group them into incremental and radical changes.

10.2 Personal and organizational strategy: defining paths and achieving goals

We will begin, then, with a simple model of change that can be applied at a strategic organizational level and at an individual level. Figures 10.1 and 10.2 are broadly similar despite small changes in the wording, because they are both designed to assess the gap between the current position and a future position, either for the organization or for the individual.

As we can observe, Figures 10.1 and 10.2 are the same models for change except that one works successfully at a strategic level and the other at an individual level. Figure 10.1, of course, requires a more complex formal analysis such as PESTLE, or

Figure 10.2 Defining personal change

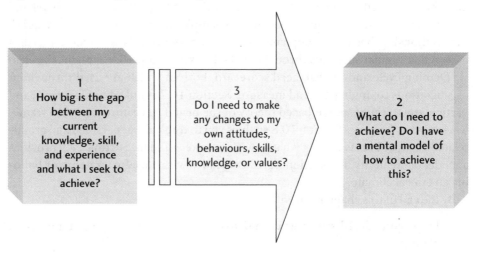

SWOT, or perhaps competitor analysis. It is also essential that you understand the arguments related to Figure 1.1. Thus each perspective offers a different pathway through change.

By contrast, Figure 10.2 is designed to question a person's knowledge, values, and attitudes. Critical to this, of course, is the level of motivation required. In Chapter 8 we noted that managers could use the Path–Goal model. This is a pragmatic model for identifying and enhancing commitment to a particular change path. Once again we can see how this could operate at a strategic level (as intended in Chapter 8), but we can also think through how we might use this at an individual level to identify and enhance our own motivations to pursue a particular path. Figure 10.3 illustrates the Path–Goal theory, which we previously linked to leadership. At a personal level we can also consider our own personal characteristics, such as level of motivation, current level of skill and knowledge, and current experience. Then we can look at the nature of the task or objective to be achieved. This raises questions about the knowledge and skill levels required and the type of experience needed in order to apply these things.

Figure 10.3 illustrates a model for personal development that looks at personal characteristics of the individual and relates these to the demands of the task. The critical question then becomes related to the psychological calculus, the extent to which the likely reward is worth the effort expended. Adopting this model for strategic leadership would require slight modifications. For example, in relation to the task, the leader needs to ask whether the directions are clear, the goals set for individuals and groups tangible, and the roles of individuals clearly defined. In relation to the demands of the task, the strategic leader needs to ask how effective the support and encouragement are for individuals and teams, and whether relationships are harmonious and professional.

Figure 10.3 Personal development based on the Path–Goal model

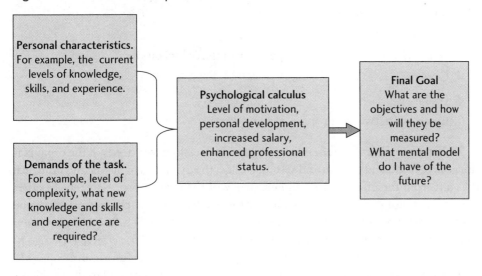

---

❶ Stop and think 10.2

Using any of the figures (10.1, 10.2 or 10.3) as a model, define a path and a course of action you might follow to plan a personal or strategic change initiative.

10.3 Cultural change

10.3.1 Tichy's change levers

In Chapter 6 we examined the 7S framework and Snyder's diagnostic model. An alternative structural-functional approach from OD is Tichy's (1983) change levers.

Tichy divided culture into three sub-systems. He considered an organization as a holistic system consisting of various sub-systems. These sub-systems were seen to reflect a functional relationship to the overall system to the extent that changes in one would influence changes to the others. Whilst these sub-systems included production, marketing, and sales, three were more influential. These were the *technical system*, the *political system*, and the *cultural system*. Because dysfunctions could occur if they were not carefully managed, each sub-system had to be influenced by change levers. Nine levers for change can be used to influence each sub-system. These are the:

1. External interface, or the organization's external environment (input).

2. Mission.

3. Strategy.

4. Engagement of key stakeholders in managing the processes that drive the mission and strategy.

5. Identification of task changes.

6. Networks prescribed for the operation of the organization.

7. Core processes, once clarified.

8. People.

9. Emergent networks, properly managed.

Whilst the technical system reflects the rational, task-driven needs of the organization, the political and the cultural systems reflect the dynamics of power and influence that underpin the effectiveness and efficiency of the change process itself. In other words, the non-rational, emotional and informal, behavioural characteristics of the latter two systems are the key to achieving the tasks required. Whilst each sub-system can be understood separately, all must be managed together for effective change to occur. The strength of this model is the weight it places on the informal, as opposed to the formal, organization. The major weakness, however, is related to the problems associated with all structural-functional models discussed throughout this book. Their use should be tempered with a knowledge of the issues and potential problems that may occur.

10.3.2 Influencing the cultural climate

As we noted in Chapter 6, cultural climate researchers are interested in measuring how people feel about their own organization. Whilst they focus on similar issues to the corporate culture and OD writers, they adopt fewer assumptions, preferring instead to test hypotheses. They measure the 'health' of an organization's climate using questionnaires. This can be done with different departments, workgroups, or entire organizations. How people feel about their working lives is seen to reflect both hygiene and motivating factors. Hygiene factors can be regarded as precursors to motivators: that is, they need to be in place before motivation can be effective. For example, it may be difficult to motivate a group of people if they are unhappy about their working environment; so the working environment is therefore a hygiene factor. Attitudes are related to perceived problems and their potential causes. Accordingly, researchers are interested in assessing the extent to which attitudes and behaviours support the core functions of the organization. Although numerous items can be added to reflect contextual issues, three are seen to be important, as illustrated in Figure 10.4.

As we noted in Chapter 6, culture can be viewed as 'a complex whole' rather than as a variable of the organization. By identifying these three features we come to recognize the importance of values, leaders, and context to an organization's culture. The starting point to any form of culture change is, first, to recognize how the organization's culture impacts on every aspect of an organization's actions. This is to suggest

Figure 10.4 Influencing the cultural climate

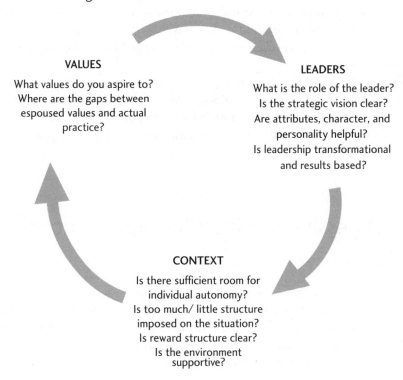

VALUES

What values do you aspire to?
Where are the gaps between
espoused values and actual
practice?

LEADERS

What is the role of the leader?
Is the strategic vision clear?
Are attributes, character, and
personality helpful?
Is leadership transformational
and results based?

CONTEXT

Is there sufficient room for
individual autonomy?
Is too much/ little structure
imposed on the situation?
Is reward structure clear?
Is the environment
supportive?

that it is not a separate entity but permeates everything. Culture change begins with establishing values. As Figure 10.4 indicates, 'to which values does the organization aspire?' is the leading question, followed by inviting organizational members to identify where there may be gaps between espoused values and actual practice. To refresh your memory you should look at section 2.5.1 above, on defensive reasoning. What we noticed there was that even leading organizations can become exposed to contradictions. Leaders need to answer four central questions:

1. What is their role?
2. Is the strategic vision clear?
3. What are their personal attributes, and how do their own character and personality help or hinder activity?
4. How might transformational and results-based leadership engage with, and get the best from, the organization's members?

Finally, context is always central. Just as we discovered that it was not possible to recommend universal criteria for leadership, so how a leader acts will also depend on context. The advice we can take from the behavioural research into leadership is that context is always the key. For this reason the Path–Goal approach is particularly useful and could easily be incorporated at this stage. But we need to ask whether there is sufficient room for individual autonomy, or too much or too little structure imposed on the situation. In addition, the reward structure must be clearly defined and seen to be transparent. Overall, people engage better when they work in a supportive environment.

Cultural climate researchers use questionnaires to find out what people feel about a number of factors, but values, leaders, and context are usually at the heart of most studies. You might find it useful to consider section 10.10 and the approach suggested there if you wish to emphasize concern for governance and ethical standards.

10.4 Assessing readiness for organizational change

Assessing an organization's readiness for change is critical to the success of any change programme. Of course, you can devise any measures for change in relation to your own business: this is to be recommended. However, as a rough guide, you might find it useful to use the case example below. This will guide you through the process and raise a number of important questions you may wish to consider.

》Case example 10.1

Assessing readiness for change

Complete the following questions
YOUR NAME............................... NAME OF ORGANIZATION............................
INDUSTRY SECTOR: service manufacturing public sector other
NUMBER OF EMPLOYEES: 0–9   10–19   20–49   50–249 250 plus

1. Can you identify the organization's vision?   1 Yes   2 No
   If yes, define it here...

2. Can you identify the organization's mission?   1 Yes   2 No
   If yes, define it here...

3. Can you identify the *critical success factors*?   1 Yes   2 No
   If yes, please list five of them here...

4. Some organizations have a *philosophy*. Does yours?   1 Yes   2 No
   If yes, then,

   A. identify the origins...

   B. identify the aims or core values...   》

>> 5. How would you describe the *management* style of the organization in terms of:

    A. power?

    B. influence—see Chapter 7?

    C. belief system?

6. Would you describe the *organizational structure* as:

    A. organic, or

    B. mechanistic (see reference in section 1.3.2 above)?

    What do you think it should be?

7. The effectiveness of *communication* can cover many areas in organizations. If you were to focus on *communicative rules*, then:

    A. can you identify examples of formal rules that regulate behaviour? Describe them here.

    B. can you identify conventions that guide behaviour? Describe them here.

8. *Quality of working life* has become a focus because of the actions of progressive employers or trades unions. Whilst this list might vary considerably from one organization to another, a comprehensive corporate quality-of-working-life programme might include four basic items. Tick which of these are applicable to your organization:

    A. continuity of employment;

    B. fair and equitable pay relationships;

    C. employee benefits;

    D. people viewed as assets and worth investing in;

    E. participation in management;

    F. the right to free speech;

    G. equal opportunity for advancement regardless of age, sex, sexual orientation, race, religion, or physical disability;

    H. other?

Additional comments

9. *Ethical issues*

    Is your organization actively promoting an ethical policy? This might include anything from environmental issues to trading relationships. Please comment.

Finally, you should review each of the issues identified by asking yourself if any changes would improve the effectiveness of the organization, then consider how you might introduce the changes and how you would monitor them.

10.5 Identifying dysfunctions

Chapter 9 focused on identifying dysfunctions. Whilst these are many and varied, there are certain types of dysfunction that are related to governance. In particular, we noted in Chapter 7 the problem of compliance. Compliance can be simply a matter of people failing to follow existing rules or agreed procedure, but it might also be related to the dynamics of power in an organization. For example, the case study at the end of Chapter 7 illustrated how compliance systems existed but were not followed in a multinational company where, clearly, reward power, as defined by French and Raven, was exercised to circumvent management systems. We also asked why there appeared to be a gap between the espoused values of the company and the practices that led to the problem. Evidence from the court case from which this study was developed also indicates that defensive reasoning was used to justify some actions. As the organizational sociologist Etzioni (1964) indicated, it is possible to construct a typology of compliance. We can see from his three-by-three matrix that the use of power influences a particular type of follower behaviour. Figure 10.5 illustrates a model that identifies nine types of compliance.

The reasons why people comply are illustrated by Etzioni's compliance structures. For example, coercive structures require overt physical and possibly psychological power. The most extreme example is a prison, but we could also think of military regimes, high-security psychiatric hospitals, or other institutions in which coercion is the main goal. Remunerative or utilitarian power illustrates the wage–effort bargain based on rewards and sanctions. Normative power is based on the belief in legitimacy, and may be based on bureaucratic authority, but also reflect a belief in ideology, including religion. When we examine involvement, we can see that coercive power is the most alienating type of involvement, remunerative or utilitarian power is the most calculative type, and normative power leads not only to a belief in legitimacy

Figure 10.5 Compliance structures

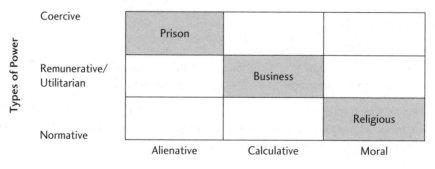

but, in the case of religious organizations, also to moral involvement. This model of compliance influenced the work of Peters and Waterman (1982). However, Peters and Waterman are only interested in the normative dimension and the desire to move the psychological contract of employees towards moral conviction through core values. It is precisely for this reason that they develop their 7S framework, as illustrated in Chapter 6.

❗ Stop and think 10.3

Think of an organization in which you have worked. Then consider how power is used or abused in that organization. Using the matrix in Figure 10.5 explain the consequences this has for the type of involvement that results. Another way of saying this is to refer to the psychological contract and consider why it changes.

10.6 Implementing and measuring change

10.6.1 Implementing change: the Deming cycle

Implementing change depends upon effective planning: consideration of what is being planned, why a particular intervention is necessary, its timing, and how it will be implemented. Planning an intervention in this way involves a logical sequence. A good example of this is the Deming cycle, in which consideration is given to planning, execution, measurement, and action, or *plan*, *do*, *check*, and *act* (or PDCA), as illustrated in Figure 10.6.

Figure 10.6 The Deming cycle: plan, do, check, and act

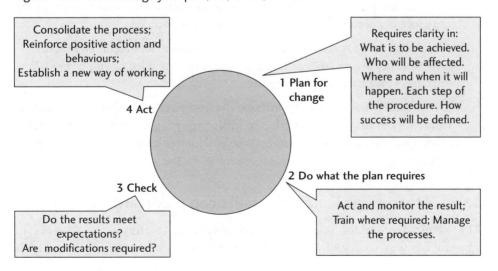

The Deming cycle is a useful technique for working methodically through a procedure. It is very useful for doing things right. The difficulty is that it will be of little value in doing the right thing. This is an important distinction. Consequently, the strategy for change you plan to implement must clearly delineate the critical processes and the principles for success.

In this, processes can be divided into two categories. These are:

1. Core processes that are critical to the delivery of the service or the product.

2. Supporting processes that enable the effective and efficient delivery of the service or product to the customer.

Assuming that the core processes are relevant and reliable, then implementing change depends upon human resources focusing on effective and efficient delivery to the customer. This is an important point requiring further clarification. Effectiveness is the measure you identify to ascertain that the product or service is 'fit for the purpose for which it was intended': in other words, that you can meet the customer's specification. This does not mean that you are delivering the product or service efficiently. It does mean, however, that you may become uncompetitive in comparison to your competitors. Being effective is therefore only 50 percent of the task of implementing change. The other 50 percent calls for efficient delivery. Being efficient, therefore, requires the organization to identify delivery processes that are SMART: that is, the task should be *specific* or clear to all. It must be *measurable*, with the intention of keeping costs to a minimum. The criteria for progress must demonstrate how each goal will be *attained* or *achieved*. The task must be *realistic*, so that effectiveness is related to efficiency in the delivery of the service or product. Finally, the delivery must be *timely*, within a realistic and practical time frame that meets both the customer's needs and the organization's ability to deliver.

Being both effective and efficient at the task depends upon three things:

1. The *people*—their skills, motivation, creativity, leadership, and how they own the processes required to deliver the product or service.

2. The *systems* used to perform the operations (we can include technology in this)—how well they are understood, whether they are controlled or empowered, how effectively the processes are integrated.

3. The *structures* put in place to manage the processes—whether a bureaucratic framework or rules are required to control an operation, or a matrix structure is more appropriate because an empowered solution to an organizational problem is required.

10.6.2 Measuring change: the balanced scorecard

The balanced scorecard is a method for measuring performance. It seeks to appraise business strategy by using a balance of measures that satisfy a variety of

Figure 10.7 The balanced scorecard

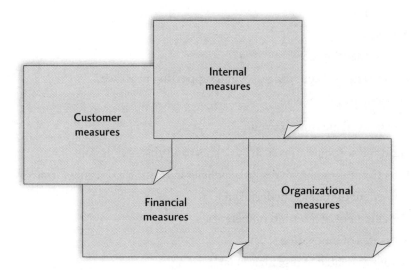

stakeholders. Firstly, financial measures must satisfy shareholders. Secondly, customer measures must satisfy customers. Thirdly, internal measures seek to focus on the results of core processes, particularly creativity and adding value. Finally, organizational measures seek to ensure effective human resource policies and development initiatives. Consequently, by balancing these four measures we arrive at the balanced scorecard. In Chapter 7 the discussion of results-based leadership proposes using a balanced scorecard to establish and measure the successful implementation of such leadership. Figure 10.7 illustrates this.

The four perspectives in detail reflect the following.

Financial measures include:

- Sales and revenue growth.
- Operating income.
- Sales cost as a percentage of total costs.
- Cost per unit.
- Measures of profitability.
- Repeat sales as a percentage of total sales volume.

Customer measures include:

- Satisfaction data from surveys.
- Pareto analysis of customers.
- Customer loyalty.
- Product returns.

Internal measures include:

- Total sales.
- New sales.
- Product development.
- Effectiveness of core processes and supporting processes.
- Service enhancement.

Organizational measures include:

- Hard and soft measures such as sickness and absence, morale.
- Effectiveness of human resource policies in relation to business strategy.
- The extent of training undertaken.
- Development of internal competencies.
- Measures of innovation.
- Activities related to organizational learning.

10.7 Building and developing strategic advantage

In Chapter 5 we discussed building competitive advantage by developing internal forces for change. Because strategy and tactics cannot work in isolation from the processes that generate performance, we have to cultivate forces for change that experiment and develop new opportunities, to exploit strategic advantages. This is illustrated in Figure 10.8.

10.7.1 Identify strategic capability

As we discussed in Chapter 5, the resource-based theory views organizations as composed of distinctive capabilities. Used effectively, human resources can be regarded as assets and can be developed to give the organization a competitive edge over its rivals. In this way, we can regard strategic change as a method for identifying and improving an organization's capabilities. There are three aspects to this: *architecture*, *reputation*, and *innovation*.

The architecture is the way in which a network of relational contracts is constructed, via internal networks of employees who interface with external networks of suppliers. Reputation is similar to branding. Both represent a particular quality that is consistently provided for the customer. The reputation of a product or company enables the customer to expect a particular standard. The key aspect of reputation is to ensure that the quality standard is not compromised. Innovation, as we noted in Chapter 5,

Figure 10.8 Building and developing strategic advantage

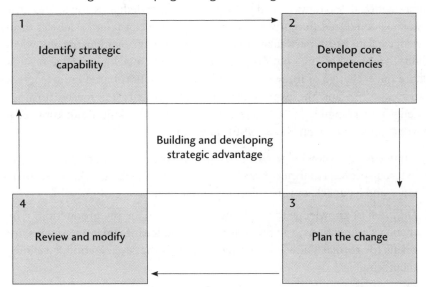

requires creativity and a culture to support it. The difficulty with innovation is that it carries risk; but so might the failure to innovate. The risk associated with innovation is usually linked to uncertainty over the demand for a product or service, and the length of time it will take competitors to develop a similar innovative product or service.

10.7.2 Develop core competencies

In Chapter 5 we noted that the development of core competencies is critical to transformational change. You should know your existing core competencies, but this is not always the case: as an organization develops, sometimes it loses sight of its original distinctive edge. Alternatively, you might be in a position to develop new core competencies in the production of products or services. Following the work of Hamel and Prahalad (2002), foresight (the term they use for thinking ahead) requires two things:

1. To think of the organization, not as a series of business units, but as a collection of core competencies.
2. To think about the functional interrelationships enabling the delivery of products, processes, and services, in order to determine the organization's core competencies.

Core competencies represent the knowledge and the specialist skills applied by people in the manufacture of a product or in the production of a service. This in itself is insufficient to remain progressive. Organizations therefore need to engage in organizational learning in order to enhance knowledge. Knowledge, however, can be considered in different ways. For example, we can refer to subject or expert knowledge related to a particular discipline, profession or industry; knowledge of methods, problem solving, and project management; social knowledge designed to facilitate the exchange of information and ideas; or action-based knowledge, which requires expertise and the experience and willingness to engage by turning tacit knowledge into a tangible asset. There are four ways of thinking about knowledge as a resource (Sprenger and ten Have, 1996). These are:

1. *Absorption* of knowledge from outside the organization, through developing external professional networks, through conferences, regular customer contacts, and feedback, or through competitive analysis.

2. *Diffusion* of knowledge through the organization, by the production of quality manuals, regulations, and procedures, knowledge information systems, mechanisms for regular knowledge exchange within the organization, coaching, and mentoring.

3. *Generation*, building capacity for generating knowledge within the organization. One of the most obvious ways is through regular quality reviews and action-learning groups.

4. *Exploitation* of knowledge about developing products and services. Techniques for exploiting knowledge include cross-disciplinary teams, market research, and enhancing the skill and knowledge levels of individuals through Action Research.

10.7.3 Plan the change

In Chapter 3 we noticed two predominant types of change model: *empirical–rational* and *normative re-educative*. The first was associated with change in linear sequence. Such models are marginally successful and work well only when the task is clear and there are no other potential problems that could emerge (litigation, ethical dilemmas, problems of leadership, politics, and so forth). Situations that do not involve such issues are rare. Kotter (1990) suggested that there were many reasons for this, but provided a model for planning change in eight stages, based on the need to:

1. *Establish a sense of urgency.* Usually this is undertaken through market research, analysis of competition, or because a crisis has recently arisen for the organization.

2. *Create a coalition*, usually by identifying influential people who will act as champions of the change process.

3. *Develop a clear vision* that is achievable and clearly articulated to everyone throughout the organization.

4. *Share the vision.* This relies on effective channels of communication, which, of course, differ in relation to the size of the organization. In this process, the coalition of influential individuals can be particularly persuasive.

5. *Empower people and remove barriers or obstacles to progress.* This may require changing structures, systems, or processes that are no longer as useful as they once were.

6. *Secure short-term wins* as visible evidence that things are changing, and also that people are rewarded appropriately for their efforts.

7. *Consolidate and move forward,* building on success and continuing to remove barriers to change. Most importantly, it requires the change process to be refreshed and given new vigour.

8. *Anchor the change programme.* In other words, this final stage requires that everyone understands the new routines and work practices.

10.7.4 Review and modify

We noted in Chapter 3 that writers about processual or emergent change argue that change emerges from unplanned processes that could not be anticipated; that planned change models oversimplify reality and tend to ignore relationships between individuals, groups, and organizations, as well as decision-making processes. They raise the question, for those planning change, of how to identify problems as they emerge, and how to redirect the change efforts to achieve a solution. A partial answer to this question is to monitor change. For example, in Chapter 3, we saw that Buchanan and Dawson suggest that we combine four elements to produce a processual narrative approach. We can therefore be vigilant of four types of potential conflict:

1. *Conflicts of attribution,* which often occur between different stakeholders.

2. *Conflicts of assessment,* which reveal the contestable quality of change outcomes.

3. *Conflicts of interpretation,* which cause confusion.

4. *Conflicts of audience,* which suggest that different messages are being communicated to different audiences.

You should also read section 3.5 on problems faced by planned change programmes. These problems were only indicative of the types of problem that might arise at different stages, but we need to be mindful of them. Stage one might involve contestable definitions. Difficulties at stage two (analysing and planning) might reflect inaccurate or insufficient data to make a qualified analysis, or lack of expertise by those responsible for managing the change process. At stage three (implementation), difficulties might include resistance to change, lack of management support, or resource issues. At stage four (steering), difficulties might be characterized by loss of key people, change adopted for the wrong reasons, or loss of momentum. Difficulties at stage five might include failures to involve relevant knowledgeable people in the evaluation, and to deal with people with different political agendas. You should remember that many other potential problems cannot be anticipated. Therefore the purpose of review is to correct problems that have emerged in the change process. Regular review sessions should be arranged in order to manage the change process.

10.8 Force Field Analysis: analysing and changing underlying behaviours

Since the success of any change initiative depends upon recognizing the importance of underlying behaviours and attitudes at the beginning when defining the problem, we need to consider the psychological and social factors that can either become barriers to change, or enable successful implementation. Force Field Analysis is one of the most appropriate vehicles for transforming the processes that underpin most tasks. However, we need to be cautious about how we use it.

Lewin was concerned to demonstrate how individuals, as members of social groups, move through transitions by dealing with psychological and social barriers. FFA was devised as a three-step process to assist people to manage behavioural change. Others who followed these research interests later include Kübler-Ross (1973), who researched psychologically extreme transitions such as bereavement, Adams *et al* (1976), and Menninger (1975), all of whom were concerned with discontinuity and transition (see Chapter 11).

Consequently, there is both a driving and an opposing force. In most situations of this kind it may be possible to reduce the opposing force. A successful change involves unfreezing existing behaviours by challenging assumptions and prejudice.

Because Lewin saw the idea of a force field as a tension (or series of related tensions) that affects the personal (psychological) or social (group) context, FFA is his voluntary analytic method for enabling change. Lewin was interested in the emotional and cognitive forces that block change, such as perception, attitudes and behaviours, and habits. One of the difficulties is that cultural norms often inhibit change: any practical change desired by individuals or groups first requires a willingness to challenge attitudes, and resistance to change is in fact concerned with internal barriers. How does this work? First, a stable equilibrium represents a balance of forces for and against change. The positive force might be represented by the desire or motivation to give up a habit. However, if this motivation is blocked (or resisted) by a need to persist in the habit, then no change will occur. Second, the desire to eliminate the habit will have greater success in achieving its objective if the negative forces causing resistance are destabilized in some way; and an even greater chance of success if the positive force (for example, motivation) can be increased. Third, the movement towards eliminating the habit will have a higher chance of being sustained if the new equilibrium is reinforced. In other words, the new pattern of behaviour must become frozen as a new habit driven by repetition and routine. To understand this, consider the following case example.

> ## » Case example 10.2
>
> ### Changing behaviours or attitudes using Force Field Analysis
>
> Force Field Analysis is a sophisticated technique for dealing with change at a personal or group level. To understand this process, undertake the following task.
>
> #### Step one
>
> Identify a personal problem that you are prepared to share with others. This should relate to an attitude or a behaviour you want to, but find difficult to, change. For example, giving up smoking, changing your driving behaviour, changing your eating habits, getting fit, improving your work behaviour to pass exams, and so on.
>
> #### Step two
>
> Using the Force Field diagram (Figure 10.9), identify the driving forces beneath each arrow. These will be related to your motivation to succeed and will include potential positive outcomes. Now identify all issues that cause you to resist changing.
>
> #### Step three
>
> The question you need to ask is: 'how can I minimize the resisting forces and increase the driving forces?' Remember, for Lewin, a successful change project involved three steps:
>
> 1. unfreezing the present level;
> 2. moving to the new level;
> 3. refreezing the new level.
>
> Now draw up an action plan to unfreeze your current situation: state how you will proceed. Then, when you have visualized the change you want (the new level), state how you will freeze the new behaviours and attitudes so that they become habits.

Groups should use FFA by first deciding on the nature of the problem to be addressed. A problem-tree analysis can be used for this purpose. This can be undertaken as follows:

1. Agree the definition of the problem.
2. Write the problem focus (or trunk of the tree) in the centre of a flip chart.
3. Identify potential causes or things that contribute to the problem. These are written below the defined problem and are regarded as the roots of the tree.

Figure 10.9 Force Field diagram

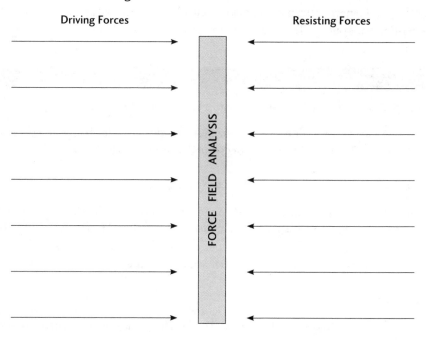

The problem tree can be regarded as a simple technique for stating or confirming the issues related to a defined problem. This will enable the group to define its objective, which then becomes the focus for the FFA. Thus, if we take our illustration above as an example, the objective will be written into the central vertical box and the driving and resisting forces are then identified. This is relatively straightforward. The problem comes next when we critically appraise the reasons or motives behind the driving and resisting forces. In order to engage in a voluntary process in which people feel involved and in control, answers to the following questions may be required:

- Whose interest is served by meeting this objective?
- Who loses in the process?
- What are the costs to individuals?
- What are the benefits to individuals?
- Will achieving the objective be divisive in any way?
- What will the advantages be?

Unless agreement can be reached on these matters, then attempting a FFA with a group will have uncertain results.

10.9 A model of creativity

Creativity is essential for the development of unique competencies. We noted in Chapter 5 that sustained competitive advantage results from the acquisition and effective use of bundles of distinctive resources that competitors cannot imitate. High-performance work systems and the resource-based view of the firm require creativity and innovation. We can visualize the process in Figure 10.10.

Armstrong and Baron (2003) refer to three types of capital that make organizations unique. These are:

Human capital—the knowledge, skills, and abilities of the employees who are hired and developed by an organization.

Social capital—first, the way that an organization structures itself to achieve maximum benefit from human resource development; second, the 'stocks and flows of knowledge derived from networks of relationships' within and outside the organization.

Organizational capital— 'the institutionalized knowledge possessed by an organization that is stored in databases, manuals, etc. It is alternatively called structural capital' (Edvinson and Malone, 1997: 14), and 'organizational capital'.

Figure 10.10 Preconditions for creativity

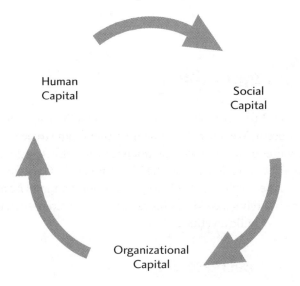

Human
Capital

Social
Capital

Organizational
Capital

Figure 10.11 A creative event: rapid movement between two cognitive states

Inspiration ◄─────────────────────────► Elaboration

These types of capital are preconditions for creativity. Individual and group creativity appears to oscillate between two cognitive states. This often triggers a creative event, as illustrated in Figure 10.11.

Creative people appear more open to incoming stimuli—the senses are continually feeding information. The creative event might be solving a problem, inventing a product, or developing an idea, but in each case the process is stimulated by the application of something meaningful.

Developing creative synthesis with a group or team requires:

1. A well-structured learning environment.

2. That managers create opportunities and facilitate creative thinking through the support they give. They should also act as mentors or coaches.

3. That a group shares similar values and objectives.

4. Applied decision making for a particular purpose. For example, some decisions need a highly prescriptive approach, whereas others require a greater degree of flexibility.

❗ Stop and think 10.4

Write down what you think are the main barriers to individual creativity; and to creativity in groups.

10.10 Building an ethical climate

We noted in Chapter 2 that compliance, by itself, is insufficient to deal with ethical problems that may occur. We must also remember that failing to deal effectively with ethical issues is a matter of governance: that not practising effective governance leaves an organization open to litigation and, as the Siemens case in Germany in 2008 illustrated, it also leaves the employees liable to prosecution and imprisonment. Simply pleading ignorance is rarely successful. This raises two questions—what is moral reasoning? And how do we build an ethical climate?

10.10.1 What is moral reasoning?

The first question is a matter of philosophical debate, but we can reasonably assume that moral reasoning is part of our upbringing. This is a continuous process throughout our lives, and we can identify critical periods, such as childhood, adolescence, and during working life. In each stage we are socialized to adopt and test out cultural standards. The process of socialization allows us to understand social rules and how we are prepared to respond to them.

For example, most parents believe that one of their most important duties is to guide their children to be of sound moral character. Does this stop at the workplace or should managers also act responsibly? In Chapter 2 we saw problems associated with the failure to consider ethical responsibility for change, and noted (in the end-of-chapter case study in Chapter 7) that it is not unusual to find a gap between espoused values of the organization and the actual practices that occur. As the case study suggested, managers are responsible when they do not provide moral guidance or allow collusion to develop. We can therefore understand how we enter an organization or a profession and adopt ethical standards. Perhaps a better way of putting this would be to suggest that we can learn unethical behaviour from work colleagues and this might be classified as immoral; or learn amoral behaviour largely because no governance is practised at all. At the other extreme, when an organization practises effective governance through training designed to raise our level of awareness, then we can consider that to be ethical practice.

Kohlberg (1981) argued that individuals develop moral reasoning and that this happens in a particular sequence. His model of moral development suggests that there are three levels of development, each with two stages.

Level 1—The Preconventional Level (Self-Focused Morality)

Stage one is characterized by punishment and obedience. Morality is simply about obeying rules because of the sanctions and consequences imposed. Young children learn to avoid punishment.

Stage two is characterized by developing behaviour that best satisfies needs.

Level 2—The Conventional Level (Other-Focused Morality)

Stage three is characterized by meeting the expectations of parents and significant others by trying to please.

Stage four is characterized by respecting authority and by meeting obligations, which in turn further motivates behaviour.

Level 3—Postconventional Level (Higher-Focused Morality)

Stage five is characterized by an awareness of the principle of reciprocity. That is, we come to recognize 'give and take' or that compromise reflects a win–win solution for two or more parties.

Stage six is characterized by a universal orientation to ethical principles. This encourages greater reflection about how the individual wishes to see him- or herself acting in the world. Not everyone is equipped to undertake this journey to level six but those that do develop a sense of justice, fairness, and respect for human dignity.

10.10.2 What can managers do to build an ethical climate?

Evolving moral awareness is a lifelong process. Managers can help to identify good choices. We do not necessarily need to provide solutions, but should engage in critical thinking about consequences. Kohlberg (1981) suggested that some people could undergo moral regression. Thus the individual becomes disaffected with the arbitrary application of rules and contradictory reasoning. In this case the organization or its leadership may be seen to be culpable. Kohlberg's theory suggests that a view of justice is central to moral reasoning. In organizations we could suggest that justice depends on the type of reasoning that occurs when people are faced with difficult situations. Thus, when practice contradicts formal rules, the sense of justice or fairness required for moral reasoning becomes contradictory because the principles are unsound. This is illustrated in the following case example.

There are two responses to the question raised above. The first is to ask what are an organization's responsibilities to its stakeholders, a question typical of the multiple constituencies perspective and illustrated in Figure 10.12. The second response is to suggest eight things that can be done to develop an ethical climate, as illustrated in Figure 10.13.

Criticism of Kohlberg's stages suggests that both culture and gender may be important variables in moral reasoning. Furthermore, it may be possible to make moral judgements without resorting to concepts of fairness, corporate rules, law, or human rights. Nevertheless, Kohlberg's theory suggests that managers should give thought to stages five and six when thinking about change.

Figure 10.12 Ethical responsibilities to stakeholders

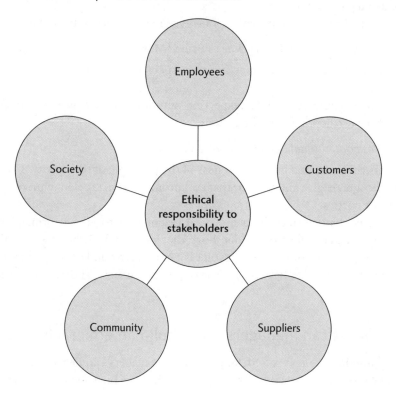

》 Case example 10.3

Moral reasoning or moral regression?

Reinhard Siekaczek, a 57-year-old manager, was accused along with 299 other Siemens employees of corruption. In his defence he admitted to siphoning off €1.3bn. He told a Munich court that he had 'informed his entire divisional board about the system and assumed that the whole group executive board knew about it…' On the opening day of Germany's biggest corporate corruption trial, 'Siekaczek described how managers signed off "commissions" on yellow Post-It notes which could be easily removed in case of raids or investigations'. He claimed that he tried to stop 'the widespread bribery at Siemens' fixed-line telecommunications equipment division where he was a sales manager' but had 'fallen foul of his superiors who "didn't want to hear"'.

Sources: David Gow, *The Guardian*, 27 May 2008; Maria Marquat, *The Huffington Post*, 26 May 2008; Carter Dougherty, *New York Times*, 26 May 2008.

Figure 10.13 Building an ethical climate

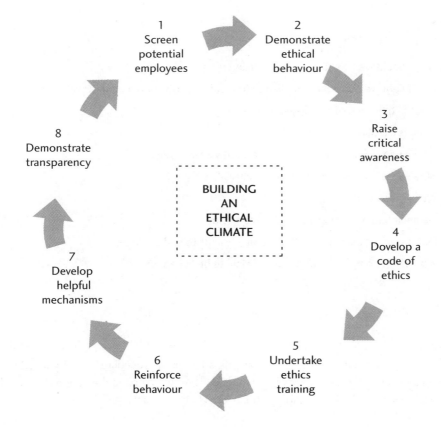

> **❶ Stop and think 10.5**
>
> Have you ever seen examples of unethical behaviour in an organization? Considering Kohlberg's stages, do you think that such people have not developed in some respects or are you aware of any evidence to suggest moral regression?

10.11 Summary

The models illustrated in this chapter are related to the themes and issues of the book. They are related to relevant chapters as stated in the introduction to this chapter. Throughout the book you will already have come across different models. You should remember, however, that any model is related to a perspective and should be chosen carefully or not at all. Equally, you may find it more productive to construct your own models and methodology based on your understanding and knowledge. The models provided in this chapter are therefore complementary to those elsewhere in the book.

◼ Study questions

1. Why should we be cautious about using models of change?
2. Why might we consider compliance to create a problem of commitment?
3. What is the value of the Deming cycle?
4. What is a balanced scorecard?
5. How might a Force Field Analysis be used well or badly?
6. Why might you use a Force Field Analysis?
7. What is creativity?
8. Define moral reasoning and moral regression.
9. Outline an organization's ethical commitment to stakeholders.
10. Why might compliance and cultural climate be linked?

◼ Exercises

Exercise 1
The Deming cycle is a technique for changing a technical procedure. Identify a technical procedure in an organization known to you and illustrate in a table the actions you would undertake using each of the headings (plan, do, check, and act).

Exercise 2
Think of a particular organizational setting and make a list of dysfunctional behaviours you have either observed or could imagine occurring. State why you would consider them to be dysfunctional and justify why you consider your view to be objective.

Exercise 3
Organizational structure creates role demands. Illustrate with examples how this happens. Then demonstrate how role conflicts could occur. You should consider how this affects groups and individuals.

Exercise 4
Think of a change situation and apply any of the models in this chapter to it. When you have done this, critically appraise your own efforts.

Exercise 5
Construct a personal change journey as described by Figures 10.2 and 10.3.

■ Further reading

Etzioni, A. (1964), *Modern Organizations*, Englewood Cliffs, NJ: Prentice-Hall. Although the date of the book may deter some readers, the text remains a classic because of the type of compliance structures it identifies. I would recommend reading this text alongside the text by Kets de Vries and Miller (1984) recommended below.

Hamel, G. and Prahalad, C.K. (2002), 'Competing for the Future' in Henry, J. and Mayle, D. (eds), *Managing Innovation and Change*, London: Sage, 23–35. The text is recommended for the challenge the authors provide by suggesting organizations reorganize around core competencies.

Kets de Vries, M.F.R. and Miller, D. (1984), *The Neurotic Organization, Diagnosing and Changing Counterproductive Styles of Management*, London: Jossey-Bass. Another classic and unorthodox text the reader should read for the relationship it suggests between leadership, culture, and the use and abuse of power.

Patterson, M.G., West, M.A., Shackleton, V.V.J., Dawson, J.F., Lawthom, R., Maitlis, S., Robinson, D.L., and Wallace, A.M. (2005), 'Validating the cultural climate measure: links to managerial practices, productivity and innovation', *Journal of Organizational Behavior*, 26, 379–408. Recommended for the methodological instrument—the Cultural Climate Measure—used to assess an organization's culture.

Woodward, C. (2005), *Winning*, London: Hodder Paperbacks. Recommended for the practical approach Sir Clive Woodward took to transforming the culture of the English rugby 'establishment' whilst also focusing on the nature of the task, the objective to be achieved, and the skill levels required to achieve success.

■ References

Adams, J.D., Hayes, J., and Hobson, B. (1976), *Transition: Understanding and Managing Personal Change*, London: Martin Robertson.

Armstrong, M. and Baron, A. (2003), *Strategic HRM: The key to improved business performance*, London: Chartered Institute of Personnel and Development.

Beckhard, R.(1969), *Organization Development: Strategies And Models*, Reading, MA: Addison-Wesley.

Burke, W.W. (2002), *Organization Change : Theory and Practice*, London: Sage.

Deming, W. E. (1986), *Out of the Crisis*, Boston, MA: MIT Center for Advanced Engineering Study.

Edvinson, L. and Malone, M.S. (1997), *Intellectual Capital: Realizing your company's true value by finding its hidden brainpower*, New York: HarperCollins.

Etzioni, A. (1964), *Modern Organizations*, Englewood Cliffs, NJ: Prentice-Hall.

Greiner, L (1972) 'Evolution and revolution as organizations grow', *Harvard Business Review*, July/August, 37–46, reprinted May/June 1998.

Hamel, G. and Prahalad, C.K. (2002), 'Competing for the Future' in Henry, J. and Mayle, D., *Managing Innovation and Change*, London: Sage, 23–35.

Kohlberg, L. (1981) *Essays on Moral Development, Vol. I: The Philosophy of Moral Development*, San Francisco, CA: Harper & Row.

Kohlberg, L., Levine, C., and Hewer, A. (1983) *Moral stages: a current formulation and a response to critics*, Basel: Karger.

Kotter, J.P. (1990), *A Force for Change, How leadership differs from management*, New York: Free Press.

Kübler-Ross, E. (1973), *On Death and Dying*, London: Routledge.

Menninger, W.X. (1975), 'The meaning of morale: a Peace Corps model', in Moyniham, D.P. (ed), *Business and Society in Change*, New York: American Telephone and Telegraph Co.

Peters, T.J. and Waterman, R.H. (1982), *In Search of Excellence: Lessons From America's Best Run Companies*, New York: Harper & Row.

Sprenger, C. and ten Have, S. (1996), 'Kennismanagement als moter van de lerende organisatie', *Holland Management Review*, Sept–Oct, 73–89.

Tichy, N.M. (1983) *Managing Strategic Change: Technical, Political, and Cultural Dynamics*, New York: John Wiley & Sons.

Weisbord, M.R. (1976) 'Organizational Diagnosis: Six Places to Look for Trouble With or Without a Theory', *Group and Organization Studies*, 1, New York: Wiley, 430–447.

 Take your learning further: Online Resource Centre
http://www.oxfordtextbooks.co.uk/orc/grieves/

Visit the Online Resource Centre that accompanies this book to enrich your understanding of this chapter. Explore case study updates and answers to questions, test yourself using an interactive flashcard glossary, and keep up to date with the latest developments in the area.

CHAPTER 11

Resistance to change

11.1 Introduction

In this chapter we explore the concept of resistance to change. It is often assumed that people resist change but this is not necessarily the case. We need to remember that change can be either positive or negative. When we look at social change, for example, we can identify many aspects that are negative, such as white-collar crime or deviance. These examples are not seen in the usual context of positive and purposeful activity. Conversely, when we examine the development of popular movements, or internet activity such as chatrooms, Facebook, and MySpace, we discover the trends triggered by a sudden development of enthusiasm and popularity.

We begin the chapter by considering the 'conventional wisdom' that reflects the managerialist or task-driven approach to changing things. Broadly speaking, this can be associated with the structural-functionalist perspective, which focuses on the redesign of structures and work processes. We also look at the concept of the tipping point, which is derived from the book of that name by Malcolm Gladwell. Although we cannot directly relate this to organizational change, it is clear that, by implication, we might consider these ideas to be associated with the multiple constituencies perspective and its emphasis on negotiated meaning. In particular, we explore a case example involving the Singapore LTA, which successfully anticipated and 'managed out' potential resistance to change. We then explore the idea of socio-psychological stress and resistance. What we need to understand here is that there are personal situations in which people are severely affected by what happens to them. These are usually extreme situations but it can be the case that even within everyday situations people undergo stress or trauma as a result of the work they do. For example, police officers, fire prevention offices, or paramedics often have to deal with very difficult situations that can have traumatic effects on their own lives. It is no surprise, therefore, that such professions often have very high incidences of stress-related illness in comparison to other professional or work groups. Finally, we explore the critical perspective on resistance to change. This is concerned in particular with the way in which the concept of labelling occurs and also with the way in which those in positions of power might actually cause the problems of resistance they seek to eliminate.

In this chapter we will:

- Explore the managerialist assumptions of resistance associated with the conventional wisdom.
- Discover the meaning of 'tipping point' in relation to social change and organizational change.
- Learn what is meant by resistance in situations of stress and trauma.
- Critically analyse the nature of resistance to change.

11.2 Conventional wisdom

Many managerialist texts regard the subject of resistance to change as unproblematic. These often provide change aphorisms related to perceptions, structures, and anxiety. For example:

- Perceptions often refer to things such as motivation—'the risk of change is perceived to be greater than the risk of standing still', or 'people relate to others who identify with the old ways of doing things', or 'people do not feel connected to the change strategy'.

- Structural issues often suggest a problem with cognition or skill, such as 'people lack role models for the action required', or 'people feel overloaded and overwhelmed'.

- Anxiety often refers to fear, such as 'people fear change', or 'they lack skill', or 'they lack the competence to change'.

Many of these are genuine reflections of consultants and managers who may be concerned with the issues of alienation, as for example when an employee is required to use automated instruments in place of active engagement in the task. Since all organizations require change to be managed, it is reasonable to expect the willing participation of all members. Thus, by planning change actions, managers seek to expedite the change process. The difficulty emerges when different perceptions give rise to what is considered to be a desirable or undesirable change. This is essentially a matter of legitimacy.

---

❶ Stop and think 11.1

Think of a change situation and identify different views from the positions of different stakeholders. Identify those who advocate the change and consider their motives. Then identify those who support the change advocated. Finally, identify those who openly challenge the change, as well as those who covertly reject it. How many different motives can you identify?

The difficulty for most managers responsible for a change initiative is convincing people that change is required. It has been argued that most large-scale change programmes go through phases that characterize the success or failure of a programme. A useful example of this is illustrated by Harvey and Brown (2001) and summarized as follows:

Phase 1 is characterized by an informed minority who see the need for change. The difficulty is that they see the potential opposition or resistance to the change as large and necessary to overcome.

Phase 2 represents the movement for change in which converts are acquired and come to be identified with the change initiative. This appears to represent a polarization between supporters and opponents.

Phase 3 reflects conflict that is likely to emerge between supporters and opponents. How this phase is managed becomes critical because it represents the pivotal point between success and failure.

Phase 4 is characterized by success to the extent that supporters outnumber resisters. Thus remaining resistance is considered as irritating rather than critical to success.

Phase 5 reflects the alienation of resisters who become increasingly marginalized by the successful efforts of the majority.

This idea of resistance to change reflects the application of work psychology, in which resistance is seen as functionally undesirable yet often an inevitable consequence in people whose work patterns or comfort zones are disrupted. If resistance is therefore seen as undesirable but understandable, then it becomes pathological only when the movement to successful change is significantly disrupted or abandoned. This view of resistance to change is rooted in the structural-functional perspective and has become characteristic of Organizational Development (OD) consultants. Thus, managers may believe the change to be desirable or necessary. Consequently, the negative reactions of participants must be addressed by views that increase the perceived desirability of the initiative. Thus, following Kotter (1996), managers need to communicate a compelling vision, such that negative aspects of the change are de-emphasized. Such arguments seek to appeal to the emotional states of participants who are confronted by a change initiative that has no appeal for them.

The first direct reference to resistance to change in the organizational change literature was Coch and French's (1948) 'Overcoming Resistance to Change', which was concerned to address resistance in the workplace. Resistance was manifested in measurable signs such as high staff turnover rates, grievances, and low output rates. Symptoms were harder to detect, but associated with attitudes to work. The adoption of the open-systems model by OD practitioners involved a helping relationship in which the facilitator of change sought to identify barriers to perception. For example, by using Force Field Analysis, facilitators can identify barriers to perceptions and, with the willing involvement of participants, help to strengthen motivations and weaken negative responses. There are many situations in which this may be the case, as we will come to understand below.

11.3 The tipping point and negotiated meaning

The tipping point is a term used by Gladwell (2005), who associates the metaphor of epidemic with social change. Thus criminality, fashion, and religious and social movements can spread like a virus to epidemic proportions. If this process is associated with trends, then it may explain how, when enough people are hooked by a product or persuaded of the need to join in, the momentum for change becomes overwhelming. When enough people become a critical mass, a tipping point is reached and the pace of change increases dramatically. This is because a critical mass of adopters want to become associated with change. It should be noted, however, that this change can be either positive or negative. The tipping point can move the critical mass to voice its negative concerns, in which case the social epidemic can become dysfunctional. Conversely, the tipping point can become a force for positive change.

Gladwell (2005: 29) articulates three rules for those social changes that take off like epidemics. The first is 'the law of the few'; the second, the 'stickiness factor'; and the third is 'the power of context'. Each of these, he claims, 'provides us with a direction for how to go about reaching the tipping point. Social changes that occur like epidemics are changes that happen in a hurry.' This is because change can be infectious, providing the right circumstances exist for the transmission of social change. A second point he makes is that little causes can have big effects and that 'change happens not gradually but at one dramatic moment'. He provides a number of varied examples of social epidemics. For example, he points out that 'a handful of East Village kids started the Hush Puppies epidemic' and a scattering of the residents of a few housing projects was sufficient to start the Baltimore syphilis epidemic. Certain people are critical to the transmission of social problems or, more creatively, to the transmission of ideas. As he therefore points out, the number of people who drive epidemics is usually very small and this appears to conform to the Pareto principle (or 80/20 rule). As Gladwell (2005: 21) argues:

> Social epidemics work like biological epidemics. They are also driven by the efforts of a handful of exceptional people. In this case, it's not sexual appetites that set them apart, it's things like how sociable they are, or how energetic or knowledgeable or more influential someone is among their peers. In the case of Hush Puppies, the great mystery is how those shoes went from something worn by a few fashion-forward downtown Manhattan hipsters to being sold in malls across the country.

The 'law of the few' suggests the answer is that one of these exceptional people found out about the trend and, through social connections, energy, enthusiasm, and personality, spread the word. Central to the progression of change is the idea of 'stickiness'. This phrase refers to a message that carries a big impact. Like a good, or sometimes bad, tune, you can't get it out of your head. It sticks in your memory. The implication is that there are specific ways of making a contagious message memorable and these are relatively simple changes to the presentation or structuring of information that somehow make a big impact.

Once a sticky message has been created, it appears to pick up pace and speed by means of people with special abilities, whom he refers to as 'connectors', 'mavens', and 'salesmen'. He cites the psychologist Stanley Milgram's experiments, which have become commonly known for '6 degrees of separation'. Known officially as the small-world experiment, Milgram's study sought to test a long-standing assertion about the average length of a path: the likelihood that two people selected at random would know each other, based on the probability that someone in their social network would be known to both of them. Milgram's experiment took the population of the USA as a social network, and sought to identify the number of people it would take to get a letter to its destination from one coast of the USA to the other. In each of his experiments he found that, despite the distance, most of the letters reached their destination in five or six steps.

Finally, the power of context suggests that we are all sensitive to the conditions and circumstances in which events occur. An example used by Gladwell is the broken window theory, devised by the criminologists James Wilson and George Kelling. Wilson and Kelling argue that crime is the inevitable result of disorder. If a window in a neighbourhood is left and not repaired, people walking by conclude that no one cares and no one is in charge. So more windows will be broken, and the sense of anarchy will spread from the building to the rest of the street. This sends a signal that anything goes. Although this is a negative example, it also works in reverse. An epidemic can emerge from the smallest details, but context is the key. The power of context is an environmental argument suggesting that we pick up subtle but important cues about behaviour from the social context in which it occurs.

Although Gladwell does not refer to organizational change, others have used his metaphor to suggest that change occurs in organizations in precisely this way. For example, Burke (2002) argues that the processes are similar to those in organizational change. Similarly, when enough people are persuaded by the wisdom of change, a tipping point occurs. The three types of people—'connectors', 'mavens', and 'salesmen'—that Gladwell refers to are essential to this process. Connectors have a special gift for bringing the world together. These people are facilitators of change. Mavens collect information and are good at sharing what they know. Salesmen are, of course, persuaders who promote the cause of change.

Gladwell's argument suggests that organizational change, like social change, may sometimes occur in small ways and eventually reach epidemic proportions. This, of course, can mean that an organization's strategy can be successful. And conversely, the tipping point may also reflect a sudden increase in resistance to change. Some organizations have been very successful in managing change because they appear to have undertaken change strategies in a methodical manner that reflects the attention to detail that Gladwell refers to. One example is illustrated in the following.

❯❯ Case example 11.1

How Singapore LTA successfully managed resistance to change

Planning change in Singapore

The concept plan of the Singapore Urban Redevelopment Authority considers all aspects of land use for commerce, housing, recreation, nature areas, infrastructure and defence. The management of these requires an integrated plan. As part of this ❯❯

❯ planning process, the Land Transport Authority (LTA) planned to provide 'convenient access without creating excessive congestion'.[1]

The role of the LTA

The LTA is the public transport system of Singapore and was established on 1 September 1995 through the merger of four public sector entities: Registry of Vehicles (ROV), Mass Rapid Transit Corporation (MRTC), Roads & Transportation Division of the Public Works Department, and Land Transport Division of the then-Ministry of Communications. The LTA's ultimate goal is to provide 'a smooth and seamless journey for all'.[2]

The Authority is a statutory board of the Republic of Singapore Ministry of Transport. This has overall responsibility for overseeing Singapore's growing transport needs, whilst the LTA plans long-term transport requirements for the country's citizens, who make 8.9 million journeys daily. Planning change is achieved through its 'vision for a people-centred land transport system'.[3]

It was founded in 1995 as a public (governmental) agency to plan and regulate land transportation. Its remit was to expand public transportation networks by developing new routes and light rail systems. Existing integration of the transport networks relied on a Farecard, which commuters inserted into slots in a machine that then deducted money from the card. Commuters were also able to transfer funds electronically from their bank accounts to top up the stored value on their Farecards.

Soon after its formation the LTA recognized that the solution was to move the entire transport system to an integrated smart-card system. In this, it represented the three public transport organizations in Singapore. The way the LTA managed the change was seen to be successful due to the way it sought to minimize potential resistance to change. At an early stage it consulted with and involved key stakeholders in the decision-making process. This is always difficult in the public sector, largely because a public authority is charged with responsibility to the public. Yet at the same time it has to work with other providers to deliver an effective service. In other words, although the ultimate goal is public satisfaction, in order to earn this it is necessary to work with other stakeholders to achieve that outcome. The stakeholders had to be convinced of the merits of a new integrated system in place of the existing one, and the public had to be satisfied that the new system would have benefits for them. This meant moving from a slow magnetic system to a fast, smart-card system.

The problem

The first light-rail system in Singapore was built in 1997. The public transport network was expanding rapidly and both a light-rail system and a north-east line were added to the existing train system. The need for change, in order to ensure the future ❯

>> development and growth of Singapore's public transport system, was therefore very strong. The difficulty was that the magnetic Farecard had too little data storage and processing capacity for a new system to operate effectively.

The LTA successfully anticipated potential resistance to the change by communicating its intentions to key stakeholder groups. These were:

- The public transport organizations (PTOs).
- The general public.
- Organizations that were affected by the change.

For example, Goh Gin Howe, Deputy Director, IT Planning and Quality Assurance, stated that 'one of the important mandates in developing our future plans is to create a people-centered transport system'. As such, it was critical for LTA to have a platform where it could deliver timely information, showcase its vision and aspirations, and inform the public about future land transport development and possibilities in Singapore. This platform would also serve to channel feedback from the public back to LTA.[3]

A study of how resistance was managed suggested that resistance was minimized by:[4]

- Involving key stakeholders (primarily PTOs) from the beginning of the project.
- Influencing public opinion leaders.
- Educating the public through comprehensive publicity designed to train and educate.
- Developing a critical mass of support.

The strategy sought to influence all key stakeholders at a very early stage when the project was considered and designed. It was vital that any anticipated resistance to the change was minimized by creating a shared vision from the point of view of all stakeholders. The PTOs were involved in order to identify any issues they had with the project. The general public was informed and the publicity generated at a later stage was designed to educate and train Singaporeans in how to use the new system. For example, the public were educated through sustained publicity, which focused, not just on training them to use the system, but also on its advantages. But the LTA was aware from the very beginning that it required a critical mass of public support. It was aware, for example, that grass-roots opinion leaders were essential to its success. To do this it organized a public relations steering committee that set about organizing a competition for the public to identify the name of the new smart card. After the winner was identified, approximately 45,000 participants were invited to review the new EZ-link card before it was officially launched. These participants were then able to buy and use the new card on the mass rapid/light-rail transit system and selected other services.   >>

> » The main strategic problem for the LTA was its own sphere of control and influence. For example, the LTA also communicated effectively to its 3,600 employees, who were 'located at four main offices and many other mini offices at different geographical locations across the island. Operating from multiple locations made it difficult for LTA to deliver its corporate messages to all its employees'; hence the need to develop an effective electronic communications system. Consequently, the LTA senior IT analyst, Hester Tan, suggested that whilst 'it is not possible for us to expect total participation from all our internal corporate events, the solution was to make organization-wide announcements available in CD format and screen the announcements to employees at a pre-arranged time.' Whilst this 'was not an ideal communication method', it appeared to deliver the message to enough people to make it reasonably successful.[3]

Sources:
[1] Singapore LTA Land Transport Masterplan Part 1 of 2 <http://www.youtube.com/watch?v=sr7nlx-qAFl>.
[2] LTA (<http://sg.ksdb.com>) is located at 1 Hampshire Road (Old KK Hospital) Singapore 219428.
[3] Available at <http://www.microsoft.com/casestudies/Case_Study_Detail.aspx?CaseStudyID=4000003265>.
[4]Sutanto, J., Kankanhalli, A., Tay, J., Raman, K.S., and Tan, B.C.Y. (2009), 'Change Management in Interorganizational Systems for the Public', *Journal of Management Information Systems*, 25(3), 133–175.

This case example illustrates that organizational change can be managed successfully, providing that attention to detail is considered and problems, such as the potential sources of resistance to change, are anticipated. It also means that not only are such people involved at an early stage in a project or change strategy, so that their concerns can be addressed, but the message for change is constructed well through what Gladwell refers to as 'stickiness'. There is one final point worth remembering. This is that, when attempting to address change in what is a very large public undertaking involving inter-organizational change, it is wise to communicate the message to the public through key opinion leaders. Therefore, the final message from Gladwell is his reference to what psychologists have understood for some time. That is, to be successful any change strategy must work through groups or networks of opinion leaders whose objectives are related to the overall strategy. The case example above illustrates how the Singapore LTA intelligently involved small groups of opinion leaders, or stakeholders, at an early stage, thus avoiding or minimizing resistance.

11.4 Socio-psychological stress and resistance to change

Socio-psychological stress and resistance stem from situations in which individuals experience psychological trauma or reality disjunctions in which their personal social world is turned upside-down. The causes may be social (situations that carry specific dynamics) but the experience is personal. One of the first approaches to deal with the relationship between stress and resistance was Menninger's (1975) studies of the American Peace Corps between the years 1963 and 1971. Menninger interviewed Peace Corps volunteers who had resigned. The change curve he constructed to illustrate this process indicated that morale was affected by cultural disruptions. For example, on returning to their native American culture the volunteers exhibited emotional feelings similar to those they had felt when they left it. Such stress and feelings of uncertainty occurred after periods of stability had been disrupted. Menninger suggested that other situations that involve psychological disruption are also explained by his change curve.

11.4.1 Dealing with crisis

The book by Elizabeth Kübler-Ross, *On Death and Dying* (1973), was the first text to address psychological traumas of people when faced with crisis. She documented the phases people pass through when coping with personal loss, grief, trauma, or serious illness. The stages are:

1. *Denial*: examples—'I feel fine', 'This can't be happening, not to me!'
2. *Anger*: examples—'Why me? It's not fair!', 'How can this happen to me?', 'Who is to blame?'
3. *Bargaining*: examples—'Just let me live to see my children graduate', 'I'd do anything for a few more years', 'I will give my life savings if...'
4. *Depression*: examples—'I'm so sad, why bother with anything?', 'I'm going to die... What's the point?', 'I miss my loved one, why go on?'
5. *Acceptance*: examples—'It's going to be okay', 'I can handle it with change', 'I can't fight it, I may as well prepare for it'.

The catastrophic reactions that Kübler-Ross refers to have been noted in other types of personal loss. For example, loss of employment, loss of home caused by fire or repossession, are also examples of stress and trauma. Parents who 'lose' their child to drug addiction may perceive that their world has come to an end when they see the aspirations they had for their child dissolve into insignificance. The stages do not always follow the sequence described. People may switch between stages, or never achieve acceptance, the final stage, because they cannot move out of depression. It is possible that some people stick in the denial stage, in which case resistance to change is manifested in various ways.

Others, such as Adams, Hayes, and Hobson (1976), suggest that general life transitions, such as marriage, divorce, bereavement, moving house, and so on all fall within a similar change model. Essentially, the process begins with a sense of 'immobilization' in which individuals feel numbed by their experience. This is followed by a very slight improvement in the second stage, during which individuals attempt to minimize the effects. This is followed by a third stage—'depression'—once the sense of loss is felt as a permanent fact of life. At the bottom of the depression individuals either 'accept and let go' (stage four), or fail to move on. The fifth stage reflects a successful transition by 'testing' new possibilities. The sixth stage involves 'search for meaning', which is eventually consolidated through a process of internalization (stage seven).

Some writers, such as Harvey (1990), suggest that all change involves some sort of loss, and Maurer (1996) identified eight ways in which people intentionally or unintentionally resist change (confusion, criticism, denial, malicious compliance, sabotage, easy agreement, deflection, and silence). The real issue here is not how many steps or phases there are, or which model is the best, but how change can be perceived as emotional rather than simply a failure of people to recognize rational economic man embodied in the view of dysfunctional employees. The dominant tendency of the conventional wisdom is that resisters are dysfunctional employees whose attitudes need to change for success to occur. In this view, as change progresses positively, dysfunctional attitudes and actions are reduced by the success of the initiative.

> ### ❶ Stop and think 11.2
>
> Imagine that you visit medical professionals in your capacity as an organizational consultant. You are told by a manager that the 'resisters' are a problem for the change initiative. However, in discussion with the 'resisters' you discover that they feel their own personal control and judgement over patient decisions has been removed as a result of the introduction of insurance company mechanisms such as detailed flowcharts, spreadsheets, and computer programs. Thus you discover that the professional ethic that was the main motivation for becoming a medical professional is undermined because the medical staff feel less involved in treating patients and more answerable to an impersonal managerial control system. The medical staff therefore perceive that they have become 'processors of information' who have become deskilled in the process. What verdict will you come to? Are the medical professionals 'resisters' or are they disillusioned professionals? Furthermore, do you regard power as a dimension of change or do you see it as simply a strategic necessity? How would you deal with this situation?

Burke (2002), like many other writers, tends to see the Kübler-Ross model (or variants of it) as the natural explanation for resisting change. This type of argument assumes a politically neutral process in which strategic enlightenment is confronted by the dark forces of irrationality, self-interest, and dysfunction. However, this is controversial and we need to consider a critical assessment of the definition 'resistance to change'.

Research into the models of stress, grief, and trauma has not provided conclusive evidence that they occur exactly as these theorists describe. For example, the stress and trauma theories derived from Kübler-Ross do not address cultural differences and context—the role and type of support offered by significant others in the process. Nevertheless, such models do play a part in our understanding of a complex process, but we need to be cautious about the type of organizational resistance we equate such models with.

❗ Stop and think 11.3

Do you think that studies into trauma and stress sufficiently explain the concept of resistance to change in the workplace? Do they explain the underlying dynamics of resistance sufficiently to apply the model to all categories of resistance? Try to write down an argument for the use of these models, then write down an argument against.

11.5 A critical analysis of resistance

A critical analysis to resistance argues two things: first, that resistance results from labelling by people in positions of power; and second, that agents of change themselves may be the cause of resistance. The first point suggests that what others might call 'differences of opinion' are themselves legitimate but become defined as illegitimate by people in positions of power. If we refer back to Chapter 7, we noted that the dark side of leadership can give rise to the amplification of conflict, the mental life of the organization, and the neurotic organization. Such arguments suggest that what managers might call resistance may in fact be a function of their own attitudes and actions. Indeed, they may contribute to their own problem by so defining attitudes that are not in harmony with their own. For example, if employees object to a course of action and that objection is defined as disruptive or bloody-minded, it becomes labelled as resistance. The situation becomes a self-fulfilling prophecy. Consequently, it has been suggested that the perspective on resistance to change 'is decidedly one sided' (Ford, Ford, and D'Amelio, 2008). Consider the case example below. This illustrates the possibility that the road to resistance might be constructed by a manager who uses 'rewards power' to achieve ambiguous results.

» Case example 11.2

The road to resistance is not always paved with good intentions

In order to reduce costs and increase efficiency, John Mathews, the general manager of Worktools, a tool hire company, decided to create work teams. This had the advantage of enabling the delegation of decisions previously made by managers. At a general »

>> meeting that all staff were asked to attend he stated his goal of creating effective teams and argued passionately for a system based on trust and responsibility. Bill Bradley reports directly to John Mathews and is John's deputy. He is responsible for sales and marketing. Bill was given the task of implementing the changes and personally overseeing their success. At a second general meeting Bill repeated the need for teamwork and argued that everyone must be more open about information sharing.

In a later one-to-one meeting, Bill asked an employee to 'keep him posted' about the performance of another employee. In a further one-to-one meeting, Bill told Clarissa Denby that she was the most loyal member of his staff and he relied on her to keep a watchful eye on who was really cooperating and who was resisting. Two days later Bill interviewed Lynne Jennings, who had applied for the job of team leader. During the interview Bill said, 'I think you are an attractive candidate and ideal for this position. You will be aware that the role of team leader requires flexibility and a desire to please both customers and management. If you took on this job I have a good deal of authority regarding salary and this would be based on your willingness to be flexible and to please.'

Reflection

Bill Bradley is defining reality as he sees it. Any action or point of view that does not correspond with his is therefore seen as resistance. Both the concept of organizational reality and resistance to change are egocentric and managerialist. As a result of his failure to reflect on his management style, we encounter three problems that are not conducive to openness and trust. First, during his second general meeting he stated that everyone must be more open about information sharing and yet his own management style contradicts this. Asking an employee to 'keep him posted' about the performance of another employee is secretive and undermines the essence of openness and trust. Second, Bill asked Clarissa Denby to keep a watchful eye on who was really cooperating and who was resisting. Third, the words he uses to Lynne Jennings during her interview contain *double entendres*. For example, phrases such as 'attractive candidate', 'desire to please', 'I have a good deal of authority', and 'willingness to be flexible and to please' are suggestive connotations beyond what one would expect in a work situation. We must conclude that the change strategy desired by John Mathews is doomed to failure.

The case example illustrates how people in positions of power can define reality to their advantage. If employees react negatively to the change initiatives because of the contradictions and mixed messages, then they are likely to be labelled resisters. Consider therefore the possible implications of the examples in the stop and think activity below.

> ❗ Stop and think 11.4
>
> **What resistance might the manager cause?**
>
> What a manager sees as resistance might result from his or her own language. Such language might reflect deeper attitudes, or simply reflect inappropriate comments. Some of the examples may be *double entendres*. Others are ambiguous but might cause offence. Consider what problems of resistance the examples might cause.
>
> 1. I will expect it on my desk first thing in the morning.
> 2. You'll just have to work on it over the weekend to complete it.
> 3. I wouldn't want you to think me sexist, but...
> 4. Don't shout at me!
> 5. Who the hell do you think you are?
> 6. You're as useful as a chocolate fireguard.
> 7. I shouldn't really be telling you this but I overheard Mandy say that...
> 8. You look gorgeous.
> 9. You couldn't organize a piss-up in a brewery.
> 10. I can swing some things in your favour if you come on board on this. If 'my staff' cause a problem, then I want to know about it.
> 11. It's the third time you've asked me for this and I've already told you it was sent ages ago...
> 12. We don't pay you to make mistakes.
> 13. I want your resignation on my desk by Friday.
> 14. I'm sick of taking the flak for you guys.

Some researchers have pointed out that change agents may cause resistance by breaking agreements and psychological contracts, violating trust, misrepresenting situations, or creating communication breakdowns. Broken agreements and the violation of trust have been cited as a major cause of resistance by various researchers (Andersson, 1996; Cobb, Wooten, and Folger, 1995; Reichers, Wanous, and Austin, 1997; all cited in Ford, Ford and D'Amelio, 2008). As we noted in Chapter 9, we must be careful about attributing cause and effect to situations. We observed, for example, that managers often treat manifestations as if they are the root causes of problems, which leads to misdiagnosis. In fact, the real causes of most problems are latent or underlying, that is, they are often deeper than the manifestation. There are many problems that give rise to resistance to change in organizations, but we can identify six to illustrate the point about who defines reality and the motives for doing so. It would be useful to reflect on each of these and attempt the stop and think activity immediately after the list.

Six examples in which resistance to change can be misdiagnosed:

- The introduction of new technology.
- The design of work practices.
- The dynamics of workgroups or teams.

- How a message is communicated.
- Culture change.
- Contradictions between policy and practice.

❗ **Stop and think 11.5**

In each of the examples listed above, consider opposing positions between a manager seeking to introduce change and a group of employees who resist it. The manager has encountered negative attitudes and defines these people as 'resisters': review his/her view. Then turn to people who may be subjected to these change situations and consider the type of objections they might have. When you have done this, think about why the concept of resistance to change is problematic.

In each of the situations listed above, people might be subjected to the imposition of change initiatives in a way that causes genuine grievances. For example, the failure to observe the principles of socio-technical systems when introducing new technology can cause objection. Thus we can see this as a position polarized between a manager's need for flexibility and employees who experience alienation. Each of the examples has the potential to arouse resistance. Furthermore, whilst resistance may be precipitated by anticipated perception of unwelcome change, poor implementation of an initiative that lacks employee involvement can result in a variety of social and psychological pressures.

The design of the built environment is often a cause for concern, especially when the people who are to spend their working lives in it are not involved in the design or implementation of the plans. Two useful contrasting examples are provided by Barnes (2007). She illustrates the redesign of two call centres, one in Tasmania and the other in Queensland. The differences are striking. Both sites featured improved lighting (natural and diffused to cut glare), ceiling tiles designed to reduce noise, and adjustable workstations, but there were physical differences between the Tasmanian and Queensland sites. Evidence suggested a difference in attitudes between the two sites. For example, the site surveys indicated that 62 percent of Austravel Tasmania employees and 100 per cent of IOC (that is Queensland) workers were satisfied with their physical conditions of work (Barnes, 2007: 250). Why were 38 percent of Tasmanian employees dissatisfied? The answer appears to reflect management's claim that, whilst a 'nice environment makes staff happy', they failed to appreciate that professional financial dealers or brokers did not see themselves as call-centre workers. Their professional standing as 'high-status finance brokers' was not in keeping with the call-centre design, nor the relocation to what was referred to as the 'ghetto end of town'. Thus, as Barnes notes, their 'improved physical conditions had not compensated for the perceived decline in status that resulted from relocation' (ibid.). She concludes by saying that the issue was really about power and control (ibid.):

Although the Queensland and Tasmanian sites were similar in design, the differing reactions of staff underscored the importance employees attached to exercising control over their working environment. Where they had had input into the design, as in Queensland, they accommodated to the built environment. Where it was absent, as in Tasmania, the employee response was one of aggravation. Implicit in comments about the windows was an attitude of hostility to managerial control. Workers perceived management to be taunting them—'it's here but you can't see it'—or attempting to make them work harder by removing all distractions, or infantilising them by assuming that their work effort would decline if they were provided with a view.

The intersection between change introduced through new technology and work practice has also been highlighted in research. For example, Clark and Preece's (2005) study of the introduction of a company intranet illustrates different perceptions of change between the 'shapers and makers' of technological change and those who are less enthusiastic. The implementation of the change initiative began with an expression of how the intranet was a radical innovation, reflected how things had changed, and why 'they needed to change'. As Clark and Preece point out, the change was defined by management and was used to legitimize a 'top-down' imposition of radical change with tight time schedules. Why was everyone not as enthusiastic about a tool that, at least in theory, would improve their communications? This is partly answered by recognizing that, whilst the shapers and makers may have viewed it as radical change, the rest saw it as incremental change, 'being suitable for some people and jobs and not for others (who obtained more 'functionality' from the old technology)'. Consequently, it had 'little meaning for some staff (for example, those who had Taylorised, rulebound jobs) as against others who were expected to be innovative'. Many such people reverted to traditional means of communication by using the telephone more. Whilst this might be seen as a subtle form of resistance, what is perhaps more useful to note is the genuine concerns people had about operational dangers:

> Others had identified some dangers here, such as the information on the Web pages having not been 'validated' or being 'misinterpreted' by users. There were indications that there may be self-serving purposes behind what people were saying through their Web pages ('Look how entrepreneurial and up-to-date we are'). Change was being represented on the computer screen by some people, and not, for example, necessarily manifested by job changes or the physical movement of staff.

(Clark and Preece, 2005: 162)

As we observed in Chapters 1 and 2, the structural-functional perspective is concerned with controlling things through technical expediency. In particular, we noted that limiting our attention to technical solutions to complex problems can be problematic and, on occasions, dangerous. This is the problem of rationality. Whilst some work tasks are predominantly technical and require rational procedures, the failure to consider other non-rational consequences (psychological, social, ethical, political) can give rise to resistance. For example, BPR processes are usually considered as predominantly technical rational instruments for change, yet they can underplay or ignore 'conflict, resistance, resignation, or manoeuvre, in order to avoid the implementation of redesigned processes etc' (Hagedorn-Rasmussen and Vogelius, 2003: 20). In their study of BPR in Denmark, Hagedorn-Rasmussen and Vogelius point out that BPR uses 'rationalistic tools for breaking up the labour process, and mapping and measuring processes have also been a high priority'. Thus, 'by applying those tools detailed analysis of the process flow is conducted'. A generic problem appears to be that when the labour process is divided into small entities and re-engineered, 'the technical rational approach is favoured, and the inherited politics in the change processes is often neglected' (Knights and McCabe, 1998) and this contributes to marginalization of human and socio-political dimensions (Willcocks and Currie, 1996; Willcocks, Currie, and Jackson, 1997; Taylor, Snellen, and Zuurmond, 1997; Willmott, 1994a, b; all cited in Hagedorn-Rasmussen and Vogelius, 2003). In their own research Hagedorn-Rasmussen and Vogelius illustrate how meaning and the avoidance of alienation become neglected in the redesign in favour of technical expediency:

> Our case demonstrates that job satisfaction was actually part of the commission at the beginning of the change programme. But in the ongoing process of change the theme was disassociated and excluded in terms of the changes that materialised. The limited approach to 'value' and 'customer' which is often applied, also in our case study, excludes the broader themes from the change programmes agenda.

(Hagedorn-Rasmussen and Vogelius, 2003: 30)

In contrast to the managerialist approach to resistance, the critical perspective has been much more concerned with addressing sociological questions pertaining to what people experience and why they resist managerially driven change. Most studies of this type relate to the labour process debate about the effects of management strategies. Indeed, it has been argued that Sewell and Wilkinson (1992) have drawn attention to 'the apparent paradox that modern developments in the labour process and managerial strategies have given rise to decentralisation and devolution of responsibility for tactical decision-making while at the same time generating higher levels of centralised, strategic control and surveillance' (Button, Mason, and Sharrock, 2003: 50). The critical labour process debate tends to view management change-interventions as extensions of management control in which resistance occurs as a means to defend a traditional position.

In their study of disempowerment and resistance in the print industry, Button, Mason, and Sharrock (2003) suggest that the theoretically driven analysis of labour process theorists is too simple because it reduces and simplifies or 'reifies both social relations and technology in ways which mask the complexity of the everyday experience of work'. The thesis tends to 'overlook the possibility that employees may simultaneously resist some aspects of management control of their activities and nevertheless seek to perform their allocated tasks to the best of their abilities' (ibid.: 12). Thus the idea of resistance to change is a much more complex series of interweaving motives and social practices that often seeks to achieve organizational goals and, at the same time, maximize the intrinsic satisfaction of the work experience. Their study of the implementation of new technology to control the process of workflow in a printing factory illustrates how employees and managers work out a joint solution to an organizational problem. The employees' resistance to a new control system was imaginative in finding a negotiated solution:

Re-establishing the order of the print room

> Faced with a situation in which their well-established practices for controlling work and maximising production were challenged by the introduction of SUR-VALANT, operators responded by devising new ways of organising their work. They reacted to the system by selectively switching it off for certain parts of the day's work. On the face of it this might appear to be just the sort of resistance to technology that Sewell and Wilkinson (1992) regard as increasingly difficult in the context of ever more sophisticated regimes of managerial control but which Thompson and Ackroyd (1995) insist remains a central feature of the industrial landscape. Neither of these characterisations is, however, adequate to describe what occurred at Establishment Printers. Their work around of the technology was not simply an attempt on operators' parts to preserve their autonomy and control in the face of a surveillance-capable technology. Nor can it reasonably be seen as an effort to thwart the continual march of technology. Rather their actions displayed an orientation to using the system in such a way that they could overcome the problems we have described above yet also achieve the organisational goals that motivated its deployment in the first place. Their activities thus took on the cast of solving a problem caused by the system, rather than simple resistance to management and technological control.

(Button, Mason, and Sharrock, 2003: 57)

11.6 Summary

We have explored the subject of resistance to change by looking at it from different perspectives. We noted, for example, that the conventional wisdom of managerialism tends to assume that resistance is a natural process because it's what humans do. Second, it suggests that resistance is dysfunctional and should be eliminated. This chapter, however, has attempted to open up this debate by questioning the concept of resistance to change. We can see how stakeholders might be involved productively in the process, thus minimizing potential resistance. For example, Case Example 11.1 shows what can be done in complex situations that require interagency or inter-organizational change. This particular case also exemplifies how the concept of the tipping point and the implications associated with it might successfully be applied. We have also explored the psychological characteristics that affect individuals who have experienced stressful or traumatic situations. We can recognize how the work originally developed by Menninger followed by Kübler-Ross helps us to understand the difficulties people face when the certainties they took for granted collapse around them. Finally, the section on a critical analysis of change illustrated that managers sometimes do inadvertently become the cause of their own problems. We also noted how change can be managed badly and lead to forms of resistance, no matter how subtle. This often occurs when new technologies are introduced, or when the built environment is reconstructed, without any consideration of socio-technical systems. It still appears to be the case today that not enough architects, planners, or computer systems analysts have learned the lessons of the past. In other words, we continue to see such professions failing to observe their own dictum that form follows function. As the end-of-chapter case study indicates, when we reverse form and function it can have serious consequences for the social and cultural environments in which people work. The problem is that those within become labelled as resisters. And yet, we should not neglect the fact that senior managers themselves are often naive agents of change, or seek politically expedient motives for short-term gain.

⊛ Case study

The Big Move

We sat in our staff room looking around us. We had been told that the 'big move' was to take place on Wednesday and we 'had two days to finish packing and clear out'. We were surrounded by boxes; those marked 'home' far outnumbered those marked 'staff room'. We were about to be moved to a multi-million-pound new build just outside of town. As with many FE colleges, this was the way forward: out with the old and in with the new, regardless of cost, both financially and personally. Prior to the move we had already lost many good experienced staff, from housekeeping through to senior management, due to restructuring. However the executive group, or senior management team, remained the same.

I should set the scene by explaining that our old college was largely functional and 'fit for purpose' as a place to engage with students. For example, students could visit staff rooms when they needed advice, and staff engaged in dialogue with students in a self-managed way. In our staff room, four tutors shared the office. Each had a large desk, a four-drawer filing cabinet, there was shelving to the ceiling, two phones, two computers, a printer, a kettle, and access to an Aladdin's cave of a resource room. We always had a supply of tissues and spare cups to accommodate our needy and ⊗

occasionally upset students. Here comes the mathematical equation that was never going to work—our new staff room!

The staff room is designed like a call centre. We moved to an open-plan staff room shared with 100 staff called the Service Sector. This includes a mishmash of departments: Childcare, Health and Social Care, Hair and Beauty, Catering, Sport, Leisure and Tourism, our sector director, four assistant directors, and two admin staff. We each have one desk (unless you are unlucky enough to be part-time and then you have to 'hot desk'); we also have one very small shelf that can take eight medium-sized text books or twelve A4 files. The reason for most of our boxes being marked 'home' was precisely because there is no space to store anything. The planning of the room does not include bookshelves! This lack of space is ridiculous and I could cope only by filling the contents of my home with the contents of two filing cabinets and what I could accommodate from the old resource room. This change in space usage would have made sense if we had been moving to a paperless office where materials from exam boards and other programme details were digitized. But no one involved in the new space design had thought of that. Because most of us run more than one programme and teach on numerous programmes, we require much more allotted shelf space. Filing is taken home. We're allowed to put a filing tray on our desks (which measure 1 metre by 60 centimetres), but they have to be blue, and we have to buy them ourselves, replacing any we had already bought.

Morale was low, yet our philosophy was 'think positively and see what the working environment was like when we were there and settled in'. On arrival at the new build we found there were ten computers (that is, one for every ten people) and, if you are unlucky enough to sit on the end of a row, you have one on your desk to be used by everyone in that row. One hundred staff share one black-and-white and one colour printer, although the colour printer is monitored and we are instructed 'not to use it "willy nilly" '. We get regular emails complaining that the toner is running low too quickly, and we are using too much paper. There is also a photocopier which is out of bounds to all staff other than the managers or administrators. We *are* provided with a kettle, but you can imagine the difficulty of sharing this with another 99 people. So, if you have a 15-minute break, you are lucky to get any hot water for a coffee.

We are seated in rows of eight and in alphabetical order. We share one telephone, No one feels ownership of the staff room as we were never consulted about the lay-out or the design of the working environment. Although we were told that nothing is allowed on the floor, over time we've devised filing and storage space where our legs should go under the desk. Every now and then we are given a 'telling off' and threatened with 'exec' inspecting our untidiness but most of us are past caring. After all, it is an FE college and we do have students' work to mark and lessons to prepare.

Management styles have become dictatorial. Our director, who had been a hairdresser and to my knowledge has had no management training, holds weekly meetings. Our Friday morning meetings cannot be avoided. We are signed in and would have to account for why we were not there. This meeting is used as a stick to beat

❯ us with. It is rarely positive and we are usually berated and told how little we do. Sometimes we're told that 'what we are doing will upset the exec'. Our director has poor people skills. She talks as she thinks and uses inappropriate language and communication. Four-letter words are not just confined to factories; or perhaps we have just become a people-processing factory. Her team (if you can call it that) have little respect for her. She offers no encouragement and motivation is a matter of simply following orders. Of course, all of this exposes the myth that women are instinctively better managers than men. However, she does supply us with breakfast now and again at meetings, but also treats us like children. A group of tutors working in my sector are ex-army and ex-police and their facial expressions during these meetings regularly reveal amazement at this management style. An example of this style is the commanding emails she regularly sends. On one occasion she demanded that we observe a dress code. She stated that, when in college, staff should act in a professional manner and should not wear baseball caps, coats, or dirty and worn clothes, and if we needed advice on what to wear, to contact her! I looked around the room at my colleagues to see if anyone was wearing such items. Of course, this was completely erroneous. There were only smart professional people at their desks and no baseball caps in sight.

Change should be a positive experience, offering personal and professional development, allowing staff to come together and share good practice. However, this change brought stress and anxiety to staff both young and old. Many have gone off sick and some have thrown in the towel altogether. Morale became even lower. Our professional status and our competence in teaching are continually scrutinized. The college brings in outside consultants to 'observe' us, although no managers are ever observed for their managerial ability. We are observed, so it's said, in a 'non-threatening way' and for our own 'professional development', but, strangely, we are graded, and this is recorded on our appraisal, and logged with HR. If we did not get a 1 or 2 we'd have to be reobserved. Grade 3 is 'satisfactory', but in the eyes of our college this is a failure. This contradiction has caused many staff even more stress.

Of course, an FE college is not just about tutors; we do have the responsibility to teach students. They have also had a raw deal. Many courses were axed in the move to the new build: performing arts, music, languages, to name but a few. Some of these could not have continued, simply because the new build does not have a hall and stage to perform on. Nor was it designed with music rooms. But no staff were consulted in advance, and those who taught such subjects suddenly found their employment prospects diminish. Student facilities have also been squeezed. The old college had a large refectory and common room. This was replaced with a few tables and chairs in the entrance foyer. There are not enough seats to accommodate all the students at break times and, even though the times are staggered, many have to sit in the corridors on the floor eating their chips and gravy. There is nowhere for them to 'chill out' and often this results in them getting up to 'mischief'. ❯

❯ Government initiatives have forced FE colleges to make provision for 14- to 19-year-olds in the drive to offer vocational subjects. However, we find that many of the 14-year-olds are, in fact, pupils who've been excluded from mainstream education. The executive group or senior team of the college, in their wisdom, decided to put all these pupils into one group and offer them skills for life! Needless to say that's not a good idea. We end up with overcrowded classrooms filled with the excluded pupils from a variety of schools, all under one roof. The results were that the police have to make frequent visits to college to 'sort them out'. Our caretakers are close to assaulting the 'little darlings' because of the inappropriate language and behaviour directed at them. Our posh new college has come under siege from a silly, alienated schoolchild mentality. Lifts are urinated in, condoms are left lying around the place with little notes meant to shock the tutors, and there are daily fights. All adults have become powerless: we have no rights. After all, as we're frequently told by management, 'we are here to offer a service'. Of course, this causes more stress to the workforce. Management always side with student complaints and are ready to bring disciplinary action against any staff member who complains about a student. On many occasions staff have to accept bullying or harassment from students, because they are our 'customers'. This crazy logic of quality management somehow gets used as a stick; managers who do not concern themselves with the facts or the process, simply because they work with limited objectives, can use it to beat people with.

During the first year many staff left the college; they'd had enough. The whole educational ethos is changing. Money rather than education has become the strategy. The new focus replaced the quality of the student experience with 'bums on seats'. Senior management insists that no potential student can be turned away, regardless of their GCSE results. Their suitability for working next to other children or vulnerable adults isn't something we should question; even if at interview they say things like 'they ain't filling in another f****ing form', we have to smile at them sweetly; after all, respect is old fashioned, and they are the new customers.

This year Ofsted was looming, so all the i's were dotted and the t's crossed. Management became obsessed with Ofsted inspection and, because they required the college to achieve a high grade, all staff were instructed how to perform during the inspection week. Impression management was practised as a high art during that week. Classrooms had to be decorated with displays of students' work, even though previously we were not allowed to put anything on the walls because it would make the insurance on the new plaster null and void. Expensive canvas prints showing students and staff involved in the learning process and extracurricular activities were hung around all the corridors. Money, which was tight, was miraculously found to send the 14-year-old 'difficult' students off on an Outward Bound week in the hills. Meeting after meeting was held to remind us how to write schemes of work and session plans, despite the fact that we all do this routinely anyway. We were instructed to use every piece of ICT equipment available because we were a 'college for the future'. The chosen few, students and staff, were briefed on what to say to the inspectors ❯

❯ when interviewed by them. The scene was set; did it matter to us? Were we, the staff, going to have anything to gain from this performance? The college received a grade 1 'outstanding in every area' Ofsted report.

Three years have passed since the 'big move' and management have achieved their strategic objectives. Staff offered little formal resistance, myself included, and we have collectively become passive and complacent. This whole change represents a victory of form over substance: a building non-functional for educational purposes; quantity over quality; impression instead of genuine engagement. Staff are controlled rather than consulted. If you measure the success of change by short-term objectives, then management were successful in achieving what they wanted: prestige led to rapid promotion for managers, the façade of the college looks elegant; senior management were mentioned in dispatches. On the other hand, the cultural climate is poor. There is a high incidence of absenteeism and long-term sickness. There is a good deal of negativity from staff towards senior management. There are also high incidences of stress and harassment from management. Psychological bullying is commonplace, from both middle and senior management. Staff are talked down to at meetings and occasionally humiliated if they express criticism. The blame culture is passed down the line from senior management to middle management, who then blame staff for any inadequacy. If you measure success by longer-term objectives, then the quality of the educational experience for students is questionable and the problems that lie below the surface raise doubts over efficiency and effectiveness.

Questions

1. How would you personally measure the success of this change initiative?

2. Do you regard any issues as dysfunctional?

3. What socio-technical issues are raised by this case study?

4. What management issues are raised by the case study?

■ Study questions

1. From your own experience, make a list of as many examples of resistance to change as you can think of.

2. What is a tipping point and how does it occur?

3. Provide two examples of tipping points.

4. Define socio-psychological stress and explain why people undergoing such an experience might resist change.

5. What characteristics define a critical analysis of resistance to change?

6. How can resistance to change result from a self-fulfilling prophecy?

7. How might people in positions of power cause resistance?

8. Provide four examples of how resistance to change can be misdiagnosed.

9. What is a socio-technical system?

10. What is meant by the managerialist approach to change?

■ Exercises

1. In May 2009 the scandal of Members of the British Parliament fiddling expense claims reached epidemic proportions, with *The Daily Telegraph* providing new revelations daily. By the end of May the 'epidemic' tore through cabinet ministers and members of all parties like a tornado. Voters were outraged and Members of Parliament became figures of ridicule. The democratic process was undermined by the revelations, to the extent that a tipping point for change emerged. Explain what happened. Research newspapers of the time to understand the extent of the problem. Then relate this to Malcolm Gladwell's argument that change occurs in small ways. When you have done this, identify what change emerged and identify resistance to the change.

2. Read Case Example 11.1. Then say how change was well managed by anticipating resistance to change. What are the lessons we might learn from this case?

3. What arguments would you put to suggest that those employees who resist change are dysfunctional employees?

4. What arguments would you put to suggest that managers can be the cause of resistance to change?

5. Find examples of the failure to observe the principles of socio-technical systems in relation to (a) the built environment and (b) the introduction of new technology. Say why this might lead to resistance.

■ Further reading

Barnes, A. (2007), 'The construction of control: the physical environment and the development of resistance and accommodation within call centres', *New Technology, Work and Employment*, 22(3), 246–259. This illustrates the redesign of two call centres, one in Tasmania and the other in Queensland. This is a good study of how resistance emerged in one but not the other. It illustrates how resistance is tied to perceptions of profession and context, and the failure to apply a socio-technical approach to the built environment.

Clarke, K. and Preece, D. (2005), 'Constructing and using a company Intranet: "it's a very cultural thing" ', *New Technology, Work and Employment*, 20(2), 150–165. A useful account of the introduction of a company intranet that illustrates different perceptions of change between the 'shapers and makers' and the users of technological change.

Coch, L. and French, J. (1948), 'Overcoming Resistance to Change', *Human Relations*, 1, 512–532. A classic text on overcoming resistance to change.

Gladwell, M. (2005), *The Tipping Point*, London: Abacus. A topical conversation on the theme of how big change occurs.

Sutanto, J., Kankanhalli, A., Tay, J., Raman, K.S., and Tan, B.C.Y. (2009), 'Change Management in Inter-organizational Systems for the Public', *Journal of Management Information Systems*, 25(3), 133–175. This is a good detailed example of how to successfully manage potential resistance to change.

■ References

Adams, J.D., Hayes, J., and Hobson, B. (1976), *Transition: Understanding and Managing Personal Change*, London: Martin Robertson.

Andersson, L.M. (1996), 'Employee cynicism: An examination using a contract violation framework', *Human Relations*, 49, 1395–1417.

Barnes, A. (2007), 'The construction of control: the physical environment and the development of resistance and accommodation within call centres', *New Technology, Work and Employment*, 22(3), 246–259.

Burke, W.W. (2002), *Organization Change, theory and practice*, Thousand Oaks, CA: Sage.

Button, G., Mason, D., and Sharrock, W. (2003), 'Disempowerment and resistance in the print industry? Reactions to surveillance-capable technology', *New Technology, Work and Employment*, 18(1), 50–61.

Caldwell, C., and Clapham, S.E. (2003). 'Organizational trustworthiness: An international perspective', *Journal of Business Ethics*, 47, 349–364.

Clarke, K. and Preece, D. (2005), 'Constructing and using a company Intranet: "it's a very cultural thing"', *New Technology, Work and Employment*, 20(2), 150–165.

Cobb, A.T., Wooten, K.C., and Folger, R. (1995). 'Justice in the making: Toward understanding the theory and practice of justice in organizational change and development', *Research in Organizational Change and Development*, 8, 243–295.

Coch, L. and French, J. (1948), 'Overcoming Resistance to Change', *Human Relations*, 1, 512–532.

Ford, J.D., Ford, L.W., and D'Amelio, A. (2008), 'Resistance to Change: the rest of the story', *Academy of Management Review*, 33(2), 362–377.

Gladwell, M. (2005), *The Tipping Point*, London: Abacus.

Hagedorn-Rasmussen, P. and Vogelius, P. (2003), 'What is value-adding? Contradictions in the practice of BPR in a Danish Social Service Administration', *New Technology, Work and Employment*, 18(1), 20–34.

Harvey, D.E and Brown, D.R. (2005) *An Experiential Approach to Organisation Development*, Sixth edition, London: Prentice-Hall.

Harvey, T.R. (1990), *Checklist for Change: A Pragmatic Approach to Creating and Controlling Change*, Boston, MA: Allyn and Bacon.

Knights, D. and McCabe, D. (1998), 'When "Life is but a Dream": Obliterating Politics through Business Process Reengineering', *Human Relations*, 51, 6.

Kotter, J.P. (1996) *Leading Change*, Boston, MA: Harvard Business School Press.

Kübler-Ross, E. (1973), *On Death and Dying*, London: Routledge.

Maurer, R (1996), *Beyond the Wall of Resistance: Unconventional Strategies that Build Support for Change*, Austin, TX: Bard Press.

Menninger, W.X. (1975), 'The meaning of morale: a Peace Corps model', in Moyniham, D.P. (ed), *Business and Society in Change*, New York: American Telephone and Telegraph Co.

Reichers, A., Wanous, J., and Austin, J. (1997), 'Understanding and managing cynicism about organizational change', *Academy of Management Executive*, 11(1), 48–59.

Rousseau, D.M., Sitkin, S.B., Burt, R.S., and Camerer, C. (1998), 'Not so different after all: A cross-discipline view of trust', *Academy of Management Review*, 23, 393–405.

Sewell, G. and Wilkinson, B. (1992), ' "Someone to Watch Over Me": Surveillance, Discipline and the Just-in-time Labour Process', *Sociology*, 26(2), 271–289.

Spencer, S. and Adams, A. (1990), *Life Changes: Growing through Personal Transitions*, San Luis Obispo, CA: Impact Publishers.

Sutanto, J., Kankanhalli, A., Tay, J., Raman, K.S., and Tan, B.C.Y. (2009), 'Change Management in Inter-organizational Systems for the Public', *Journal of Management Information Systems*, 25(3), 133–175.

Tannenbaum, R. and Hanna, R.W. (1985), 'Holding on, letting go, and moving on: understanding a neglected perspective in change', in Tannenbaum, R. *et al* (eds), *Human Systems Development*, San Francisco, CA: Jossey-Bass.

Taylor, J.A., Snellen, I.T.M., and Zuurmond, A. (eds) (1997), *Beyond BPR in Public Administration—Institutional Transformation in an Information Age*, Amsterdam: IOS Press.

Thompson, P. and Ackroyd, S. (1995), 'All Quiet on the Workplace Front? A Critique of Recent Trends in British Industrial Sociology', *Sociology*, 29(4), 615–633.

Willcocks, L.P. and Currie, W.L. (1996), 'Information Technology and Radical Re-engineering: Emerging Issues in Major Projects', *European Journal of Work and Organizational Psychology*, 5(3), 325–350.

Willcocks, L.P., Currie, W.L., and Jackson, S. (1997), 'In Pursuit of the Reengineering Agenda: Research Evidence from UK Public Services', in Taylor *et al* (eds), *Beyond BPR in Public Administration—Institutional Transformation in an Information Age*, Amsterdam: IOS Press, 103–132.

Willmott, H. (1994a), 'Business Process Re-engineering and Human Resource Management', *Personnel Review*, 23(3), 34–46.

—— (1994b), 'The Odd Couple? Re-engineering Business Processes; Managing Human Relations', *New Technology, Work and Employment*, 10(2), 89–98.

Take your learning further: Online Resource Centre
http://www.oxfordtextbooks.co.uk/orc/grieves/

Visit the Online Resource Centre that accompanies this book to enrich your understanding of this chapter. Explore case study updates and answers to questions, test yourself using an interactive flashcard glossary, and keep up to date with the latest developments in the area.

CHAPTER 12

The themes and issues of future organizational change

12.1 Introduction

How might we be guided in our study of organizational change? For my part, I hope that you, the reader, are now aware that the study and practice of organizational change rest upon a mixture of art and science. What I mean by 'art' is the reflective appreciation that comes from applying knowledge and skill and, in the process, becoming sensitive to the issues of change. What I mean by 'science' is the appreciation that other knowledgeable people have applied the rigours of different social science disciplines to their studies. In other words, to apply change and make a well-crafted intervention is a skilful or, to be more precise, an artful accomplishment. But this cannot be done without a level of understanding that embraces both method and critique. We would do well to remember the saying, 'in the land of the blind the one-eyed man is king'. For this reason we need a sense of perspective or, more precisely, we need four perspectives to guide us.

Each of the four perspectives introduced in Chapter 1 creates a direction for under-standing the subject matter of organizational change. The material on change could be presented simply as a series of uncontested facts driven home by clichés and a few funny stories along the way, but that would ignore the arguments and warnings required for an intellectual appreciation of the subject. Therefore the central message of the book is that we need to understand these perspectives to appreciate how to apply organizational change to complex organizations. There are four reasons for this:

1. *Because some things need to be controlled.* For example, health and safety systems, financial systems, engineering systems, and quality control systems need to be controlled, centrally and better. This therefore requires an understanding of the *structural-functional perspective,* because the main issue is the efficiency and effectiveness of compliance systems and procedures.

2. *Other situations require the maximum input from key stakeholder groups,* as sug-gested by the *multiple constituencies perspective.* This is normally the case in the public sector, but it is also increasingly the case in the private sector, where engagement with stakeholders is required in order to maximize the success of a change initiative. In such cases there is usually a heavy emphasis on governance. This should, of course, be one of the lessons we learned from the international banking crisis of 2008–2009.

3. *Ethical consideration of strategic actions and decisions.* In this respect we noted how the perspective of *Organizational Development* (OD) is the only perspec-tive on change that proactively engages an ethical position. As Chapter 2 also emphasizes, it is very dangerous to exclude ethical implications from deci-sions about change, especially when potentially libellous situations might arise. Besides, this is a matter of governance (or good housekeeping) in relation to human resource practices, marketing, sales, and health and safety.

4. Finally, *we need to be reflective in any change initiative.* For this reason we need to subject our own reasoning and decisions to critical scrutiny. There are essen-tially two versions of critical debate. The first is derived from traditional studies of organizational behaviour, such as groupthink or risky shift, or from studies of leadership that raise difficult questions. The second is associated with schol-ars of critical theory who do not intend to provide advice but are able to explain and challenge the processes we take as normal practice. This version raises questions about how legitimacy is constructed and, indeed, can be deconstruct-ed. It also suggests that power lies behind all organizational activities. It is less concerned, therefore, with power structures and more concerned to illustrate how power is practised through speech (for example by giving orders or by con-torting facts to suit a preferred outcome) and various language games, many of which are legitimized by appeals to efficiency, competition, profit, shareholder value, and so on. We referred to this perspective as *Creativity and Volition: a Critical Theory of Change.*

If we understand these perspectives, we can free ourselves from the limits of igno-rance derived from a simple instrumental approach to the subject of organizational change. We can understand the issues that constrain us, but we can also find a path through difficulties that often resemble a minefield. If you would not walk through a minefield without special equipment—at the very least a mine detector—then why engage in change initiatives without the conceptual equipment to make that journey successful? If we apply the themes and issues identified in this book to the future, then we can raise some interesting questions and reveal challenging new possibilities for organizational change. These are described below.

12.2 Efficiency and effectiveness

In the private sector efficiency may be the most important criterion, as organizations compete for position in their relentless pursuit of profit and branding. However, the public sector is much more concerned with effectiveness. To explain this it would be useful to remind ourselves of the British Parliament's difficulty in justifying MPs' expenses. What occurred between May and June of 2009 was a crisis of confidence in the morals and social responsibility of British MPs. The issue was only superfi-cially about expenses. The underlying problem was the poorly constructed system that enables MPs to exploit public finances to their own advantage. Therefore, to view organizational change simply as a matter of instrumentality neglects bigger questions about values. Look at the stop-and-think exercise below to consider your own views on this relationship.

❗ Stop and think 12.1

- Should organizations add value to society? If so, what values would you identify beyond economic ones?

- Do organizations have economic, social, or moral responsibilities in a world increas-ingly dominated by the global exchange of goods and services?

- Can activities of organizations contradict the pursuit of democratic goals and, if so, does this matter?

- To what extent might the actions of leaders in complex organizations intrude on the lives of ordinary people?

Your answers to the questions in this stop-and-think activity may be varied but they should enable you to recognize the complexity of the argument. In reality, it is difficult to be negative about these questions. That is, it is increasingly difficult to view organi-zations simply as a matter of economic expediency. For example, if we were to review the history of industrial legislation from the period of the first Industrial Revolution in Great Britain from the 1750s onwards, we would discover the development of the Factory Acts, the involvement of pressure groups, environmental legislation, and social legislation in relation to public order. In the twenty-first century the process of globalization has virtually shrunk the world in time and space. We have become dependent upon each other in ecological terms. Global capital, whatever the form and shape it continues to take, requires trust so that exchange relationships do not break down. But we have also come to recognize our responsibilities towards developing countries, or towards underdeveloped countries that suffer from drought and famine. It is therefore inevitable that we question the extent to which the relationship between economic rationality on the one hand and values on the other is likely to change in the future.

Figure 12.1 illustrates this balance between the four perspectives introduced in Chapter 1.

Figure 12.1 suggests that these four perspectives ultimately identify different positions in relation to organizational change, yet in reality these different positions reflect movements back and forward between efficiency on the one hand and values on the other. For example, to view organizations simply as a matter of managing or manipulating systems through the structural-functional perspective is rather

Figure 12.1 A model for dealing with complex change

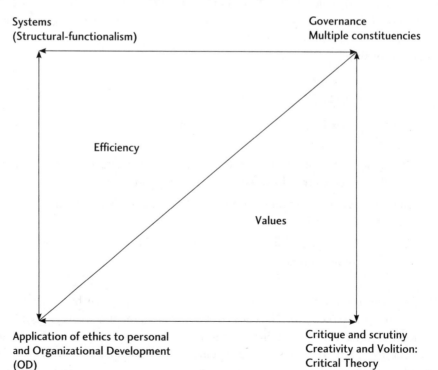

like viewing a tennis match as nothing more than two people passing a ball back and forth over a net in order to decide a winner. Of course, seeing tennis purely as a functional exchange ignores various incidental aspects that provide the real value. For example, it cannot account for the intrigue and drama constructed by spectators and news commentators. The fact that spectators value it as an activity they wish to spend time viewing is what makes the event a meaningful drama. And yet, tennis coaches would no doubt advise their protégés which aspects of their performance they need to control. When a number of tennis players become a team, who may then represent their country, they might form an organization. In this case we might consider OD as a means to link personal development with the objectives of the organization. We can therefore see that the vertical axis in Figure 12.1 between systems and Organizational Development reflects efficiency. To improve performance we either control things better or we develop people skills. The means for achieving such an improvement moves downwards from simple controls to complex internal controls, and in doing so becomes a matter of personal and organizational development (the OD perspective). In this diagram we can see how the horizontal axis from systems to governance reflects a movement towards meeting and agreeing the objectives of different stakeholders. We can also see how the vertical direction from issues of governance requires greater critical scrutiny of actions. Since the purpose of critical theory is to investigate the process of legitimation by enquiring into forms of domination and control, we come to understand how different stakeholder groups define their own positions. Finally, if we look along the bottom horizontal axis from Organizational Development to critical theory, we increasingly move away from the focus on efficiency to the focus on values. In other words, we can ask questions such as who legitimizes efficiency, and why they do it? Understanding organizational change in this way enables us to appreciate how to deal with complexity. These perspectives inform the themes of the book, which are identified by the chapter titles.

12.3 Will planned change be replaced by a better methodology?

Planned change is one of the most contentious themes in the organizational change literature, as we discovered in Chapter 3. Planned change has been heavily criticized and can easily be critiqued. However, we also need to enquire into the extent to which the criticisms can resolve the problems they raise. There are two related difficulties with these criticisms. The first is the assumption, by critics of planned change, that everything that is not processual or emergent change must be defined as planned change. This is an error of judgement, because we can find theories with different knowledge claims. Thus, we can identify *empirical–rational* strategies that are essentially managerialist and exemplify a simple technically expedient linear destination model of change; but we can also identify *normative re-educative* approaches based on models that are intended to develop an organization's capacity to learn. In contrast, these cannot be described as linear destination models because they are not mechanistic, nor do they create a simple causal sequence.

The second problem is the paradox raised by advocates of processual or emergent change theory. Their valuable contribution is to recognize that historical, political, and contextual processes unfold as change progresses. These are difficult to identify at a planning stage but are the main causes of change failure. Yet, despite the value of their contribution, processual theorists do not provide a model for managing change. Nor will such a theory provide an alternative, because its epistemological position is born out of critique. Such an epistemology is not intended to be aligned to the needs of management, nor is it intended to produce a methodology.

12.4 Organizational adaptations driven by political, economic, social, and technological needs

Organizations adapt to their environments in two ways: by reacting to changes in the marketplace; or by proactively influencing change and creating new opportunities in the marketplace (these are discussed in Chapters 4 and 5 respectively). The first is driven by a response to perceived threats whilst the second is driven by a desire to innovate. It should be obvious that, whilst threats are negative, opportunities are positive. Whilst both involve risk, it is the former that often reflect limited control or weakness in determining the course of strategic change. Another way of thinking about this is to argue that, in each case, change is desired in order to enhance further control. Strategic change that is either reactive or proactive is therefore an exercise in risk taking. There are, however, new risks and opportunities (PESTLE factors) in the future related to a possible reorganization of capital and changes to capitalism itself.

The current state of globalization reflects significant transformations in economic and industrial power away from traditional economies such as the USA and Europe. India and China between them represent approximately 40 percent of the world's population. Since both countries are rapidly industrializing, they have a huge supply of relatively cheap labour, as well as reflecting huge markets for the growth of consumer products. China's economy, for example, has doubled over the last decade. It is likely that India's economy will grow in the future by a similar amount. The Chinese, Indian, and other Asian economies are likely to become major players in the future of corporate capitalism.

Joseph Schumpeter, the Austrian economist, noticed that capitalism renews itself by going through recessions and economic upturns. He used the phrase 'creative destruction' to illustrate how new technologies and new markets emerge from recessionary spirals. For example, the Great Depression of the 1930s spawned new technological innovations. Companies like EMI and DuPont, which became associated with the production of coated plastics and polyester film products, came into existence in the 1930s. In 1931 EMI opened the Abbey Road Studios in London in order to make gramophone records. The emergence of plastics, nylon, and a variety of photosensitive products enabled companies such as Kodak and DuPont to create new markets. In the recessionary period of the 1970s entrepreneurs such as Bill Gates created software solutions when he developed Microsoft and Steve Jobs of Apple enhanced the potential of the microcomputer. In the 1990s, recession appeared to enhance new technologies such as mobile phones and digital technologies, leading ultimately to the redevelopment of various industries, including music.

It is therefore likely that new technologies and markets will emerge as a result of proactive change, especially in organizations that have deliberately developed slack resources. One of the most likely impacts in the future will no doubt be technologies and services driven by the need to demonstrate sustainable business and environmentally friendly transformations. Just as the car industry emerged in the 1920s as new technologies facilitated growth, the pressure of these forces is already spawning electric cars powered by lithium ion cells. These are likely to stimulate demand in the attempt to resolve the problems associated with fossil-fuel technology.

›› Case example 12.1

Tesla, sports car for the future?

Tesla is an American company that makes an electric roadster. The current version runs off lithium ion cells equivalent to 6,831 laptop batteries. It takes 16 hours to charge the batteries from a 13-amp electricity supply. The car itself is driven by a 250-brake-horsepower (bhp) electric motor and achieves 125 miles per hour with acceleration similar to that of a Ferrari. It has a range of 200 miles between battery charges. It appears to be the ecological sports car of choice for celebrities such as Leonardo DiCaprio, Dustin Hoffman, and George Clooney. The Tesla has already outperformed the large motor car manufacturers with the speed with which it has delivered the car to market. The car is a product of the electronics industry in Silicon Valley. The cars are all built by Lotus in the UK and they use the chassis of the Lotus Elise. Bigger companies such as Daimler (which has a 10 percent stake in Tesla and owns Mercedes) are likely to follow with their own small electric cars. A 300-bhp electric motor will power the next model. This combination of power and electric fuel cells may well be a mini-revolution. Such vehicles have a high chance of becoming the transport of the future, since many governments are creating financial subsidies to encourage consumers to buy green technology.

In Chapter 5 we discussed how high-performance work systems, organizational learning, and strategic human resource development encourage creativity by focusing on the quality and expertise of intangible assets. It is also likely that more subtle supporting structures will emerge, related to the development of human resources. For example, performance-related pay might well be linked to targets imposed on directors to achieve green solutions. Many companies are already undertaking detailed audits of emissions in order to demonstrate to consumers that they are acting responsibly by minimizing the impact on the environment. In the future it is likely that executive pay and bonuses will be linked to environmental targets. Being a sustainable business is likely to be a factor that positively influences shareholder value in the future. It is also likely that demonstrating green credentials is required by a supply chain, similar to the huge increase in quality improvements and international standards that occurred in the 1990s.

» Case example 12.2

Sustainable culture change at National Grid

National Grid has set new carbon dioxide reduction targets. These will be used as criteria for executive bonus payments. The National Grid will measure the tonnes of carbon dioxide it emits from each of its businesses. Sustainable targets will become one of a series of items measured, which already include customer service attitudes, reliability measures, and operational and financial measures. National Grid believes that building a sustainable business is itself a major culture change. Currently the organization has a medium-term objective to reduce greenhouse gas emissions by 45 percent by 2020, and a long-term target to reduce them by 80 percent by 2050. In addition, National Grid is introducing low-emission vehicles into its vehicle fleet and incorporating carbon targets into its investment criteria.

12.5 Corporate social responsibility

Corporate social responsibility (CSR) originally emerged from activities related to work with charities, community action, or through concerns about exploitation and the use of child labour in the Third World. Its growth was provoked by the reaction of various pressure groups or individuals who coalesced around the growing power of big business, on the one hand, and as a reaction to the failure of multinationals to act responsibly, on the other. Examples of corporate power also emerged with Monsanto's technological revolution in genetically modifying various crops, beginning with soya beans. Similarly, Nike and Adidas were heavily criticized for their loosely regulated supply chains, which regularly used child labour in contradiction to those companies' espoused values. The rise in corporate power became increasingly linked to globalization, often because such corporations have higher incomes than the national product of many medium-sized countries. At the same time, summits of international leaders were regularly targeted.

The challenge to corporate power has been overtly manifested in a variety of riots, beginning in Gothenburg with the European Union's summit of business and political leaders in June 2001. Such protests have become regular in reaction to meetings of world leaders. At the G20 London meeting in 2009 the situation was further exacerbated by the banking crisis and the seemingly unfair treatment of various people, who had suffered as a result of negligent corporate actions and greed. Dissatisfaction has also been crystallized by the power of the pharmaceutical industry in not responding to the AIDS crisis in countries like South Africa that cannot afford expensive drugs. It is possible that similar arguments may emerge in the future over the supply of basic services such as power, water, transport, and food.

The actions of pressure groups and their campaigns against the growth in corporate power resulted in the launch of an 'action plan for CSR', and in 2005 being designated by the EU as the CSR year. We have also seen the development of international standards in relation to the UN Declaration of Human Rights and the Rights of Children. Furthermore, the behaviour of multinationals has been questioned by the Organisation for Economic Co-operation and Development, which continually seeks to draw up codes of practice. In the UK, the Institute for Social and Ethical Accountability has recently emerged as a new professional body concerned with social auditing. The Ethical Trading Initiative in the UK has also attempted to construct labour codes of conduct. It is clear that international regulation is desired in the ebb and flow of international markets. Despite recessionary pressures, governments and multinationals will continue to move further in the direction of corporate social responsibility.

12.6 Compliance or culture?

In Chapter 2 we discovered that there are various issues related to ethics that we ignore at our peril, such as the problem of omniscience, through which bad and occasionally dangerous decisions emerge by simply applying an instrumental approach to change. Whilst these are related to CSR, it is the issue of compliance or culture that lies at the heart of organizational change.

The theme of organizational culture is developed in Chapter 6. The analysis of culture revolves around two perspectives: the structural-functional perspective and the critical perspective (Creativity and Volition: a Critical Theory of Change). The structural-functional perspective includes three approaches: the 'strong' or corporate culture writers; Organizational Development (OD) writers; and cultural climate researchers. The critical perspective (Creativity and Volition: a Critical Theory of Change) challenges these approaches by arguing that the organic analogy upon which the structural-functional perspective and OD are based leads to inappropriate analyses. We can see this in the idea that culture is not a variable to be manipulated and is, in keeping with Tylor's original definition, 'a complex whole'. Seen this way, it enables us to discern a paradox: that the strong corporate culture writers would find satisfaction with the development of 'strong' corporate cultures in the banking industry prior to the credit crunch of 2008–2009, or in the Siemens case. However, by failing to see culture as the complex whole we call 'organization', they neglect the existence of countercultures that contradict the official or preferred cultural definition. As we saw, in the Siemens case (Case study at the end of Chapter 2) the official (strong) culture was circumvented with the aid of Post-It notes that indicated what was to happen next in the sequence of illegal transactions (Post-It notes were used because they could be removed quickly should auditors turn up unexpectedly). When this was discovered, the German court case suggested a number of interesting possibilities, but it is the debate between compliance and culture that proves to be the most enduring and interesting for the future.

Unlike the past, there are international change drivers today, such as the desire for international regulation in relation to the interconnectedness of the banking system, and the need to embrace sustainable development. We can recognize these arguments today when, for example, it is argued that the uncontrolled excesses of the banking system in the first decade of the twenty-first century led to the 'credit crunch' or banking crisis of 2008–2009. Some political leaders were castigated for freeing up regulatory controls. This so-called 'light touch', some argue, enabled the worst excesses of unethical practice. The reality is that both regulation and culture are important: but over-increase of regulation in the wrong situations leads to a diminution of culture. In other words, people feel less appreciated, less involved, become more mechanistic in their work, and alienated in their labour. But the opposite can also be counterproductive, because an organization cannot have too much culture, although it *can* be sloppy in the way in which it engages with customers, clients, and other stakeholders. We can easily find examples of defensive reasoning, which is, in fact, a cultural phenomenon. To that extent it is argued that moral awareness needs to be defined and cultivated as a change initiative. We can see the problem of defensive reasoning in the Siemens example, in which an ethical climate was circumvented by devious activities designed to avoid existing compliance systems.

12.7 Power and the unstated discourse in organizational change

The theme of Chapter 7 indicates that organizational change is itself a political intervention. The critics of change suggest that change interventions are little more than an exercise in managerial control. Whilst this is often the case, this argument ignores the multiple constituencies perspective, which helps us to see that many organizations have to exercise governance on behalf of stakeholders. A Health Trust would be a good example, in which a counterargument might suggest that not all situations are exploitative, and that a variety of stakeholders must be involved (by law) in the interests of public scrutiny. However, we can also understand how managerial control might appear as a neutral process even though decisions are made by and in the interests of dominant coalitions. Challenging questions are raised by psychodynamic issues because organizations are arenas in which complex interactions are played out, and where motives may reflect deep psychological traits. Such power is often subtle but may indicate that the neurotic traits of leaders, as illustrated in Chapter 8, lead to neurotic organizations in which compulsive behaviours are played out in ritual performances. One of the more interesting aspects of the postmodern argument is the way that the activity of deconstruction challenges legitimating discourses. Deconstruction searches for the hidden assumptions behind discourses and it can also reveal potential unstated motives. In this sense, power resides in discourse. Thus, how reality is framed is as important as who frames it, and the reasons for doing so. Once we recognize this, then we come to understand that values are inseparable from any discourse. But the real point is not simply the engagement with ethical issues, but the silences that lie behind managerialist discourse. In other words, everything is related to values: personal, social, and economic.

An example of this argument can be illustrated by reference to the Climate Change Act introduced in the UK in 2008. This seeks to reduce greenhouse gas emissions in the UK to at least 80 percent below the 1990 levels by 2050. If government undertook a cost/benefit analysis and included the social and environmental costs of not taking action, then policy would not be determined solely by traditional economic criteria. For example, what would be the benefits to the environment if government subsidized railways to a greater extent and moved significantly more people away from using petrol and diesel vehicles? What are the social and environmental costs of not doing this? This argument can be applied to the activities of many public utilities, such as the use of water meters in houses, or the subsidized development of alternative energy sources. Each of these can easily be achieved, but we need to ask what the political reasons are for government not moving away from traditional economic calculations focused purely on economic costs. We can also ask what motives might be revealed among various lobby groups who would oppose alternative strategies. This form of critique can be turned on the idea of governance itself (informed, of course, by a multiple constituencies perspective) by asking what are the unstated discourses of power that lie behind the practice of governance. This type of analysis could also become part of a diagnostic framework, as explained in Chapter 9. The discourses of stakeholders would include external constituencies and the client system itself. Attempting to triangulate perceptions and underlying assumptions of power lying silent behind stakeholder preferences would enable a critical turn that challenges traditional OD methodology. This is best illustrated in Case example 9.3. We might also use a methodology of deconstruction to challenge most of the managerialist literature on change management. Nowhere is this argument more apparent than in the idea of resistance to change (Chapter 11). Thus it is not difficult to see how traditional managerial concepts normalize the topic and, in so doing, construct definitions of problems (that is, they problematize challenges to a preferred definition of reality). This is another example of silent discourse, because sets of binary opposites are constructed in such a way that they appear non-contentious, as we noted in Case Example 11.2.

Finally, it is worth emphasizing that this concluding chapter has suggested that we are near a tipping point on a number of these big issues. Because we are currently undergoing political, economic, social, and technical change, it is difficult to visualize the more tangible outcomes of subtle processes. But they are emerging. In many cases we are likely to see a critical mass of adopters. What we need to bear in mind in this process is that critique does not end just because a critical mass of adopters wants to become associated with change. Remember that organizational change can be either positive or negative, but that depends on values. And what was the unstated discourse in this text? It should be clear by now that this is an argument against the instrumental view of change.

Glossary

Action Research Developed by Lewin to improve organizational performance through collaboration to understand the causes of a problem. Although there are variations, it can be described as an eight-step model: (1) problem identification; (2) consultation with key stakeholders; (3) data gathering and diagnosis; (4) feedback to stakeholders; (5) action planning—setting objectives and goals; (6) taking action; (7) data gathering to determine effectiveness of intervention; (8) a feedback loop to step (1) to allow effective evaluation.

Anti-foundationalist The representation of agency as also involving the researcher's ethical discrimination between the acts of identifying something as a problem, and endorsing the definition of it.

Behaviour modification theory Also 'Behaviourism' and 'Operant Technologies'. The model described by Luthans and Kreitner (1985) is a five-step process of behavioural change: (1) identify the key behaviour; (2) measure its baseline frequency; (3) identify its antecedents and consequences; (4) change the antecedents and consequences to encourage desired behaviours and discourage undesirable behaviours; (5) evaluate to determine whether the behaviour and performance have changed in the desired direction.

Behavioural Styles theory This attempts to create profiles of effective leader behaviours. A leadership style is a general pattern of behaviour that favours either tasks or people in making decisions. This research emerged from traits theory and focuses on training and developing leaders by getting them to identify and reflect on the relationship between performance and people.

Bounded rationality The view that rational decision making is constrained because no individual can possess all the situational facts; so one can never fully appreciate each option until it is experienced. Bounded rationality challenges the assumption of objective rationality that a clear, unambiguous decision can be made providing one is in possession of all the facts, which ignores the importance of people's values in making decisions.

Business Process Re-engineering (BRP) A methodology for redesigning work around core processes. The idea was initiated by Michael Hammer in 1990 when he argued that managers need to obliterate work that does not add value, rather than using technology to automate it.

Business strategy Describes the mechanism of competition in markets within preferred industries in which an organization has chosen to compete.

Change agent Occasionally used loosely to describe stimulus for change; more often, to refer to an individual given a key role in implementing change.

Change intervention Change actions taken at a strategic level to help an organization become more effective.

Client system The wider organization, as distinct from the client with whom an intervention and contract are negotiated. Some investigation of the client system is recommended before the contract is defined.

Cognitive dissonance Holding two contradictory ideas, attitudes, or beliefs simultaneously. The theory proposes that people need to reduce dissonance by changing their attitudes and beliefs, which leads to changed behaviour.

Conflict The driving force for organizational change, because competition is a necessary feature of capitalism. Nations and organizations compete for scarce resources and this forces change. Organizations structure inequality to grant differential benefits to particular groups of people, which gives rise to disenchantment and conflict, and use managers to resolve these conflicts.

Congruence analysis A method that explicitly seeks to consider the impact of a given corporate strategy upon key stakeholders.

Corporate social responsibility Considering the interests of society by accounting for the impact of activities on customers, suppliers, employees, shareholders, communities, and other stakeholders. More recently, an obligation to sustainability and the environment have been included. Because it seeks proactive practices rather than reacting to legislation, the approach is seen as a method of governing powerful MNEs.

Corporate strategy Describes the goal(s) to be achieved in industries in which the organization chooses to compete.

Creativity and Volition: a Critical Theory of Change Challenges the assumption that change is produced by consensus, and argues that modernist change theories reduce people to mere operations within a system with its own objectives. In contrast, Critical Theory implies we must listen to people in the change process. It is critical in particular of the linear view of planned change, suggesting that change occurs in a circular manner.

Critical Theory A description of diverse theoretical traditions that include the Frankfurt School of social science, Foucault's analysis of power, and phenomenology's focus on meaning systems.

Cultural climate Regarded as 'an intervening variable' between the context of an organization and the behaviour of its members.

Cultural control The view that culture is a variable of the organization that can be controlled. Exponents refer to the relationship between leadership and corporate values, and the need to develop strong cultures. Critics argue that culture cannot be used to manage change, and that organizational analysis should identify political issues related to interventions.

Design School of strategy The School views the CEO as the organizational strate-gist. Strategic leadership involves making internal and external SWOT analyses within the organization's context.

Dominant coalition One over-riding group or a mixture of fluctuating interests that seeks to exert authority in some way, such as management, trades union interests, and, in complex public sector organizations, committees that take on executive roles to develop policy initiatives.

Emergent or processual change Associated with critics of planned change, who argue that it is impossible to plan for all contingencies. The approach is only an alternative inasmuch as it rejects the linearity of change programmes.

Empirical–rational strategies By applying rational principles to all debate and investigation, they replace ignorance or superstition with objective and scientific methods for extending knowledge. Empirical–rational strategies of planned change are typically large schemes such as the planning of a built environment, military campaigns, and the design of large-scale public services such as the National Health Service, education, social services, and so forth.

Epistemology The study and limits of knowledge. For example, each perspective outlined in this book makes knowledge claims but each also has its limitations and contradictions.

Ethnocentric Criticism of a nineteenth-century world view, which judged other cultures as primitive or advanced; making biased judgements based on a privileged position, rather than trying to understand the indigenous culture.

Excellence Movement A group of writers associated with the McKinsey consultancy firm and Harvard's Graduate School of Education, whose ideas were influential in promoting the neo-functionalist argument that a strong corporate culture is a key variable of an organization.

Expectancy theory Motivation is determined by the amount of effort required to obtain a reward and the likelihood of achieving the reward.

External forces for change The range and scope of factors external to an organization (over which they will have little influence or control) that can significantly shape that organization's competitive position.

FAR analysis Scenario-based morphological forecasting method.

Fitness for purpose A test for quality: a product or service must be seen as fit for the purpose for which it was intended.

Five Forces of competition Focused evaluation of the competitive context of an organization within the structures of its market(s) and its industry.

Force Field Analysis Lewin's technique for managing organizational transitions using a collaborative approach involving education, mentoring, and coaching.

Fordism The system of mass production introduced by Henry Ford, which simplified production methods through standardizing parts and introducing the production line. The phrase has since acquired negative connotations associated with deskilling such as 'knowledge mining', in which the knowledge and skills of individuals are built into computer programs, leading to a simpler system using fewer people.

Gestalt methods/morphological methods Analytical methods where the overall outcome needs to be considered, rather than a particular part of that outcome. Such methods are usefully applied to complex, multivariable problems.

Group dynamics Term first used by Lewin to describe groups appearing to take on a personality of their own, related to their unique composition. Lewin argued that opportunities for re-education (today, 'organizational learning') increase when individuals strongly identify with the group. The most successful change strategies occur when a group collectively decides to change its behaviours. This is a much more powerful and effective change strategy than traditional forms of instruction. Lewin's work on group dynamics became the foundation for group development and training—which focused on skills, sensitivity training, and team building—and ultimately Organization Development.

High-performance work systems Systems said to demonstrate the characteristics of high involvement and high performance. Organizations adopting innovative work systems were described as High-Performance Work Organizations by Osterman (2000). This was described as 'a shift from fixed systems of production to a flexible process of organizational development'.

Ideology Variously used: for example, 'organizational ideology' usually means a set of principles such as rules or conventions that guide thinking; conflict theorists use the Marxist definition 'false consciousness', which implies that the presentation of selective ideas seeks to mask an underlying reality.

Impact wheel A simple analytical method where the user considers the potential consequences of a given action or decision.

Kaizen A Japanese word with no direct English equivalent, generally taken to refer to social activities or cultural work practices that underpin quality management; in the West, associated with empowerment, teamworking, and participative management.

Law of the situation Derived from Follett's argument that simply ordering people to do things effectively may not always cause them to do so. Even appeals to reason and to intellectual persuasion might not work, because people bring emotions, habits, attitudes, prejudices, and behaviours into the workplace. The law of the situation requires understanding how these mental attitudes impinge upon any given situation and, most importantly, upon how orders are perceived. Follett argued that orders must be depersonalized to avoid negative resistance.

Logical incrementalism A term introduced by Quinn (1978) to describe what really happens when change occurs, rather than what leaders might claim occurred, which tends to focus on events rather than processes.

It suggests that change occurs in a circular manner and that many processes critical to change go unnoticed.

Machine control The analogy of organizations with machines that require a variety of control mechanisms. The Classical School of Management saw organizations as composed of little more than control mechanisms, a mechanistic and one-dimensional view.

Manifest and Latent functions Manifest functions are a deliberately designed aspect of an organization: often component areas such as leadership, strategy, systems, skills, structure; or an intended purpose (a policy initiative). We may refer to a department as a functional unit or a policy as being in line with a manifest (functional) intention. Latent functions are processes that are unintended, or have not been deliberately designed into a system or into a policy. These may be positive but, if they give rise to negative consequences, are referred to as dysfunctions.

Modernism Originally described the machine age of the early twentieth century and progressive movements in art and architecture. Gradually applied to the processes that characterize the management of large organizations. Modernism or modernity is no longer viewed as progressive and is linked to rigid forms of control exemplified by bureaucracy, Taylorism, and Fordism: managerialism focused on measurement and calculation rather than on process. Organizations were therefore viewed as machines and people as cogs in a machine technology that emphasized rational calculation at the expense of humanistic principles.

Multinational enterprise (MNE) An organization that has productive capacity in a number of countries.

Multiple constituencies perspective Derived from the theory articulated by Cyert and March (1963), which reflects how people in social systems act to maximize their own interests. The theory implies that a change effort requires leaders to mobilize support by appealing to rational principles through negotiation, because different stakeholders bring motivations and prefer positions that suit their own interests.

Normative re-educative strategies Described by Chin and Benne (1976) as a form of re-education or organizational learning that seeks to establish pragmatic results in contrast to those achieved by scientific experiments; also as a normative process of enquiry seeking agreement over ideas and emotions. The most obvious methodology is Action Research.

Oligarchy A group of decision makers and power brokers at the top of organizations. Even in democratic organizations an elite group emerges and eventually controls executive power.

Omniscience Infinite knowledge; wisdom to know everything.

Open-systems model Introduced by von Bertalanffy (1956). Katz and Kahn (1966) described an organization as an open system in which change is represented by a continuous flow of inputs that are transformed into outputs. The open-systems model is more sophisticated than the closed systems of physical science since it is based on living systems, which interact with their environment.

Optimizing solutions Ideal solutions; usually unrealistic, because organizations consist of coalitions of interests. See **satisficing solutions**.

Organic analogy Originating with Durkheim's structural functionalism, an analogy in which a society or an organization is viewed as an system constructed of functionally interrelated parts, like a human body.

Organizational Development A synthesis of the systems thinking of the structural-functional perspective with the behavioural research of human resource theory. OD is characterized by humanistic principles and methods informed by Action Research, organizational diagnosis, process consultation, promoting personal growth and organizational learning, and a focus on the roles of groups within an organization's culture. Central to OD is the idea of planned change.

Organizational learning The deliberate practices that take place in an organization in order to enhance the organization's stock of knowledge and to explore how best to facilitate change.

Paradigm A guiding perspective containing rules for interpretation; how thinking can be either guided or inhibited by the assumptions it contains.

Pareto analysis Sometimes referred to as the 80/20 rule: a rough approximation suggesting that 80 percent of problems are related to 20 percent of customers. It can be applied to many things and its purpose is to draw attention to which customers to deal with first.

Path–Goal theory Emerging from Behavioural Styles research, via Expectancy theory, it argued that individuals (and by implication teams) calculate and compare the effort required to obtain a reward and the likelihood of achieving the outcome. The theory suggests that a leader can influence this process by identifying challenging pathways to goals, and valued rewards.

PEST; PESTLE or BPEST An analytical method that considers political, economic, sociodemographic, and technological factors (and others) shaping an organization's external environment.

Phenomenology, –ological Associated with Edmund Husserl. A radical challenge to structuralism and functionalism that, applied to organizations, sees them as arbitrary social constructions that are precarious and fragile rather than solid structural entities. Phenomenology therefore challenges the idea of constraint and is better able to explain change than structural-functionalism. See Berger and Luckman (1966), which illustrates how our understanding of reality is socially constructed by the definitions we use; and Wittgenstein (1953), which demonstrated how language use defines both our sense of reality and the limits of our world.

Pluralism Emerged from consent theories. Modern organizations are complex and contain different interests whose views and differences must be accommodated in order to achieve a psychological contract in which people are motivated to perform effectively and efficiently. Thus, effective change is seen to result from involving employees in the decision-making process. Participative management is a feature of this approach.

Power-coercive strategies Interventions that exert power overtly, such as management or trades union industrial relations strategies, and using government legislation and company rules to exert maximum control in seeking compliance.

Proactive change Anticipatory organizational strategic responses to external forces for change (their pursuit is required to extend and improve competitiveness).

Process consultation Part of the methodology of OD consultants. Sometimes referred to as the clinical or medical model, it distinguishes between symptoms and signs on one hand, and underlying or root causes on the other, as a diagnostic process to separate cause and effect.

Psychological contract An informal agreement related to motivation of individuals, based on conventions or ways or working, stated or unstated, but never existing as policy statements. Usually contrasted with the formal contract of employment.

Punctuated Equilibrium This model suggests that evolution tends to move from relatively stable periods, where little appears to happen, to sudden spurts of rapid development.

Rationalizations Cognitive strategies that enable managers and employees to justify their illegal or unethical behaviour. Rationalizations often become associated with normative behaviour and part of a group's dynamics. These behaviours are sanctioned by attitudes that appear to neutralize objections to or regrets about participation in unethical acts.

Reactive change Passive organizational strategic responses to external forces for change (their pursuit is required to sustain competitiveness).

Reflexivist A methodology of self-awareness; a phenomenological process of critical self-examination of ideas or actions.

Reify, reification Simplifying reality with conceptual models. For convenience, when complex phenomena are presented, only selected elements are outlined or abstracted. Similarly, for clarity an ideal type is used to polarize examples. In language, when we create categories we tend to look for examples that fit, and often ignore or overlook those that are fuzzy or do not fit our categories exactly. This is much more so when we build a theory. Thus, to regard an organization as an organism has its uses, but the danger is that we miss its limitations.

Resource-based view of the firm (RBV) An economic theory that seeks to identify a firm's potential key resources, which must be rare and based on a value-creating strategy. If they are difficult to repeat, then they provide competitive advantage.

Reverse osmosis A process that forces a solution through a filter, which traps the solute on one side but enables the solvent to flow to the other.

Satisficing solutions Satisfactory but not ideal solutions to problems.

Self-efficacy A process of learning what knowledge, skills, and experience to apply to particular situations; the gradual acquisition of complex cognitive, social, linguistic, and/or physical skills through experience.

Self-fulfilling prophecy A form of negative labelling that, when applied routinely, has the effect of defining, stigmatizing, and creating the outcome predicted. Schoolchildren who are continually defined as lazy internalize such labels, and come to act out the role.

Situational control The extent to which leaders have control over three critical variables: leader–follower relations; task structure; and position power.

Situational/contingency theory Examines the situation and other variables (contingencies) that determine the success of a task. Part of the Behavioural Styles approach to understanding what makes an effective leader.

Socio-technical systems A term referring to the dangers of introducing a technical system without the clear understanding and involvement of the people who are to use it.

Change agents, therefore, should investigate work methods and preferences, motivations and social relationships, and designers should always investigate use before they design it.

Specialization The extent to which highly skilled operations and individuals are required.

Strategic leadership In Selznick (1957), the leader was seen to act as a strategist responsible for developing a 'distinctive competence' by aligning the 'internal state' of the organization with its 'external expectations'. The idea of the strategic leader gained currency with the Design School of strategy, which gave rise to the strategic management discipline.

Strategic Planning School Emerged out of the Design School of strategy. It sees the strategic leader's role as objective setting and undertaking external followed by internal audits.

Strong culture Promoted by the 'Excellence Movement', the argument that excellent organizations possess a strong values-driven culture.

Structural functionalism Sometimes simply referred to as functionalism. Associated with Malinowski and Radcliffe-Brown (anthropology), Durkheim (sociology). Requires identification of the functions things perform in any structural arrangement. Culture represents institutional forms, such as decision-making procedure, and the construction of functional areas such as a department, but also holds the key role in creating a unified whole (the organism).

Structural-functional perspective Uses the 'open-systems' model to describe and analyse how change results from transforming inputs into outputs. The perspective is useful in examining simple changes to a production process. Its value lies in its ability to change the arrangement of tasks and procedures. A contemporary version of this is Business Process Re-engineering.

Structured Impact Wheel A simple analytical method that adapts the impact wheel to consider the potential consequences of a given action or a decision using PESTLE factors to guide that consideration.

SWOT analysis A method of identifying how the external forces for change can be addressed by potential within an organization (quantifying **T**hreats, minimizing organizational **W**eaknesses, addressing and exploiting **O**pportunities and **S**trengths).

Taylorism An alternative name for scientific management. Developed by Frederick Winslow Taylor, it investigates the most efficient execution of tasks in terms of speed and time, and led to HR specialist job analysis. It is heavily criticized for ignoring social phenomena such as age, motivation, leadership, and group dynamics.

Traits theory Sought to identify innate characteristics, internal mechanisms that determine how individuals act. Whilst in some areas (e.g. personality testing) clear (although not uncontested) results have emerged, in leadership no significant determinants have been found, and the theory was abandoned for the Behavioural Styles theories, though it re-emerged under the guise of leadership attributes analysis. This investigates followers' perceptions rather than leaders' traits.

Transactional leadership Term used by Burns (1978) to compare with transformational leadership. The balance a leader strikes between the rewards and punishment directed at a team. No effort is made to develop employees: it has a purely functional role.

Transformational leadership Term attributed to the sociologist Jim Downton, meaning an effective leadership style in situations where leaders and followers raise each other's performance through motivation and moral commitment. Developed further by Burns (1978), who contrasted the term with transactional leadership.

Triangulate A technique for obtaining information by employing different methods to corroborate or refute a particular hypothesis, or obtaining different views or perceptions in a client system.

Unitarism Emerged from force and elite theories. Political governance in which power is centralized. In organizations, a unitary system of management expects that decision making is centralized, and HR strategy is based on all employees sharing and committed to the goals of the organization.

Whistleblowing The unauthorized disclosure of illegal or unethical conduct within an organization or institution.

Zero-sum game Parties in a competitive situation adopt win–lose tactics. They do not accept or have not worked out that compromise may be a better (win–win) solution.

Subject index

Author index